Besfort T. Rrecaj

Politics of Legal Regimes of Nuclear Energy in the Aspect of International Security

AF827715

Besfort T. Rrecaj

Politics of Legal Regimes of Nuclear Energy in the Aspect of International Security

The NPT Regime, International Security, Nuclear Terrorism and International Cooperation

LIT

This book is printed on acid-free paper.

Bibliographic information published by the Deutsche Nationalbibliothek
The Deutsche Nationalbibliothek lists this publication in the Deutsche Nationalbibliografie; detailed bibliographic data are available in the Internet at http://dnb.d-nb.de.

ISBN 978-3-643-90545-1
Zugl.: Prishtina (Kosovo), Univ., Diss., 2014

A catalogue record for this book is available from the British Library

©LIT VERLAG GmbH & Co. KG Wien,
Zweigniederlassung Zürich 2014
Klosbachstr. 107
CH-8032 Zürich
Tel. +41 (0) 44-251 75 05
Fax +41 (0) 44-251 75 06
E-Mail: zuerich@lit-verlag.ch
http://www.lit-verlag.ch

LIT VERLAG Dr. W. Hopf
Berlin 2014
Fresnostr. 2
D-48159 Münster
Tel. +49 (0) 2 51-62 03 20
Fax +49 (0) 2 51-23 19 72
E-Mail: lit@lit-verlag.de
http://www.lit-verlag.de

Distribution:

In the UK: Global Book Marketing, e-mail: mo@centralbooks.com
In North America: International Specialized Book Services, e-mail: orders@isbs.com
In Germany: LIT Verlag Fresnostr. 2, D-48159 Münster
Tel. +49 (0) 2 51-620 32 22, Fax +49 (0) 2 51-922 60 99, E-mail: vertrieb@lit-verlag.de

In Austria: Medienlogistik Pichler-ÖBZ, e-mail: mlo@medien-logistik.at
e-books are available at www.litwebshop.de

TABLE OF CONTENT

FOREWORD 11

CHAPTER I: INTRODUCTION 13

CHAPTER II: NUCLEAR ENERGY: FROM INVENTION TO ITS MULTIPLE USE 23

II.1 INVENTION AND DEVELOPMENT OF THE FISSION PROCESS AND NUCLEAR ENERGY 23
II.2 MULTIPLE USE, PRODUCTION AND RISKS FROM RADIOACTIVE MATERIALS 33
II.3 NUCLEAR ENERGY AS AN ALTERNATIVE AGAINST GLOBAL WARMING 44
II.4 NUCLEAR ENERGY AS AN IMPORTANT COMPONENT OF THE NUCLEAR ARSENAL AND A GUARANTOR OF NATIONAL SECURITY 51

CHAPTER III: REGULATION OF THE USE OF FORCE IN INTERNATIONAL LAW AND NUCLEAR WEAPONS COUNUNDRUM 63

III.1 FROM JUS AD BELLUM TO JUS IN BELLA AND DEVELOPMENT OF RULES OF THE USE OF FORCE BEFORE THE UN 63
III.2 THE USE OF FORCE IN THE UN ORDER 71
III.3 THE RIGHT TO SELF-DEFENCE, IMPLICATION OF NCULEAR WEAPONS AND ITS LIMITS 78
III.4 NUCLEAR WEAPONS AND MILITARY DOCTRINES 89

CHAPTER IV: THE LEGALITY OF THREAT OR USE OF NUCLEAR WEAPONS AND THE ICJ LEGAL ADVISORY OPINION 97

IV.1 THE COMPETENCES OF ICJ AND ITS ROLE IN INTERPRETATION OF INTERNATIONAL LAW 97
IV.2 THE WORLD COURT PROJECT 106
IV.3 THE FAILURE OF ICJ TO GIVE A CLEAR OPINION REGARDING THE LEGALITY OF THREAT OR USE OF NUCLEAR WEAPONS 114
IV.4 OUTSIDE OF THE ICJ OPTION AND SEPARATE OPINONS OF JUDGES 127

CHAPTER V: INTERNATIONAL LEGAL REGIME OF NUCLEAR ENERGY 135

V.1 FROM THE BARUCH PLAN TO THE TREATY ON NUCLEAR NON-PROLIFERATION (NPT) 135
V.2 THE SAFEGUARD GUARANTEES AND THE ROLE OF THE INTERNATIONAL ATOMIC ENERGY AGENCY (IAEA) 145
V.3 NUCLEAR FREE ZONES AS A MODEL TOWARDS THE CREATION OF A UNIVERSAL ZONE FREE OF NUCLEAR WEAPONS 154
V.4 NUCLEAR TEST BAN 163

CHAPTER VI: THE PROLIFERATION OF NUCLEAR WEAPONS AND TECHNOLOGY IN CONTEMPORARY CASES AND ISSUES REVOLVING AROUND THEM 173

VI.1 THE ROLE OF AN INDIVIDUAL AND THE NEED FOR IMPROVEMENT OF MEASURES AND INTERNATIONAL COOPERATION IN REGULATING INDIVIDUAL ACTIVITIES: THE CASE OF A.Q.KHAN 173
VI.2 NUCLEAR PROGRAMMES FOR PEACEFUL USE OR MORE PRECISELY: THE CASE OF IRAN 181
VI.3 A BLOW FROM INSIDE AGAINST THE NON-PROLIFERATION TREATY: THE CASE OF THE DEMOCRATIC PEOPLE'S REPUBLIC OF KOREA 190
VI.4 THE RISK OF PROLIFERATION FROM WEAK STATES 199

CHAPTER VII: NUCLEAR TERRORISM: PREVENTION AND THE FIGHT AGAINST IT 209

VII.1 NUCLEAR TERRORISM AS A REAL INTERNATIONAL CONCERN IN THE CONTEMPORARY WORLD 209
VII.2 THE PREVENTION AND FIGHT AGAINST NUCLEAR TERRORISM THROUGH INTERNAITONAL LAW 217
VII.3 PREVENTION AND FIGHTING NUCLEAR TERRORISM BY OTHER INTERNATIONAL ACTS 225
VII.4 OTHER BILATERAL AND OTHER MULTILATERAL APPROACHES IN PREVENTION AND THE FIGHT AGAINST NUCLEAR TERRORISM 233

CHAPTER VIII: CONCLUSION 243

LITERATURE 251

Index 287

Table of figures

Table 2.1.: Uranium exploitation and costs 36
Table 2.2.: Nuclear energy capacity in the world 39
Pic. 2.1. Chain reaction of atom nuclei splitting – The fission process 25
Pic. 2.2.: Projection of installed nuclear capacities by 2035 presented in MWe net 47
Pic. 2.3.: Yearly needs for nuclear reactors by 2035 presented in tU 48

To my wife Arlinda and for a peaceful and hopeful growing of our son and daughter Rroni and Ambla!

FOREWORD

I have developed the interest in the topic of nuclear energy and international security while in my post-graduate studies in the US in the year 2005-2006. Important developments happened around this time with Iranian nuclear program being "busted" forcing the Iranian regime to confess the existence of its nuclear programme. In another development, North Korea earlier announced its withdrawal from the NPT regime, a major blow from inside, just to move later with its first nuclear test in 2006. Other important events evolved around this time revolving around Russia facing major issues with the safety of its nuclear energy stockpiles and also Pakistan having issues around the safety of its nuclear energy stockpiles and perhaps even of its nuclear weapons. The whole international community was focused in finding solution on how to stop further proliferation activities of nuclear energy which might be used for military purposes. Perhaps to the good side, Libya confessed to possessing a nuclear programme and in 2003 decided to abandon its nuclear ambitions due to concerted international pressure. After the 9/11 nothing was granted anymore and the idea that terrorists and criminal organizations may well go ahead and seek way to get hold of nuclear energy to use it for their agendas. The US was the placed to be at that time where news headlines, many academic writings, professional and political discussion were focused on how to cope with the developing situation and that is where I realized that the nuclear energy issues is a challenging, interesting and important topic to write about.

However, at that time I was already into the mode and interest of another important topic of international law revolving around the principle of sovereignty and territorial integrity and self-determination related mainly to secessionist movements. In the academia, it is sometimes referred to as the remedial secession. I was mainly interested in the case of Kosovo and why Kosovo gained that right to self-determination and statehood due to its legal, political and historical past. Entering my PhD studies, I had to decide my focus area and here comes that earlier interest on nuclear energy and international security and it was the right time to do it. Another factor was, I believe, was my earlier high school education in natural sciences that was the Gymnasium Xhevdet Doda in Prishtina. Nuclear energy juxtaposes natural sciences such as physics, math or chemistry with social sciences such a law in trying to control what nature gave us in order to use it to our benefit and not to our destruction. The interest, motivation and necessary impetus was there to produce this work.

In the end I would like to thank Professor Enver Hasani, University of Prishtina with whom I have worked closely in this book and Professor Rainer Arnold, University of Regensburg for reviewing it and recommending it for publication.

I would be very happy to receive any comment on the following email address: besfort.rrecaj@uni-pr.edu

Author

CHAPTER I

INTRODUCTION

"The world that we have made as a result of the level of thinking we have done thus far creates problems that we cannot solve at the same level as the level we created them at."[1] Man, from his creation has been faced with various challenges and the overcoming of which has required the use of the thinking process, a process which has lead man to the developments we are living with today. Means and methods by which man managed to overcome the different challenges, in turn, created their challenges for which a new process of thinking was required to overcome them. This is best explained by the quote of a Nobel Prize winner and one of the individuals who contributed a lot to the process of developing nuclear weapons, Albert Einstein. The nuclear weapon was created to stop a great evil of the time that mankind was facing, to stop World War II (WW II). In itself, this idea sounded very appealing taking into consideration that this war was causing huge human suffering but also great material damage. The use of a weapon with a high destruction capacity, not seen before by mankind, was thought to prevent further suffering. However, the invention of the process of splitting atoms into smaller parts followed by the release of energy occurred a few years earlier. This process has given huge advantages to mankind for example, in the field of medicine while today this process is used more and more to produce electricity for peaceful use. Anyhow, parallel to its use for peaceful purposes man has invented ways to control it and use it for military purposes, to build nuclear weapons.

The dropping of the two bombs on Japan ultimately forced Japan to surrender in September of 1945.[2] Overcoming this huge challenge to mankind, through the invention of a devastating instrument, would cre-

[1] For more on Einstein Quotes see "Albert Einstein Site Online", visited on 30 December 2012 http://www.alberteinsteinsite.com/quotes/einsteinquotes.html.

[2] The two bombs hit cities of Hiroshima and Nagasaki on 6 respectively 9 November of 1945. Germany had surrendered earlier in May. For more on the WW II see Martin Gilbert, *The Second World War: A Complete History* (Henry Holt and Company, New York, 2004).

ate other complicated problems with more devastating potential which man is still facing today. Now that the devil was out of the bottle, many scientists who were involved in the Manhattan Project, including Albert Einstein, saw the potential risk and timely warned the decision makers of that time. In another rather ironic quote, Einstein expressed that *"I do not know how the Third World War will be fought, but I can tell you what they will use in the Fourth — rocks!"*.[3] In a situation where time and knowledge could not be retrieved, accompanied by the great will of many states to have such a weapon in their possession, would, in itself, create the problem of how to manage the new situation where the main focus is that such a weapon attracts as little attention as possible for states and as few as possible states possess such a weapon. Possession of nuclear weapons, in the first place, would be considered as a guarantee for national security thus making it highly attractive to have one.

One problem presents itself immediately and that is the knowhow of producing nuclear energy and that of the technology for delivering of nuclear weapons. States who have the knowhow in these two processes can easily combine them and create nuclear weapons and the means of delivering them as a basis to accommodate military requirements. Today, many states have the knowledge of how to enrich Uranium, as one of the key elements in the production of nuclear energy. Enriched Uranium at a certain low level serves for the production of electricity, the demand for which is increasing every day. But, the same technology may be used to enrich Uranium to a higher level which can then be used for military use. This increases, to a maximum level the risk of nuclear weapons proliferation, taking into consideration that applicable international legislation allows states to possess the knowhow and technology for the production of nuclear energy that is for peaceful use.

Today, the key problem lies with this issue, how to allow states to produce nuclear energy freely for peaceful use while the same states are prohibited from using their capacities to produce nuclear weapons and at the same time to stop the transfer of knowhow and technology from those states to others who intend to produce nuclear weapons. The main objective of this dissertation is to analyse this issue and how production of nuclear energy and related technology is managed at the international level. It analyses the work of main international actors

[3] Supra note 1.

that is states and international organisations, and their functions and competences in the international management of nuclear energy. This dissertation will try to give some answers to what the role of states and international organisations is, what their competences are and what should the changes be at the institutional and legislative level to fill loopholes for effective international management of nuclear energy. The international system is still state oriented and states still guard their independence jealously through principles of sovereignty and territorial integrity. Having no clear international hierarchy, it still remains with the willingness of states and their *bona fides* stance to fulfil international obligations. The issue becomes more complicated in cases pertaining to international security where any lack of will or sincerity may be a cause of raising tension and distrust among states.

The role of the individual in their personal capacity is seen to be very important and essential in the management of this process. The case of A.Q. Khan shows that an individual with an international network managed by persons in an individual capacity may cause huge problems. This unveils the need, but also shows a big gap at the international level, for regulation of individual capacities in this field. An individual should be treated much more as an international subject, with responsibility towards the international community for his/her activities related to the transfer of knowhow and technology for the production of nuclear energy.

The purpose of this dissertation is to analyse judicial regimes which regulate the production and use of fission material and its management. The main focus in this aspect is Highly Enriched Uranium, knowhow and technology for its production which despite its major benefits in different fields of life, may be used for military purposes with a direct impact on international security. Another element used for the production of nuclear energy is plutonium, which is a by-product obtained during the process of Uranium enrichment so, in order to come upon this element, states should first of all gain knowhow and technology for Uranium enrichment. With plutonium, the risk relates to states that already possess stocks of plutonium, but this will be discussed with the topic of securing stockpiles with radioactive elements, where plutonium is a part of the inventory. The method of producing nuclear energy is through the use of Helium elements. But, the problem with this way of producing energy is that, still, there is no technology available to control and manage it safely enough, thus this still remains outside the reality of states' agenda.

Enriching Uranium and the fission process also known as the splitting of atoms will be the main focus of this dissertation. The fusion process or the process of joining atomic nuclei will be analysed just as one of the processes for the production of energy which is a more complicated and hardly manageable process from the technical point of view and that is why states avoid the use of this methodology for the production of nuclear energy. With regards to nuclear technology, it has been concluded that it is very hard, almost impossible at this stage of development, to safely separate technologies which are used exclusively for peaceful use from that which is used exclusively for military use.

The proliferation of nuclear weapons by states creates a chain of problems because, in the first place, it endangers international security and peace. It is very logical that states do not want to live next to a nuclear weapons state. This may raise tension. Possession of nuclear weapons by one state may incite the other to have one, thus creating a sort of vicious cycle of spiralling escalation where each state wants to keep its advantage even if it is necessary to enter into an armed conflict. The Nuclear Non-Proliferation Treaty (NPT) tries to control the proliferation of nuclear energy for military use but as to how successful it has been still remains an issue of debate. Today, nevertheless this treaty has a universal membership but in particular situations it allows states to withdraw which makes a huge impact on the treaty. In the end, the proliferation of nuclear weapons multiplies the abilities of criminal and terrorist organisations to put such a weapon into their hands and thus realize their objectives. This last option would be the worst nightmare that anybody could imagine.

If states possess nuclear weapons then it is implied that those serve a particular purpose, that of securing their national security thus they consider their use as legal. But, how real is a nuclear weapons conflict and what are the international rules relating to the use of force and how is the use of nuclear weapons defined are topics which will be analysed here. A more specific analysis will be done on the concept of the use of preventive force followed by concrete examples which possess a very controversial issue leaving lots of room for interpretation. Seeing the eventual high risk to mankind in the event of nuclear conflict, a wide international initiative was taken under the name of the World Court Project through which it is meant to delegitimize these weapons. This project targeted the International Court of Justice through the UN General Assembly but in its advisory opinion this court could not approve the claims of those who brought this issue before it.

To manage the control of nuclear energy, man, acting on behalf of the state has designed concepts, means and methods, the purpose of which was to, at least, prevent the further proliferation of nuclear weapons. The starting point, of course, is the international legal infrastructure by which states mutually agree to designing provisions dealing with nuclear energy and weapons and their control. At the core is the NPT, the objective of which is the prevention of proliferation of nuclear energy for military use without infringing upon the right of each state to use it for peaceful purposes. For the realisation of the objectives of the treaty, states established other technical provisions and institutions with the consent of Member States. Still, it remains a big issue as to what to do with states which choose not to be part of the Treaty while this Treaty recognised five nuclear weapons states as such. This dissertation will discuss the main international legislation dealing with nuclear energy. It will try to give some answers as to why the regime of this Treaty is considered to respect double standards and why some nuclear states still remain outside the regime. In this way conclusions will follow on what this means for international security and the proliferation of nuclear weapons and material and is this regime too fragile taking into consideration the fact that states may at any time withdraw from this regime by respecting certain procedures which seem to be easy to justify.

While at the global level it still remains an illusion, different regions saw the creation of international regimes which expressly prohibit, in general, the use of nuclear weapons and the existence of such programmes. These regimes present very important steps which imply that, today, peace on the planet, at least legally, is protected from nuclear weapons. It is hardly imaginable that in the near future we can see a world free of such weapons, but, maybe we can see other similar regimes reducing the areas of land without such a regime. In an interview given by Mohamed El Baradei, former head of the International Atomic Energy Agency, he stated that the world may move forward towards reducing the amount of nuclear weapons but they will not be totally eliminated. According to him, those [nuclear weapon] which remain should be supervised internationally, maybe by the Security Council.[4] This dissertation will try to give some answers to the role of these regional regimes in the prevention of nuclear proliferation. Important aspects which will be discussed are constraints put on nuclear states outside of these regimes. What are these constraints and how applicable are they? It seems that these regimes, nevertheless, remain too fragile in cases of involvement of high national interests as interpreted by powerful states which possess nuclear weapons. A good example is with the nuclear free regimes in East Asia which will be discussed in this work.

From the philosophical aspect the work used qualitative methodology by interpreting the international legislation in regulating this field and also quantitative methodology by comparing different factors presented in numbers which deal with the number of nuclear weapons, amount of nuclear energy produced in the world and also the main sources of Uranium as the main element for production of nuclear energy today. The historical aspect of the development of current issue is very important and through which the work tries to explain the essence of the existence of nuclear energy today and reasons why man has focused on developing such programmes. The dissertation will aim to explain in a critical aspect the state of international legislation related to nuclear energy and to research the field of law which needs to be changed or to be strengthened to achieve international security and peace.

The dissertation is divided into six main chapters while the first and the last deal with the introduction and conclusion respectively. The second chapter gives a brief overview of the development of the concept fission process up to production and its use. This chapter uses technical resources in trying to explain how nuclear energy is produced, Uranium resources, Uranium enrichment technology and also a brief description of states which possess or are believed to possess nuclear weapons.

[4] "It was Others Who Failed", Intervista e Mohamed Elbaradei, *Spiegel,* 18 May 2009, visited on 15 January 2012, http://www.spiegel.de/international/world/0,1518,625600,00.html.

States possess nuclear weapons to use them for the protection of their national interests. The legal regime of the use of force is regulated by the UN Charter. The third chapter explains when states may use force. In principle, the use of force is forbidden by the Charter, nevertheless, states, in exceptional cases may, however, use it. But, even when they are allowed to use force, states are constrained in the use of means of warfare according to humanitarian law. The use of nuclear weapons is not expressly prohibited by humanitarian law, but what may be the effect of the Martens clause and how may this clause be applied in the case of nuclear weapons? The military doctrines play an important role in this aspect and which will be analysed in this chapter for the purpose of clarifying ambiguous situations at international level. By analysing military doctrines, this chapter will try to determine more accurately what the circumstance are and what leads states by their way of interpretation consider to be necessary and leave no other option to the utilization of their nuclear weapons arsenal.

The fourth chapter analyses key international agreements which regulate the use of nuclear energy starting with the NPTas the main pillar of this perspective. The main objective of this agreement is to create an international regime for preventing the proliferation of nuclear energy and technology for military use. Nevertheless, this regime is criticized for applying double standards by allowing five states to possess nuclear weapons while prohibiting this privilege to others. What are the limitations of this regime and what are the guarantees provided by the five nuclear states given to other states which are party to the regime? Why a state outside the regime should be part of it and limit its right to possess nuclear weapons or to develop technology and knowhow to produce it? The regime is not designed to regulate the use of force but the mere fact that a state possesses nuclear weapons implies that they have reserved their right to use them in a particular situation which is determined by their own interpretation. This dissertation will analyse nuclear weapon free zones and their role in the creation of a safer environment from nuclear weapons.

The International Court of Justice is the main institution for the interpretation of international law. After the end of the Cold War, this court was faced with a request to give an advisory opinion on the legality of the threat or use of nuclear weapons. Still, this opinion will be considered as very controversial which left a lot to be desired if one wanted to have greater clarification. With regard the main issue, the judges were split 7/7 while the drafting of the opinion was too general and vague. Maybe this court should deal with this issue once more, because, after some time, it could reason and handle such a request in a different manner and be more precise. The role of humanitarian law and the protection of the individual and environment are becoming more important every day in all aspects of international regulation. A wider interpretation in scope could have a direct impact on the further limitation of the use of nuclear weapons in a state of affairs where reaching an international consensus on delegitimizing them seems to be unreachable, even in the foreseeable future. The fifth chapter analyses the opinion of the International Court of Justice related to nuclear weapons and whether this court could have drafted its opinion differently. To reflect on the background of this opinion, this chapter will analyse separate opinions of judges in a situation where the majority of them have criticised the opinion as too general and too vague.

The NPTmay be said to be in a way, a failure because it has not yet achieved its objective taking into consideration that some states have developed their nuclear programmes and today possess nuclear weapons after its entry into force. The regime of this Treaty and guarantees given by the five nuclear weapons states have not made it attractive for states like India, Pakistan and Israel to become part of it, while North Korea withdrew completely from the regime to carry out its first nuclear test in 2005. A very controversial issue remains with Iran which still remains within the regime. The sixth chapter will analyse issues related to proliferation and how nuclear weapons and programmes proliferated after the entry into force of the NPT. A particular emphasis will be given to the role of the individual and the clandestine network of A.Q. Khan, which contributed a lot to their proliferation. International legislation deals mainly with states, while actions of individuals in their personal capacity still remain mostly in the exclusive domain of the state as an internal matter and it seems that states should do more in this direction focusing on further improvement of internal legislation and also in better cooperation at international level to fight such phenomenon.

The seventh chapter focuses on the issue which is a concern and related with nuclear energy; on the possibility of criminal and terrorist organisation being able to possess a nuclear weapon or enough material to produce an improvised nuclear weapon. The attacks of 11 September show that terrorist networks, such as Al Qaeda, are capable of using all possible means to realize their objectives. This chapter will analyse how states are doing in fighting international nuclear terrorism. The lack of will of states to sign key agreements followed by the lack of international consensus on defining terrorism will be analysed as a major issue in this aspect. It will also analyse other international instruments which help to fight nuclear terrorism and the role of international bilateral and multilateral cooperation in this perspective. It will try to present an answer to the possibilities of such organisations obtaining such weapons or their capabilities of building one.

Due to the complexity of issues related to nuclear energy and weapons and its technology it is very often regarded as idealistic to find a common long term solution because we are dealing here with a problem which interlocks high national interests, where states hesitate, at the highest level possible, to cooperate with each other thus embracing a more extreme mood regarded as *real politik* where the main objective is how to increase your power to the detriment of the other state. The eighth chapter will present conclusions drawn upon the analysing issues from different perspectives with the main conclusion that at this state of affairs at international level, the best way of controlling and managing nuclear materials is to centralise its production and distribution. This would enable the establishment of a global reserve which would offer enough enriched Uranium for peaceful use to all states that need it. The International Atomic Energy Agency would have the main role in supervising this reserve while the main suppliers of enriched Uranium would be the five nuclear states which are accepted as such by the NPT.

This dissertation uses the term nuclear energy but literature and different agreements also use the technical term "fission material" to reflect on the way nuclear energy is produced by splitting the nuclei of atoms. In specific cases, however, this term is also used. The reference for peaceful use is used to describe all ways of the use of nuclear energy which excludes the military aspect of it. The term nuclear states is used for those states who have potential nuclear military capabilities. A large part of this work analyses with the interpretation of international provision of international agreements. During its interpretation, in specific cases, the original language of the provision is inserted within the text with italic lettering. To better explain the technical aspect the dissertation uses illustrations which are taken from official web pages of different agencies which deal with nuclear energy. The names of different personalities are written in original. During the research, a visit was paid to the main headquarters of the International Atomic Energy Agency in Vienna where discussions were held with legal experts contributing a lot in orienting and explaining different issues related to the topic and its importance. Also, an interview was held with the Director of the International Peace Institute in Vienna and with the representatives of the Hungarian Mission in UN Organisations in Vienna, including the International Atomic Energy Agency.

CHAPTER II

NUCLEAR ENERGY: FROM INVENTION TO ITS MULTIPLE USE

II.1 INVENTION AND DEVELOPMENT OF THE FISSION PROCESS AND NUCLEAR ENERGY

The development of the concept to produce nuclear energy by splitting the nuclei of atoms, in technical language known as the fission process, started in the first decade of the XX century by British physicist Ernest Rutherford.[1] While the industrial development accelerated at that time, production of energy in this way marked a very important step for the development of mankind. But, if that could be controlled, to be used to meet the requirement of development in general, the samc could be used for its destruction. This concern was spinning around heads of scientists such as Ernest Rutherford, Ernest Lawrence, Albert Einstein etc., who invented it, from the beginning and later worked in the fission process. Very soon, this concern would reach other layers of society such as the political elite and has continued up to the present. Therefore it is a simple fact that the fission process and its technology is the same for military and civilian development which colours this process with two facets, which, at least morally, juxtapose to each other. These are two facets of the same medal where the one has to do with using that energy for peaceful purposes[2] while the other one has to do with the possibility of its use for destructive military purposes.[3]

The theoretical concept invented by Rutherford was developed at the beginning of the XX century but realization of the splitting of the

[1] Sarah J. Diehl and James Clay Moltz, *History of Nuclear Weapons and Non-Proliferation: A Reference Handbook* (ABC Clio, California; Colorado; England 2002) pp. 1-2.

[2] The term for peaceful use is used in this work to refer to the process where the Uranium is used mainly for the production of electricity but also for other purposes other than military.

[3] Supra note 5 p. 2.

atom nuclei in practice would come much later. Necessity is the mother of all invention and in this case the need to end WWII pushed the US to accelerate the realization of this process, in a bid to create a weapon of mass destruction which would force the enemy to surrender. From the technical and technological point of view, the main issue was to invent a device which would help to split the nuclei of the atom. Physician Ernes Lawrence from the US had invented a concept which would be used as the basis for building a device called cyclotron in the University of California-Berkley at the beginning of the 1930's. Cyclotron would help to realize the process of splitting the atom nuclei.[4] On the other hand, in Hungary, scientist Leo Szilard had developed the concept of "chain reaction" in 1934 which is initiated when a neutron hits the atom nuclei, thus making it highly unstable and splitting it into two pieces and at the same time releasing free neutrons. Free neutrons from the previous splitting hit the nuclei of other atoms thus generating other processes of fission which is the process known as the "chain reaction". [5] Two pieces of the split nuclei known as products of the fission process are turned into radioactive isotopes. Despite the creation of these isotopes and the release of free neutrons, this process also releases energy. For military use in building nuclear weapons, this energy is released impulsively with a devastating effect while for peaceful uses for example with nuclear civilian reactors, this chain reaction is controlled to produce electricity according to the needs of the citizens.[6]

To understand the fission process we need to understand the structure of the atom. The atomic number of Uranium is 92, which represents the number of protons in this element, which remains unchanged in all types of atoms of this element. But, the number of neutrons distinguishes two types of Uranium isotopes. In nature, there are two types where one has 143 while the other has 146 neutrons. The sum of the numbers of protons and neutrons give a specific isotope of the

---

[4] *Ibid.* The Cyclotrone is a device which enables acceleration of sub atomic particles. In the case of nuclear energy this device enables delivering of proton flocks which are collided at high velocity inside the Uranium atomic nuclei and splitting the nuclei thus changing the physical characteristics of the initial material. For more see "*Jefferson Lab Glossary*" visited on 25 April 2012, http:www.education.jlab.orgwglossary/index.html.

[5] Frank Barnaby, *How Nuclear Weapons Spread: Nuclear Weapons Proliferation in the 1990s* (Routledge, New York, 2005), Introduction. In this case we have to do with the atmoci nuclei of Uranium U-235 as one of the isotopes of this element.

[6] *Ibid.*

atom of Uranium known as U-235 and U-238.[7] Of these two Uranium isotopes, U-235 is the object of interest in this dissertation because its nuclei is highly unstable and can be split very easily if hit by a neutron during the fission process, even in cases where it is hit by neutrons at low velocity. This makes the realisation of the chain reaction and release of energy very easy. The isotopes which go through the fission process are known as the fission material.[8] In nature, the concentration of U-235 isotopes in Uranium is on average around 0.72%. In order to increase this concentration the so called Uranium enrichment process is carried out. Uranium enrichment is carried out in three ways: gaseous diffusion; use of ordinary centrifuges; and gas centrifuges. Today, the most common way and the cheapest form of enriching Uranium is performed by using big gas centrifuges.[9]

Pic. 2.1. Chain reaction of atom nuclei splitting – The fission process

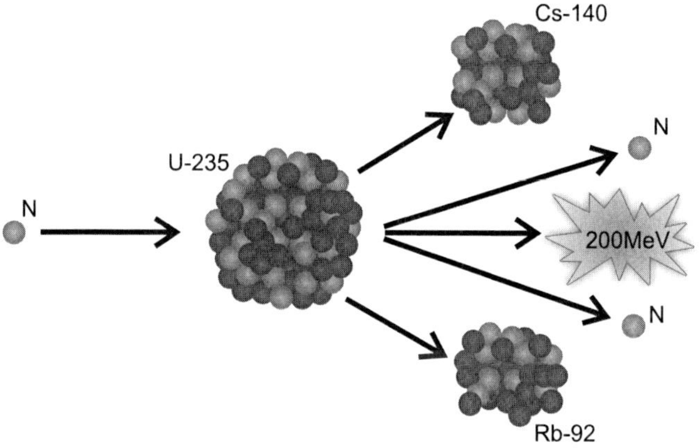

$U^{235} + n \rightarrow$ fission + 2 or 3 n + 200 MeV[10]

[7] Supra note 9 p. 5.

[8] The Uranium isotope U-238 can undergo a fission process only in cases when neutrons colliding with its nuclei move at a certain velocity which makes the whole process more complicated to achieve the result. See supra note 9 pp. 5-7.

[9] Joseph Cirincione, *Bomb Scare: The History and Future of Nuclear Weapons* (Columbia University Press, New York, 2007) pp. 7-8.

[10] *"Nuclear Chain Reactions"*, Atomic Archive, visited on 20 March 2012, www.atomicarchive.com/Fission/Fission2.shtml.

Another very important element for the production of nuclear energy is Plutonium. This element cannot be found in nature, but it is produced as a by-product during the process of Uranium enrichment. This was invented by scientists from the University of California-Berkley, Glen Seaborg and Emilio Segre. They realized that when the Uranium isotope U-238 absorbs one neutron it turns into a new element with 147 neutrons and with the atomic number 239, now known as Plutonium. This element is also highly unstable. In fact, in comparison to Uranium, a smaller amount of this element is needed to initiate a chain reaction and thus release of huge amount of energy.[11]

Another process, opposite to fission, is the process of the joining of atomic nuclei or the fusion process.[12] This process is realized when two nuclei of light elements, such as Hydrogen, are joined to create a heavier element. The energy released in the fusion process is bigger than the one produced during the fission process. In addition, this process requires more energy to initiate it. Elements which are used to realize the fusion process are Tritium (H-3) and Deuterium (H-2).[13] Through the fusion process a so called plasma energy is released similar to the sun, but the production of such energy is very complex and complicated in that man still could not device a safe enough reactor for peaceful use.[14] Due to the high complexity, states are focused on the production of energy through the fission process by using Uranium, so this dissertation will focus on this process.[15] From the military point of view, the first hydrogen bomb was created using the fusion process and tested in 1952 in the US.[16]

The development of the atomic bomb is closely related to the name of the scientist Albert Einstein, who sent a letter to President

[11] Supra note13, pp. 8-9.

[12] Supra note 8.

[13] In this process it is also used Lithium-6 Deuteride which when heated at high temperatures disintegrates by creating Tritium and Deuterium. For more see supra note 5, pp. 199-200.

[14] It was thought that through this process they would be able to produce and inexhaustible source of energy meeting the demand of mankind even in a future distance. However they would need more time to work in this direction, see Robin Herman, *Fusion: The Search for Endless Energy* (Cambridge University Press, US, 1990 Reprinted 1991), pp. 3-4.

[15] Ernes Rutherford, regarding the fussion process, expressed that *"We cannot control atomic energy to an extent that would be of any use commercially, and I believe we are not ever likely to do so"*, see Garry McCracken & Peter Stott, *Fusion: The Energy of Universe* (Elsevier Academic Press, Massachusets, USA, 2005), p. 3

[16] *Id,* p. 4.

Franklin Roosevelt presenting findings by two of his colleagues on nuclear energy and the possibilities of creating a bomb, which can release a huge amount of energy by using the technology of splitting Uranium atoms.[17] Nevertheless, despite this enthusiasm, Einstein also showed his concern for the future of mankind in case of its misuse. In the same letter dated 2 August 1939, Einstein expresses that *"it may become possible to set up a nuclear chain reaction in a large mass of Uranium, by which vast amounts of power and large quantities of new radium-like elements would be generated"*[18]. The letter mentions that the invention of such a phenomenon would help to create a bomb with a highly devastating effect which at the same time can be transported by ship but with the capability of destroying the whole seaport.[19]

On the other side of the Atlantic, in Great Britain, two scientists, Otto Frisch and Rudolf Peierls had calculated the destruction capacity of a nuclear bomb. According to them, if 1 kg of Uranium were used, it would be possible to use a bomb, the effect of which would be equal to several thousand tons of ordinary dynamite TNT.[20] In their memorandum, drafted in March 1940, among others, they expressed their deep concern on the possibility that Nazi Germany may possess such a bomb *"if one works on the assumption that Germany is, or will be, in the possession of this weapon, it must be realized that no shelters are available that would be effective and that could be used on a large scale. The most effective reply would be a counter-threat with a similar bomb. Therefore it seems to us important to start production as soon and as rapidly as possible, even if it is not intended to use the bomb as a means of attack"*.[21] Various intelligent sources from western countries

---

[17] Einstein collaborators, Enrico Fermi dhe Leo Szilard conducted new research showing that the Uranium elements may be turnd into an important source of energy, see supra note 13 p. 1.

[18] Einstein letter to President Roosevelt, 2 August 1939, p. 1, Atomic Archive, visited on 10 March 2012, http://www.atomicarchive.com/Docs/Begin/Einstein.shtml.

[19] At he same time the concern was expressed here for the possibility of the Nazi Germany getting hold of such an important research data or perhaps it is already working on such a weapon. This is due to the fact that Germany at that time had stopped selling of Uranium for the Czech mines after occupying it and that in the Kaise-Wilehelm in Berlin they are working on the American invention regarding Uranium, see *Ibid.*

[20] Supra note 13, p. 8.

[21] The two scientists had escaped earlier from Germany in Great Britain as refugees and had solid knowledge about the German programmes and its affinities for production of such a weapon, see The Frisch-Peierls Memorandum, March 1940, Atomic Archive, visited on 8 September 2012, http://www.atomicarchive.com/Docs/Begin/FrischPeierls.shtml.

believed that the atomic industry of Nazi Germany, under the leadership of Werner Heisenberg,[22] may make considerable progress in developing atomic energy.[23] In the Far East, Japan was also planning to carry out research on the production of nuclear material, including the development of the cyclotron.[24]

Such remarks, flooding in to him from the academic world, and also the impact that British Prime Minister Winston Churchill had upon him, made President Roosevelt go ahead with the support of the project to build the atomic bomb also known by the code name "The Manhattan Project" or in a more formal way "The Manhattan Engineering District". In Great Britain a committee was established with the name MAUD[25] with the purpose of evaluating advise from Frisch-Peierls who pretended that *"material for building of the bomb may be ready by the end of 1943"*.[26] On 9 October 1941, President Roosevelt had authorized the project to build the first atomic bomb. One of the key persons supporting the project was Vannevar Bush, who would head the US National Defence Research Committee. The surprise attack on Pearl Harbour in December of 1941 increased the political pressure even further to accelerate activities for building the nuclear bomb as an imperative for self-defence and to end the war.

The Manhattan Project was a joint American-British endeavour but all of the activities to realize it took place in the US. Separate specialized activities were dispersed in cities like Chicago, Handfor (Washington), Oak Ridge (Tennessee) and Los Alamos (New Mexico).[27] J. Robert Oppenheimer, physics professor at the University of California-Berkley, was assigned to head the project while General Lieutenant Leslie

[22] Werner Heizenbert won a Nobel Peace Price in the field of Quantum Mecahnics and its application in detection of allotropic forms of Hydrogen.

[23] Supra note 5, p. 3.

[24] Cyclotrone accelerate particles through its magnetic field. See supra note 8.

[25] MAUD took the name after a british nurse who worked with the Danish physicist Niels Bohr. For more see supra note 13, p. 3.

[26] Supra note 13, p. 3.

[27] Facilities for the production of Plutonium were installed in Hanford; In Oak Ridge was istalled the Calutron for the fission process; while the laboratory of designing and building the nuclear bomb was located in Los Almos. In 1944, another reactor for the production of Uranium U-235 was constructed in Clinton, Tenesse. For more see "Timeline of the Nuclear Age", Nuclear Files, visited on 8 September 2012, http://www.nuclearfiles.org/menu/timeline/timeline_page.php?year=1943.

Groves from the US army was to become the head of administration.[28] The project engaged various scientists who, in principle, new nothing more other than that they were working on an important project but not its final objective. Robert Serber, a scientist engaged in the project, held some lectures for other scientists which were to be known as the Los Alamos Primer. These lectures contained instructions on how to build a bomb for military use using the principle of a controlled chain reaction to achieve the release of a high amount of energy.[29] The focus of Serber, in particular, was Uranium U-235. According to his calculations, 1 kg of Uranium U-235 could be used to build a bomb capable of releasing energy equal to 20,000 metric tons of TNT.[30] The first radioactive material to build the atomic bomb containing U-235 came from Oak Ridge in Los Alamos on 2 February 1945, and the weight of which was 200 metric grams.[31]

During the process, scientists had to deal with two problems: realization of the chain reaction on one hand and development of a bomb capable of handling the chain reaction on the other hand. This project managed to come up with designs which are still used in nuclear weapons technology. The one used the so called gun-type fission while the other implosion-type technique.[32] The first design is suitable to use Uranium while the other one uses Plutonium. The first one was used in the bomb which was dropped on Hiroshima, while the other one was used in the bomb dropped on Nagasaki.[33] The first atomic bomb test would be realized on 16 July 1945 in Trinity Alamogordo, New Mexico.[34] News of the success of this test first reached the ears of the new President Harry Truman while he was present at the Potsdam Conference discussing the fate of Germany after the war.[35]

[28] It was the American general who chose Oppenaheimer to head the project, see supra note 13, p. 4.

[29] Notess from his lectures are now declassified and may be found at the official webpage of the American Federation of Scientists, visited on 9 September 2012, http://www.fas.org/sgp/othergov/doe/lanl/docs1/00349710.pdf.

[30] *Id.*

[31] Supra note 13, p. 9.

[32] *Id*, p. 10.

[33] *Id*, pp. 10-11.

[34] Despited earlier mathematical calculations on the effect of nuclear energy the first test surprised all of them who were involved in the Manhattan Project when seein it in reality. For more see "Timeline of Nuclear Age", Atomic Archive, visited on 9 Septebmer 2012, http://www.atomicarchive.com/Timeline/Time1940.shtml.

[35] Supra note 13, p. 11.

Maybe Nazi Germany was the main reason behind the accelerated efforts to build an atomic bomb however it would be used against the other enemy of the time, Japan, because Germany surrendered earlier, before the bomb was built.[36] After the successful test, the US continued to build the atomic bomb to use in a real war situation. As a result, two bombs would be built. The one known as "the Little Boy" used Uranium and was dropped on Hiroshima, and the other one known as "the Fat Man" used Plutonium and was dropped on Nagasaki.[37]

The decision to drop the atomic bomb on Japanese cities was taken by the US President Harry Truman. President Truman created a provisional committee to formulate the politics of using atomic bombs. This committee, in its politics had designated that the atomic bomb should be used against a factory which is used for military purposes and without any warning.[38] The decision to drop the bombs was not made without objections. The scientists of the Metallurgical Laboratory in Chicago headed by Leo Szilard, seeing the devastating effect of such a bomb and the proliferation risk in other states, asked President Truman to reconsider his decision and to give Japan another chance to surrender. They clearly presented their concerns of nuclear weapons proliferation in the future which would pose a threat to the US, considering that the Manhattan Project was only the first step in an unstoppable process which could produce similar bombs with even greater devastating capabilities.[39]

On 6 August 1945 the first bomb "Little Boy", with a capacity of 15 metric kilotons was dropped on Hiroshima, and three days later the second bomb "Fat Man" with a capacity of 21 metric kilotons was dropped on Nagasaki. Their effect proved to be devastating, while the decision to drop them remains a hot debate. Many personalities including US high ranking heads had different opinions on the war against Japan. Among them was the US army general who became later the US

[36] Supra note 5, p. 5.

[37] *Ibid.*

[38] Notes from the meeting of Provisional Committee of 1 June 1945 para. VI. For more see "The Manhattan Project", Nuclear Files, visited on 9 September 2012, http://www.nuclearfiles.org/menu/key-issues/nuclear-weapons/history/pre-cold-war/manhattan-project/index.htm.

[39] Records of the Chief of Enginneers, Manhattan Enginneer District, Harrison-Bundy File, US National archive, Record Group 77, folder #76, publikuar në Nuclear Files, visited on 9 September 2012, http://www.nuclearfiles.org/menu/key-issues/ethics/issues/scientific/petition-chicago-metallurgical-laboratory.htm.

President, Dwight Eisenhower, who expressed that *"I had been conscious of depression and so I voiced to (Sec. Of War Stimson) my grave misgivings, first on the basis of my belief that Japan was already defeated and that dropping the bomb was completely unnecessary, and secondly because I thought that our country should avoid shocking world opinion by the use of a weapon whose employment was, I thought, no longer mandatory as a measure to save American lives. It was my belief that Japan was, at this very moment, seeking a way to surrender with a minimum loss of face."*[40] In these words we can see his scepticism against dropping the bomb as not necessary from the military point of view and the protection of American citizens but also morally not necessary. According to research conducted in 1946 on the Strategic Bombardment of the USA it was concluded that *"Certainly prior to 31 December 1945, and in all probability prior to 1 November 1945, Japan would have surrendered even if the atomic bombs had not been dropped, even if Russia had not entered the war, and even if no invasion had been planned or contemplated."*[41] The research confirms concerns the American President had had earlier. However, maybe Japan would have surrendered later, but it would still remain a relative and even conspirative issue as to how many lives could be saved from the war, taking into conisation that the two bombs dropped on Hiroshima and Nagasaki took the lives of around 200,000 humans.[42] In other words, would there be fewer victims if the war dragged on for a few more months without dropping the atomic bombs. In this case, we have to take account of other indirect effects which are very hard to be ascertained in time and space.

Looking at reality the devastating effect and possibilities of other states running to get hold of one of them, President Truman in his address to congress stated that: *"The hope of civilization lies in international arrangements looking, if possible, to the renunciation of the use and development of the atomic bomb, and directing and encouraging the use of atomic energy and all future scientific information toward peaceful and humanitarian ends"*.[43] This was a message of hope when

[40] General Dwight Eisenhower, US Responses to Dropping the Bomb, 1945, Nuclear Files , visited on 5 June 2012, http://www.nuclearfiles.org/menu/key-issues/nuclear-/eapons/history/pre-cold-/ar/hiroshima-nagasaki/us-responses-to-bomb.htm.

[41] *Ibid.*

[42] *Weapons of Terror: Freeing the World of Nuclear, Biological and Chemical Arms, Weapons of Mass Destruction Commission* (EO Grafiska, Stockholm, 2006), p. 32.

[43] President Harry S. Truman Message to Congress on the Atomic Bomb, Washington

nearing the end of WW II but it was also a message of deep concern that the development of such weapons would not only be the privilege of the US. Nevertheless, the greatest concern relates to the possibility of such weapons falling into the hands of states or other non-governmental organisations which would not hesitate to use them for aggressive purposes. Also, the emphasis here is laid upon the potential benefit of using his source of energy for *"peaceful and humanitarian end"*, meaning on the possibilities of its use for the production of electricity, the need for which would increase every year to support the development of mankind.

Today, we can still ask the question what if the dropping of the nuclear bombs had not been considered as necessary to stop Japan and end WW II. Would the world revile the existence of these weapons or would that still remain a military secret? Considering the devastating effect on Hiroshima and Nagasaki, every state started to feel threatened by their existence and started hankering for their possession which could be used at least as a deterrent. Had the states not been able to see this devastating effect, maybe states would not have raced for such weapons, in which case the nuclear proliferation would be stopped. This argument is hardly plausible considering that some states, already had such programmes and a considerable number of scientists had the knowledge about such a process. It is more plausible that had the bombs not been dropped, it could have delayed nuclear weapon proliferation but probably it could not have stopped it forever.

DC, 03 October 1945, published in Harry S. Truman Library and Museum, Public Papers of the Presidents: Harry Truman 1945-1953, visited on 10 September 2012, http://www.trumanlibrary.org/publicpapers/index.php.

II.2 MULTIPLE USE, PRODUCTION AND RISKS FROM RADIOACTIVE MATERIALS

The benefits from radioactive materials, the invention of the chain reaction and its control and also the ability to enrich Uranium had an important impact on different fields of life in applied sciences, military, civil engineering, medicine, agriculture etc.[44] The military industry managed to produce nuclear weapons which, upon activation, release a high amount of energy while civil engineering managed to produce electricity in a process controlled by specific reactors which is used by the wide population.[45] According to Hannes Alven, a winner of a Nobel Peace Prize in nuclear physics, *"the military atom and the civil atom are the Siamese Twins"*.[46]

In the applied sciences, radioactive isotopes are used to cure or to detect particular diseases. Radioactive isotopes are produced in reactors through the splitting of atoms and are also known as radioisotopes such as for example, technetium-99.[47] Today, these radioisotopes are used, especially, in detecting heart and brain diseases through the scanning process. In treating diseases, radioisotopes are used to cure cancer for example, by injecting a filament of radioactive material directly in the place where the cancer has developed in the human body in order to dissipate the tumour and to kill cancerous cells. Other methods to cure diseases include the swallowing of such a radioisotope for example, radioactive iodine in curing thyroid glands or its direct placement in a body cavity with cancer such as cobalt-60.[48]

In industry, radioisotopes are used to scan thick sections of steel to check its structure for eventual cracks especially in the case of railway tracks where the density and strength of steel should be highly precise to withhold heavy weights. Radioisotope caesium-137 is used in this process. In agriculture, radioisotopes with for example Cobalt-60

---

[44] "What is nuclear fission", Nuclear Files, visited on 10 March2012, http://www.nuclearfiles.org/menu/key-issues/nuclear-weapons/basics/what-is-fission.htm.

[45] Supra note 9, Introduction.

[46] Miles A. Pomber "Editor's Note", Arms Control Association, visited on 18 Juley 2012 http://www.armscontrol.org/act/2008_04/EditorsNote.

[47] Supra note 49, Introduction.

[48] *Ibid.*

are used mostly in developing countries to control insects which destroy agricultural crops.[49]

Radioactive materials are used for the production of electricity which is so important to support various industries in the industrialized world which are faced with an increasing demand for additional and sustainable sources of energy. The spectrum usage of this energy stretches even further. Russia is in the end phase of producing a locomotive which will run on nuclear energy.[50] Also, the European Space Agency, in cooperation with NASA, is working on constructing a spaceship to explore Mars and it is believed that it will be realized in the not too distance future.[51] Among such projects, research robots have been constructed which are sent to Mars and are energized by nuclear energy.[52] This makes the mission of a robot very efficient because it supplies the robot with a sustainable and constant source of energy.

Despite the multiple use of the fission process, the key issue which relates to international security, deals with the specific relations between the use of this energy for peaceful purposes in the production of electricity on one hand in its use for military use on the other hand. This is so because, while in medicine the quantity needed for radioactive elements is very small, the need is for a much higher production of such elements for peaceful use for the production of electricity both in quantity and quality (the concentration of radioactive isotopes). This means that states that possess nuclear reactors to enrich Uranium to be used for the production of electricity then, the same technique and technology can be used to enrich Uranium up to the level needed for military use and the production of nuclear weapons.

Uranium is a common element in nature. It is dispersed between the stones of the earth's crust but it is not mainly concentrated in ore, making it difficult to exploit. The Uranium deposits, which are econom-

---

[49] *Ibid.*

[50] "Revolutionary railroad: Atomic train being developed in Russia", *RT*, 20 February 2011, visited on 10 July 2012, http://rt.com/news/sci-tech/revolutionary-locomotive-russia-atomic/.

[51] Martin Lamonica, "How nuke power bested solar in latest March mission", *CBS News*, 22 November 2011, visted on 10 July 2012, http://www.cbsnews.com/8301-205_162-57329453/how-nuke-power-bested-solar-in-latest-March-mission/.

[52] NASA has build its March research laboratory called "Curiosity" which is now in Maqrch and is energized using Plutonium dioxide, see *Ibid.*

ically favourable for exploitation, are in stones conglomerates of quartz, phosphates and sand stones etc.[53] Exploitation of Uranium in these cases is not very difficult and it can be mined by the opening of underground or open pits (open cast) and also by the process of soil drainage. After extracting the ore, it is sent to special mills which extract Uranium in the oxidized form is known by the formula U_3O_8, which has a yellow colour. Because of the colour it is called *"Yellow Cake"*. After its production, *"Yellow Cake"* moves further along the process of purification and refining.[54] Presented below are tables representing Uranium sources in the world according to the OECD.

[53] Supranote 49, p. 3.

[54] *Id*, p. 4.

Table 2.1.: Uranium exploitation and costs[55]

Costs according to states

	<USD 40WKg U	**<USD 80WKg U**	**<USD 130WKg U**	**<USD 260WKg U**
Algeria	0	0	19 500	19 500
Argentina	0	7 000	10 400	10 400
Australia NA	1	163 000	1 176 000	1 179 000
Brazil	139 900	157 700	157 700	157 700
Canada	267 100	336 800	361 100	387 400
Central African Republic	0	0	12 000	12 000
Chile	0	0	0	800
China	52 000	100 900	115 900	115 900
Congo, Dem. Rep. of	0	0	0	1 400
Czech Republic	0	400	400	400
Finland	0	0	1 100	1 100
France	0	0	0	9 000
Gabon	0	0	4 800	4 800
Germany	0	0	0	3 000
Greece	0	0	0	1 000
India	0	0	55 200	55 200
Indonesia	0	0	4 800	4 800
Iran, Islamic Republic of	0	0	0	700
Italy	0	0	4 800	4 800
Japan	0	0	6 600	6 600
Jordan	0	44 000	44 000	44 000
Kazakhstan	14 600	233 900	336 200	414 200
Malaysia	0	8 100	13 600	13 600
Mexico	0	0	0	1 300
Mongolia	0	37 500	37 500	37 500
Namibia	0	2 000	157 000	157 000
Niger	17 000	42 500	242 000	244 600
Peru	0	0	1 300	1 300
Portugal	0	4 500	6 000	6 000
Romania	0	0	3 100	3 100
Russian Federation	0	100 400	181 400	181 400
Slovakia	0	0	0	5 100
Slovenia	0	0	1 700	1 700
Somalia	0	0	0	5 000
South Africa	76 800	142 000	195 200	195 200
Spain	0	2 500	4 900	4 900
Sweden	0	0	4 000	4 000
Tanzania	0	0	0	8 900
Turkey	0	0	7 300	7 300
Ukraine	2 500	38 700	76 000	142 400
United States	0	39 000	207 400	472 100
Uzbekistan	0	55 200	76 000	76 000
Vietnam	0	0	0	1 000
Zimbabwe	0	0	0	1 400

[55] For more detailed approach see, Uranium 2009: Resources, Production and Demand, (OECD NEA & IAEA, 2010).

Uranium enrichment is a process carried out to increase the concentration of U-235 isotopes in natural Uranium as base material.[56] In nature, Uranium is mostly found with a concentration of this isotope at around 0.7%. For military use and production of nuclear weapons, the concentration of these isotopes should be at around 93%, while for the production of electricity this percentage ranges from between 20% to 25%.[57]

In one nuclear reactor, the fuel, which is also known as the element for the production of energy, is presented in a cylindrical form in multiple parts which are cooled through water passing over them. The water, then flows through an energy convertor which converts it into steam passing it through a secondary circuit, thus making it possible for the turbines to be rotated by the steam released. The reactor is encased with a material composed of graphite or natural Uranium which has the role of reflecting the neutrons which could escape freely back into the core but in this way they are returned to facilitate the fission process. An important element is the moderator which controls the Uranium isotopes U-238 by not allowing them to capture fee neutrons which are needed to split the Uranium U-235.[58] The fuel is usually replaced between 3 and 4 years. This is done in the first place because the neutrons which have the key role in the process are gradually absorbed by the fission products. With their elimination, the chain reaction comes to an end.[59]

After its extraction from the reactor, the unused Uranium, Plutonium and the fission products remain as a residue from the fuel.[60] These elements can be isolated by a reprocessing factory in a highly complex process where different acids, such as tribute phosphate and water are used.[61] The Plutonium is produced when, during the fission process, Ura-

[56] Multilateral Approaches to the Nuclear Fuel Cycle, The report of the Independent Expert Group on Multilateral Approaches to the Nuclear Fuel Cycle, Commissioned by the Director General, p. 45, IAEA Doc. INFCIRC/640, 22 February 2005. This process is conducted in specific reactors the capacity of which is measured on specific working units.

[57] John Tabak, *Nuclear Energy*, (Energy and the Environment, New York, 2009), p. 3-4. In electricity production, the role of the nuclea energy is to convert thermal energy created in the fission process into kinetic energy which is further converted into electricity.

[58] Different states used various reactors such as France and the United Kingdom uses graphite moderated reactors and which are cooled by gas while Canada uses heavy water moderated reactors and which are cooled by heavy water or gass. The most used reactors however are those graphite moderated reactors which are cooled by light water, see supranote 49, p. 8.

[59] *Id*, pp. 7-9.

[60] The fission products are atomic fragments created after the split of atomic nuclei during the process, see *Ibid.*

[61] *Id*, p. 10.

nium isotopes U-238 absorb one neutron and transform it into U-239 or Pu-239. Plutonium is also very radioactive and can be used for the production of energy to be used for peaceful or military purposes.[62]

Nuclear energy plays a very important role in the production of electricity throughout the world and is present in many developed states and to some extent with increasing trends in the developing world. The trend of using this source of energy is increasing every day and it appears that it will continue so during the XXI century.[63] At the beginning of 2007, 30 states in the world possessed 435 nuclear reactors for electricity production which altogether produced 370 GW3 of energy, while 30 other reactors were in the process of construction in 13 states. During the year 2006, two units with a production capacity of 1,5GWe came online in China and India. In the same year, China, the Republic of Korea and Russia started to construct 7 new reactors.[64] The first nuclear reactor to produce electricity started its operation in 1956 in Calder Hall, Sellafield, England with a capacity of 50 MWe. In 1985 there were 33 new reactors, while during the 1990's the number or new reactors remained below 10 every year.[65]

Nuclear energy in the developed world and members of the OECD contributes 16% of the total electricity production. Around 90% of nuclear reactors operate in these states.[66] The trend of electricity production by nuclear energy has increased steadily from the 1960's. A large increase was marked especially during 1970-1990 when a small decrease in the pace of building new reactors was noticed, as can be seen in the table below.

[62] Supra note 49, p. 9.

[63] Risks and Benefits of Nuclear Energy, Report nga OECD NEA, (OECD 2007), p. 10.

[64] *Id*, p. 17.

[65] *Id*, pp. 18-19.

[66] *Id*, p. 17.

Table 2.2.: Nuclear energy capacity in the world[67]

Country	Operating Reactors	Generating Capacity (GWe net)	2008 Uranium Requirements (tU)	Reactors under Constructions	Reactors Started up during 2007 and 2008	Reactors shut down during 2007 and 2008	Reactors using MOX
Argentina	2	0.935	160	1	0	0	0
Armenia	1	0.375	90	0	0	0	0
Argentina	2	0.935	160	1	0	0	0
Armenia	1	0.375	90	0	0	0	0
Belgium	7	5.865	1 030 (c)	0	0	0	1
Brazil	2	1.766	450	0	0	0	0
Bulgaria	2	1.906	255	2	0	0	0
Canada	18	12.700	1 600	0	0	0	0
China	11	8.438	1 800	12	1	0	0
Czech Republic	6	3.634	635	0	0	0	0
Finland	4	2.680	485	1	0	0	0
France	59	63.130	9 000 (c)	1	0	0	20
Germany	17	20.470	2 300 (c)	0	0	0	4
Hungary	4	1.860	420	0	0	0	0
India	17	3.782	750	6	1	0	1
Iran	0	0.00	0	1	0	0	0
Japan	55	47.94	6 915	3	0	0	1
Korea	20	17.70	3 400	5	0	0	0
Lithuania	1	1.185	210	0	0	0	0
Mexico	2	1.365	+ 160 +	0	0	0	0
Netherlands	1	0.480	60	0	0	0	0
Pakistan	2	0.425	65*	1	0	0	0
Romania	2	1.300	200*	0	1	0	0
Russia	31	21.743	4 100	8	0	0	NA
Slovak Republic	4	1.710	380	0	0	1	0
Slovenia	1	0.666	230	0	0	0	0
South Africa	2	1.800	280	0	0	0	0
Spain	8	7.450	1 515	0	0	0	0
Sweden	10	9.000	1 575	0	0	0	0
Switzerland	5	3.238	280	0	0	0	0
Ukraine	15	13.100	2 480	2	0	0	0
UK	19	10.100	950	0	0	0	0
United States	104	101.000	16 425	1	1	0	0
OECD	343	310.322	47 130	11	1	1	26
TOTAL	438	372.692	59 065	46	4	1	27

[67] *Ibid*

At the close of the XX century and the beginning of the XXI century there was a decrease in demand for the production of electricity by nuclear energy. It seems that nuclear incidents and accidents have had a great influence in this perspective. The most well-known incident is the one on Three Mile Island in the US in 1979 while the accident of Chernobyl in 1986 in the Ukraine marks the other feature.[68] In 2011, another major accident occurred in Japan, Fukushima, which was a result of a tsunami in the Pacific Ocean causing irregularities in the function of the nuclear reactor resulting in an explosion and leak of radioactive material.

After the accident in Fukushima many states started to review their nuclear programmes. Among them for example, Germany published a new energy plan on 3 March 2011, which foresees that all nuclear reactors in Germany be closed down by 2021 or 2022 at the latest.[69] This plan came not more than a year after Germany had drafted a strategy, published in June 2010 which foresaw the extension of the lifespan of nuclear reactors in Germany by up to 14 years.[70] Fukushima had a similar impact in Switzerland, where the Federal Council recommended the gradual decommissioning of 5 existing nuclear reactors by 2019, respectively 2034 when their warranty expires. However, the Swiss stance does not seem to be definitive because it allowed a door open to extend the life span of its nuclear reactors if it can be done in a secure enough manner.[71] But, on the other hand, for example the US took a decision to build new nuclear reactors while China and India are also doing the same thing.[72]

[68] *Id*, p. 19.

[69] "Nuclear Phaseout is an historic Moment", *International Spiegel Online*, 30 May 2011, visited on 11 March 2012, http://www.spiegel.de/international/germany/0,1518,765681,00.html.

[70] "Merkel's Government Extends Nuclear Plants Lifespan" *International Spiegel Online*, 30 May 2011, visited on 11 March 2012, http://www.spiegel.de/international/germany/0,1518,715833,00.html.

[71] "Switzerland Decides on Nuclear Phase-out", *The New York Times*, visited on 25 May 2011, http://www.nytimes.com/2011/05/26/business/global/26nuclear.html.

[72] From 1978 the US has not build any nuclear reactor in their territory, see Michael Marchhall, "US to resume building nuclear plants", *New Scientists,* visited on 14 February 2012, http://www.newscientist.com/article/dn21476-us-to-resume-building-nuclear-plants.html.

The Fukushima accident came as a result of a tsunami in the Pacific Ocean, following an earthquake measuring 9 on the Richter Scale. The earthquake created high ocean waves reaching up to 38.9 meters, which hit the eastern coast of Japan.[73] Some of these waves hit the nuclear reactor used for the production of electricity in Fukushima, Dai-Ichi. These waves reached the height of 14 m, which supersedes by almost three times the protection capabilities of the reactors which were designed to withstand waves up to 5.7 meters in height. The impact destroyed the energy supply of almost all parts of the control system making it impossible to control reactors 1-4.[74] The impact also destroyed important infrastructure elements, thus initiating a chain of destructive and explosive reactions and ultimately the leak of radioactive material which spread around the environment.[75]

The mission of experts, assigned by the IAEA in cooperation with the Japanese experts, studied the circumstances leading to the accident and came to the conclusion that the management of the Dai-Ichi reactor reacted according to the standard operating procedures. The accident came as a result of the design of the reactor which did not foresee withstanding such high waves accompanied by the lack of adequate emergency administrative procedures to cope with similar accidents.[76] The leak of radioactive material caused earth, water and air contamination, the effects of which are very hard to determine, even today.[77]

In the case of Three Mile Island, Pennsylvania, in the US, on 28 March 1979, the nuclear reactors suffered damage in its unit 2 valves causing the loss of cooling water from the core of the reactor which lead to high increase in the level of temperature. The core started to melt

---

[73] For more details see IAEA Mission Report of the Great East Japan Earthquake Expert Mission, IAEA International Fact Finding Expert Mission of the Fukushima Dai-Ichi NPP Accident Following the Great East Japan Earthquake and Tsunami, 24 May-02 June 2011, 16 June 2011. See in general the report on nuclear security for the year 2012, Nuclear Safety Review of the Year 2012, IAEA Doc. GC (56)/INF/2.

[74] *Id*, p. 11.

[75] *Ibid.*

[76] This report cames iwth 15 conclussions and 16 lessonlearned points on how to face similar situations in the futures, for more see the report, supra note 78.

[77] The waves and their destruction effect cased death of some persons but none of them has died as a result of radioactivity expossuret, "Fukushima Accident 2011", World Nuclear Association, November 2012, http://www.world-nuclear.org/info/fukushima_accident_inf129.html.

leading to the leak of radioactive materials.[78] A robot was launched three years later to examine the environment and came to the conclusion that half the core had melted or was destroyed and 20 metric tons of Uranium had leaked from the bottom part of the valve.[79] This accident did not have any effect on humans because the radioactivity of leaked materials was at a low level. The average level of radioactivity at 17 km radius was at 0.08 milisieverts which equals the radioactivity which is released after normal X-ray scanning in ordinary hospitals.[80] However, there was the psychological effect and financial aspect, as the cleaning operation dragged on for 12 years at a cost of $973 million.[81] The first unit of the reactor restarted its work in 1985 and it has not faced any problems thus far.[82]

The Chernobyl accident happened on 26 April 1986 and was mainly a result of human error.[83] The accident happened on a testing day to check the electronic control system during routine maintenance. During this process the reactor operators had switched off the control system which affected the instability of the reactor and the reduction of energy. In the meantime it was faced with a rapid increase of energy causing the explosion of steam and consequently the blocking of reactor valves. Ultimately, the core of the reactor and a large part of its body was damaged leading to a fire which lasted for 10 days.[84]

Radioactive material released from this accident spread in all directions in a few days, mainly by wind. Also, contamination in humans spread through dairy products and leafy plants which absorbed gas with radioactive material. From the territorial perspective, the most affected states were the Ukraine, Belorussia and the western part of Russia.[85] Out of 600 employees present on that day, 28 died within 3 months because

[78] "Cold War: A Brief History" Atom Archive, p. 28, vvisited on 20 September 2012, http://www.atomicarchive.com/History/coldwar/page19.shtml.

[79] *Ibid.*

[80] "Three Mile Island Accident", World Nuclear Association, 30 May 2011, visited on 20 September 2012, http://www.world-nuclear.org/info/default.aspx?id=500&terms=three%20miles%20island.

[81] *Ibid.*

[82] *Ibid.*

[83] "The Chernobyl Accident", United Nations Scientific Committee on the Effect of Atomic Radiation, 30 May 2011, visited on 20 September 2012, http://www.unscear.org/unscear/en/chernobyl.html.

[84] *Ibid.*

[85] *Ibid.*

of radiation exposure. Longer effects to the population living in the vicinity of the reactor started to show up later. An increase in leukaemia and thyroid cancer as well as diseases to the eye cataract was noticed.[86] Hundreds of thousands of individuals were forced to evacuate and build their new homes in safer areas. As to the financial aspect this accident caused damage valued at more than $200 billion. Today, a confining structure is being built around the area to replace the previous shield built immediately after the accident and which was designed to confine the effects of radioactivity still leaking from the area where the reactor was placed. This project is planned to be completed in 2014.[87]

Accidents are things waiting to happen and man is accommodated to live with them. The way of life entails risks at certain levels. Looking at them from a statistical point of view, we can conclude that the number of nuclear incidents and accidents is low. Not all incidents and accidents cause major damage, but their destructive potential is so great that it causes nightmares in every individual. Destructive images of Chernobyl and Fukushima are conjured up in the minds of individuals. In a way it can be compared with the air traffic which even though from the statistical aspect is the safest means of transport, a single accident can cause breaking news and distracts the mind of man who develop different sorts of paranoia related to air transport, preferring road transportation, which according to statistics causes more victims than air transport.[88] By the same logic we can raise the question as to which is the safest way of energy production for peaceful use? Is it energy produced by fossil fuels or the one produced using nuclear energy? The first form has been used for a long time however, today we see its impact in the environment. Greenhouse gas emissions have directly caused the increase of the earth's temperature and it has also incited climate change in general which could be devastating for mankind. Man, only in recent decades has become aware of this. In the end, emanating from these arguments, it is very hard to calculate which method of elec-

---

[86] *Ibid.*

[87] "Chernobyl Accident, 1986",World Nuclear Association, December 2012, visited on 20 September 2012 http://www.world-nuclear.org/info/chernobyl/inf07.html.

[88] Kreshnik Gashi, Head of the Aeronautical Accident and Incident Investigation Commission in Kosovo, Interview with the author on air traffic safety, Prishtina, 15 Julay 2012. For more on this issue see, John A. Stoop and James P. Kahan, "Flying is the Safest Way to Trave: How Aviation was a Pioneer in Independent Accident Investigation", *European Journal of Transport and Infrastructure Research*, EJTIR, Vol. 5, no. 2, 2005, pp. 115-128.

tricity production is safer in the long term taking into consideration the facts we know today.

Nuclear accidents which have occurred up to now will nevertheless not cause a decrease of interest and need for nuclear energy. This is ascertained by the statistics presented above where in all aspects we can see an increase in the need for Uranium. Even Japan, which suffered the latest nuclear accident decided to revitalise the same reactor and continue on with the production of electricity using nuclear energy.

II.3 NUCLEAR ENERGY AS AN ALTERNATIVE AGAINST GLOBAL WARMING

The needs for nuclear energy have increased over time. Three main reasons may be responsible for this trend: the development of modern, safe and secure technologies for electricity production using the fission process; the relatively low cost of Uranium in the international market; and the ability to produce so called clean energy. This is so, even at a time when man has seen three major accidents among which two had devastating effects. Man has always been faced with similar challenges creating a need to find proper solutions to overcome them. Man lives from nature and the goods it has to offer. The use of natural resources should stay in equilibrium with the needs of mankind and the protection of the environment. The human brain has timely developed and so the sensitivity towards rationalizing the use of natural resources in an attempt to protect the environment in which we live. This, of course, takes into consideration technical and technological abilities which have improved activities of man also including the use of nuclear energy.

Accidents such as that of Chernobyl and Fukushima have shocked mankind due to their devastating effects but it seems that in the long-term they will not be able to slowdown or bring to halt the construction of new nuclear reactors all around the world. Such accidents should be studied well and in an objective manner to avoid as much as possible their repetition. Total avoidance is probably not possible but a decrease in the number of accident may be possible.

One of the main reasons which has increased the needs for the use of Uranium for the production of electricity is the concern of global warming. Global warming, to a large extent, is a result of human activities.[89] Even today, the largest share of global electricity comes from fossil fuel created over millions of years, such as oil, gas and coal which are based on the common element of carbon.[90] To better explain the relations between the uses of these resources of energy one should look at the atmospheric and the geological factors of the earth. The sun is the main source of heat on earth. A part of the total amount of heat that comes from this source is retained in the earth's atmosphere. The amount of this captured heat depends on the chemical composition of the atmosphere.[91] An increase in heat capacity affects the increase of the earth's temperature, creating in this way the so called greenhouse effect. In one aspect this process seems very important because in a contrary situation the temperatures on the earth would decrease to a level which could not support life here.[92]

One of the chemical components affecting the increase of heat capacity is carbon dioxide. By burning fossil fuels, used by mankind for many years, it releases this element into the atmosphere. This long-term process has today caused a significant increase of carbon dioxide thus causing an increase of the atmospheric coefficient to capture heat coming from the sun and consequently an increase of the earth's temperature.[93] The impact of this phenomenon can be seen in many natural events starting with hurricanes, the likes of which have never been seen before, a change of ocean currents, high level of the incidents of flooding in certain areas while droughts in other. A result of such phenomena is the cause of natural disasters, ice melt and an increase in the sea level etc.[94]

[89] "Fact Sheet: Climate change science-the status of climate change today", UN Framework Convention on Climate Change, visited on 26 March 2012, http://unfccc.int/press/fact_sheets/items/4987.php.

[90] For more information regarding the use of different sources of energy see "2011 Key World Energy Statistics", International Energy Agency, visited on 20 September 2012, http://www.iea.org/textbase/nppdf/free/2011/key_world_energy_stats.pdf.

[91] Supranote 62, p. 18.

[92] *Ibid.*

[93] *Ibid.*

[94] For more see activities of the Intergovernmental Panel on Climate Change established by the UN Environment Programme and the World Meteorological Organization to provide the world with scientific data on current global warming and climate changes and its

The use of nuclear reactors to produce electricity does not produce any carbon dioxide. This makes it possible to produce large amounts of electricity without affecting the heat capacity of the atmosphere.[95] Due to this fact, many states, especially in the developed world, produce a part of their electricity using nuclear energy. Among them France for example, produces 78% of its needs from 58 nuclear reactors.[96] At the same time, France is the biggest beneficiary from exporting nuclear energy by earning around $3 billion a year. In its plans, France has foreseen to continue constructing new reactors of Generation III.[97] According to the OECD and IAEA report, exploration and construction of new Uranium mines in 2008 had increased by 133% when compared to 2006 data. Around $1,642 billion had been spent on these activities. [98] Most of the states have reported an increase in activities of Uranium exploration as well as an increase in the financing of Uranium ore extraction after 2003 when the price of Uranium started to increase. Around 80% of exploration and development costs had to do with national activities while others included activities outside the state.[99]

The total volume of identified Uranium ore at the beginning of 2009 was estimated at 5,404,000 metric tons. Sources of this ore which may be extracted at low cost decreased while there was an increase in the amount of ore which is more expensive to extract.[100] The total amount of undiscovered resources, which include expected and speculative resources are foreseen to be at around 10,400,000 metric tons.[101]

economic and social impact, visited on 13 October 2012, http://www.ipcc.ch/.

[95] If we make a comparison between an average nuclear actor and a central which uses coal to produce electricity ita can be calculated that the later would have to use 2,5 million metric tons fo coal thus realeasing a huge amound of carbon dioxide with direct effect in increasing the atmospheric coefficient thus impacting in raising global temperatures in the world, see supranote 95, p 19.

[96] "Nuclear Power in France" World Nuclear Association, April 2011, visited on 20 September 2012, http://www.world-nuclear.org/info/inf40.html.

[97] *Ibid.* France has not marked any significant nuclear accident in its nuclear ractors. On 12 September 2012, they marked an accidend in Marcoule caused by a small explosion and caused one victim of a worker in the plant while injuring four others. There was not any significant radioactive leak which could have any impact in the environment, see John Lichfield, "France on edge after accident at nuclear site", *The Independent*, 13 February 2011, visited on 20 September 2012, http://www.independent.co.uk/news/world/europe/france-on-edge-after-accident-at-nuclear-site-2353692.html.

[98] Supranoe 59, p. 9.

[99] *Ibid.*

[100] *Id*, fp. 10.

[101] The identified sources refer to the Uranium deposition determined by direct measurement and where a pre-feasibility or even a feasibility study can be done. Data on other sources are relied on the geological composition of the land compared to ealier mining and knowledge and regional geo-

Uranium production reached its peak of 43,880 metric tons in 2008, which presents an increase of 6% and around 11% when compared to production volumes in 2007 and 2006 respectively. All states have reported an increase in the production of this element. A considerable increase was presented by Kazakhstan (around 671%) while the smallest increases were presented by Australia, Brazil, Namibia and Russia. A reduced production was reported by Canada, Nigeria and the US because of smaller amounts of Uranium ore extraction, technical difficulties and preparation for mine expansions.[102]

With regards to the Uranium needs, 438 nuclear reactors were connected to electricity grids in 2008 producing a total amount of electricity of 373 GWe. To produce this amount of electricity 59,065 metric tons of Uranium were needed.[103] By 2035, total nuclear capacity is projected to increase to 511 GWe in the most conservative case and up to 782 GWe in the best case scenario, would mean an increase of 37% respectively 110% of 2009 capacity. This would also mean an increase in the demand for Uranium to a level of 87,370 metric tons respectively 138,165 metric tons up to the year 2035.[104]

Pic. 2.2.: Projection of installed nuclear capacities by 2035 presented in MWe net

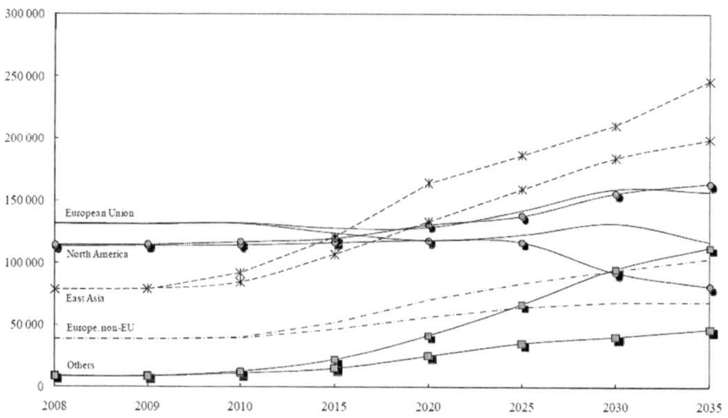

logical maps. Not all states are oblidged to report prognosed or speculative sources, see *Id*, pp. 9-10.

[102] *Id*, p. 10.

[103] *Id*, p. 11.

[104] *Id*, p. 11.

Pic. 2.3.: Yearly needs for nuclear reactors by 2035 presented in tU

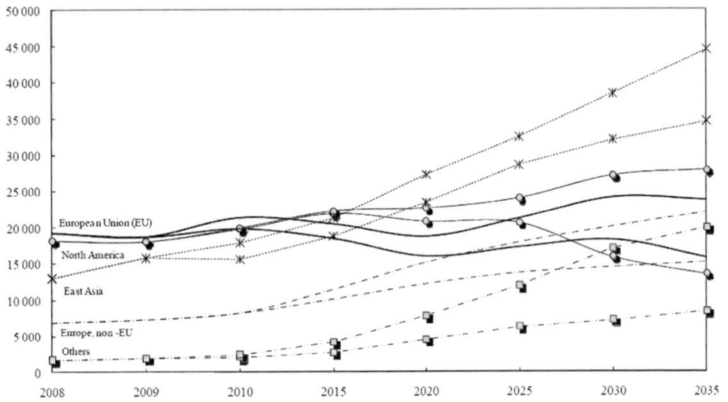

In geographic terms, the demands show a different spread. The East Asia region will present the largest increase in the demand for Uranium as a result of an increased need for electricity related to the economic development of this region, mainly China. This region is expected to increase its needs by 150%. The European non EU region is expected to increase its needs by between 75% and 175 % while an increase is also expected to be presented for the regions of the Middle East, South Asia, Central and South America, Africa and South-East Asia. In the regions of North America and the EU, data varies from 30% up to 40% or its contraction by 10% or 20% respectively.[105] These statistics, for the moment, are only projections and may vary in the future. Many factors may impact on the decrease of needs such as different nuclear accidents such as the one in Fukushima. The effects of this accident still remain to be seen however, it seems that some states such as Germany, Austria etc. have decreased their projections for Uranium needs due to this accident.

The reports on the state of climate change increases pressure to find alternative sources of energy and in this perspective one of the options may be nuclear energy. In July 2009, the G8 leaders agreed to lower the level of emission of greenhouse gasses by 2050 to 50% of the level in 1990. If we refer to current trends of electricity production

[105] *Id*, p. 12.

and its politics to use fossil fuels it may be said that the impact on the environment in the future would be very big.[106] With the development of ambitious programmes of producing electricity by using nuclear energy it can decrease the level of carbon dioxide by 11,6 Gtwit, in particular in the period from 2030 up to 2050.[107]

Another factor which can lead to increase the need for nuclear energy is the development of new modern reactors with increased levels of performance. The security factor is key to the development of such reactors. The new reactors for example have increased their lifespan by around 60%. This means that the refuelling time has increased to a point almost equalling the lifespan of nuclear reactor.[108] The current status of nuclear technology shows a high level of complementarity between the sustainable development of mankind and that of improved performance as compared to other energetic alternatives.[109] Factors which impact the development and improvement of nuclear technology may be divided into three groups: market, public/politics and technology.[110] The free market increases competition between companies to produce better nuclear reactors and also the awareness of buyers who want sustainable reactors with low maintenance costs, always to the highest security standards. The public/political factor is very complex and it is related to different pressures coming from the public and reflected in political relations. Different disasters, no matter what causes them, may very easily impact on the oscillation of public opinion and with this its political support for governments. In this way, political forces may be compelled to withdraw from nuclear plans in cases of a drop in public support. The technological aspect is related closely to the competition between different companies to produce advanced nuclear reactors while also preserving the image of the company producing them.

In 2008, Uranium production satisfied 74% of nuclear reactors demands in the world. The rest was supplied by other resources of Uranium, the so called secondary Uranium resources such as from Highly Enriched Uranium warehouses coming from the dismantling of military nuclear heads, enrichment of depleted Uranium and reprocessing of nu-

[106] World Energy Outlook: 2009, OECD/IEA (OECD, Paris, 2009), p. 9.

[107] *Ibid.*

[108] Supra note 59, p. 76.

[109] Supra note 112, p. 10.

[110] Innovation in Nuclear Technology, NEA/OECD (OECD, Paris, 2007), p. 11.

clear waste used for electricity production.[111] The development of mines to extract Uranium is being adapted to the needs for this ore through existing centres of production, committed and those in perspective. However the price of Uranium could become high at the same time due to increased costs of exploring and extracting this ore.[112]

II.4 NUCLEAR ENERGY AS AN IMPORTANT COMPONENT OF THE NUCLEAR ARSENAL AND A GUARANTOR OF NATIONAL SECURITY

Nuclear energy would probably not receive this great attention if it were used for peaceful purposes only. The great concern revolving around it has to do with the possibility of its use for military purposes in terms of building nuclear weapons and their proliferation within different states. The possible possession of nuclear weapons by various international criminal and terrorists organisations to serve their aims is the worst nightmare any individual can dream of. The concern is real taking into account that the same technology used to enrich Uranium for peaceful purposes can be used to enrich it to high levels (more that 90%) which can then be used to build nuclear weapons. This concern was expressed by President Truman as early as 1945 in his speech addressed to the American congress. From that time, activities to control the production and possession of nuclear energy would reconcile with the fact that ultimately every state had the right of using the same source of energy for peaceful purposes. The main international document which tries to prevent the proliferation of nuclear energy for military use but without infringing a state's right to use it for peaceful purposes is the NPT which will be analysed later.

The world after WWII created blocks with opposing ideologies which were reflected in relations between them.[113] One was the west-

[111] Supra note 59, p. 12.

[112] *Ibid.*

[113] For more on this issue see David Held & Anthony McGrew, *David Goldblatt & Jonathan Perraton, Global Transformations: Politics, Economics and Culture* (Stanford University Press, California, 1999).

ern block under the leadership of the US with a liberal-democratic ideology, while the other was the east block under the leadership of the former USSR with a communist-centralist ideology. To a great extent, relations between these two blocks would be reflected in a constant improvement and advancement of military nuclear programmes and technologies for the delivery of nuclear war heads. With the possession of nuclear weapons by the US, the same would be highly attractive for the former USSR. The arms race, developed between these two blocks, created a vicious cycle without any easy escape, the result of which was the ever modernisation and advancement of military nuclear arsenals. With the invention of nuclear energy, the clock could not be turned back.[114] States, looking to their destruction capacities, struggled to put them in their possession or to improve them if they possessed one. This was closely connected to national interests and guaranteeing a concept of preventing any eventual nuclear attack, known as the nuclear deterrent.[115] After the end of the Cold War international relations relaxed to a great extent and this was directly reflected in various initiatives to concretely and mutually reduce nuclear military arsenals after having established a thread of trust, even though there was a reduction of such arsenals earlier and attempts to mutually agree on their reduction.[116]

Establishing the United Nations Organisation (UN) after WWII created a thread of hope for international cooperation according to the principles enshrined in the UN Charter for international peace and security. But, very soon it was realized that this was just an illusion because of antagonism between the eastern and western worlds which were reflected mainly in the work of the Security Council (SC) as the

---

[114] Supra note 46, p. 17.

[115] In English language this term is known as "*Nuclear Deterrence*" and has accompanied international relations during the Cold War. Nuclear deterrence has to do with the psychological effect int he mind of your enemy thus influencing its behaviour. This concept entails physical and psychological factors. By physical factor it is meant the hardware capacities of a states that is having nuclear weapons ready to be launched thus intimidating the enemy that if it attacks it will be responded by a huge and overwhelming counterattack. See Lieutenant Colonel Charles W. Durr Jr. *United States Army, Nuclear Deterrence in the third Millennium* (USAWC Strategy Research Project, US Army War College Carlisle Barracks, Pennsylvania, 2002), p. 1.

[116] The main emphesis is put on the US-USSR relationship which had the absolute highest number of nuclear weapons, around 90% , see"Ten Fact About Nuclear Weapons", Nuclear Age Peace Foundation, visited on 10 January 2012, http://www.wagingpeace.org/articles/2009/09/facts_myths.pdf. An avarage capacity bomb in the US has eight times more effect that the one dropped on Hiroshima which killed over 90,000 people.

main body engaged in securing international peace and security.[117] The Charter gave to the General Assembly (GA) its role to regulate disarmament however, its success would fall prey to its competence of approving only recommendation resolutions, which from the legal point of view are not obligatory.[118] In this way, the greatest success in preventing the proliferation of weapons of mass destruction, in particular nuclear weapons would result more from bilateral cooperation between the US and the former USSR.

Conscious of the issues related to nuclear energy and the possibility of beginning an arms race, the US, right after the end of WWII took their first steps to finding mechanisms to control nuclear energy. People, who contributed to the development of nuclear weapons and those who gave orders to use them against Japan, now started to think as to how to control nuclear energy. One of the personalities who lead this process was Oppenheimer, who oversaw the programmes for the development of the nuclear weapons together with Dean Acheson and David Lilienthal.[119] President Truman had established a commission composed of Acheson and Lilienthal but headed by Oppenheimer, which drafted a report to be known as the Acheson-Lilienthal Report.[120] The report, handed to President Truman in March 1946 appealed for the establishment of an international authority to regulate all nuclear activities through a system of international inspections so that such activities were only used for peaceful purposes. The report, also, called for the elimination of all nuclear weapons after the establishment of that authority. It placed special emphasis on cooperation between the US and the USSR, taking into consideration that, at the time, the latter seemed to have enough capacities to develop a nuclear weapon soon.[121]

In the meantime, President Truman, together with the British and Canadian Prime Ministers Atlee and King, in November 1945, issued a declaration which requested the establishment of a commission within the UN to oversee nuclear activities. According to this declaration "*This can only be brought about by giving wholehearted support*

[117] Charter of the United Nations, 59 Stat. 1031, T.S. 993, 26 June 1945, Kapitulli VIII.

[118] For the GA competence see *Id*, Kapitulli II.

[119] Supra note 5, p, 6.

[120] "The Acheson-Lilienthal & Baruch Plans, 1946", US Department of State, Office of the Historian, visited on 15 January 2012, http://history.state.gov/milestones/1945-1952/BaruchPlans.

[121] *Id*, p. 6. Shih also *Ibid.*

to the United Nations Organisation and by consolidating and extending its authority, thus creating conditions of mutual trust in which all peoples will be free to devote themselves to the arts of peace. It is our firm resolve to work without reservation to achieve these ends".[122]

Based on these stances and reports, President Truman assigned Bernard Baruch to represent the US on the UN Commission for Atomic Energy meeting held on 14 June 1946. At this meeting, Baruch presented a project for the establishment of an international authority for the Development of Nuclear Energy. The Baruch Plan, as it was later known, included changes from the earlier plan proposed by Acheson-Lilienthal. According to the Baruch Plan, the Authority for Atomic Development would have had competences to oversee the development and use of nuclear energy; to manage any of the nuclear installations with capacity to produce nuclear weapons; and to inspect any nuclear object which deals with research for peaceful purposes.[123] According to this plan, the authority would report only to the Security Council where none of the five permanent Member States would have the right to veto the decision taken in this body.[124] In the Baruch speech he expresses his concern that *"if we fail, then we have damned every man to be the slave of fear".*[125]

Despite American attempts and approval by the UN commission on Atomic Energy, the American plan could not get enough support from the former USSR. In a world under the thumb of real politics it was very hard to believe that such a plan would be accepted by Stalin at a time when the balance of power was a crucial issue. At this time, ideological divisions were growing, while the loss of strength and the balance of power meant an unacceptable loss. Stalin had seen the American achievement in building a nuclear weapon as more than ordinary news. It had to do with industrial strength, scientific achievements and national prestige. Stalin had addressed the scientific community in the former USSR to build such a weapon, because, now, the balance of

[122] "Declaration on Atomic Bomb by President Truman, and Prime Ministers Atlee and King", 15 November 1946, Nuclear Files, visited on 15 Januart 2012, http://www.nuclear-files.org/menu/key-issues/nuclear-energy/history/dec-truma-atlee-king_1945-11-15.htm.

[123] Supra note 124.

[124] *Ibid.*

[125] The way the proposal was presented was intended to correspond to the US concers in securing that no other state would be able to possess such a weapon. Only after other states, and in particular the USSR, are halted to produce such a weapon the US expressed its readiness to demolish its military nuclear capacities, see Supra note 13, p. 16.

power was broken as he expressed himself *"Build the Bomb-it will remove the great danger from us"*.[126] This was a major slap to an international attempt in trying to prevent nuclear weapons proliferation. The arms race would increase every year, be it in the quantitative aspect in the number of nuclear weapons, be it in the qualitative aspect in the increase of power, their design, the use and delivery of such weapons.

The Russian programme of building nuclear weapons started in 1943. It was headed by Igor Kurchatov. At the beginning, the Russian scientist was faced with the lack of financial and political support from the Soviet leadership.[127] The support would come after WWII and American advances in the possession of such a weapon. At one point, the Soviet leader when addressing his scientists stated that "*ask for whatever you like. You won't be refused*" anything to achieve the expected success.[128] After four years, they achieved a concrete result when on 29 August 1949 the Soviets tested for the first time their first nuclear weapon in Kazakhstan at a site called Semi-Palatinsk-21.[129]

The production and possession of nuclear weapons would not be contained to only these two states. By 1964, such weapons would fall into the hands of the United Kingdom (1952), France (1960) and China (1964) which, at the same time, represented the first wave of proliferation. Later, it would be Israel, Pakistan and India which would develop such a weapon. Many other states would develop military nuclear programmes such as South Africa, Libya, Iraq, North Korea and Iran.[130] Some of these states have already renounced them, while others have not and have become a matter of international concern.[131]

Today, eight states are believed to possess nuclear weapons: the US, Russia, China, France, Great Britain, India, Pakistan and Israel. A brief analysis regarding the nuclear military arsenals of states possessing nuclear weapons will be given below.

[126] David Halloway, *Entering the Nuclear Arms Race: The Soviet Decision to Build the Atomic Bomb 1939-1945* (Wilson Center, Washington, D.C, 1979), p. 41.

[127] Supra note 13, p. 18-19.

[128] *Ibid.*

[129] *Ibid.*

[130] Supra note 46, p. 60.

[131] South Afrika developed its programme in secrecy and its is believed that it was in possession of some nuclear warheads but were destroyed at the end of the apartheid regime, see "Nuclear Weapons: Who Has What at a Glance", Arms Control Association, 8 June 2011, visited on 15 January 2012, http://www.armscontrol.org/factsheets/Nuclearweaponswhohaswhat.

USA

The USA, for the first time, in 2009, made public its quantity of weapons in its nuclear arsenal. According to official notification, it possesses 5,113 nuclear warheads which included tactical, strategic and non-deployed weapons. The number of nuclear warheads has changed over the years with the maximum reached in 1967 and numbering 31,255 such warheads.[132]

Up to now, the US has conducted 1,030 nuclear tests, more than any other state. Recently the US declared that they had stopped producing nuclear material for military use. Of late, the US declared to be in possession of 54 metric tons of Plutonium and 250 metric tons of HEU.[133] In the agreement reached with Russia in 2000, the US committed itself to removing 34 metric tons of surplus Plutonium. This agreement was amended with an additional protocol in 2010 with concrete guidelines as to the way this radioactive material is to be removed by 2018.[134] The US has close cooperation with nuclear programmes in Great Britain, which entails the supply, by the US, of ballistic missiles launched from submarines. The US, also, is the only state to station nuclear weapons in another state such as those stationed in Belgium, Germany, Italy, Holland and Turkey. These are of the tactical weapons type and are deployed based on cooperation within NATO membership.[135]

---

[132] "Increasing Transparency in the U.S. Nuclear Stockpile", US Departmet of Defence Fact Sheet, 03 May 2011, visited on 15 January 2012, http://www.defence.gov/npr/docs/10-05-03_Fact_Sheet_US_Nuclear_Transparency__FINAL_w_Date.pdf.

[133] This policy of halting HEU production started in 1964 while from 1992 they halted also the process of Plutonium production for military use, see "Arms Control and Proliferation: The United States", Arms Control Association, visited on 8 July 2011, http://www.armscontrol.org/factsheets/unitedstatesprofile.

[134] For more see Agreement Between the Government of the United States of America and the Government of the Russian Federation Concerning the Management and Disposition of Plutionium Designated as no Longer Required for Defence Purposes and Related Coopeartion, 1 September 2000.

[135] It is believed that the US has deployed 200 other nuclear weapons in other states under which remain under their custody during peace time but in cases of war they may be put ander the NATO control for self-defense, see "Arms Control and Proliferation: The United States", Arms Control Association, visited on 8 June 2011, http://www.armscontrol.org/factsheets/unitedstatesprofile.

Russia

Russia has not yet disclosed its data of nuclear material and its arsenal. It is believed to have around 2,430 strategic weapons and around 3,700 up to 5,400 other nuclear non-strategic warheads. It also includes around 3,000 other warheads on the dismantling list.[136] Up to now, Russia (including the former USSR) conducted 715 nuclear tests, with the first one taking place on 29 August 1949 and the last one on 25 October 1990. Russia has declared that it is no longer producing HEU or Plutonium for military use. According to one study conducted in 2009, Russia is believed to possess 750 metric tons of HEU and 120-170 metric tons of Plutonium for military use.[137]

With help from the US, Russia is currently implementing a programme, for the depletion of 500 metric tons of surplus HEU which will be used for peaceful purposes. Russia signed an agreement with the US to remove 34 metric tons of surplus Plutonium by 2018.[138] Russia is seen, especially by the US, as a potential threat for the proliferation of nuclear technology and exporting ways of production of HEU to states such as Iran or Syria. Another very real concern relates to scientists and other persons who have worked directly in the Russian nuclear industry, who may be easily manipulated and pass on sensitive information, due to the poor economic conditions at home, to the benefit of various states but also non-state actors connected to terrorist or criminal activities.[139]

[136] Hans M. Kristensen and Robert S. Norris, "Russian Nuclear Forces 2011", *Bulletin of the Atomic Scientist*, 67(3), (SAGE, 2011), pp. 67-68.

[137] Global Fissile Material Report 2011, (International Panel on Fission Material, September 2011), p. 178. Data found in this report may not be very accurate dute to lacking of information.

[138] "Arms Control and Proliferation: Russia", Arms Control Association, visited on 9 June 2011, http://www.armscontrol.org/factsheets/russiaprofile.

[139] *Ibid.*

China

China prefers total secrecy on the number of nuclear weapons in their arsenal and material. According to independent organisations, China has around 100-200 nuclear warheads. In 2004, China only published that it has the smallest nuclear arsenal out of the 5 nuclear weapons states which signed the NPT.[140] Up to now, China has conducted 45 nuclear tests, out of which, the first was conducted on 16 October 1965 and the last one on 29 July 1996. China has never declared anything about stopping production of HEU or Plutonium for military use. According to independent sources, China has accumulated around 25 metric tons of HEU and around 6 metric tons of Plutonium for military use.[141] China has helped Pakistan in its nuclear and missile programmes. Libya, North Korea and Saudi Arabia have also benefitted from help given by China in their nuclear programmes. Lately, it is believed that such activities are becoming rarer.[142]

United Kingdom

The United Kingdom published in December 2006 that it would reduce its nuclear arsenal from 200 nuclear warheads to less than 160.[143] Up to now, it has conducted 45 nuclear tests, the first one of which was carried out on 3 October 1952 and the last on 26 November 1991.[144] In April 1995, the British government declared that it is no longer producing HEU or Plutonium for military use. The government has also declared that it possesses 3.5 metric tons of Plutonium and 17.4 metric tons of HEU for military use.[145]

---

[140] "Arms Control and Proliferation: China", Arms Control Association, visited on 9 June 2011, http://www.armscontrol.org/factsheets/chinaprofile.

[141] *Ibid.*

[142] *Ibid.*

[143] "Arms Control and Proliferation: United Kingdom", Arms Control Association, visited on 10 June 2011, http://www.armscontrol.org/factsheets/ukprofile. Nuclear warheads are placed in military submarines know as the Vanguard Submarines one of which is always in the move as part of the UK military doctrine.

[144] *Ibid.*

[145] *Ibid.*

France

France is believed to have around 350 nuclear warheads. France has conducted 210 nuclear tests the first of which was conducted on 13 August 1960 and the last one on 27 January 1996. In 1996, President Chirac made public that France was no longer producing HEU or Plutonium for military use. Also, according to him, France would destroy all its factories used to produce this material. France is believed to be in possession of 30 metric tons of HEU and around 5 metric tons of Plutonium for military use.[146] With regards to its role on proliferation, France helped to build a nuclear reactor in Osiraq, Iraq, which was destroyed by Israel in 1981.[147]

India

India is believed to have around 100 nuclear warheads. This state is expanding its activities to produce ballistic missiles, which could deliver nuclear warheads from land or submarines.[148] India conducted 3 nuclear tests, the first of which was on 18 May 1974 and the last one on 13 May 1998. India continues to produce nuclear material for military purposes.[149] This state is believed to have played a key role in the proliferation of technology and methods of production of nuclear material in Iraq and Iran, and it is feared that nuclear programmes information may have been leaked to other states and non-state actors.[150]

[146] Supra note 143, p. 164.

[147] "Arms Control and Proliferation: France", Arms Control Association, visited on 10 June 2011, http://www.armscontrol.org/factsheets/franceprofile.

[148] "Arms Control and Proliferation: India", Arms Control Association, visited on 10 June 2011, http://www.armscontrol.org/factsheets/indiaprofile.

[149] Mian, Zia, A. H. Nayyar, R. Rajaraman, and M. V. Ramana, *Fissile Materials in South Asia: The Implications of the U.S.-Indian Nuclear Deal*, (International Panel on Fissile Materials, September 2006), p.36.

[150] David Albright, Susan Basu, "Neither a Determined Proliferator Nor a Responsible Nuclear State: India's Record Needs Scrutiny", *Institute for Science and International Security*, 5 April 2006, p. 4.

Pakistan

Pakistan is believed to have around 60 nuclear warheads. Pakistani nuclear programmes are closely linked with the name Abdul Qhadeer Khan (A.Q. Khan) who is known as the father of these Pakistani programmes. Pakistan has conducted two nuclear tests, the first of which was on 28 May 1998 and the second one on 20 May 1998. Pakistan continues to produce nuclear materials for military purposes and is attempting to expand it capacities with other related programmes. Pakistan is believed to have around 1,300 kg of HEU and around 90 kg of Plutonium for military use.[151]

A.Q. Khan has developed a black marked through which he transferred nuclear knowhow for the production of nuclear energy to other states such as Iran, Libya and North Korea.[152] This was ascertained when a cargo ship sailing towards Libya was captured in October 2003. After this, Pakistan has taken concrete measures, including legislative ones, to control the proliferation of nuclear energy in a more rigid manner.[153]

North Korea

The North Korea nuclear programmes are accompanied by high controversies in international relations. In 1994, the US signed an agreement with this country to put a halt to the production of Plutonium in Yongbyon, in exchange for the construction of two reactors with light water and other forms of help in electricity production.[154] However, that agreement was never implemented. Lately, in January 2010, North Korea expressed that it is ready to stop enmity with the US and to continue

[151] "Arms Control and Proliferation: Pakistan", Arms Control Association, visited on 10 June 2011, http://www.armscontrol.org/factsheets/pakistanprofile.

[152] For more see the Chapter below.

[153] Supra note 157.

[154] "Arms Control and Proliferation: North Korea: Arms Control association, visited on 10 June 2011, http://www.armscontrol.org/factsheets/northkoreaprofile.

with attempts to build a nuclear free Korean peninsula.[155] The new leader Kim Jong-un, the son of Kim Jon-il, accepted suspending Uranium enrichment and mid-range missile tests.[156]

North Korea conducted one nuclear test on 9 October 2006. Because of well kept secrets by the government, it is not possible to know the amount of nuclear material that North Korea may possess to produce nuclear weapons. According to the IAEA, North Korea possesses 8 kg of Plutonium and 25 kg of HEU. North Korea has contributed in the transfer of technology.[157] North Korea became part of the NPT regime at the beginning of 1990s, but withdrew later inciting great international concern.

Israel

Israel has not officially recognized being in possession of nuclear weapons nevertheless, it is believed that it may be in possession of around 75-200 nuclear warheads. The official policy of Israel is that it *"will not be the first country to introduce nuclear weapons in the Middle East"* and that for this reason it will not admit or negate anything.[158] However, former Israeli Prime Minister Ehud Olmert, in an interview with the German channel N24, indicated, indirectly, that Israel possesses nuclear weapons stating that the US, Russia, France and Britain have nuclear weapons and are civilized people who do not threaten anyone. According to him Israel is a civilized nation leaving open to all to answer and for which he was later criticized in Israel.[159] Israel has a fleet of military airplanes F-16 and F-15 capable of carrying nuclear warheads. Also, Israel, according to an independent analysis, possesses a submarine, known as the Dolfin, which can also carry nuclear warheads.[160]

[155] "Country Profile: North Korea", Nuclear Threat Initiative, visited on 10 October 2012, http://www.nti.org/e_research/profiles/NK/Nuclear/chronology.html.

[156] North Korea agrees to nuclear moratorium, *BBC*, 11 March 2012, visited on 10 October 2012, http://www.bbc.co.uk/news/world-asia-pacific-17208755.

[157] Supra note 161.

[158] David Eshel, "Israeli's Nuclear Deterrence Faces First Scrutiny", *Jane's Intelligence Review*, Vol. 12, No. 7, July 2000, p. 14.

[159] Greg Myre, "Olmert Inadvertently acknowledges Israel has the bomb", World Security Network, 13 December 2006, visited on 15 January 2012, http://www.globalsecuritynews.com/showArticle3.cfm?article_id=13787.

[160] "Arms Control and Proliferation: Israel", Arms Control Association, visited on 10

Israel is believed to have Uranium enrichment programmes, but it is not known at what capacity but it is believed to have around 600 kg of Plutonium for military use.[161] Israel is not believed to have played any part in the proliferation of nuclear programmes for military use aside from suspicions to the contribution of nuclear programmes in South Africa, which currently does not present any concern taking into consideration that this state halted its nuclear programmes during the 1980s.[162]

Iran

Iran signed the NPT in 1970, but has developed its nuclear programmes for peaceful use for more than 50 years. In the last 10 years these programmes have advanced to a great extent giving Iran the capability of producing nuclear material on its own.[163] The problem with the Iranian nuclear programme revolves around the secrecy under which it was developed up to the last decade, when it was discovered by the IAEA. In the second part of 2002, the IAEA started to investigate Iranian installation for the enrichment of Uranium, the factory for production of heavy water in Arak and gas centrifuges in Natanz.[164] The Iranian programme has relied on information taken from the A.Q. Khan network. Disclosure of nuclear programmes, kept in high secrecy for a long time, raised international concerns, mainly from western states and related to the real purpose of the programmes.[165] In 2009, Iran made public, information regarding the existence of another installation in the city of Qom used to enrich Uranium.[166] International concerns regarding Iranian nuclear programmes have to do with the real purpose of its existence without disputing the right of Iran to produce nuclear energy for peaceful use.

June 2011, http://www.armscontrol.org/factsheets/israelprofile.

[161] Albright, David, "Global Stocks of Nuclear Explosive Materials", *Institute for Science and International Security,* 30 June 2005.

[162] Supra note 166.

[163] Supra note 161.

[164] "Arms Control and Proliferation: Iran", Arms Control Association, visited on 10 June 2011, http://www.armscontrol.org/factsheets/iranprofile.

[165] *Ibid.*

[166] *Ibid.*

Nuclear military arsenals in existence today in the world are enough to destroy mankind many times over, despite initiatives, mainly at the bilateral level, to reduce it. These arsenals present a real concern for the whole of mankind and at the same time it spells out the paradox of its existence.

CHAPTER III

REGULATION OF THE USE OF FORCE IN INTERNATIONAL LAW AND NUCLEAR WEAPONS COUNUNDRUM

III.1 FROM JUS AD BELLUM TO JUS IN BELLA AND DEVELOPMENT OF RULES OF THE USE OF FORCE BEFORE THE UN

The history of mankind is associated with years of wars which were incited by various reasons. History perhaps notes more years of war than peace.[1] In our conscience, we focus more on the First World War (WWI) and the Second World War (WWII) which took so many lives of both civilian and military personnel in addition to material damage. They remain in our mind also because of their proximity in time. However, the history notes other major wars such as "the Hundred Years War" between France and England (1353-1453)[2] or "the Thirty Years War" (1618-1648)[3] in Europe. Such wars have been conducted in other parts of the world from the beginning of the modern civilizations of Babylonia, China, Ancient Greece and the Roman Empire. But, for the first time, war was outlawed by the General Treaty for the Renunciation of War.[4]

From ancient times, man has tried to regulate means and methods of warfare in a bid to confine their destructive effects. During medieval times, religion played an important role in this aspect.[5] Up to the

[1] For more see Geoffrey Parker ed., *The Cambridge History of Warfare* (Cambridge University Press, New York, 2005).

[2] *Id*, p. 158.

[3] *Id.* p. 88.

[4] L. F. L. Oppenheim, *International Law: A Treatise* (Vol. 2, 7th edition, London, 1952), pp. 177-78.

[5] For more see David R. Snock *Religious Perspectives on War: Christian, Muslim and Jewish Attitudes Toward Force* (Revised Edition, US Institute of Peace, Washington, 2002).

"Thirty Years War", the conduct of warfare was regulated by informal means and on many occasions they were not followed.[6] This was so particularly in times of the so called total war, according to which, a very small or no difference existed between the combatants and civilians, because every individual, combatant or civilian, may be considered as part of the enemy and a potential threat.[7]

Conduct of war was a means in the states hands to realize their "rights"[8] in an anarchic system with no higher authority to regulate the behaviour of states. Thus a concept was developed of the right to war or *jus ad bellum*.[9] In international relations theory this is known as realism according to which the world is an anarchic system and states fight to realize their interests defined in power.[10] Speaking from the legal perspective, war was an inherent right of a state's prerogative of its absolute sovereignty.[11]

Formalisation of the right to war did not take place until the Dutch lawyer Hugo de Groot, known as Grotius, wrote his book *De Jure Belli Ac Pacis*.[12] This book was written during the "Thirty Years War" and the author was greatly influenced by witnessing the massive destruction caused by this war in Europe. In his book, Grotius acknowledged that war is an unavoidable part of the anarchic system of international relations. However, even in such a system, according to him, states ought to be conscious and apply constraining measures in their rights to go to war, *jus ad bellum*, and also in the way and means they

[6] Jill M. Sheldon, "Nuclear Weapons and the Laws of War: Does Customary International Law Prohibit the Use of Nculear Weapons in all Circumstance", *Fordham International Law Journal*, 20 Fordham Int'l L.J. 1891, 1996, pp. 210-211.

[7] Edward Gunn, "The Moral Dilemma of Atomic Warfare", *Aegis, The Otterbein College Humanities Journal*, Spring (2006), p. 67.

[8] The concept of having a right in international relations seems to always entail controversies in international law especially in cases involving national interests where states are ready to use force in which case the determination of circumstances is subjective a symbol of sovereignty.

[9] States many times have used this concept to realize their interests by interpreting the right to wage war according to their own determination, supra note 176, p. 178.

[10] Paul R. Viotti, Mark V. Kauppi, *International Relations Theory*, (Pearson, 2010, New York), p. 52- 53. For more on this issue see Hans J. Morgenthao, *Politics Among Nations*, (Knopf, New York, 1948).

[11] Supra note 176, p. 178.

[12] Supra note 178, p. 216. See also Hugo Grotius, *De Jure Belli Ac Pacis Libri Tres*, Francis W. Kesley ed. And James B. Scott trans.,The Classics of International Law (1964). The book of Grotius is devided in three part where the first one analyzes *ju ad bellum*, the second one causes behind war and the third one *jus in bello*.

conduct war, *jus in bello.*[1] According to him, *"War ought to be undertaken except for the enforcement of rights; when once undertaken, it should be carried on only within the bounds of law and good faith".*[2]

The purpose of regulating the way of use of force was used during times of war was to humanize the war itself, and hence the concept of humanitarian law started to be developed with the main objective of protecting individuals caught up in war, in particular the civilians, women, children, the wounded and also prisoners of war.[3] After Grotius, other authors wrote about humane war. Jean Jacques Rousseau argued that the purpose of states entering wars is to destroy the enemy state.[4] According to him, the state may consider the defenders of an enemy state as legitimate targets only when they use their weapons. At the moment of submission they turn into an illegitimate target for the attack to continue.[5] It seems that this struggle of different scholars to humanize as much as possible the damages of war failed to exert its impact in reality.[6] However, these struggles would not go in vain without leaving its impact on the consciousness of different statesman to be revealed years later. During the XIX and beginning of the XX century some important documents would be approved such as the St. Petersburg Declaration and The Hague Conferences would take place to deal with the issues of warfare.[7]

In 1868, statesmen of that time on the European continent would agree to sign a declaration during an international conference in St. Petersburg.[8] The main reason behind this conference was to halt the pro-

[1] Hugo Grotius, *De Jure Belli Ac Pacis Libri Tres*, in Francis W. Kesley ed. dhe James B. Scott trans.,The Classics of International Law (1964), p. 18.

[2] *Ibid.*

[3] "International Humanitarian Law and Related Legal Regimes", International Committee of Red Cross, visited on 26 October 2011, www.icrc.org.

[4] Jean Jacques Rousseau, *Social Contract* (1972), in Donald A. Cress ed. & trans, Basic Political Writings, (Hacket Publishing, IndianapolisëCambridge,1987), p 145.

[5] *Ibid.*

[6] According to the ICJ statute, the role of writings of prominent jurists are a subisidary source of international law besides the judicial decissions, see the ICJ Statute Art. 38

[7] In the St. Petersburg declaration it can be notices the influence Grotius and Rousous had in defining the use of exesive force and that the purpose of the use of force is only to weaken the enemy and not its total destruction, see "Declaration Renouncing the Use, in Time of War, of Explosive Projectiles Under 400 Grammes Weight. Saint Petersburg, 29 November/11 December 1868", ICRC International Humanitarian Law: Treaties & Documents, visiten on 15 June 2012, http://www.icrc.org/ihl.nsf/INTRO/130.

[8] Supra note 178, p. 216. This converence was initiated by Russia.

duction and use of bullets which were able to explode when hitting the target.[9] The Russian Kingdom called this conference to agree that such a weapon should no longer be produced and its use forbidden during armed conflicts and which resulted in the adoption of the St. Petersburg Declaration.[10] According to this declaration, "*the only legitimate object which status should endeavour to accomplish during war is to weaken the military force of the enemy*". A force should be used to demobilize armed personnel but care should be paid to the excessive use of force by the "*employment of arms which uselessly aggregate the sufferings of disabled men, or render their death inevitable*".[11] By this declaration, states committed themselves to renounce the use of any kind of projectile of a weight below 400 grams capable of exploding when hitting the target or when it possesses a flammable material.[12] The use of such weapons may cause unnecessary injuries or total decomposition of bodies which would be in contradiction with principles of humanism.[13]

The St. Petersburg Declaration marked an important moment in the movement of states to codify the rules to humanize war. The Russian Kingdom once more called another conference in 1899 to discuss issues related to international security and peace and also the control of war.[14] This conference was held in The Hague and would be known as The Hague Conference. The same would be held in 1907 and together would be known as The Hague Conferences.[15] The objective of these conferences was to achieve global peace by controlling the development and further modernization of weapons in quality and as well as quantity. This objective failed to realize its aims due to the lack of will of the participating states to achieve a consensus, but, formally, they accepted the

[9] These types of bullets would be used to penetrated armoured vehicles. But with further modifications it was made pssibile for such bullets to explode upon touching softer surfaces such as body of a person, see Dietrich Schindler & Jiri Toman, *The Laws of Armed Conflicts* (BRILL, Leiden, 1988) p. 101, also Hilaire McCoubrey & Nigel D. White, *International Law and Armed Conflicts* (Ashgate Publishing Group, Aldershot & London, 1992) p. 219.

[10] 19 states had signed or became later party including France, Russia, Great Britain etc., see Dietrich Schindler & Jiri Toman, *The Laws of Armed Conflicts* (BRILL, Leiden, 1988), pp. 297-298.

[11] Supra note 191.

[12] *Ibid.*

[13] Supra note 178, p. 217.

[14] *Ibid.*

[15] Final Act of the International Peace Conference Hague 1899, publikuar në ICRC, International Humanitarian Law: Treaties and Documents, visiton on 16 Januaryy 2012, http://www.icrc.org/ihl.nsf/INTRO/145?OpenDocument.

regulation of armed conflicts.[16] The result of the conference of 1899 was the adoption of three covenants and a final protocol regulating: 1) pacific settlement of international disputes; 2) laws and customs of war on land; 3) maritime warfare.[17] Another declaration which came out of the conference and also very important, was the declaration which dealt with the prohibition of the use of specific weapons, including dum-dum bullets, asphyxiating gases and projectiles and explosives discharged from balloons or other new analogous method.[18] However, these conventions were not regarded as legally binding because they only expressed the will of states to adopt provisions foreseen in those conventions and the declaration in which case, states were hesitating to do so.[19]

In the second conference, proposed by the US President and prepared by the Queen of Holland at the invitation of the Russian Czar, and held in the same city in 1907, the three conventions were reviewed and a declaration was issued. Also, 10 new conventions were adopted here.[20] The same as the first time, states failed to make any progress with regards to disarmament, but some new principles of humanitarian law were affirmed such as the principle of obligatory resort to arbitration in cases of disagreements between states the purpose of which was to prevent the use of force without trying to deal with it in a peaceful manner.[21]

A common achievement of these two conferences was the adoption of two conventions (that of 1899 and 1907) which defined the principles of customary international law which are to be followed during land warfare between enemy parties.[22] Both of these conventions are based on the so called *"Martens Clause"*.[23] In a modified version of The Hague Convention of 1907, this provision stated that "*Until a more complete code of the laws of war has been issued, the High Contracting Parties*

[16] Supra note 178, p. 217.

[17] For more see, ICRC, International Humanitarian Law: Treaties and Documents, visited on16 Januaryy 2012, http://www.icrc.org/ihl.

[18] The Hague Declaration 1899, ICRC International Humanitarian Law: Treaties and Documents, visited on 30 November 2011, http://www.icrc.org/ihl.nsf/TOPICS?OpenView.

[19] Supra note 199.

[20] Supra note 178, pp. 217-218.

[21] Final Act of the Second Peace Conference Hague 1907, ICRC International Humanitarian Law: Treaties and Documents, visited on 28 October 2011, http://www.icrc.org/ihl.nsf/FULL/185?OpenDocument.

[22] Supra note 178, p. 218.

[23] Convention Respecting the Laws and Customs of War in Land, Hague 1899, U.S.T.S. 539, 2 A.J.I.L. Supp. 90.

deem it expedient to declare that, in cases not included in the Regulations adopted by them, the inhabitants and the belligerents remain under the protection and the rule of the principles of the law of nations, as they result from the usages established among civilized peoples, from the laws of humanity, and the dictates of the public conscience".[24]

According to The Hague Conventions, the belligerents have limited rights to hurt the enemy (Article 22) and the aggressor is not allowed to cause unnecessary injuries by using weapons, projectiles or exclusive related materials designed to cause injuries (Article 23(e)). Belligerent parties should protect the enemy who has surrendered and should not cause any wound upon them (Article 23(c)), while according to Article 25 it is forbidden to attack a neutral state or any defenceless city, village or building.[25] Many authors of international law think that the rules defined by The Hague Conferences manifest general customary law and from this aspect they are binding on all states no matter whether they become a formal party to them or not.[26] Another very important achievement of The Hague Conference of 1907 was the establishment of the Permanent Court of International Justice[27] the predecessor of the International Court of Justice.[28]

Despite their good purposes, WWI brought a major blow to these conferences. During this war, to a large extent, chemical substances were used, especially by Germany and England.[29] The use of such substances caused massive deaths of people with different body injuries

[24] According to the 1899 convention, this provision was formulated as *"Until a more complete code of the laws of war is issued, the High Contracting Parties think it right to declare that in cases not included in the Regulations adopted by them, populations and belligerents remain under the protection and empire of the principles of international law, as they result from the usages established between civilized nations, from the laws of humanity and the requirements of the public conscience"*, krahaso *Id* me Convention Respecting the Laws and Customs of War in Land, Hague 1907, ICRC International Humanitarian Law: Treaties and Documents, visited on 28 October 2011, http://www.icrc.org/ihl.

[25] *Ibid.*

[26] Geoffrey Best, *War and Law Since 1945* (Clarendon Press, Oxford, 1994), p.8.

[27] For more see "International Court of Justice, Permanent Court of International Justice", visited on 03 November 2011, http://www.icj-cij.org/pcij/index.php?p1=9.

[28] Maybe the only organ which could be said to have being a successful story during the LN was the PCIJ while the ICJ would be regarded as its successor which would build its practices based on the achievements of the PCIJ, see "International Court of Justice", visited on 03 November 2011, http://www.icj-cij.org/homepage/index.php.

[29] For more see "Weapons of Mass Destruction",US Arms Control and Disarmament Agency Fact Sheet, which describes the use of poisonous gasses during the WW I, visited on 2 November 2011, http://dosfan.lib.uic.edu/acda/factsht.htm.

contrary to all previous norms established by The Hague Conferences and customs of war developed that far.[30] Seeing the extent of destruction caused by the use of toxic gases and other similar substances as means of war,[31] the world leaders, once more agreed to hold an international conference to control the international trade of arms, ammunition and means of war, which was held in Geneva in 1925.[32]

In the Geneva Conference of 1925, participants adopted the Protocol for the Prohibition of the Use in War of Asphyxiating, Poisonous or other Gases, and of Bacteriological Methods of Warfare.[33] According to this protocol, the prohibition of the use of asphyxiating, poisonous and other gases is part of the international law which is applied against the consciousness and state practice.[34] By signing this protocol, states have agreed that the same constraints be applied against bacteriological methods of warfare, which entails the use of bacteriological means to cause injuries to the belligerent party.[35]

Three years later, in 1928, the first attempt was made to renounce war as a means of achieving the interests of one state and to delegitimize it in international relations aside from self-defence. This was achieved by the Paris Pact also known as the General Treaty on Renunciation of War as an Instrument of National Policy or as the Act on Global Peace. Today it is more known as the Kellogg-Briand Pact.[36] This pact was signed by 63 states. The pact, in its essence, has changed to recognise the concepts of just and unjust wars. According to its sec-

---

[30] Adam Robert & Richard Guelff ed., *Documents on the Laws of War* (Oxford University Press, New York, 1989), p. 138.

[31] For more on this issue see Arms Control Association vizituar më, www.armscontrol.org.

[32] For more on this issue see "1925 Geneva Protocol", United Nations Office for Disarmament Affairs, visited on 3 November 2011, http://www.un.org/disarmament/WMD/Bio/1925GenevaProtocol.shtml.

[33] *Ibid.*

[34] *Protocol* for the Prohibition of the Use of Asphyxiating, Poisonous or Other *Gases*, and of Bacteriological Methods of Warfare, 94 L.N.T.S. 65, 17 June 1925, para. 2, 3, 4.

[35] *Id*, para. 5. This protocol, nevertheless, left some loopholes in precisely categorizing poisonous gases and other biological means (such as tear gass, other non letha gases or herbicides) but to which this protocol applies within the wordin "other". 13 states stated tha this Protocol also applies aginst tear gases when handed their instruments of ratifications. On the other side, the US deposited a declaration after it ratified the protocol in 1975 stating that this protocol does not apply agains t chemical herbicides and related agents, see supra note 214, p. 137.

[36] Emri Kellogg-Briand comes from the main initiator of thi pact, the US Secretary of State Frank B. Kellogg and the French Foreing Minister Aristide Briand.

ond paragraph *"the time has come when a frank renunciation of war as an instrument of national policy should be made to the end"*.[37] The pact calls states to use pacific means because *"all changes in their relations with one another should be sought only by pacific means and be the result of a peaceful and orderly process"*.[38] Anyhow, the attempts of states failed to prevent another great war with global impact and known as WWII. The League of Nations Covenant did not delegitimize war, while the attempts to regulate disarmament did not yield any results.

All of the above mentioned activities to define the rules of warfare were done by international state cooperation. These activities are important because states are the main actors of international law and only they can impose restraints upon themselves by entering specific agreements or by way of established customary law.

Outside state initiatives, an important role was played by the Red Cross Movement, as a non-governmental organisation established by Henri Dunant. He witnessed great sufferings of people during the war in Solferino in 1859 and in 1863 and managed to bring together some personalities from Switzerland who were engaged in humanitarian activities to create the Red Cross Movement, which would soon gain international character.[39] The initial aim of this movement was to ameliorate the condition of wounded on the battlefield and in 1864 the movement managed to organize an international conference which approved the Geneva First Convention for the Amelioration of the Condition of the Wounded and Sick in Armed Forces in the Field.[40] Later, in 1949, Four Geneva Conventions would be adopted which would codify the rules for treating the wounded on land and sea, prisoners of war and the status of civilians and neutrals in war.[41] The Geneva Conventions will be analysed in detail in the following chapters.

---

[37] Kellogg-Briand Pact 1928, 93 LNTS 343, para 2, Yale Law School Avalon Project, visited on 15 November 2011, http://www.yale.edu/lawweb/avalon/imt/kbpact.htm.

[38] *Id*, para 3.

[39] David Armstrong, Lorna Lloyd & John Redmond, *International Organizations in World Politics* (third edition, Palgrave Macmillan, New York, 2004), p. 5.

[40] *Ibid.*

[41] *Ibid.*

III.2 THE USE OF FORCE IN THE UN ORDER

The UN Charter (the Charter) presents the foundation for the new world order after WWII.[42] The main objective and purpose of the Charter is to preserve international peace and security through a system of collective security[43] and development of friendly relations among states.[44] The main principles to realize objectives and purposes of the Charter are enshrined mainly in Article 2 at the core of which lies the preservation of sovereignty and territorial integrity of states. Considering the great destruction caused during the two world wars, the main concern of drafters of the charter was to prevent another war, at least of that character. The main focus on sovereignty and territorial integrity as the basic principle presented a way of avoiding another war, through a system where no state has the right to intervene in the internal matters of another state or to infringe upon its territorial integrity. Article 2(4) forbids the use of force in international relations accordingly *"All Members shall refrain in their international relations from the threat or use of force against the territorial integrity or political independence of any state, or in any other manner inconsistent with the Purposes of the United Nations"*.[45]

Besides this paragraph which refers to inter-state relations, Article 2(7) of the Charter, forbids the use of force also by the UN itself accordingly *"Nothing contained in the present Charter shall authorize*

[42] The Charter expressed the will of states allied agains the Central Axis and at the beginning it was sigend from those states only. Later it was opened for signing by other states and today it has 193 Member States , see Lori F. Damrosch, Louis Henkin, Richards Crawford Pugh, Oscar Schachter, Hans Smit, *International Law: Cases and Materials* (Fourth edition, West Group, St. Paul, 2001) p. 934.

[43] Supra note 121, Art. 1 para 1.

[44] *Id*, Art. 1 para 2.

[45] A complex problem related to the implementation of this principle is the definition of the term force used in Art. 2(4). This article uses this term departing from the term "war" used by Kellogg-Briand pack and LN Covenant. This term was intentional used because states have often engaged in different types of warfare without declaring it beforehand. The term "force" as a more general term is used in the Charter to also embrace ofther forms of warfare. But on the other side, this term in itself contains ambiguities such as for example may the use of economic, political or psychological meas be considered as force, see Oscar Shcachter, *International Law in Theory and Practice*, (Martinus Njihoff Publishers, Dordrecht-Boston-London,1991) pp. 110-113, also supra note 228 Art. 2 para. 4.

the United Nations to intervene in matters which are essentially within the domestic jurisdiction of any state or shall require the Members to submit such matters to settlement under the present Charter...".[46]

The principles of the Charter on the prohibition of the use of force have now become part of imperative provisions to which there is no deviation permitted, also known as *jus cogens* provisions.[47] These norms are applicable against all states with universal character, *erga omnes*, which means that states cannot justify the use of force even in cases where high national interests are involved also entailing security aspects.[48] Despite this, during the Cold War, the world was frequently faced with situations involving the use of force and intervention in international relations, which led many to reconsider whether Article 2(4) on the prohibition of the use of force still has its universal binding character due to the frequent violations by states. However, none of the states in their minds or in their public stance have positioned themselves in contradiction to this article which negates the existence of the element of *opinion juris* to depreciate this principle.[49] In the case of military activities within and against Nicaragua, the ICJ stated that *"...the Court has however to be satisfied that there exists in customary international law... the Binding character of such abstention (non-use of force).*[50] This behavioural norm on the non-use of force, according to the ICJ is extracted from the stance of states during discussing and adopting different GA resolutions, in particular the Declaration on Friendly relations of 1970, which was approved by unanimity by members of the GA.[51]

The Declaration on the Principles of International Law in Relation to the Friendly Relations among States in Harmony with the UN Charter,

---

[46] Supra note 228, Art. 2 para, 7.

[47] Lori F. Damrosch, Louis Henkin, Richards Crawford Pugh, Oscar Schachter, Hans Smit, *International Law: Cases and Materials* (Fourth edition, West Group, St. Paul, 2001) p. 934.

[48] Louis Henkin, *How Nations Behave: Law and Foreign Policy*, (2nd edition, Columbia University Press, New York, 1979) pp. 137-38.

[49] Compare for example Franck, "Who Killed Article 2(4)? Or Changing Norms Governing the Use of Article 2(4)", *American Journal of International Law"*, 64 A.J.I.L. 809 (1970) and Louis Henkin, "The Reports of the Death of Article 2(4) Are Greatly Exaggerated", *American Journal of International Law*, 65 A.J.I.L. 544, 1971. The SC inability to discharge its duties during the Cold War contributed in raising these issues, see also supra note 224, pp. 40-42.

[50] *Military and Paramilitary Activities in and Against Nicaragua* (Nicaragua v. United States), Jurisdiction and Admissibility, 1984 ICJ REP, 392., 27 June 1986, para 188.

[51] *Ibid.*

also known as the Declaration on Friendly Relations,[52] defines more precisely the notion of the use of force. This declaration is based on other UN documents which deal with the use of force and tries to interpret them.[53] The declaration, in its introduction, defines more precisely the use of force and the way it is manifested and drawing attention at the same time to the fact that states should *"refrain in their international relations from military, political, economic or any other form of coercion aimed against the political independence or territorial integrity of any State"*.[54] According to this declaration, the use or threat to use force presents a violation of international law and Charter, confirming in this way that states have never relied on the use of force to resolve their international disputes.[55] The principles of the Charter which are part of this declaration, present founding principles of international law and it appeals on all states to *"be guided by these principles in their international conduct and to develop their mutual relations on the basis of the strict observance of these principles"*.[56]

In 1987, the GA approved another declaration which clarifies the prohibition clauses of the Charter on the use of force even more. This declaration is known as the Declaration on the Effectiveness of the Principle of Refraining from Threat or Use of Force in International Relations.[57] This declaration defines the obligation of states to refrain from the use of armed forces against other states. According to it *"States have the duty to abstain from armed intervention and all other forms of interference or attempted threats against the personality of the State or against its political, economic and cultural elements"*.[58] Accordingly, states in international relations should use pacific means for the resolution of international disputes to preserve international peace and security.[59]

[52] The GA Resolutions have no binding effect. But, nevertheless, the importance of this declaration relies on the fact that it reconfirms the principles which are part of the Charter and also it was approved by a consenus by the GA members.

[53] William R. Slomanson, *Fundamental Principles of International Law* (Fourth edition, Clark Baxter, California 2003), p. 461.

[54] Declaration on Principles of International Law concerning Friendly Relations and Co-operation Among States in accordance with the Charter of the United Nations, 24 October 1970, p 3, UN. Doc. A/RES/25/2625.

[55] *Id*, p. 4.

[56] *Id*, p. 11.

[57] Declaration on the Enahancement of the Effectiveness of the Principle of Refraining from the Threat or Use of Force in Internaitonal Relations, 18 November 1987, UN. Doc. A/RES/42/22.

[58] *Id*, pika 7.

[59] *Id*. point 17.

If we go from the principles of main international documents starting with the Charter on the prohibition of the use of force, it would be very paradoxical to see the existence of large and small armies all around the world. The existence of such armies and their different arsenals is itself is *prima facie* not in violation of these international documents. If this is so, then the use of force is permissible in some cases. In line with this the Charter makes some exceptions from the main principle on the prohibition of the use of force. According to Article 39 *"The Security Council shall determine the existence of any threat to the peace, breach of the peace, or act of aggression and shall make recommendations, or decide what measures shall be taken in accordance with Articles 41 and 42, to maintain or restore international peace and security"*.[60] Article 42 defines which measures may be taken by the SC to reinstate international peace and security which includes *"...such action by air, sea, or land forces as may be necessary...* which *...may include demonstrations, blockade, and other operations by air, sea, or land forces of Members of the United Nations"*.[61] This article allows the SC council to decide on different measures *"as may be necessary"*.

Besides the SC, the right to use force, according to the Charter, was given to states which may use it for self-defence. This is foreseen with Article 51 accordingly, *"Nothing in the present Charter shall impair the inherent right of individual or collective self-defence if an armed attack occurs against a Member of the United Nations, until the Security Council has taken measures necessary to maintain international peace and security..."*[62]. In cases of self-defence, the SC should be notified immediately which then may decide on further measures on how to reinstate international peace and security, *"Measures taken by Members in the exercise of this right of self-defence shall be immediately reported to the Security Council"*.[63]

An important issue related to the use of force is the threat to use force, which is an enshrined part of the concept of the use of force in the Charter and other GA resolutions mentioned above. This issue

---

[60] Supra note 228, Art. 39.

[61] *Id*, Art. 42. The Charter has foressen for the SC to use other massures stated in Art. 41 before resorting to Art. 42 which include all other measures short of the use of force such as restraining economic relations, air, railway, road, postal, telegraphic, radio communication etc.

[62] Supra note 228, Art. 51.

[63] *Ibid.*

was analysed to a certain extent by the ICJ in rendering its opinion on nuclear weapons which will be analysed later. In principle, the threat to use force in international relations is prohibited by the same documents mentioned above on the prohibition to use force. But, while in the latter case the issue is the definition of the term "force", in the former the issue revolves around the definition of the term "threat". States many times, take actions which easily may be qualified as threat for example military exercises or dislocation of ships and submarines in the so called *"gun boat diplomacy"*[64]. Another example is possession of nuclear weapons. Does equipment with nuclear weapons necessarily mean threat to another state?[65] The US and Israel and also other western European states see as a serious threat possible equipment with nuclear weapons by Iran.[66] In September 2007, Israel attacked a nuclear reactor in Syria under the pretext of Syria having its nuclear weapons programmes under development which may present a threat to the very existence of Israel.[67] The same measure by Israel was taken in 1981 when it attached the Iraqi nuclear reactor in Baghdad.[68]

When analysing such situations, attention should be paid to international relations regarding the particular states concerned. In the case of Israel in the Middle East, any action by neighbouring states towards increasing its military capacities may be viewed as a potential threat due to the lack of trust between states and the general history of enmity in the region. The perception of national security in such regions is very sensitive where the tolerance of what in other circumstances would be viewed in a different manner, is very low. Today, relations between Israel and Iran are considered with high concern due to the Iranian nuclear programme. The development of nuclear energy by Iran would be viewed as a serious threat to the national security of Israel.

[64] Mbi nocionin *"gunboat diplomacy"* see Michael Graham Fry, Eric Goldstein, Richard Langhorne, *Guide to International Relations and Diplomacy* (Continuum, New York, 2002), p. 442.

[65] Supra note 232, p. 948.

[66] "Israeli PM warns about danger of nuclear Iran", *CBS News*, visited on 31 October 2011, http://www.cbsnews.com/8301-501713_162-20127919/israeli-pm-warns-about-danger-of-nuclear-iran/; "Excerpts from Obama Interview for New York Times", *New York Times*, visited on 9 November 2011, http://www.nytimes.com/2010/04/06//orld/06armstext.html?pagewanted=2&sq=obama%20interview&st=cse&scp=1.

[67] "Israel's Airstrike on Syria's Nuclear Reactor: Preventive War and the Nonproliferation Regime", Arms Control Association, visited on 9 November 2011, http://www.armscontrol.org/node/3404.

[68] Anthony Fainbert, "Osirak and International Security", *The Bulletin of Atomic Scientists* (Educational Foundation for Nuclear Science Inc., 1981), p. 37.

Israeli concern becomes very vivid at the moment when the Iranian President Mahmoud Ahmedinejad states that Israel should be wiped off the map.[69]

A similar situation occurred during the Cuban Crisis in 1961 when the US discovered the placement of soviet nuclear missiles in Cuba. Under the auspices of the Organisation of American States[70], the US managed to put into place a maritime blockade on the high seas around Cuba, stopping further movement of Russian submarines directed towards Cuba. The US considered that the existence of nuclear missiles so close to its territory presents a direct risk to its national security.[71] Such situations always remain an object of analysis with different interpretations coming from different parties. Some authors believe that the actions taken by the US were not in compliance with the principles and purpose of the UN, because the blockade was placed on the high seas which, according to the law of the sea, are open and free for navigation by all ships and other navigational vehicles.[72]

When talking about threat, it is important to check on the purpose of the state as to why it decided to take a particular action which may be viewed as a potential threat by another state. The purpose is a subjective element and it is very hard to determine because states may take particular actions such as for example, dislocation of military troops or show of military strength as a normal behaviour in international relations through which a state shows its military force as a preventive measure against a potential attack by another state. In this way, states also keep their dominant position against other states, which does not mean a threat in the form of a stick and waiting to attack.[73] But, such an action followed by other elements such as for example a concrete and direct threat with the purpose of coercing another state to

---

[69] "Iranian Leader: Wipe out Israel", *CNN,* visited on 27 October 2005, http://articles.cnn.com/2005-10-26/world/ahmadinejad_1_israel-jerusalem-day-islamic-world?_s=PM:WORLD.

[70] In its meeting of 23 October 1962, the OAS Council took a decissio for *"immediate dismantling and withdrawal from Cuba of all missiles and other weapons with any offensive capability"*, UN Doc. S/5193.

[71] Marjoie Whiteman, "Threat or Use of Limited Force: The Cuban Missile Crisis, 1962", *Digest of International Law*, Vol 4, 1965, pp. 523-24.

[72] Maac Chesney, "Some Comments on the "Quarantine" of Cuba", *American Journal of International Law*, 57 A.J.I.L. 592 (1963), p. 596, Louis Henkin, "The UN and Its Supporters", *Political Science Quarterly,* 78 Pol. Sci. Q. 504 (1963), pp. 527-528.

[73] Supra note 232, pp. 948-949.

leave its territory or to make any other substantial political concessions, which are not based on international agreements, may be considered as a threat to use force in violation of Article 2(4) of the Charter.[74]

States never use force as a means of aggression instead justifying it with the right to use it. This further strengthens the principle of the prohibition to use force in such cases, despite the fact that the world still faces different conflicts. The principle of the prohibition to use force seems that, at least, up to now has managed to prevent a major conflict with global repercussions, even though this argument may be challenged as to whether states merely stayed faithful to this principle or whether they considered that losses in the event of another global war would be greater than attempts to solve their disputes by using pacific means, diplomatic and judicial. Nevertheless, in cases of the use of force, states always rely on their inherent right to self-defence due to some sort of action by another state viewed as a potential direct or indirect threat. Even the concept of self-defence entails in itself, very confusing problems and situations which become a source of serious international disagreements and may lead to the spiralling of conflicts up to a real armed conflict. Here, the issue that arises is, what are the limits to the use of force as an inherent and inviolable right of each state, in cases of self-defence.

[74] *Id*, p. 949, see also UN Secretary-General on the Question of Defining Aggression, UN. Doc. A/2211, 3 October 1952, p. 52, para. 367-374.

III.3 THE RIGHT TO SELF-DEFENCE, IMPLICATION OF NCULEAR WEAPONS AND ITS LIMITS

Self-defence is an institution which allows, exceptionally, states to resort to the use of force. This concept takes on an important place especially in cases where nuclear weapons might be involved due to their massive destruction capacities taking with them legal as well as moral dilemmas. Individual or collective self-defence is defined by Article 51 of the Charter, *"Nothing in the present Charter shall impair the inherent right of individual or collective self-defence if an armed attack occurs against a Member of the United Nations, until the Security Council has taken measures necessary to maintain international peace and security"*.[75] According to this provision, individual and collective self-defence should be taken as a temporary measure until the SC takes its responsibilities for the preservation of international peace and security.[76]

Self-defence and the moment of its activation is one of the most controversial issues in international law. Article 51 of the Charter entails two real concepts approached with different interpretations.[77] According to the first one, the right to self-defence entails the right to use force only after the attack from the enemy has been realised, which is also known as reactive self-defence. According to the second concept, the right to self-defence allows a state to take its action on self-defence before the realisation of an eventual attack.[78] Both concepts have their flaws. According to the first one, the state would have to wait until the attack had finished and its effect seen to be real and measurable. However, it would be very hard to imagine that a state would wait until the attack occurred in reality and react in self-defence as a counter measure. This would be even mor-

[75] Supra note 228, neni 51.

[76] *Ibid.*

[77] Anthony Clark Arend, "International Law and the Preemptive Use of Military Force", *The Washington Quarterly*, 26(2) The Wash. Quarterly 89, 91 (2003), p. 92 , see also, Roxana Vatanparast, "International Law Versus the Preemptive Use of Force: Racing to Confront the Specter of a Nuclear Iran", *Hastings International and Comparative Law*, 31 Hastings Int'l & Comp. L. Rev. 783, summer 2008, p. 788.

[78] Roxana Vatanparast, "International Law Versus the Preemptive Use of Force: Racing to Confront the Specter of a Nuclear Iran", *Hastings International and Comparative Law*, 31 Hastings Int'l & Comp. L. Rev. 783, summer 2008, p. 788.

ally absurd because a state has the right and duty to protect its citizens, obliging it to take all necessary measures to fulfil its rights and duties. This leads us towards embracing the second concept as a more real and reasonable tool. Today, there are advanced techniques and methods of gathering information and intelligence to intercept a possible attack from a particular state, in which case it would be quite reasonable that a state takes adequate measures to neutralise totally or to minimize as much as possible, damage which might be caused by an eventual attack. A real concern attached to this concept relates to the fact that states might be misinformed because of certain facts regarding an eventual attack waiting to happen, leading it to take particular counter measures which might not be able to be justified later. In the best case scenario, the other state would ask for justification of that state's actions while in the worst case scenario it would lead to a spiralling of the conflict and possible start of an armed conflict, in which case, in fact, the other state would act in self-defence.

The right to self-defence to prevent an eventual attack comes from the customary law reflected in Article 51.[79] The language used in this Article, with reference to *"inherent"*, is the same one used in the *Caroline* case between the US and Great Britain.[80] In the *travzux preparatoire* of the San Francisco conference commission it states that *"the use of arms in legitimate self-defence remains admitted and unimpaired"*.[81] The UN General Secretary, Koffi Annan, in its speech addressed to the GA in 2003, stated that states "keep" their inherent right to self-defence according to the charter.[82] Also, similar language was used in the Chapultepec Treaty, which foresees the right to collective self-defence in case of an armed attack.[83]

The risks of misusing Article 51 according to the second concept are very possible. This is so, because states, intentionally or not,

---

[79] *Ibid.*

[80] *Ibid.*

[81] Schaster, "The Right of States to Use Armed Force", *Michigan Law Review*, 82 Mich. L. Rev. 1620, 1984, p 1633-1635.

[82] The Secretary-Genearal Address to the General Assembly, New York, Sept. 23, 2003. See also Bowet D.W., *Self-Defence in International Law* (Praeger, Manchester, 1958), p. 185 *"It is ... fallacious to assume that members have only those rights wich the Charter accords to them; on the contrary they have those rights which general international law accords to them exept in so far as they have surrendered them under the Charter"*.

[83] This treaty deals with the interamerican agreement on reciprocal assistance and solidarity, supra note 255, pp. 1633-1635.

may misuse it to launch an attack against one state under the pretext of preventing the realization of an eventual attack, but in fact it covers the realization of another interest.[84] This takes us to another dilemma which is developed within this concept of self-defence which has to do with anticipatory self-defence and preventive self-defence. According to the first one, the attack has started to be realized and very soon it is expected to realize it effects, while according to the second one, the attack has not started yet, but according to circumstances it may be understood that an aggressive attack may be about to start.

In the Caroline[85] case two conditions were defined as crucial to be cumulatively existent in order to legitimize the right to self-defence: necessity and proportionality.[86] In 1837 the Canadian people living in the British colony revolted and rebelled against British control. They managed to put Navy Island in the Niagara River under their control. On 29 December of the same year they fired shots against a British ship which was sailing along the river while another ship with the name of Caroline was carrying people and ammunition to that island. From this island the Canadian bank was in sight.[87] This pushed the British soldiers to attack, on the same day, the Caroline causing the death of some persons while the rest managed to escape.[88] According to the British side, the attack against the Caroline was taken because it was a necessity to stop the supply of people and ammunition to the rebels on Navy Island which would eventually enable them to mount an attack and capture the Canadian side of the Niagara River.[89]

This event was followed by a chain of communication between the US and Great Britain, with the US not ready to accept British reasoning that the use of force and sinking of the Caroline was a nec-

[84] The missue of this principle was partly due to theinability of the UN and in particular the SC to discharge its duties in the maintenance of peace and security in the world. In this situation, it allowed states to intepred on their own their right to take measures for self-defense as they determined according individual criteria, Philip C. Jessup, *A Modern Law of Nations: An Introduction* (Mac Millan, New York, 1948), pp. 166-167.

[85] On the incident in Niagra River between the Great Britain and the US see "The Caroline", Max Planck Encyclopedia of Public International Law, visited on13 April 2012, http://www.mpepil.com/sample_article?id=/epil/entries/la/-9780199231690-e261&recno=12&.

[86] Matthew Allen Fitzgerald, "Seizing Weapons of Mass Destruction from Foreign-Flagged Ships on the High Seas Under Article 51 of the UN Charter", *Vancouver Journal of International Law*, 49 Va. J. Int'l L. 473, 2008, pp. 478-79.

[87] *Ibid.*

[88] *Ibid.*

[89] R. Y. Jennings, "The Carline and McLeado Cases", *American Journal of International Law*, 32 Am. J. Int. L 82, 1938, pp. 83-84.

essary action to protect its territorial integrity.[90] The then Secretary of State Daniel Webster, in 1841 presented conditions which should be fulfilled in order for one state to justify self-defence measures, according to which a state should present the *"necessity of self-defence, instant, overwhelming, leaving no choice of means, and no moment for deliberation...and that it do nothing unreasonable or excessive; since that act, justified by the necessity of self-defence, must be limited by the necessity, and kept clearly within it"*.[91] Lord Ashburton agreed with the interpretation of the Secretary of State stating that the British attack remained under those boundaries, because the US failed to take any actions to prevent illegal activities of the Caroline leaving it to the British soldiers to intervene as a matter of necessity.[92] The Caroline case embraces the right to self-defence taken against an imminent attack. The standard determined in this case was interpreted later by international institutions namely after WWII. In 1947 the Military Tribunal of Nuremberg stated that *"preventive action in foreign territory is justified only in case of an instant and overwhelming necessity for self-defence, leaving no choice of means and no moment for deliberation"*.[93]

According to this standard the issue of necessity of the use of force is confined within a real attack which is instant and overwhelming which leaves no other choice or means and no moment for deliberation. An instant attack means that there is a high level of certainty that the attacking state is about to or already has launched an attack against the state in a position of self-defence, or that the attack has already started but has not yet finished. This is still a relative issue which depends on a specific case and circumstance and one should take many factors into consideration such as: military doctrines of attacking states, attacking capabilities, readiness, military exercises, official stance against particular state etc. The level of the certainty of the attack occurring depends

[90] Supra note 271, pp. 478-79.

[91] The letter of American Secretary Daniel Webster addressed to Lord Ashburton, dated 27 July 1842, Yale Law School Avalon Project, visited on 13 April 2012, http://www.yale.edu/lawweb/avalon/diplomacy/britian/br-1842d.htm.

[92] *Ibid.* The letter was closed with a sincere apology which meant that he in a way admitted the wrongfull doing for excessive reaction an not in line with what was the understading of Secretary Webster. See also supra note 271, pp. 478-79.

[93] Uri Shoham, "The Israeli Aerial Raid Upon the Iraqi Nuclear Reactor and the Right of Self-Defence", *Military Law Review*, 109 Mil. L. Rev. 191, 1985, p. 196. For a more extensive view on this issue see the San Remo Manual on International Law Applicable to Armed Conflicts at Sea, 12 June 1994, section II.

on the general capabilities of a state and technical and technological development of a state. This level of certainty shifts proportionally as we consider the timing of the attack when it happens.[94] Today, states use different military technologies to realize their aggressive attacks in a very short period of time, while weapons have much greater range of effectiveness and are more lethal. From the viewpoint of nuclear weapons which are capable of killing millions of people and destroying large cities, states, in order to protect their territorial integrity and sovereignty and ultimately their citizens, may be very sensitive and accordingly much more prone to use the concept of preventive self-defence than wait and see if an attack by nuclear weapons is imminent or already on the way to becoming reality. So in this perspective, states tend to move away from the standard as defined by the Caroline case.

The level of risk of misusing the preventive self-defence is even greater. It would be very dangerous if states counter reacted against actions of another state which has to do with for example the redeployment of its military forces or because it had started the modernization of its military potential.[95] In the Nicaragua case, the ICJ stated that lacking prior arrangements defined by states by an agreement, international law does not put any constraints upon the right of states to decide about the level of security they keep and this is valid *erga omnes*.[96] On the other hand, it would be very naïve if we were to say that a state should stand twiddling their thumbs and wait until a bomb was dropped on its land before reacting because, at least morally, this would not be the correct thing to do.[97] According to Louis Henkin, a state may react with counter measures against a captured attack.[98] According to this, a captured

[94] Mark E. Newcomb, "Non-Proliferation, Self-Defence, and the Korean Crisis", *Vanderbilt Journal of Transnational Law*, 27 Vand. J. Transat'l L. 603, October 1994, pp. 619-620.

[95] The US and Japan have expressed their concern about information regarding the increase of military budged by China to be used for moderinizing its military hardware. China on the other side expressed its concern related to the American military presence in the region and their relations with Taiwan, see Jane Perlez, "Continuing Buildup, China Boosts Military Spending More Than 11 Percent", *The New York Times*, 4 March 2012, http://www.nytimes.com/2012/03/05/world/asia/china-boosts-military-spending-more-than-11-percent.html?_r=0 , see also Gardner, "Commentary on the Law of Self-Defence", në *Law and Force in the New International Order,* ed. Damrosch & Scheffer, (Westview Press, San Francisco, 1991) pp. 51-52.

[96] Supra note 235, p 135, para. 269.

[97] Gardner, "Commentary on the Law of Self-Defence", në *Law and Force in the New International Order,* ed. Damrosch & Scheffer, (Westview Press, San Francisco, 1991), pp. 51-52.

[98] Yoram Dinstein, *War, Aggression and Self-Defence*, (2nd ed. Cambridge University Press, Cambridge, 1994), p. 190.

attack would be when the belligerent party has taken a clear stance of resolution for an armed attack in an open and irreversible way.[99]

Due to the high risk of an eventual attack involving nuclear weapons, the standard of self-defence would be lower than that of an eventual attack by conventional weapons. According to Christopher Greenwood *"where the threat is an attack by weapons of mass destruction, the risk imposed upon a state by waiting until that attack actually takes place compounded by the impossibility for that state to afford its population any effective protection once that attach has been launched, mean that such an attack can reasonably be treated as imminent in circumstances where an attack by conventional means would not be so regarded.*[100] States are much more prone to accept an attack by conventional weapons before they resort to self-defence than they are in cases when nuclear weapons might be used.

History has shown some cases when states resorted to preventive self-defence. But, very often, those actions became a matter of hot debates on key issue of their legitimacy. In 1967, Egypt nationalised the Suez Canal and decided to block the passage of ships along this canal which was considered by Israel as a violation of its security and decided to launch an attack against Egypt and its allies.[101] In 1981, Israel bombed a nuclear reactor under construction in Iraq under the right to anticipate self-defence.[102] While in the first case Israeli actions did not draw much international reaction, in the second case the reactions were prompt and great considering that such an action presents a very wide interpretation of Article 51 of the Charter and the standard set in the Caroline case.[103] During 1980s the US intervened in Nicaragua under the right to collective self-defence because Nicaragua was engaged in

---

[99] Can this statement by the Iranian President be regarded as a clear and resolute stance against Israel which would somehow legitimize an eventual attack in self-defense at this particular stage, see *Ibid.*

[100] Christopher Greenwood, "International Law and the Pre-emptive Use of Force: Afghanistan, Al-Qaida, and Iraq", *San Diego International Law Journal*, 4 San Diego Int'l L.J. 7, 2003, p. 16.

[101] Supra note 282, p. 51-52.

[102] For more see Helmut Philip Aust, *Complicity and the Law of State Responsibility* (Cambridge University Press, New York, 2011).

[103] Supra note 282, pp. 51-52. For more compare D'Amato, "Israel's Air Strike Upn the Iraqi Nuclear Reactor", *American Journal of International Law*, 77 A.J.I.L 584 dhe Stanimir A. Alexandrov, *Self-Defence Against the use of Force in International Law* (Kluwer International, The Hague, 1996).

some disturbing activities from the American viewpoint, including the massive accumulation of armaments. This intervention was referred to the ICJ, which deplored US activities as illegal and not properly based on the concept of individual or collective self-defence.[104]

Perhaps the most important recent case relates to the US invasion of Iraq. In analysing this situation one has to take into consideration the 9/11 attacks which basically emphasised the destructive potential that one terrorist network can cause. This, to a certain extent, may have had its influence in taking the decision to invade Iraq in 2003. Iraq was already under some certain types of economic sanctions continuously from 1991when it was forced to pull out of Kuwait which it had invaded and conquered at the end of 1990.[105] According to the SC Resolution 687, Iraq was obliged to destroy, remove or render harmless under international supervision the weapons of mass destruction the world believed that the regime of Saddam Hussein had in his possession.[106] As time passed it seemed that the regime of Saddam Husain was not willing to give in and economic sanctions were effecting only the civilian population, in particular the poor and vulnerable.[107] In the meantime, in order to prevent an attack of the regime against the Kurdish and Shia populations in the north and south of the country respectively, the UN determined no-fly zones which to a large extent were implemented through the military support of the US and Great Britain.[108]

The Saddam Hussein regime managed to misuse the "Oil for Peace, UN programmes in which they used money secured by selling oil mainly to secure for the regime its needs which gave a lot of headaches to the international community.[109] On the other side, Iraq presented ob-

---

[104] Supra note 235, p 135, para. 269.

[105] Supra note 224, p. 109-110.

[106] Security Council Resolution 687, UN. Doc. S/RES/687 (1991), 8 April 1991, para 14.

[107] To ease on the situation of civili population the UN in December of 1996 approved a "Oil for Food" programme which foresaw for Iraq to be able to sell a specific quantity of oil in order to provide for food and other sanitary and medcial means for its population, see "UN Oil for Food Programmes" in http://www.un.org/depts/oip/, visited on 15 November 2011, also supra note 224, pp. 109-10.

[108] Supra note 224, pp. 109-10.

[109] See "Report on the Manipulation of the Oil-for-Food Programmes", Independent Inquiry Committee, 27 October 2005. More than 2000 differen companies were involved in corruption scheme in cooperation witht he Iraqi officials. This report has criticized a lot SG Kofi Annan for mismanagement. For an executive summary and analysisi of this programme see report of the *BBC*, visited on15 November 2011, http://news.bbc.co.uk/2/shared/bsp/hi/pdfs/27_10_05_summary.pdf.

stacles in allowing international inspectors to check the situation on the weapons of mass destruction facilities and programmes in accordance with the SC Resolution 687. In these circumstances, in September of 2002, the American President managed to push through SC Resolution 1441[110] which obliges Saddam Hussein to let the UN inspectors in to check weapons of mass destruction facilities and programmes as a last chance for international cooperation.[111] The regime once more failed to cooperate at the desired level with inspectors who were used by the US to justify its decision to attack Iraq. The US was supported by other states in a coalition called "The Coalition of the Willing".[112] The US justified its attack on their right to self-defence from an expected attack because of the aggressive rhetoric of the Iraqi regime, the existence of nuclear programmes, failure to cooperate with the UN inspectors and possibly the most dangerous, the possibility of the Iraqi regime cooperating with Al Qaeda and with it the possibility of transferring weapons of mass destruction into the hands of this network. However, a commission formed by the American Department of Defence to investigate weapons of mass destruction programmes in Iraq under the name of "Iraqi Observation Group", did not manage to find any evidence of the existence of the production or the gathering of weapons of mass destruction from 1991.[113] This was a huge blow in legitimizing the American invasion of Iraq under the pretext of preventive self-defence.

The concept of necessity as an integral part of the notion of self-defence entails two elements: 1) the level of certainty of the military potential of one state to cause serious damage; 2) the lack of other pacific options to deal with the case.[114] According to Hugo Grotius "*In order that self-defence may be lawful, it must be necessary; and it is not necessary unless we are certain, not only regarding the power of*

[110] According to the Resolution 1441, Iraq had failed to comply witht he SC Resolution 687, see Security Council Resolution 1441, UN. Doc. S/RES/1441 (2002), 8 November 2002.

[111] Supra note 224, pp. 109-110.

[112] The attack started in mid of March 2003 with military support coming only from the United Kingdom and to a certain extend by Australia out of 45 states which openly supported this attack, supra note 224, p. 36.

[113] "Comprehensive Report of the Special Advisor to the Director of Central Intelligence on Iraq's Weapons of Mass Destructions", 30 September 2004, CIA-s https://www.cia.gov/library/reports/general-reports-1/iraq_wmd_2004/index.html#sect1.

[114] Kristen E. Eichensehr, "Targeting Teheran: Assessing the Lawfulness of Preemptive Strikes Agianst Nuclear Facilities", *University of California Los Angeles Journal of International Law*, 11 UCLA J. Int'l L. & For. Aff. 59, 2008, p. 66.

our neighbour, but also regarding his intention."[115] While according to Christopher Greenwood, *"the right of self-defence will justify action only where there is sufficient evidence that the threat of attack exists. That will require evidence not only of the possession of weapons but also of an intention to use them."*[116] Both of these conclusions put into perspective that an important element of reliability for the eventual use of preventive self-defence is the resolute stance of the supposed attacking state to use force and basically it remains only a matter of time as to when it will start. To ascertain the resolute stance of one state to attack, the time is a determining factor for a state which pretends to react in self-defence. The greater the time between the supposed expected attack and that of self-defence the harder it becomes to ascertain the attack.[117] In these cases, to define the purpose of determining the use of force, states rely on auxiliary means and methods such as the engagement of different intelligence structures to gather information related to the stance of one state in a particular situation, public declarations by high level officials, the existence of nuclear plans and programmes, military doctrines etc.

The use of auxiliary means to evaluate the realization of an eventual attack sometimes may fail as for example the American and its allies attack against Iraq which was based on intelligence on the existence of weapons of mass destruction programmes in Iraq which later proved to be wrong. The intelligence data were presented by the American President George Bush at the SC session to win the approval of the use of force by this organ.[118] With regards to declarations of states and their official stance, many times states give declarations which have nothing to do with the reality but in this way they tend to achieve some particular political aims which may have to do with the strengthening of its internal regime or cohesion or in relations to other particular states. Thus it is important to pay attention to internal political or regional constellations in which a particular state is situated in order to clarify the motive of issuing official declarations.

In addition to what was said above, an important factor to legitimize self-defence has to do with exhaustion of diplomatic means

[115] *Ibid.*

[116] *Ibid.*

[117] Miriam Sapiro, "Preempting Prevention: Lessons Learned", *New York University Journal of International Law*, 37 N.Y.U. J. Int'l L. & Pol. 357, 2005, p. 367.

[118] Nigel D. White, *Democracy Goes to War: British Military Deployments under International Law* (Oxford Univeristy Press, New York, 2009) p. 245-250.

to resolve a particular international dispute. Diplomatic means may in fact be an inexhaustible tool to resolve disputes. These means should be used within a certain framework at a particular time. This is so because a state may misuse diplomatic means to avoid attention while it continues with its agenda outside the radar to realize its objective which is a matter of dispute. In cases involving nuclear programmes, an important framework for negotiations is presented by the NPT regime. This regime foresees specific provisions for cooperation with the IAEA and for the engagement of inspectors to monitor nuclear programmes. Cooperation within the NPT framework also provides specific guarantees for benign aims of states in the regime.[119]

Another important factor in legitimizing self-defence is the time factor of realisation of the supposed attack. In the case of nuclear weapons, is it enough that a nuclear state has intentions to attack at some point or only the mere fact of possessing nuclear programmes which may be only for peaceful purposes, in order to realize self-defence? Or should there be other evidence of existence of concrete nuclear military programmes? Can one interpret the possession of ballistic missiles together with nuclear programmes as a potential threat to another state which may be used to legitimize self-defence? In 1981 Israel bombed the Osiraq nuclear reactor in Iraq, a month before it was supposed to be operational.[120] Israel justified the action in that it had made this attack at this phase because if it was to be bombed later, meaning after it had become operational, it would be a huge danger to the people due to the release of radioactive elements.[121]

In the end, states should pay attention to the principle of proportionality in cases of self-defence. This means that the level of attack for self-defence should be proportional to that of the threat.[122] This entails dilemmas in cases of anticipatory self-defence and even more in cases of preventive self-defence. Many authors think that such self-defence may never by proportional because there is no objective measure from an attack which was not yet realised.[123] In 2006, the Israelis built a mil-

---

[119] Supra note 299, pp. 70-71.

[120] *Id*, p. 74.

[121] *Id*, p. 66

[122] Bowet D.W., *Self-Defence in International Law* (Praeger, Manchester, 1958), p. 3.

[123] Ian Brownlie, *International Law and the Use of Force by States* (Clarendon Press, Oxford, 1963), pp. 158-159 *"In the great Majority of cases to commit a state to an actual con-*

itary campaign in the territory of Libya against Hezbollah with the justification of responding to missile attack from this organisation and war against terrorism. Despite questions as to how legitimate this campaign was, and which was supported by very few sates, it was a common international consensus that it was at least not proportional to the missile attacks.[124]

The concept of self-defence leaves a lot of room for interpretations. This room seems terrible in cases of preventive self-defence, based on history which has seen initiatives of preventive self-defence which later proved to be wrong. The issue becomes even more problematic when nuclear energy enters the equation because states become very sensitive to that. The Cuban Crisis or the case of Iran and North Korea today, prove this high sensitivity of states from the mere fact that a state wants to improve its military capabilities or the existence of some sort of nuclear programme event if it is declared for peaceful use. Immature actions may easily lead to the spiralling of international disputes and incitement to open conflict. The international law refers to self-defence in general terms, but it does not have any specific reference on issues involving nuclear weapons or programmes which is still considered to be a just part of the military arsenal of one state. To clarify more on self-defence and nuclear weapons and programmes it is useful to look at the military doctrines of nuclear states and see how states perceive their nuclear arsenal.

---

flict when there si only circumstancial evidence of impending attack would be to act in a manner which disregarded the requirement of proportionality".

[124] Jutta Brunnee and Stephen J. Toope, *Legitimacy and Legality in International Law: An International Account* (Cambridge Studies in International and Comparative Law, Cambridge University Press, Cambridge, 2010), pp. 298-299.

III.4 NUCLEAR WEAPONS AND MILITARY DOCTRINES

To analyse the readiness of one state to use force, it is important to look at the military doctrine designed by that state. Military doctrine is defined in different ways by different states by taking into consideration the level of potential risks it faces, technical and technological development, internal politics and its role on the military, military budget etc. According to one general definition, the military doctrine has to do with focusing military capabilities towards the realization of strategic objectives and concrete results.[125] In a more dissect way another definition attributes certain goals that a military doctrine attempts to achieve: 1) guaranteeing security at the expense of other states by reducing overall security; 2) guaranteeing national security by equalizing a threat and stabilizing overall security; 3) guaranteeing national security by increasing other countries sense of security, consequently weakening the sources of threat.[126]

Military doctrines serve specific purposes and their effect is different, depending on the object and purpose they serve. This is dependent on the level of international relations of particular states. In certain situations, a state may show its military strength to other states against which it feel threatened by increasing their military capabilities until a balance is achieved. But this in turn may incite an arms race because if the other state is persistent in retaining its military primacy. In a world of *realpolitik* which mostly corresponds to military thinking where states are eager to preserve their full independence, the increase of military capabilities may be easily viewed as a change in the balance of power further leading to the security dilemma even though the purpose of the other state is for defence purposes only.[127] Such a situation may lead ultimately to an armed conflict among states.

Military doctrine plays a crucial role in placing the balance of power through which states show their capabilities and readiness to

---

[125] Bert Chapman, *Military Doctrine: A Reference Handbook* (ABC-CLIO, California 2009), p. 1.

[126] *Ibid.*

[127] Supra note 182, p. 57.

protect their national interests against other states. Other states may constrain themselves from taking any aggressive step which, on the contrary, a state would have taken.[128] In advancing their interests, states make various calculations of potential benefits and costs it could incur by taking a certain decision to achieve a particular purpose.[129] Military doctrines are used by states to subjugate and neutralize as much as possible or totally a potential threat by a particular state

In military doctrines of nuclear states specific attention is paid to nuclear weapons which have a crucial strategic importance. This is so because states, including those who have nuclear weapons, do not want to suffer a potential attack by a nuclear weapon. This managed to maintain the balance of power during the Cold War between two blocks, the west and the east, known as the bipolar world and it seems that it achieved stopping a major conflict between nuclear states belonging to these blocks. Nuclear military doctrines were an important part and also remain to play that role of deterrence or more precisely the nuclear deterrence.[130] Nuclear deterrence has its physical and psychological effect. According to the first one, a state has to have serious military capabilities, enough to threaten the enemy at that level that would make it not think or plan any eventual attack. This is achieved when there is a resolute stance to use nuclear weapons and when that state managed to transmit this resolution to the other state that it has capacities and a will to deter any kind of attack.[131]

The possession of nuclear weapons can guarantee to a certain extent the national security of one state, which makes them very attractive. Through them, states strengthen their position in international relations vis-à-vis nuclear states and as well as those states that do not have any such weapon. This is, actually, the first and main reason that incited the proliferation of nuclear weapons. The prevention of further proliferation of such weapons is, after all, in the interests of all states, including those nuclear ones. An important step was taken with the signing of

[128] Of course military doctrines are not final in determination of military capabilities of a state because it can be manipulated by a particular state intentionally to achieve a result. For this reason states use other means to come to a more accurate data related to real military capabilities of a state.

[129] Supra note 182, pp. 55-59.

[130] "Deterrence", Project of the Nuclear Age Peace Foundation, Nuclear Files, visited on 20 April 2012 http://www.nuclearfiles.org/ .

[131] *Ibid.*

the NPT. If this treaty tries to prevent a further proliferation of nuclear weapons, non-nuclear states needed additional guarantees from nuclear weapons related to preserve their security from nuclear threat. For this reason, nuclear states have designed their nuclear military doctrines and gave guarantees[132] to non-nuclear states that they will not use their nuclear weapons against non-nuclear states even in cases when they are first attacked by those states with conventional weapons. Up to now, it seems that these guarantees have been kept, taking into consideration that history has not shown any armed conflict where a nuclear state would use its nuclear weapons against a non-nuclear state even though these states were dragged into an armed conflict. Nevertheless, it is also true that none of the nuclear states were faced with a situation where its existence came into question thus leaving it quite relative to the positioning of nuclear states as designated in their nuclear military doctrines. It would seem absurd to believe that nuclear states would not use their nuclear weapons when faced with the situation when its existence is put into question, even in cases when it is attacked by conventional weapons. France, in its military doctrine has expressed it military readiness to use it nuclear arsenal in such cases. Below is a brief analysis of the nuclear military doctrines of nuclear states.

THE US

The US acknowledged, for the first time, the quantity of nuclear material which could be used for nuclear weapons in 2009. According to the official announcement on 30 September 2009, they possessed 5,113 nuclear heads, including tactical, strategic and non-deployed weapons. This number has decreased continuously from 1967 when the US military arsenal was at its maximum level of 31,255 such weapons.[133] In their military doctrines the US states that they *"will not use or threaten to use nuclear weapons against non-nuclear weapons states that are party to the NPT(NPT) and in compliance with their nuclear non-proliferation obligations"*.[134] Anyhow, the US has reserved the

[132] With regards to safeguards given upon signing of the NPT see Chapter below.

[133] Supra note 138.

[134] Remarks at the Review Conference of the Nuclear Non Proliferation Treaty by

right to reformulate this policy in cases involving biological weapons, implying that the US would use nuclear weapons if attacked or threatened by an eventual biological attack.[135]

Russia

Russia is believed to be in possession of around 2,340 strategic nuclear weapons and around 3,700 to 5,400 other nuclear heads and also around 3,000 other nuclear heads waiting to be dismantled.[136] According to Russian military doctrine published in 2010, *"The Russian Federation reserves their right to use nuclear weapons in response to the use of nuclear and other types of weapons of mass destruction against it and (or) its allies, as well as in response to aggression against the Russian Federation that utilizes conventional weapons that threatens the very existence of the state"*.[137] In this case, we can also see that Russia reserves the right to use nuclear weapons in cases when a threat exists, not only from the use of nuclear weapons by an enemy but also when a conventional state is supported by a nuclear state. In extraordinary cases, when the existence of the Russian Federation has come into question even in cases when it is attacked by a state using conventional weapons, Russia would use nuclear weapons according to this doctrine. However it applies only in cases of attacks or threats directed towards Russia and not its allies.

China

China is covered by total secrecy as to the number of nuclear weapons and material it potentially has. According to sources from in-

---

Hillary Rodham Clinton, The US State Department, 3 May 2010, visited on13 April 2012, http://www.state.gov/secretary/rm/2010/05/141424.htm.

[135] *Ibid.*

[136] Supra note 142, p. 67-68.

[137] Alexei Arbatov, Vladimir Dvorkin, and Sergey Oznobishcheve, *Contemporary Nuclear Doctrines* (Institute of World Economy and Internaitonal Relations, Russian Academy of Sciences, Nuclear Threat Initiative, IMEMO RAN, Moscow, 2010), pp 21-22.

dependent organisations, China has around 100-200 nuclear warheads, while in 2004 it only stated that China possessed the smallest nuclear arsenal of the five nuclear states of the NPT regime.[138] In its military doctrine it declared that *"China undertakes not to use or threaten to use nuclear weapons against non-nuclear-weapon States or nuclear-weapon-free zones at any time or under any circumstances"*.[139] This doctrine is directed towards states that possess nuclear weapons and are members of the NPT or other similar arrangement. It is interesting to empathise that according to this doctrine, China has given guarantees that it will not be the first country to use nuclear weapons in an eventual conflict.[140]

United Kingdom

The United Kingdom made public in December 2006 that it would reduce its nuclear power on stand-by from around 200 nuclear warheads to less than 160. In May of 2000, the British government reaffirmed its commitment not to use nuclear weapons against a state which does not have one and is a party to the NPT. However, it made it known that it will use nuclear weapons in extreme cases involving the question of the state's existence. [141]

France

France is believed to have around 350 nuclear warheads. According to its doctrine, France reserves the right to attack with such a weapon in cases of conflict. While in 1995 it reaffirmed that it would not use nuclear weapons against a state which does not possess such a weapon and is a member of the NPT.[142] In January of 2006, the French President

---

[138] Supra note 146.

[139] "Chinas' National Statement on Security Assurances", Nuclear Threat Initiative, 5 April 1995, para. 2 http://www.nti.org/db/china/engdocs/npt0495a.htm.

[140] *Id*, para 1.

[141] Supra note 149.

[142] David S. Yost, "France's New Nuclear Doctrine", *International Affairs,* Vol. 82,

Jacques Chirac stated that the use of nuclear weapons would be an option as a countermeasure against states which plot a terrorist attack or any other attack involving a weapon of mass destruction against France.[143]

India

India is believed to be in possession of around 100 nuclear warheads. India is expanding its activities to produce ballistic missiles capable of carrying nuclear warheads and which could be launched from land or submarines.[144] The main reason for the development of its nuclear programmes according to India is to keep the lowest level possible of deterrence. Of course it can be implied that its primary target is Pakistan due to years of conflict in particular over the issue of the territories of Kashmir[145] According to its doctrine, India would not be the first to use its nuclear weapons but only as a counter measure *"Nuclear weapons will only be used in retaliation against a nuclear attack on Indian territory or on Indian forces anywhere"*.[146] The government has reserved the right to use nuclear weapons against an eventual biological or chemical attack.[147]

Pakistan

Pakistan is believed to have around 60 nuclear warheads. In its military doctrine, which is not official, Pakistan states that it developed its nuclear programme as a means of deterrence and that it has adopted the policy of the non-use of nuclear weapons first.[148]

Issue 4 (2006), pp. 701-702.

[143] "France "would use nuclear arms", *BBC*, 19 January 2006, http://news.bbc.co.uk/2/hi/europe/4627862.stm, see also supra note 153.

[144] Supra note 154.

[145] Ali Ahmed, "Reviewing India's Nuclear Doctrine", *Institute for Defence Studies and Analyses*, 24 April 2009 p. 2.

[146] *Ibid.*

[147] Supra note 154.

[148] "Pakistan Profile", Nuclear Threat Initiative, visited on10 June 2011, http://www.nti.org/e_research/profiles/Pakistan/Nuclear/index.html, see also, Peter Lavoy, "Pakistan's Nu-

Israel

Israel has never admitted to being in possession of nuclear weapons even though it is believed that this state possesses around 75-300 nuclear warheads. The official policy of Israel is that it *"will not be the first country to introduce nuclear weapons in the Middle East"* and that for this reason it will not give any negative or positive answer.[149]

Military doctrines are used to give greater clarity on the right of states to use force in cases allowed by international law. This is seen also in the nuclear doctrines of different states which refer to cases related to self-defence. But, if we look closely, these doctrines entail in themselves, some vagueness because states, by reserving their right to use them in specific cases of self-defence, they give themselves the exclusive right to determine the existence of such circumstances. The situation becomes even murkier in cases of nuclear attack of a very small capacity which may be equal to an attack by a conventional weapon or in cases of an attack by chemical or biological weapons. Military doctrines do not give sufficient clarity to this perspective; however it would seem plausible that the principle of proportionality would have to prevail in any circumstance. Also, it is still not clear what is meant by the threat to the state's existence and at what point a state may invoke this reason to use nuclear weapons. Here also, a state which is under attack would interpret it in individual manner as to what amount that attack endangers the existence of that state.

To give more clarity related to the right to use force and the role of nuclear weapons, maybe the ICJ would be the proper institution to do so however, in its advisory opinion on the legality of use or threat to use nuclear weapons, the ICJ failed to give a precise answer on the main issue still leaving it up to states to interpret it on an individual basis.

---

clear Posture: Security and Survivability," Nonproliferation Policy Education Center, January 2007, pp. 4-5, http://www.npolicy.org/article_file/Pakistans_Nuclear_Posture-Security_and_Survivability.pdf.

[149] Supra note 164, p. 14.

CHAPTER IV

THE LEGALITY OF THREAT OR USE OF NUCLEAR WEAPONS AND THE ICJ LEGAL ADVISORY OPINION

IV.1 THE COMPETENCES OF ICJ AND ITS ROLE IN INTERPRETATION OF INTERNATIONAL LAW

Ideas for the creation of a court which would solve disputes among states are not new. Those date at least from medieval times. This idea has come from different authors who believed in the development of world governance which, among others, would have in its possession a court to interpret the law and yield justice. In this aspect for example a poet, Dante Alighieri from Florence, in medieval times proposed such a thing in his book *De Monarchia.*[1] Up to the beginning of the XX century such initiatives remained mainly as ideas and writings of individuals who believed in the development of an hierarchic international system or of a super state which would function similarly to states as we know them today with their legislative, executive and judicial bodies. In this way, they thought, world peace could become a reality.[2]

The creation of a super-state entails overcoming complex issues because it would mean the intermingling of different ideologies, social systems and cultures stemming from different peoples, nations and ethnicities, which make it nearly impossible from today's perspective. For this reason, focusing on creating different institutions dealing with specific fields seems to be more feasible and acceptable. The creation of a world court which would interpret the law developed voluntarily by states presents a common interest and more easy to achieve it. The most serious attempts by states to create a world court were made at The

[1] Supra note 238, p. 392.

[2] See for example Imanuel Kant, *Perpetual Peace: A Philosophical Essay* (1795). In his book, Kant proposes three articles where one of them proposes for the creation of a federation of free states implying creation of a central government.

Hague Conference in 1907. At this conference, the US delegation had proposed the creation of a permanent tribunal, which would be composed of professional judges and whose sole job would be the delivery of justice.[3] According to the State Secretary Elihu Root "*these judges should be so selected from the different countries that the different systems of law and procedure and the principal languages shall be fairly represented*".[4] This proposal was supported by the United Kingdom delegation and Germany, but not by others thus influencing the failure to create an international court at that time. However, in the meantime, it was agreed to create the Court of International Arbitration.[5]

After WWI, the League of Nations (LN) was formed as the first universal organisation in the world, the purpose of which was to prevent wars by establishing a system of collective security.[6] The LN Covenant foresaw specific means to resolve international disputes such as negotiations and arbitration.[7] Article 14 obliged the League Council to prepare a plan for the creation of the Permanent Court of International Justice (PCIJ). According to this Article the court *"shall be competent to hear and determine any dispute of an international character which the parties thereto submit to it. The Court may also give an advisory opinion upon any dispute or question referred to it by the Council or by the Assembly"*. So, the court would have two functions, that of solving international disputes and issuing of advisory opinions.[8] In compliance with this, the League Council engaged an advisory commission of lawyers who, in August 1920, came up with a report on establishing the PCIJ.[9] The LN Assembly approved the report in its first session in December of 1920.[10]

---

[3] See "History of the ICJ Court", ICJ, visited on 28 December 2011, http://www.icj-cij.org/court/index.php?p1=1&p2=1#International.

[4] *Ibid.*

[5] The International Court of Arbitration was formed in 1913 as a result of the agreement between participating states at the 1907 Hague Conference, and it still functions today. For more on this court see www.pca-cpa.org.

[6] See The League of Nations Covenant, 13 AJIL Supp. 128 (1919). According to the notion of collective security an attack against a state is deemed to be an attack agains all other LN Member States.

[7] *Id*, Art. 15.

[8] *Id*, Art. 14.

[9] This report would serve as a basis for writing the PCIJ Statute after it was changed earlier by the LN Assembly Third Committe, see supra note 337.

[10] Earlier in 1919, with the Dutch proposal a decision was taken for Justice Palace located in the Hague to serve as the headquarter of the PCIJ, see supra note 337.

The establishment of the PCIJ marks a very important step in international law and its implementation and interpretation. This meant that from now on a permanent address was created composed of a professional body which states could address to solve their disputes. The PCIJ was not given obligatory jurisdiction but it allowed states to choose whether or not they wanted to accept the decision.[11] The PCIJ would not become an organ of the LN, which distinguishes it from its successor the ICJ. The judges of this court were elected by the LN Assembly and Council in their shared competence.[12] In its work the PCIJ would apply sources determined in Article 38: treaties; international customary law; general principles accepted by civilized nations; and, according to Article 59, judicial decisions and writings of renowned scholars from around the world as subsidiary sources of international law.[13]

The LN system would not survive for long as it failed to prevent another world war. WWII officially started in 1939.[14] The start of WWII would also mean the end of the PCIJ. Allied states against the Nazi axis and Japan started their attempt for the creation of another world organisation after the war which would function differently from the LN, but mainly with the same hope of preventing future wars. The United Nations Declaration of 1 January 1942, which as approved by 26 states including the US, United Kingdom, the USSR and China, presented the basic foundation in the establishment of the UN.[15] With this, the world leaders expressed their willingness to also establish a new court. Now the new court would become part of the UN and would be called the International Court of Justice.[16]

The establishment of the ICJ would depend on the creation of the UN. The decision was finally taken during the San Francisco conference held between April and July 1945.[17] It statute would remain

[11] The PCIJ Statued, Art. 36, Yale Law School Avalon Project, http://avalon.law.yale.edu/20th_century/decad026.asp.

[12] Supra note 337.

[13] Supra note 345, Art. 38. According to Art. 59 of this statute, "*The decision of the Court has no binding force except between the parties and in respect of that particular case*". From the procession of first case in 1922 up to 1940 the PCIJ decided on 29 cases and issued 27 adisory opinions, see supra note 337.

[14] For more on the WW II see John Keegan, *The Second World War*, (Random House, New York, 2011).

[15] Supra note 224, pp. 37-38.

[16] Supra note 238, pp. 392-393.

[17] Supra note 337.

almost the same as that of the PCIJ in accordance with the requirement of Article 92 of the Charter.[18] The selection of the first judges took place in February of 1946 during the first session of the GA, while the first case was sent to this court in May of 1947. The headquarters of this court would be the same one used by the PCIJ.[19] A positive element incorporated while establishing the ICJ was that all UN Members would formally be members of the ICJ statute.[20]

The main role of the ICJ is to interpret international law as state courts interpret national law, but it differs from state courts because, in the first place, it does not make up part of an hierarchic judicial system.[21] The decision of this court is final and cannot be subject of appeal.[22] Its revision may be possible only in cases when a new fact is presented and is so crucial that it could have played a determining factor in the decision of the court had it been presented earlier during the regular proceedings.[23] The court is not part of international governance, because the UN world order had not been created as such.[24] This affects the lack of an enforcing mechanism, by which states would be coerced to comply with its decisions. However, according to the Charter, all UN Members undertake to comply and respect decisions taken by this court.[25] In cases when states do not comply with this rule, then the ICJ or the next interested party may refer that issue to the UNSC which has the power do decide which further measures should be taken to oblige states to comply with the decision.[26]

The ICJ was thought to be the most important UN organ by the many statesmen who participated in establishing this court. During the inaugural session of this court, the first president of the GA, the Belgian Paul Henri Spaak declared that *"I would not venture to assert that the International Court of Justice is the most important organ of the United*

[18] Supra note 121, Art. 92.

[19] The first case dealt with a dispute involving the United Kingdom agains Albania related to the Corfu incident, see supra note 337.

[20] Supra note 337, Art. 93.

[21] Mohamed Shahabuden, "The World Court at the Turn of the Century" në *The International Court of Justice: Its Future Role after Fifty Years,* ed. A.S. Muller, D. Raic and J.M. Thuranszky (Martinus Njihoff Publishers, The Hague-Boston-London, 1997), pp. 3-5.

[22] The Statute of the International Court of Justice, 3 Bevans 1179, 26 June 1945, Art. 60.

[23] *Id*, Art. 61.

[24] Supra note 355,p p. 5-8.

[25] Supra note 121, Art. 94, para 1.

[26] *Id*, Art. 94 para 2.

Nations; but I think I may say that in any case there is none more important"....I am deeply convinced that peace will not finally be established until all countries have recognized the truth that there can be no civilized world nor any lasting peace, if there be not complete and absolute respect for international jurisdiction and its judgements".[27] The years following its establishment show hesitation by states to address this court, especially during the cold war.[28] There are many reasons for this. It may be because the judicial procedures needed time, it incurs financial costs and is unpredictable.[29] Anyhow, after 1996 there was a positive trend by states to use this important tool for their purposes.

One of the reasons why states hesitated to address the ICJ is that political leaders hesitate to lose control over a particular case, believing that they can solve that particular problem through negotiations or political pressure, especially in serious cases, *"States do not want to risk losing a case when the stakes are high or be troubled with litigation in minor matters."*[30] Also, another reason is that the ICJ is competent only to decide according to positive law and not create a new law. It interprets the law as it is while states, frequently, as they solve their disputes simultaneously create or amend a particular relation, which can be achieved by using diplomatic means.[31]

An important role on the work of ICJ relates to its jurisdiction. According to the statute, the ICJ does not have a compulsory jurisdiction over states.[32] In order for the ICJ to hear a case, states from both sides, claimant and respondent, should accept the jurisdiction of the court, otherwise it cannot go further with the process. Referring to this right, states, which are on the claimant side, have difficulties convincing the other party to accept the jurisdiction of the court to solve their eventual dispute. Acceptance of jurisdiction may be met by: deposition of a declaration; according to the agreement or treaty the provision/s of

[27] Supra note 355, pp. 4-5.

[28] This is shown by the fact that from 1946-1996 this court heard only 97 cases out of which 75 had to do with disputes resolution and 22 with advisory opinions, see "ICJ Yearbook", I.C.J. Yb. 1996-1997, p. 3.

[29] Oscar Schachter, *International Law in Theory and Practice* (Martinus Njihoff Publishers, Leiden, 1991) p. 218

[30] *Ibid.*

[31] *Ibid.*

[32] Supra note 356, Art. 36.

which may be a matter of dispute; *ad hoc* on a case by case basis.[33] In the majority of the cases, by accepting the jurisdiction of the ICJ, states insert the reciprocity provision by which they require that this jurisdiction be accepted by the other state at the same level as the state filing the application.[34] A state may accept tacitly the ICJ jurisdiction in cases when an application is filed against that state which takes parts in the hearing without giving any objection to the jurisdiction of the court.[35]

The ICJ is composed of 15 members/judges who are elected by the GA and SC in their shared competence voting in a separate and independent procedure.[36] Nominated candidates are persons elected by the national groups represented at the PICA.[37] The list of names of the proposed candidates is handed to the UN Secretary General (SG), who presents that list before the GA and SC in alphabetic order.[38] The candidate who wins the absolute majority separately in these two organs is elected to become a member of the ICJ.[39] During the voting, the GA and SC ought to pay attention not only to the professional capacities of the candidate but also to the representation of all worlds civilizations and different legal systems.[40] The ICJ elects its president and deputy president for a three year period with the possibility of being re-elected.[41] The decisions of the ICJ are taken by the majority of judges present and voting.[42] In cases of votes split 50/50, the president decides.[43] The quorum is made up of nine judges. The ICJ may create specific chambers to deal with a particular case composed of 3 or more judges such as for example issues related to labour, transit or communication.[44] Up to now, the majority of cases have been decided in full court. During the hearing, one party may request the nomination of an *ad hoc* judge in cases when none of the judges comes from that state.[45]

[33] *Id*, Art. 36 poin 1 and 2.
[34] Supra note 232, p. 857.
[35] *Ibid.*
[36] Supra note 356, Art. 8.
[37] *Id*, Art. 4 point 2.
[38] *Id*, Art. 7.
[39] *Id,* Art. 10.
[40] *Id,* Art. 9.
[41] *Id,* Art. 21.
[42] *Id,* Art. 55.
[43] *Id,* Art. 25 point 3.
[44] *Id,* Art. 26.
[45] *Id,* Art. 31.

The ICJ has two functions: decide on contentious matters between states; and delivering advisory opinions. In exercising its function, the ICJ is based on the sources determined in Article 38 of the Statute: international agreements; international customary law; and general principles of law. While judicial decisions and the teachings of the most highly qualified publicists of the various nations remain a subsidiary source.[46] Its decisions have effect only in relations to the particular case in dispute and between the parties involved.[47] The initiation of proceedings according to the first function is done by states exercising their rights as the subjects of international law. One has to bear in mind that states may initiate the proceedings only after the responding state has accepted in one way the jurisdiction of the court.

The ICJ may give advisory opinions on any legal issue which is initiated from the authorized organs in accordance with the Charter. This competence is given to the GA and SC and also to other UN specialized organs within the scope of their activities.[48] States may request an advisory opinion but they have to go through UN organs eligible to request it. In this perspective for example the initiative of the World Court Project went through the World Health Organisation (WHO) on the first occasion but later through the GA in a changed mode. Also, Serbia requested an advisory opinion regarding the declaration of independence of Kosovo through the GA.[49] Advisory opinions are not formally obligatory, but they represent an authoritative interpretation of international law or particular provision/s. In some cases, states by a specific provision of a particular agreement determine that in cases of dispute arising from that agreement parties will address the ICJ for an advisory opinion which shall be deemed obligatory by the parties.[50]

When registering a request for advisory opinion, the ICJ has complete discretion to decide whether to give an opinion or not.[51] The ICJ, at the beginning, checks whether it has jurisdiction to give the

[46] *Id,* Art. 38.

[47] *Id,* Art. 59.

[48] Supra note 121, Art. 96.

[49] For more regardin the advisory opinion on Kosovo see Adv. Op. Accordance with International Law of the Unilateral Declaration of Independence in Respect of Kosovo, ICJ, General List No. 141, 22 July 2010.

[50] Such a provision can be found in the Convention on the Privileges and Immunities of the United Nations, 1 U.N.T.S. 15, 13 February 1946, Art. 30.

[51] Supra note 383, p. 10 para 17.

opinion. To fulfil these criteria, the question put before it should be of legal character and be requested by an authorized party.[52] Also, the question should be within the scope of activity of the authorized organisation.[53] As to the legal character of the question, the ICJ is aware that many times the issues presented which have legal character may be linked to the political aspect. In these cases, nothing prevents the ICJ giving an opinion on those issues that raise legal concerns while avoiding the political ones.[54] At the same time, during determining whether the question raised has legal issues or not, the ICJ does not take into consideration political motives that might have influenced the request to be filed with the Court.[55]

When the court answers positively to the above mentioned issues, the ICJ may conclude that it has the jurisdiction to give the advisory opinion on the question presented. But this, still, does not mean that it is obliged to give the opinion. The legal language in the Statute, Article 65, uses the word "may", "the Court may give an advisory opinion".[56] This wording leaves discretion to the Court whether to continue further or not. This leaves room for the Court to protect its integrity if faced with a difficult question with serious political consequences.[57] But, on the other side, the ICJ is aware of its important role and in principle it should not refuse such requests in cases when they fulfil formal criteria.[58]

In the end, in exercising its function of giving advisory opinions, the ICJ decides on the purpose and the meaning of the question. It focuses on whether the question placed is clear and precise. In practice, the ICJ has departed from the language used in the question in cases when the question was not clear or when it saw it more reasonably while analysing the question and circumstance that brought the request for opinion, or when the question raised did not reflect legal issues but its purpose was to raise legal issues. In cases when the question was not clear, the ICJ has clarified it before proceeding with the opinion.[59]

---

[52] *Id*, p. 11 para 18-19.

[53] Compare *Id*, p. 11 para 19 with supra note 121, para 96 point 2.

[54] *Id*, p. 13, para 27.

[55] *Ibid.*

[56] Supra note 356, Art. 65.

[57] Supra note 383, p. 13 para 29-30.

[58] *Id*, p. 13 para 30.

[59] *Id*, p. 19 para 50

After the ICJ concludes that all conditions are fulfilled and discretionally decides to give the opinion on the request filed, it decides how to proceed with the cases, dates of the hearing and also it can give a timeframe within which interested parties may present their statements in written or oral manner.[60] After hearing all parties and analysing documents according to the request, the ICJ publishes it opinion, which is taken by the decision of the majority of judges present and voting. The opinion is published and the Court then notifies the SG and the UN Members or other states or organisations which are directly or indirectly affected by that opinion.[61] The ICJ members who participated in the decision making may give their separate opinion in concurring or dissenting with the opinion.

The ICJ still remains one of the most important international organs in interpretation of international law and the delivering of justice. Despite the increased trend of cases addressed to this court, still the ICJ suffers from the lack of work because many states could not establish the necessary trust in this court and give it the compulsory jurisdiction. The problem of addressing issues to this court, including requests for advisory opinion, may be seen with the case regarding the legality of threat or use of nuclear weapons which took many years of preparations and lobbying by different states to receive the required support to file a request for an advisory opinion. Besides the complex and tiring work, this also requires financial support which is not available all the time, especially in times of economic difficulty.

[60] Supra note 356, Art. 66.

[61] *Id*, Art. 67.

IV.2 THE WORLD COURT PROJECT

The possession of nuclear weapons is closely related to the national security of the state which possesses them. States do not want to be constrained on issues related to their national security on a voluntary basis. The fact of one state possessing nuclear weapons entails that, that state reserves the right to use them when considered necessary in its own interpretation. The right to self-defence has its loopholes, in particular the preventive self-defence which raises a number of dilemmas on the right to invoke it. Anyhow, attempts to control nuclear weapons started from the moment when such weapons were used in Hiroshima and Nagasaki. Seeing its devastating effect, an initial attempt was made to halt further production by any state but as it was becoming clear that this attempt is failing, the focus shifted to attempts to limit as much as possible their proliferation.

The UN order allows for the use of force in cases of self-defence and thus it is understood that the production and possession of such weapons is carried out for this purpose and which is legitimate. States which possess nuclear weapons have, in no known case, pretended to use such a weapon for aggression purposes. The military doctrines, in particular those pertaining to nuclear weapons, express it clearly that the possession of nuclear weapons is for self-defence purposes. Furthermore, the use of these weapons, according to those doctrines, would be done mainly when a nuclear state faces an attack from nuclear weapons or when the existence of that state is in question. Accordingly, the production and use of nuclear weapons for defence purposes would be in compliance with the UN Charter.

Equipment with nuclear weapons cause an increase in friction between states because states who lag behind feel threatened and this incites them to lay their hands on the technology and knowhow for the production of nuclear weapons and this may result in an arms race.[62] This often leads to international incidents impacting on regional and world

[62] For more on this issue see Richard Rhodes, *Arsenals of Folly: The Making of the Nuclear Arms Race* (Knopf Doubleday Publishing Group, 2008, New York).

peace and security. The NPT regulates the transfer of nuclear energy and its production technology. This treaty assigns duties to states which possess nuclear weapons and technology for the production of nuclear energy and on the other side it also assigns duties to states which do not possess them. According to this treaty the nuclear states, party to the treaty, take under obligation not to transfer the technology and know-how for the production of nuclear energy or weapons to non-nuclear states, while non-nuclear states party to the treaty take under obligation not to develop nuclear programmes for military purposes.[63] The NPT makes it illegal for states to possess nuclear weapons. It still remains a very complicated issue with states not party to the regime and which possess or are believed to be in possession of nuclear weapons such as Israel, India or Pakistan. North Korea has withdrawn from the NPT, after it first became a fully-fledged member of the regime.

The NPT accepted the reality of five nuclear Member States which are members of it (the US, Russia, China, France and the United Kingdom). This pushed non-governmental organisations and associations from all around the world to seek clarity with regards to the legality of nuclear weapons and their use from a more extensive perspective and not focus only on the NPT provisions.[64] The ICJ presented a competent organ for addressing this issue and at the beginning the idea was to go through one of the specialized UN institution, in which case they should focus only on requiring an advisory opinion.[65] To achieve this, the issue addressed would have to remain within the scope of competences of a particular institution requesting it.[66] At the end of a long and tiring process of international lobbying, convincing the GA to address the issue to the ICJ for an advisory opinion was achieved, using its competences under Article 97 of the Charter and Article 65 para. 1 of the ICJ Statute.[67] The attempts to gain support from the GA to request that advisory opinion would go on for years and pass through major difficulties.

[63] See Treaty on the Non-Proliferation of Nuclear Weapons, 729 U.N.T.S. 161, 1968 i njohur ndryshe si NPT(NPT). The NPT entered into force in 1970, for more see United Nations Office for Disarmament Affairs, visited on15 November 2012, http://www.un.org/disarmament/WMD/Nuclear/NPT.shtml.

[64] Geoffrey R. Watson, "ASIL Insight: The ICJ and the Lawfulness of the use of Nuclear Weapons", *ASIL Newsletter*, June 1995, pp. 1-2.

[65] According to Art. 96 of the Charter, the GA and SC can request an advisory opinion form the ICJ on any legal matter, supra note 121, Art. 96, para 1.

[66] *Ibid.*

[67] Supra note 356, Art. 65, para 1.

The movement for addressing the issue of nuclear weapons to the ICJ originated at the beginning of the 1980s.[68] A network of peace activists, doctors, lawyers and other NGO-s, which would be known later as the World Court Project (the Project) was interested in having an authoritative opinion on the legality of nuclear weapons. To achieve this, they should address it to one of the authorized organs of the UN, aside from the SC. In this way they would avoid the SC where it was believed that such an initiative would almost certainly not succeed because of the possible use of the veto by one of the Permanent Members who at the same time all possess nuclear weapons and are members to the NPT.[69] This initiative was not unprecedented because, in a case related to damage caused by nuclear weapons, New Zealand sued France in the ICJ accusing it of causing environmental damage by testing nuclear weapons in the South Pacific.[70] Taking the case, the ICJ issued some orders requesting France to halt its atmospheric nuclear testing until the case is closed. France refused to do so reasoning that the ICJ did not have jurisdiction over that issue.[71] However, after the conclusion of two more tests, France publicly declared that it had finished its project and that it would continue only with underground tests. In this case, the ICJ stopped its procedure even before deciding whether it had jurisdiction to decide on the case or not.[72]

The Project was initiated in 1981 by the International Peace Bureau (IPB) during a symposium on nuclear deterrence.[73] For a speedy procedure, they would have to convince one of the states to use its authority to gain support within the GA to present a resolution which would require an advisory opinion from the ICJ and to do so, they organized the so called London Tribunal for Nuclear Warfare where the

[68] Edda Kristjansdottir, "The Legality of the Threat or Use of Nuclear Weapons under Current International Law: The Arguments behind the World Court's Advisory Opinion", *New York University Journal of Internaitional Law and Politics*, 30 N.Y.U. J. Int'L. & Pol. 291, 1997-1998, p. 295. For more see World Court Project/International Law, The Lawyers Committee on Nuclear Policy, visited on 30 April 2012, http://lcnp.org/wcourt/.

[69] *Ibid.*

[70] Keith Mothersson, *From Hiroshima to the Hague: Guide to the World Court Project* (International Peace Bureau, Geneva, 1992) p. 51.

[71] Kate Dawes and Commander Robert Green RN, "The World Court Project: How a Citizen Network Can Influence the United Nations", *Pacifica Review, La Trobe University, Melbourne, Vol 7 No 2, October/November, 1995, pp. 30-40.*

[72] *Id*, p. 40.

[73] *Id.*

participants focused on Australia and New Zealand as potential states to lobby the GA.[74] Australia was not very interested while New Zealand expressed its willingness to support the project.[75] An important role was played by the IPB President Sean MacBride and by the New Zealand judge Harold Evans.[76] Harold Evans, inspired by US professor Richard Falk, had drafted an open letter of 100 pages addressed to the Prime Ministers of Australia and New Zealand. Using the support from New Zealand, Evans had appealed in writing to 71 states through their missions in Canberra and Wellington. It seemed that gradually, this initiative was taking traction because, in the meantime, 110 governments from the non-aligned movement and the USSR showed interest in joining the Project.[77] But, at a decisive moment, the New Zealand government would withdraw, because it was afraid of disturbing its relations with the western states, and other permanent SC Member States.[78] New Zealand, at this time was lobbying for a non-permanent SC member seat which required the support from Western European states and the US. In addition to that, New Zealand was emerging from a not so good experience with the ICJ when it sued France for environmental damage related to nuclear testing.[79] This would cause a huge blow to the Project.

On the other side, in 1987, the Lawyers Committee on Nuclear Energy from the US and the Soviet Lawyers Association had sponsored an NGO conference in New York to discuss nuclear weapons and international law. These two organisations would later create the International Lawyers Associations against Nuclear Weapons (ILANW) in Stockholm in April 1988.[80] Now, the front was focused in many directions. After the withdrawal of New Zealand, Evans targeted European states to lobby and to talk to other groups for support and associations. ILANW organized a World Congress in September of 1989 held in The Hague, which adopted The Hague Declaration on the illegality of nuclear weapons which appealed to all UN Member States to *"take immediate steps towards obtaining a resolution by the General Assembly, requesting the ICJ to render an advisory opinion on the illegality of*

[74] Supra note 402, p. 295.
[75] Supra note 405, p. 2.
[76] *Ibid.*
[77] *Ibid.*
[78] *Ibid.*
[79] *Ibid.*
[80] *Ibid.*

the use of nuclear weapons".[81] In 1991 the Project in the United Kingdom had drafted a "declaration of public consciousness" through which he opposed nuclear weapons as immoral and illegal.[82] This declaration was inspired by the *Martens* clause[83] which referred to the "public consciousness dictate" as a determining factor in deciding whether particular means of war, which are not specified in any treaty, are prohibited or regulated by the international law.[84]

The Project was officially formed in 1992 when ILANW joined forces with the International Physicists for the Prevention of Nuclear War (IPPNW) and with the International Peace Bureau, to be joined later by other groups and citizens from all around the world.[85] In May of 1992 the Project gained important momentum, when during the work of the World Health Organisation (WHO) some states proposed a draft-resolution on the "Health and Environmental Effects of Nuclear Weapons.[86] The WHO Assembly failed to take any steps in this meeting, postponing it for the next meeting in 1993. In May 1993, the WHO Assembly put a draft-resolution on the agenda to be voted on and on 14 May, in its 46th session, it approved the resolution requesting an advisory opinion from the ICJ to the question: *"in view of the health and environmental effects, would the use of nuclear weapons by a State in war or other armed conflict be a breach of its obligations under international law including the WHO Constitution"*.[87] As it may be seen, the question was presented in such a way so that it fulfils the Charter and the ICJ Statute criteria coming from a specialized UN institution for it to be of legal matter and within the scope of the function of that institution.

---

[81] John Burroughs, *The (Il)legality of Threat or Use of Nuclear Weapons: A Guide to the Historic Opinion of the International Court of Justice* (International Association of Lawyers Against Nuclear Weapons, Munster Lit Verlag 1997), p. 10.

[82] *Ibid.*

[83] This is a characteristic provision the the Geneva and Hague Conventions and has taken this name after the Russian Foreing Minister Feodoro de Martens who proposed it in the first place.

[84] Supra note 415, p. 10.

[85] Over 700 groups from all around the world had supported this project with most of them being active in lobbying different states to join the project, see supra note 415, p. 9.

[86] Supra note 402, p. 295,

[87] Health and Environmental Effect of Nuclear Weapons, WHA RES. 46.40, U.N. WHO, Agenda Item 33, U.N. Doc. WHA 46.40 (1993) , p2. The resolution was adopted by 73 votes in favour, 40 against and 10 abstentions.

In compliance with the ICJ Statute Article 66 para. 2, the ICJ asked states and organisations to submit their declaration in writing by 10 June 1994.[88] This deadline was moved to 20 September 1994, while states and organisations who submitted their written declaration were given up to 20 June 1995 to submit their declaration regarding written declarations of other states.[89]

Immediately after the approval of the resolution from the WHO Assembly, the question arose as to how the ICJ would respond to the request to give an advisory opinion. The concern was natural due to the requirements of Articles 91 and 65 of the Charter and Statute respectively according to which the issues in the question requested should be within the scope of competences of the institution requesting it.[90] It can be seen from the way the question was presented that the WHO focused its question on the negative effect on health and environment in general from the eventual use of nuclear weapons. Certainly, these two issues of the question relate to the function of the WHO, but in essence the issue becomes more complex. A number of states considered that the WHO competences do not stretch to the legality of use of nuclear weapons.[91] According to these states, the WHO mandate is to promote and protect human health and not regulate the use of nuclear weapons, a question which lies under the competences of other UN organs such as the SC or IAEA.[92] On the other side, many states, organisations and renowned personalities did not think of it that way. According to the supporters of the WHO resolution, the WHO has a strong interest in preventing catastrophes which may affect human health because its prevention is much more effective than its treatment. The use of merely one nuclear weapon may have such a destructive effect which cannot be dealt by any of the clinics and other medical facilities of any state and it would cause real humanitarian chaos consequently a failure to protect the human health which is the main function of this organisation.[93]

---

[88] Supra note 402, pp. 295-296.

[89] *Ibid.*

[90] Compare Art. 91 para. 1 with Art. 65 para. 1 of the Charter and ICJ Statute respectively, supra notes 121 and 356.

[91] Supra note 398, p 2. A WHO legal advisor during discussions in the WHO Assembly stated tah the issue would be outside of the WHO scope and mandate, supra note 402, p. 304.

[92] Supra note 398, p 2.

[93] *Ibid.*

To overcome concerns related to the scope of the question presented by the WHO and to avoid any eventual failure before the ICJ which may consider that the question is outside of the functions of the WHO, the members of the Project approached the non-aligned states to push for approval of a resolution within the GA requesting an advisory opinion on the use of nuclear weapons.[94] In this way, the ICJ would not be able to eventually avoid reviewing the cases because of legal matters or because of being out of the scope of the functions and competences of the institution presenting it. If we refer to history, also taking into consideration activities of the PCIJ, this court only once decided to refuse to give an advisory opinion. This was the "Eastern Karelia" case. In this dispute, one of the states involved, the USSR, was not at that time a member of the LN, and due to which the PCIJ refused to give its opinion.[95]

Accordingly, there was a belief that the ICJ would not refuse to answer the question even though, seeing it from a different perspective, the issue of the use of nuclear weapons entails high political character.[96] The belief was founded on the prestige of the court, because an eventual refusal on such an important issue would not go in its favour. On the other side, even if the ICJ considered that the question fulfilled all the formal criteria and decide to give the opinion, all the parties from the losing and the winning sides would consider it as non- binding.[97]

The non-aligned states decided to jointly support the approval of a resolution and to lobby other states to vote for them. On 9 November 1993, Indonesia representing the non-aligned states presented a draft-resolution with the First Committee of the GA under the heading *"Request for an Advisory Opinion from the International Court of Justice on the Legality of the Threat or Use of Nuclear Weapons"*.[98] In the meantime, this resolution was withdrawn during the 30th Meeting of the First Committee on the request of its sponsors in order not to disturb international discussions on nuclear disarmament which were on-going at that time.[99]

---

[94] Supra note 402, p. 296.

[95] Supra note 398, p. 2.

[96] *Id*, p 3.

[97] *Ibid.*

[98] Supra note 402, pp. 296-298.

[99] For the minutes of the meeting, see Report of the First Committee U.N. Doc. A/C.1/48/SR., 3 (1993), p. 2.

In the following year, at the 11th Conference at the level of ministers, the non-aligned movement decided to place the resolution once more for approval during the next GA plenary session. The resolution was sent to be approved by the First Committee, where debates were held on approving or disapproving the draft-resolution.[100] The Morocco, German and Hungarian delegations proposed that no decision be taken.[101] Ultimately, the committee managed to approve the draft resolution with 77 votes in favour, 33 against and 21 abstentions. 33 other states did not participate in voting.[102]

After the successful approval in the First Committee, the draft resolution was placed in the GA agenda for voting under the name "Resolution 49/75 K".[103] During discussions in the GA, the NATO members, through France, tried to convince other states not to go further with approving the resolution which did in fact fail.[104] On the same date, the GA voted in favour of the resolution, with 43 votes against, 38 abstention and 23 states not taking part in voting. The Resolution 49/75 K was entitled *"Request for an Advisory Opinion from the International Court of Justice on the Legality of the Threat or Use of Nuclear Weapons"* according to Article 96, para. 1 of the Charter and requested the ICJ to give an advisory opinion on the following issue "*Is the Threat or Use of Nuclear Weapons in any circumstances permitted under international law"*.[105]

Difficulties were great but the will was greater to put the ICJ into motion with the purpose of clarifying issues related to the use of nuclear weapons from a legal point of view. The merits go to the NGO-s which believed in this endeavour which, by engaging non-aligned states" in the end managed to have the GA address the ICJ with the request. The main objective was to delegitimize nuclear weapons in all circumstances. But the ICJ would give a very confusing opinion, and thus not satisfying the will and objective of those who had struggled years to send this issue to this court believing that this court would give a clear answer.

---

[100] Supra note 402, pp. 296-298.

[101] For minutes of the meeting see Report of the First Committee U.N. Doc. A/C.1/49/L.36 (1994), p 2. The motion by Morocco, Germany and Hungary was refused by 67 votes against, 15 abstentions and 57 did not participate in the voting. Among them, China did not vote; Ukraine abstained; Canada, Norway, Japan, Australia, Ireland, Sweden and Austria.

[102] *Ibid.*

[103] Report of the First Committee, U.N. Doc A/49/699 (1994), para. 60.

[104] Report of the First Committee U.N. Doc. A/49/PV/90 (1994), p 46.

[105] General Assembly Resolution on General and Complete Disarmament: A Prohibition of the Dumping of Radioactive Waste, UN. Doc. A/RES/49/75 (1994), pp. 15-16.

IV.3 THE FAILURE OF ICJ TO GIVE A CLEAR OPINION REGARDING THE LEGALITY OF THREAT OR USE OF NUCLEAR WEAPONS

After the GA approved the resolution requesting an advisory opinion on the legality of nuclear weapons, the SG proceeded to the ICJ which received it on 20 December 1994. The SC attached to it other important documents to be used for analysing the case.[106] After receiving the request, the ICJ, in compliance with Article 66 of its Statute, notified all interested states, including the UN, inviting them to submit their statements related to the question.[107] The deadline for submission of written statements was set to be 20 June 1995 while 20 September 1995 was the date set for submission of written statements in connection to written statements submitted earlier by other states. The 30 October 1995 was set for the session to begin and presentation of oral arguments.[108] Interested states had timely submitted their written statement[109] and many of them notified their readiness to present their oral arguments after the opening of the session.[110] During proceedings, the Republic of Nauru, which had earlier submitted a written statement, requested its statement to be struck off, which was approved and was not taken into consideration further on in the proceedings.[111]

---

[106] Adv. Op. Legality of the Threat or Use of Nuclear Weapons, 08 July 1996, ICJ General List no. 95, para 1, 2. For more on the advisory opinon and processing of the case see Legality of the Threat or Use of Nuclear Weapons, ICJ, http://www.icj-cij.org/docket/index.php?p1=3&p2=4&k=e1&p3=4&case=95.

[107] *Id*, para. 3-4.

[108] *Id*, para. 4-6.

[109] States which filed their statemen on the issue in written were: Bosnia and Herzegovina, Burundi, the Democratic Peoples Republic of Korea, Ecuador, Egypt, Finland, France, Germany, India, Ireland, the Islamic Republic of Iran, Italy, Japan, Lesoto, Malaysia, the Marshal Island, Mexico, Nauru, Holand, New Zealand, Qatar, the Russian Federation, Samoa, San Marino, the Salomon Islands, Sweden, the United Kingdom of Great Britain and Northern Ireland and the United States of America, *Id*, para. 5.

[110] States which presented verbally their argument in a session were: Egypt, France, Gjermany, Indonezia, Mexico, Iran, Italy, Japan, Malaysia, New Zealand, Philipinnes Qatar, the Russina Federation, San Marino, Samoa, the Marshal Islands, the Salomon Silands, Costa Rica, the United Kingdom of Great Britain and Northern Island, the Unites States of America and Zimbabwe., *Id*, para. 9.

[111] *Id*, para. 7.

During preliminary proceedings, the ICJ reviewed three formal issues dealing with: the competence of the organisation to request the advisory opinion; legal character of the question and the scope of the question.[112] Against these issues, states which submitted their written statements or when they presented their oral statement after the opening of the session made their comments against or in favour in a bid to convince the court not to proceed further or to support it to go ahead with the question until the end and give its advisory opinion.

In relation to the first issue, some states stated that the GA did not have the right according to Article 96 para. 1, to request an advisory opinion for issues that do not relate to its daily work.[113] According to the US, the question should have been asked by *"interested states and within their bodies of the United Nations which have an express mandate to address these matters"*.[114] According to Finland, the achievement of an effective security arrangement may come only by cooperation between states, which should take into consideration all circumstances including specific security interests of each state.[115] While according to the British statement answering the question would not help the GA *"in the exercise of its function under the Charter"*.[116] According to this statement answering the question would not only be contrary to the interests of the GA but such a thing would have a direct impact on other processes related to disarmament which were under way through bilateral and multilateral negotiations among states in which case the ICJ could put itself on the side of one or the other party when deciding to give the opinion.

Arguments against the case proceeding further also had to do with the legal character of the question. States, contesting the legal character of the question, argued that the issue of the use of nuclear weapons

[112] Compare Art. 96 and Art. 65 of the Charter and the ICJ Statute respectively, supra note 121 and 356.

[113] Supra note 441, para. 11.

[114] Letter Dated 20 June 1995 from the Acting Legal Adviser to the Department of State, together with written statement of the Government of the United States of America to the Registers Office of the ICJ, US Department of State, Washington D.C. 20520, p. 1.

[115] Letter Dated 13 June 1995 from the Ambassador of Finland, together with the written statement of the Government of Finland to the President of the ICJ, Embassy of Finland in the Hague, No. 1185, pp. 1-2.

[116] Letter dated 16 June 1995 from the Legal Adviser to the Foreign and Commonwealth Office of the United Kingdom of Great Britain and Northern Ireland, together with the written comments of the United Kingdom to the Registers Office of the ICJ, Foreign & Commonwealth Office, London SW1A 2AH, p. 1, para 1.3.

is of total political character, because the decision to use them is of political character and a sovereign act of an independent state. According to Germany, nuclear weapons are *"not only a means of warfare like other weapons. Their main purpose is political.... Their use cannot be assessed using the norms of international law without such an assessment turning from the judicial to a political one"*.[117] According to it, even though the question seems to have legal character, in fact, the ICJ was asked to review an issue which at its core entails a high political character.[118]

On the third issue, the opposing states gave different opinions arguing that the question presented was very abstract and not precise, in which case the ICJ should use its discretional right to refuse to give the opinion. An element which in particular incited reactions from opposing states regarding composition of the question was the use of the word "*permitted*". The opposing states considered that instead of this word it should have used the word *"prohibit"*, thus the composition of the question should have targeted the issue whether international law prohibits the threat or use of nuclear weapons. According to the Russian statement, states are sovereign and accordingly they, "*may accomplish any acts which are not prohibited under international law"*.[119] According to this, international law is a law that puts constraints and not permission to states, because this would mean, apriority, putting many more constraints on states. Also, according to this statement, the question does not distinguish between cases of the use of nuclear weapons in cases of self-defence from cases of using them for aggression and the difference from consequences of using nuclear weapons.[120]

The same dilemma regarding the composition of the question was presented by the United Kingdom.[121] In international law there are no rules other than those which are accepted by states through treaties or other methods by which they may regulate the level of armament.[122]

[117] Letter dated 20 June1995 from the Ambassador of the Federal Republic of Germany, together with written statement of the Government of the Federal Republic of Germany to the Registers Office of the ICJ, Der Botschafter Der Bundesrepublic Deutschland, the Hague, p. 2 para. 2.

[118] *Ibid.*

[119] Letter dated 19 June 1995 from the Ambassador of the Russian Federation together with written statement of the Government of the Russian Federation to the Registers Office of the ICJ, Russian Federation Embassy, the Hague, p. 5.

[120] *Ibid.*

[121] Supra note 451, pp. 21-22, para 3.3.

[122] *Id*, p. 21, para 3.3, see also supra note 235 case *Nicaragua v. United States*, p. 14 para 269.

According to it, the question was presented in such a way that it tacitly assumes the illegality of nuclear weapons and shifting the burden of proof from those states who would have been obliged to prove that they are illegal to the states which in the present case should prove that they are legal.[123] According to the US, the ICJ is faced with issues which are presented in a *"very general and vague question that would of necessity involve complex legal, technical, political and practical considerations"*.[124] According to them, the ICJ should go further in the proceedings because such issues cannot be answered in an abstract manner without any reference to a concrete case where states used or threatened to use nuclear weapons. In this way the ICJ would not allow itself to deal with speculations as to what could happen in the future in a hypothetic case.[125] Along the same lines, according to the German statement the composition of the question was made in such a way as if the *"eventuality of their use in the hard time could be assessed separately from their main political purpose of preventing wars"*. According to this, the use of nuclear weapons at times of war still remains within hypothetic limits.[126]

In responding to arguments presented by opposing states, the ICJ considered that there is no basis which would put into question the competences of the GA, the legal character or composition of the question. According to it, the GA is the main organ of the UN, which, according to Article 10 of the Charter, has competences to discuss any question or issue within the scope of the Charter.[127] In particular, Article 11 of the Charter gives the right to the GA to discuss any issue related to the maintenance of international security and peace including disarmament related issues.[128] While, according to Article 13, the GA has under its competence the right to initiate studies and give recommendation to facilitate the progressive development of international law.[129] On this basis, the ICJ concluded that the GA has not misused its competences in referring the question to the court.

With regards to the legal character of the question, the ICJ concluded that the question is of that character because of its requests for

[123] Supra note 451, p. 22, para 3.4.
[124] Supra note 449, p. 4.
[125] *Ibid.*
[126] Supra note 452, p. 3 para. 2.
[127] Supra note 441, para 11.
[128] *Ibid.*
[129] *Ibid.*

reviewing the threat or use of nuclear weapons against the relevant principles and rule of international law.[130] According to the court, it is not important whether the question may also have political references, taking into consideration that all issues also raise political issues at its core. This means that, during its review, the court should focus only on legal aspects and requirements of the question presented. With regards to the motive behind the question, the ICJ does not take it into consideration.[131]

Regarding the composition of the question, the ICJ was of the opinion that its objective was clear requiring it to give an opinion on the legality or illegality of the threat or use of nuclear weapons.[132] Addressing the concerns of states with the word *"permit"* instead of using the word *"prohibit"*, it stated that they are unfounded because states which possess nuclear weapons either admitted or did not put it into question that their independence to act is in fact constrained by the principles and rules of international law and in particular by humanitarian law. Arguments presented by those states and the shift of the burden of proof do not have any particular significance for the court.[133]

To proceed further, the ICJ had to identify *corpus legis* in order to work on the merits and give the opinion.[134] The main focus in preventing the use of nuclear weapons which originated from different states in their statements, written and oral, were the norms of humanitarian law. Referring to these norms, states expressed their stance that nuclear weapons are outlawed in any circumstances, even in cases of self-defence. This is particularly so due to its non-discriminatory effect and not being able to control it in cases of self-defence as a legitimate use

[130] *Id*, para. 13.

[131] *Ibid.* In another case in 1980 when the Court was requested to issue an advisory opinion on the Intepretation of Agreement of 25 March 1951 between the WHO and Egyp, the Court was of the opinion that *"in situation in which political consideration are prominent it may be particularly neccessar for an international organization to obtain an advisory opinion from the Court as to the legal principles applicable with respect to the matter under debate.."*, see Adv. Op. Interpretation of the Agreement of 25 March 1951 between the WHO and Egypt, I.C.J., Reports 1980, p. 87 para 3.

[132] Supra note 441, para. 20.

[133] *Id*, para. 21-22.

[134] It is interesting to be mentioned that the Japanese stance taking under consideration as the only country to be hit by a nuclear bobm. According Japanese government "*becuase of their [nuclear weapons] immense power to cause destruction, the death of and injury of human beings, the use of nuclear weapons is clearly contrary to the spirit of humanit that gives internacional law its philosophical foundation"*, see Letter dated 14 June 1995 from the Minister at the Embassy of Japan, together with written statement of the Government of Japan to the Registers Office of the ICJ, Embassy of Japan, the Netherlands, para II.

of force.[135] The use of such weapons may cause huge damage without any discrimination. It may cause huge human victims which may relate to particular ethnic, national or religious groups which may fulfil the genocide convention criteria taking into consideration that the purpose of committing this crime would be taken out of the fact that that particular state knew of its devastating effect but disregarded it.[136]

A number of acts exist which regulate the use of force during armed conflicts such as the St. Petersburg Declaration of 1907; the Protocol for the Prohibition of the Use of Asphyxiating, Poisonous or Other Gases, and of Bacteriological Methods of Warfare; the Geneva Convention. Due to certain interpretations it is considered that the use of nuclear weapons infringes upon the basic human right, that of life, which is protected by the Convention on the Civil and Political Rights but also with other regional human rights conventions protecting that right.[137]

Another argument that was emphasised by these states relates to the potential devastating effect that nuclear weapons have on the environment. According to Egypt *"the use of nuclear weapons is surely to cause long-term and severe damage to these resources..." (water and land under irrigation)"...making life almost impossible."*[138] The GA has approved several resolutions which delegitimized the use of nuclear weapons which presents a general opinion for the prevention of nuclear weapons such as Resolution 163 entitled "Declaration for the Prevention of the Use of Nuclear and Thermonuclear Weapons.[139]

[135] See Note Verbale dated 19 June 1995 from the Embassy of Mexico, together with written statememnt of the Government of Mexico to the President of the ICJ, Embassy of Mexico, the Hague, pp. 11-15.

[136] Communication dated 20 June 1995 from the Embassy of Egypt together with the Written Statement of the Government of Egypt, p 18-19 para 29. According to the Genocide Convention, acts which constitute genocide are Sipas Konventës për Parandalimin dhe Dënimin e Krimit të Gjenocidit, aktet të cilat përbëjnë këtë krim janë: a) Killing members of the group ; b) Causing serios bodily or mental harm to members of the gourp; c) Deliberately inflicting on the group conditions of life calculated to bring about its physical destruction in whole or in part; d) Imposing measures intended to prevent births within the group; and e) Forcibly transferring children of the group to another group. An important element here is the definition of genocide which according to this conventions should present the "purpose" as a subjective element, see Convention on the Prevention and Punishment of the Crime of Genocide, 78 U.N.T.S. 277, 9 December 1948.

[137] Compare the statements by Mexico and Egypt, supra note 470 and 471 para. 9-16 and 14-27 respectively.

[138] Compare statements by Mexico and Egyp supra note 470 and 471 para 2 and 3 respectively. See also Convention on the Prohibition of Military or Any Other Hostile Use of Environmental Modification Techniques, 1108 U.N.T.S. 151, 10 December 1976, Art. 1-3.

[139] Communication dated 20 June 1995 from the Embassy of Egypt together with the

In reviewing the case, the ICJ gave important significance to the rules of humanitarian law, included here are other human rights documents such as the International Convention on Civil and Political Rights, which does not cease to be in force even at times of war excluding some derogations as stipulated by Article 4 in cases of emergency of the ICCPR. In this perspective the right to life cannot be derogated in any circumstance.[140] Here, the ICJ refers specifically to the Geneva Conventions.[141] With regards to the Convention for the Prevention and Punishment of the Crime of Genocide, the ICJ brought forward the complexity and the significance of clarifying the "purpose" as a requirement of the Convention to establish the existence of genocide and this may be clarified only by analysing a specific case which had already happened and cannot be deduced from a hypothetic case.[142]

With regards to the environment concerns from the eventual use of nuclear weapons, the ICJ acknowledges the fact that their use would cause an environmental catastrophe.[143] However, according to the court, international agreements which deal with the protection of the environment do not pretend to constrain a state from its right to self-defence according to international law. However, states should bear in mind environmental issues when accounting for necessity and proportionality in harmony with their legitimate military targets.[144] The Rio Declaration, its first Protocol and the GA Resolution 47/37 (25 November 1992) on the Protection of Environment in Times of Armed Conflict which determine environment standards, present general obligations to protect the environment and to prevent the means and methods of warfare which are specifically used to damage the environment.[145]

Written Statement of the Government of Egypt, p 7 para 11, see also General Assembly Resolution, Un. Doc. A/RES/38/75, B 15 December 1983.

[140] Supra note 441, para 25. This was an answer to states which expressed their opinion on this point that the Civil and Political Right Covenant is applied only during peace times, *"Every human being has the inherent right to life. This right shall be protected by law. No one shall be arbitrarily deprived of his live."*, Art. 6 para. 1 of this covenant, International Covenant on Civil and Political Rights, 16 December 1966, 999 U.N.T.S. 171.

[141] Supra note 441, para. 25.

[142] *Id*, para. 26.

[143] *Id*, para. 19.

[144] *Id*, para 30. See also Rio Declaration on Environment and Development 1992, principle 24 *"Warfare is inherently destructive of sustainable development. States shall therefore respect international law providing protection for the environment in times of armed conflict and cooperate in its further development, as necessary"*.

[145] Compare the fisrt Additional Protocol of the Rio Declarationon on Environment and Development 1992, Art. 35 para. 3 and 55, and General Assembly Resolution on Protection of the Environment in Times of Armed Conflict, Un. Doc. A/RES/47/37, 25 November 1992.

After this analysis, the ICJ concluded that in order for it to give an opinion on the legality of the thrat or use of nuclear weapons, the relevant provisions are to be found in the Charter and the applicable law in armed conflicts which regulates the means and method of warfare in conjunction with specific agreements related to nuclear weapons which it determines to be relevant.[146]

The Charter prohibits the threat or use of force against the territorial integrity and sovereignty of a state.[147] No Charter provision refers to any specific weapon in this regards and the language used in Article 2(4) refers to the use of force in general and with it the employment of any kind of weapons translated into force.[148] In cases of self-defence according to Article 51, states are not constrained as to what type of weapons they may use for this purpose, but in such cases states should pay attention that its act of self-defence be necessary and proportionate. The element of proportionality, in particular is brought forward by the ICJ for the states to pay maximum respect in any case.[149] The court does not go into any quantitative details as to how this proportionality principle should be observed but it draws attention to the nature of nuclear weapons and the potential risk involved around them, thus states should think extensively before utilizing them in cases of self-defence.[150]

With regards to the threat, the ICJ subjugates it with the applicable criteria of the use of force, according to which the threat to use force would be illegal in all cases when its use would be illegal. The threat is illegal if it is directed against the territorial integrity and sovereignty of a state.[151] The ICJ did not discuss the role of the SC in the use of force according to Article 42 because it did not see it relevant for the question presented because this issue was not raised by any of the states in a written statement or orally after the opening of the session.[152]

After analysing the Charter and related provisions, the ICJ turned to other international norms shedding light on that no source of international law grants any specific authorization for the use or threat to use

[146] Supra note 441, para. 34.
[147] Supra note 121, Art. 2 para. 4.
[148] Supra note 441, para. 38-39.
[149] *Id*, para. 41-44.
[150] *Id*, para. 43.
[151] *Id*, para. 47.
[152] *Id*, para. 49-50.

nuclear weapons or any other weapons in general or in a particular situation. At the same time, it emphasises that there is no principle or rule which would, by a specific authorization, make legal the threat or use of nuclear weapons or any other type of weapon.[153] But, on the other side, if there is no principle or rule which expressly prohibits the threat or use of nuclear weapons, can one imply such a prohibition from other such provisions.

Lacking expressive provisions, states which were in favour of delegitimizing nuclear weapons, relied on the provisions prohibiting specific weapons which were codified by international agreements such as the Second Declaration of The Hague Conference 1899, The Hague Convention of 1907 and its protocol of 1925 which prohibited the use of asphyxiating and poisonous gases and an all of the similar means and materials.[154] However, according to the ICJ, it could not be implied that those specific prohibition provision also apply to nuclear weapons while the word "others" is used in those instruments, did not have the intention to refer to nuclear weapons but to other similar means and methods which have similar effects with asphyxiating and poisonous gases.[155] This may be seen from the state practice which shows that there were attempts to design similar provision which expressly refer to the prohibition of the use of weapons of mass destruction such as for example the Convention on the Prohibition of the Development, Production and Stockpiling of Bacteriological and Toxin Weapons of 1972; Convention on the Prevention of Development, Production and Stockpiling of Chemical Weapons and their Destruction of 1993.[156]

In the same manner, various activities were developed to define instruments to regulate the production, use, stockpiling, testing and destruction of nuclear energy and weapons universally or in specific areas such as the NPT; Treaty for the Prohibition of Nuclear Weapons in Latin America and the Caribbean (Tlatelolco) and the South Pacific Nuclear Free Zone Treaty (Rarotonga) etc.[157] With regards to the NPT, the ICJ re-

---

[153] *Id*, para. 52.

[154] *Id*, para. 54.

[155] *Id*, para. 55-56.

[156] *Id*, para. 57.

[157] According to Art. 3 of the Tlatelolco Treaty Protocol I"*The Government represented by the undersigned Plenipotentiaries also undertake not to use or treten to use nuclear weapons against the Cotnracting Parties of the treaty for the Prohibition of Nuclear Weapons in Latin America"*. A similar language is used in the Rarotonga Protocol II of 1985, "*Each Party undertakes not to use or threatn to use any nuclear explosive devize against: a) Parties to*

ferred to safeguards given by the five nuclear states to other states in the regime which do not possess nuclear weapons.[158] These states have given guarantees that they will not use nuclear weapons against states which do not possess such a weapon only in cases where they may be threatened by those states in alliance with states which possess nuclear weapons.[159] These stances were confirmed with the SC Resolution 948 of 1995.[160]

In analysing these provisions, the ICJ came to the conclusion that states which have undertaken not to use their nuclear weapons in specific zones or against particular states under certain conditions, have reserved their right to use them in specific cases which was not questioned by other states.[161] Even though this may show the rise of a state's consciousness to *"liberate the community of States and the international public from the dangers resulting from the existence of nuclear weapons"*[162], still it cannot be implied that a general and universal prohibition against threat or use of nuclear weapons exists.[163]

Referring to the customary law, the ICJ also could not find any such a provision which would prohibit in general and universal terms the threat or use of nuclear weapons.[164] In particular, the ICJ refers to the GA Resolution 1653 (XVI) approved on 24 November 1961. The court was of thc opinion that even the GA was aware for the non-existence of a customary law which would prohibit the use of nuclear weapons otherwise it would have addressed it to the ICJ after approval of the resolution.[165]

---

the Treaty; or b) any territory withi the South Pacific Nuclear Free Zone for which a State has become a Party to Protocol 1 is internationally responsible." Other regimes would be created later as analysed below, see Treaty for the Prohibition of Nuclear Weapons in Latin America, 634 U.N.T.S. 326, 14 February 1967, Art. 1 and Protocol II of the South Pacific Nuclear Free Zone Treaty, 24 I.L.M. 1442, 6 August 1986.

[158] These safeguards were given in 1995 when the Treaty was extended indefinitely, see supra note 441, para, 59 (c).

[159] *Id*, para. 59 (c).

[160] Security Council Resolution 984, Un. Doc. S/RES/984/1995, 11 April 1995.

[161] Supra note 441, para. 62 points a, b, c.

[162] *Id*, para. 63.

[163] *Id*, para. 63.

[164] *Id*, para. 73.

[165] *Id*, para. 72. According to states wanting to put a total ban on nucear weapons this resolution is an expression of a customary law because it was approved by majority of the states and thus reflects a nor of international customary law binding upon all states, see written statements by Egyp and Malysia for example. While other states presenting an opposing view were of the opinion that there is no such international customary law established and referring to the voting process they mention the importance of many states, incliding the nuclear states, opposed the approval of that resolution. In this way these states reserved their right ot use nu-

In the end, the ICJ focused on the provision of humanitarian law. In this corpus, it refers to The Hague Conventions of 1899 and 1907 and also the Geneva Conventions of 1864, 1906, 1929 and 1949, which it refers to as the "Hague Law" or "the Geneva Law".[166] The humanitarian law has now become a part of general customary law which determines the behaviour and actions of a state in times of armed conflict.[167] Other agreements prohibit the use of certain weapons and play an important part.[168] Specifically the ICJ refers to the *Martens* clause.[169]

The ICJ emphasises that a part of humanitarian law was developed before the invention of nuclear weapons while the other part, which has to do with the Geneva Conventions, do not refer to nuclear weapons and states did not intend to prohibit those weapons with these conventions and their related protocols.[170] However, it cannot be concluded that the rules of applicable humanitarian law in armed conflict cannot be applicable to nuclear weapon as well.[171] Such a conclusion would be in disharmony with the *intrinsically humanitarian character of the legal principles in question which permeates the entire law of armed conflict and applies to all forms of warfare and to all kinds of weapons, those of the past, those of the present and those of the future"*.[172] So, aside from the time aspect of the development of particular weapons and a law, the law applies in all cases. The ICJ puts into the spotlight that none of the declarations submitted to the court did emphasise that states have the right to use nuclear weapons in disregard of humanitarian law.[173] This relies on the *Martens* clause according to which, the principles of humanitarian law should be applied also in cases of nuclear weapons.[174] The use of nuclear weapons would go against the principle of neutrality which has now been established as part of general customary law.[175]

---

clear weapons when necessary, see in general written statements by the US, United Kingdom and Germany for example.

[166] *Id*, para. 75.

[167] *Id*, para. 82.

[168] Convention on Prohibitions or Restrictions on the use of Certain Conventional Weapons Which May Deemed to be Excessively Injurious or to Have Indiscriminate Effects, UN Doc. A/Conf.95/15, Annex I (1980), 10 October1980, The 1925 Geneva Protocol etc.

[169] Supra note 441, para. 78.

[170] *Id*, para. 85-86.

[171] *Ibid.*

[172] *Ibid.*

[173] *Ibid.*

[174] *Id*, para. 87.

[175] Compare, para. 88-89 with the Hague Convention (V) Respecting the Rights and Duties of Neutral Powers and Persons in Case of War on Land, U.S.T.S. 540, 2 A.J.I.L. Supp. 117, 18 October 1907, Art. 1 and the Hague Convention (XIII) Respecting the Rights and Duties of Neutral

In interpreting the principles of humanitarian law, states presented different opinions, in particular to self-defence situations, because, as it was mentioned above, there is no customary or written international law which prohibits in general and universal manner the use of nuclear weapons. The United Kingdom in its statement stated that the ICJ should be based on a real and concrete case in order to determine the limits on the use of nuclear weapons within the applicable provisions of humanitarian law.[176] In this way it would be more objective because nuclear weapons may be used in different ways and in particular situations they may be controlled in a certain way for example the use of nuclear weapons against military ships at sea or military troops in territories with a sparse population. This would enable the minimum amount of collateral damage.[177]

On the other hand, other states, stated that nuclear weapons violate provisions of humanitarian law in any case, because of their huge destruction capacities which cannot be controlled and an opportunity always exists for the escalation of a particular conflict into a nuclear conflict which unavoidably would entail the further use of them in that conflict. This would have an impact in lowering the chances of their controllability and much greater consequences against humans and other civilian objects. [178]

The ICJ does not accept the arguments presented by parties, because in the first case states could not give enough arguments that nuclear weapons would be used to such an extent as not to cause significant collateral damage or that a particular low scale conflict would not spiral into a large nuclear conflict.[179] On the other side, states could not present enough arguments that humanitarian law prohibits in the general and universal manner the use of such weapons. The ICJ cannot with precision conclude that the use of nuclear weapons would be against the principles and applicable rules of armed conflict in any circumstance.[180] The court cannot avoid the fundamental law of a state to exist and self-defence and also the deterrence policy which was in

Powers in Naval War, U.S.T.S. 545, 2 A.J.I.L. Supp.247, 18 October 1907, Art. 1.

[176] Supra note 451, para. 3.44, p. 40.

[177] *Id*, para. 3.70, p. 53.

[178] Supra note 441, para. 91-92.

[179] *Id*, para. 93.

[180] *Id*, para. 94.

force for many years in international relations.[181] So, the ICJ could not achieve a clear conclusion on the legality or illegality of the threat or use of nuclear weapons by a state in extreme cases of self-defence when the existence of the state is put into question.[182]

After voting, the ICJ came to the following voting results: by unanimity that there is no customary or conventional law which expressly authorises the threat or use of nuclear weapons: 11-3 that the customary or conventional provision of the international law does not place any general or universal prohibition on the threat or use of nuclear weapons; by unanimity that the threat or use of nuclear weapons which goes against Article 2 (4) of the Charter and fails to meet the criteria stipulated in Article 51 of the Charter is illegal; by unanimity that the threat or use of nuclear weapons should be in harmony with the requirement of applicable provision of humanitarian law and also specific obligations undertaken by treaties or together with obligations which expressly deal with nuclear weapons; by unanimity an obligation exits to seek, by good faith, and reach negotiations which would lead to nuclear disarmament in all aspects and for effective international control.[183]

On the most complex issue on the legality of threat or use of nuclear weapons the ICJ was divided 7 to 7, included here the casting vote of the President. According to the vote on this issue, the ICJ was of the opinion that the threat or use of nuclear weapons in "general" would be contrary to the provision of the law applicable in armed conflict and in particular that of humanitarian law. But, in view of the current standing of international law and evidence presented in the proceedings, it cannot conclude decisively whether the the threat or use of nuclear weapons in extreme situations involving self-defence when the existence of a state is put into question is illegal.[184]

The ICJ, in the main question of its advisory opinion, did not state more than that which was already known so far that the state should take care of the provision of humanitarian law when deciding to use their

---

[181] *Id*, para. 96.

[182] *Id*, para. 97.

[183] *Id*, para 105.

[184] *Id*, para. 105, operational para. E. In favour of this parapraph were President Bedjaoui and Judges: Ranjeva, Herczegh, Shi, Fleishhauer, Vereschetin, Ferrari dhe Bravo. Against were: Vice President Schwebel and Judges: Oda, Gullaume, Shahabuddeen, Weeremantry, Koroma dhe Higgins.

nuclear weapons. With this, the ICJ, in a way, put nuclear weapons on an equal footing to conventional ones for which the same rules apply. Perhaps, the ICJ had in mind the possibility of designing nuclear weapons with a similar effect as that of conventional weapons. In this way it avoided the creation of a general and universal prohibition focusing on an interpretation of general rules of international law. It can be seen that the court was focused on a strict interpretation of international law, but different stances may be seen among the ICJ members who took part in reaching the decision and also deposited their separate opinion.

IV.4 OUTSIDE OF THE ICJ OPTION AND SEPARATE OPINONS OF JUDGES

When the request for advisory opinion was submitted, the ICJ was placed with two issues dealing with its discretional power on deciding to give its advisory opinion and after a positive answer on the first issue to answer the question on specific points composing the advisory opinion. Fourteen judges participated in the proceedings, one less than the full court of 15 judges. This was in full compliance with the requirement of the Statute, Articles 24 and 254.[185] The judges taking part in voting used their right to submit their separate opinion in compliance with Article 57 of the Statute, thus making known their individual stance in favour or against the ICJ opinion. The regular voting process took place on all issues presented but the voting on two particular issues related to the substance of the opinion was very interesting. The separate opinions of judges deal mainly with these two issues.

On the first issue dealing with the admissibility of the request, only one of the judges expressed his opinion against the request. According to Judge Oda, the ICJ should have refused to give its opinion due to noncompliance of the question with Article 96 para. 1 of the Charter on the way the question was composed because it was more of

[185] Supra note 356, Art. 24 and 25 which determines the quorum for decision making in the ICJ.

a political character. In another of his arguments, he states the request lacked proper support from the UN Members.[186] But according to Judge Bedjaoui, it would be inappropriate for the ICJ to refuse to answer the question because it has to do with an issue which may involve the question of our mere existence.[187] According to him, with the invention of nuclear arms a new *"human condition"* was created and mankind is living under a suspended sentence taking into consideration the huge nuclear military potential that exists today and states had which could destroy the whole of humanity.[188]

One thing that draws the most attention is voting on point "E" of the operational paragraph 2 where the voting was split 50/50 (7 to 7). This split and submission of separate opinions by judges made this opinion one of the most controversial ones given by this court. Point "E" of the operational paragraph 2 focused specifically on the legality of the threat or use of nuclear weapons within the realm of two important fields of international law 1) humanitarian law; and 2) self-defence. On the first issue, the ICJ, to a certain extent, gives a general answer leaving a lot of room for different interpretation while on the second issue, it admits that it is not in a position to give a final conclusion as to whether the threat or use of nuclear weapons is legal or illegal in cases of extreme circumstances of self-defence when the existence of state is put into question. The way the court composed its answer shows that an ambiguity exists between the rules of international law applicable in arms conflicts and the inherent right of a state to self-defence.[189]

According to President Bedjaoui, even if the ICJ did not manage to give a clear opinion, with this it raises the awareness of the existence of a very advanced process of change in the relevant field of international law.[190] According to this, we are at the mid- stage of the creation of a new rule dealing with nuclear weapons, a stage where the old rule *"is already defunct"* while *"its successor does not exist yet"*.[191] Seeing a potential danger in such a situation, he draws attention that this, in no way, may states be incited to think that they have an authorisation to

[186] Supra note 441, dissenting opinion of Judge ODA, Diss. Op. Oda pp. 332-335.
[187] Supra note 441, declaration of Judge, Decl. Bedjaoui, pp. 268-269.
[188] *Id*, p. 268.
[189] Supra note 441, separate opinion of Judge Fleichhauer, Sep. Op. Fleichhauer, p. 305.
[190] Supra note 523, p. 272 para. 16.
[191] *Ibid.*

use nuclear weapons at their will.[192] In the end, he comes to protect the ICJ emphasising that the general composition of the opinion is not due to its incompetence to interpret the right, *"The Court cannot be blamed for indecisiveness or evasiveness where the law, upon which it is called to pronounce, itself is inconclusive"*.[193] This means that the guilt should be found at the lack of a specific international rule before it is to be sought within the ICJ.

According to Judge Vereshchetin, the issue of nuclear weapons is an issue which, had it been possible to give maximum clarity in the opinion, would be very suspicious while giving a partial answer would serve at best as a guide for states to regulate this issue better.[194] According to him, the ICJ has shown ambiguities in international law with regards to the threat or use of nuclear weapons and states should sit together and find a common and clearer meaning through diplomacy and negotiations.

The composition of the answers in two issues of point "E" seems to have been done in such a way as to give as much comfort as possible to the stance of states which took on this initiative in a bid to gain a general ban on nuclear weapons. It includes very moral and legal dilemmas. The ICJ interprets only the positive law as it is and not the way it should be. On the other hand, the judges should expunge their moral/public pressure coming from different states and international organisations lobbying for delegitimizing nuclear weapons in all circumstances.[195] On the first issue of this point, the ICJ uses the word "in general" stating that nuclear weapons are in general against humanitarian law applicable in armed conflicts and in particular against the principles and rules of humanitarian law. Here we have a so called weak legal language which leaves a lot of room for interpretation by different states trying to accommodate it to their particular understanding and interests. The language was so because there is no international document or agreement which expressly delegitimizes nuclear weapons. On the other hand, humanitarian law prohibits in general those weapons which have an indiscriminative effect and cause unnecessary damage to people and material objects. With this reason as a base, in an ideal theoretical situation, nuclear weapons would be totally in compliance with international law in cases when they hit only military facilities and avoided civilian losses.

---

[192] *Ibid.*

[193] Supra note 441, declaration of Judge Vereshchetin, Decl. Vereshchetin, p. 280.

[194] *Id*, p. 281.

[195] Supra note 523, pp. 269-270, para 6-13.

On other issues the ICJ is much clearer. In subparagraphs "B", "C" and "D" of the operational paragraph 2, by looking at the language used, it can be seen very clearly that the use of nuclear weapons should not go against Article 2(4) of the Charter[196] and eventual use of force should stay within the limits of international law applicable in armed conflicts and humanitarian law[197] and that there is not a general prohibition[198] by international customary law or conventional law regarding the threat or use of nuclear weapons.[199] While in the second part of the subparagraph "E", the ICJ expresses that it cannot come to a conclusion in cases of the threat or use of nuclear weapons in extreme circumstances of self-defence when the existence of a state comes into question.[200]

From one point of view, it is a nonsense as to how the court could refer to a situation of "*non liqet*" and fail to give a clear answer thus leaving a sort of ambiguity within itself.[201] The composition of subparagraph "E" of the operational paragraph 2 does not ignore the technological developments taking into consideration that states may produce, in the future, such nuclear weapons and cause effects which may be controlled in a more certain way or with a very low effect equal to a conventional weapon. In fact, states, while the ICJ was discussing the question, developed tactical nuclear weapons, the effect of which is very small compared to the ones which were dropped on Hiroshima and Nagasaki.[202]

The ICJ, before everything, was faced with a situation which was based in a hypothetical situation which may happen in the future, which entails more psychological modalities creating a particular situation but which had some real reference to the events of WWII with the dropping of two bomb on Hiroshima and Nagasaki. By not having a concrete situation to refer to, the ICJ was pushed to give a general opinion. In the worst case scenario, it would have refused to give an answer at

[196] Supra note 441, operational paragraph 2.C., p. 266.

[197] Supra note 441, operational paragraph 2.D., p. 266.

[198] Supra note 441, operational paragraph 2.B., p. 266.

[199] On this aspect see also the dissenting opinion of Judge Shahabudeen, Diss. Op. Shahabuddeen, p. 376-378, supra note 441.

[200] Supra note 441, operational paragraph 2.E. p. 266.

[201] Supra note 535, pp. 376-378.

[202] Micah Zenko, "Controlling Tactical Nuclear Weapons", International Relations and Security Network, 11 November 2010, visited on16 September 2012, http://www.isn.ethz.ch/isn/Current-Affairs/ISN-Insights/Detail?lng=en&ots627=fce62fe0-528d-4884-9cdf-283c282cf-0b2&id=123743&contextid734=123743&contextid735=123741&tabid=123741.

all. But the ICJ decided to answer the question and in this case, maybe it would have been better for the court to base its analysis on a hypothetical case especially in a self-defence situation and in this case the military doctrines of nuclear states should have been taken into consideration. In this aspect, the court could have made greater effort in analysing and distinguishing circumstances in which a state is attacked by another state with nuclear weapon or in alliance with a nuclear state from those circumstances involving an attack by a state with conventional weapons.

The military doctrines and statements given by nuclear states as part of the NPT regime give guarantees to not use their nuclear weapons even in cases of self-defence or to protect their allies in a case of collective self-defence against states which did not use such a weapon in realisation of their attack, aside from cases when the existence of a state was brought into question.[203] The court, in this way, could have confirmed this standing by saying that the use of nuclear weapons in these cases in not legal. With this, the ICJ would influence in extracting a more *opinion juris* and eventually contributing to the development of a customary international law which would have a more binding effect than the unilateral promises and undertakings by nuclear states. Up to now no state has ever used nuclear weapons against another state, even though there were many conflicts where nuclear states were involved. The lack of action, which in this case presents the material factor, together with the *opinion juris* for the non-use of nuclear weapons would comprise two necessary elements for the creation of a new customary law. With this, the ICJ would have given a much clearer opinion on a very important issue.[204]

The eventual creation of such a customary law would be supported by the GA resolutions, in particular by Resolution 1653 (XVI) which could have been invoked and greater analysed by the ICJ. Even though formally the GA resolutions are of no binding effect, they, however, represent the stance of the majority of UN Member States if most of them participated in voting. In this case the method of voting and the number of states participating in voting would be very important in the eventual creation of a customary law.[205]

---

[203] This issue is discussed more detail in Chapter II.

[204] A problem related to this is that some staets did not submit such safeguards or do not apply similar military doctrines such as Israel or North Korea. For more see Chapter II.

[205] Supra note 522, pp. 340-345.

With regards to nuclear weapons, in cases when a state is attacked by another state or states with such a weapon, it would be highly implausible for the court to delegitimize the use of such weapons in self-defence. In the political aspect, states would never accept such a reason and would also be counter to the "*raison d'etre*" of existence of those weapons. From the legal aspect, one cannot refer to any document which would establish one of the key elements of an eventual customary law which would delegitimize such weapons in these cases.

In their separate opinions, pertaining mostly to the operational paragraph 2, there are 6 judges who in their opinions criticise the conclusion of the court related to subparagraph "E".[206] Their critic is based mainly on a doctrine according to which the international law allows everything if it does not expressly prohibit. It is also known as the Lotus principle.[207] According to this principle, states have never agreed expressly or tacitly to prohibit the threat or use of nuclear weapons, referring to The Hague Conventions or the Geneva Conventions and its protocols.[208] Many year of state practice have shown that states in continuity have considered that the threat or use of nuclear weapons is legal within the confines of general rules of the use of force. This has to do with the five nuclear states and also their allies which are supported by them in for example, the deployment of weapons in their territories and accordingly accepting such circumstances by them later.[209] In this aspect, if one refers to the NPT, it can be seen that it deals with the possession of nuclear weapons and its proliferation but not with their utilisation.[210] The mere existence of many treaties which have declared zones free of nuclear weapons and guarantees given by the five nuclear states show that the threat or use of nuclear weapons is something real and possible without any *"expressis verbis"* obstacles in constraining them.[211]

The ICJ is criticized for not giving a definitive opinion related to cases of self-defence relying on the existence of *"non liqet"* in this

[206] For more see supra note 441.

[207] *The Case of the S.S. "Lotus"*, PCIJ Series A.-No. 10, 7 September 1927, http://www.icj-cij.org/pcij/serie_A/A_10/30_Lotus_Arret.pdf.

[208] Supra note 441, dissenting opinion of Vice President Schwebel, Diss. Op. Schwebel, p. 311.

[209] *Id*, pp. 312-314.

[210] *Ibid.*

[211] Compare *Id*, pp. 315-320 with dissenting opinion of Judge ODA, supra note 522, pp. 355-370.

field. Here reference is made to the Charter and particularly to Article 51 based on which the ICJ should have given its clear opinion. If it were not possible to find any written agreement or customary law then it could have used another source of law on the general principles accepted by civilized nations to fill the gap.[212] According to Judge Weeramantry, the threat or use of nuclear weapons is illegal in all circumstances. This is against international law and presents the negation of humanitarian concerns which confine the structure of international law.[213]

Judge Koroma was of the opinion that *"it is wholly incoherent in the light of the material before the Court to say that it cannot rule definitely on the matter now before it in view of current state of the law"*.[214] Sufficient and clear provisions exist which the court could have referred to in order to give a clear opinion.[215] According to him, the collision of important international principles (self-defence and humanitarian law) should not have impacted the court to give a clear answer because those do not exclude one another and the court in its opinion should have given more priority and substance to one or the other principle.[216]

The ICJ confirmed that there are no rules of international law which delegitimize nuclear weapons aside from general prohibitions placed by humanitarian law. In this case the focus is put on the international regimes which tend to put control on the management of nuclear weapons, programmes of states possessing them or in the physical protection of available nuclear material. A rich legal framework exists which relies on the adequate application and meaningful cooperation between states which depend on establishing faith between states and avoiding disagreements in cases involving nuclear energy.

---

[212] Supra note 544, p. 323.

[213] Supra note 441, dissenting opinion of Judge Weeramantry, Diss. Op. Weeramantry, p. 433.

[214] Supra note 441, dissenting opinikon of Judge Koroma, Diss. Op. Koroma, pp. 557-558.

[215] *Id*, p. 558.

[216] *Id*, p. 559.

CHAPTER V

INTERNATIONAL LEGAL REGIME OF NUCLEAR ENERGY

V.1 FROM THE BARUCH PLAN TO THE TREATY ON NUCLEAR NON-PROLIFERATION (NPT)

The Treaty on Nuclear Non-Proliferation (NPT) is the backbone of the global regime regulating nuclear energy, the object of which is to prevent further proliferation of nuclear energy for military purposes. This treaty presents a specific regime for controlling the production of nuclear energy and it technology. At the same time, it presents a tool available to states for dispute management between the five nuclear Member States and the rest which committed themselves to not contributing to the proliferation of nuclear weapons and technology. The main purpose of this treaty is to lower a non-nuclear state's motivation to want to have in their possession a nuclear weapon in two ways: offering of nuclear technology for peaceful use to non-nuclear states and the encouragement of nuclear states to move towards complete and full disarmament.[1] The realization of this purpose is very difficult bearing in mind that we have to deal with a very complicated issue which entails elements of national security, the need for the production of energy, state prestige etc. Above all, the nuclear states consider that their national security is protected to the greatest level by possession of such nuclear weapons. Starting from this concept, it seems rather normal that all other states would want to be in possession of a nuclear weapon or more.[2]

The need to control nuclear weapons and energy was brought to ones attention immediately after the Hiroshima and Nagasaki attacks which showed their devastating effect in reality. The proliferation risk

---

[1] Arsalan M. Suleman, "Bargaining in the Shadow of Violence: The NPT, IAEA, and Nuclear Non-Proliferation Negotiations", *Berkley Journal of International Law*, 25 Berkley J. Int'l L. 206, 2008, p. 209.

[2] *Ibid.*

became the primary concern of every statesman. For this reason, in June of 1946, the US proposed the so called "Baruch Plan" to the UN Commission on Atomic Energy.[3] This plan proposed the creation of an international authority with the primary role of controlling nuclear energy.[4] It also foresaw sanctions on any state which violated the principle of producing nuclear energy for peaceful purposes only.[5] After full functionalising of such an authority, the plan foresaw the destruction of all nuclear weapons which states might possess and to stop further production.[6]

For this initiative to be successful it needed support by other states and in particular Soviet support which had already started their activities to produce their nuclear weapons. The Soviets were sceptical at the beginning because first of all they wanted the US to disarm itself of such weapons if they wanted to have the USSR on board which on the other hand was against the US interests and with the proposal presented.[7] In the meantime, the USSR had toughened its stance expressing that no one may put any constraints upon its independence to build nuclear weapons.[8] This would mark the beginning of the acceleration in the proliferation of nuclear weapons in the USSR which managed to achieve this in 1949.[9] In such circumstances, where a stumble appears in international cooperation with the Cold War in its initial stage, the US, unilaterally, passed an act in Congress by which it prohibited the export of nuclear materials and technology in an attempt to stop the proliferation of the "American bomb".[10]

In another initiative also taken by the US in 1953, proved to be successful and resulted in the establishment of the International Atomic Energy Agency (IAEA) in 1957 under the UN umbrella.[11] This initiative had a very symbolic slogan "Atoms for Peace" under the leadership of President Eisenhower. In the meantime, France achieved the production of its nuclear weapon and together with the USSR, no longer

[3] "The Nuclear Non-Prolieferation Treaty and Global Non-Proliferation Regime: A U.S. Policy Agenda", *Boston University International Law Journal*, 12 B.U. Int'l L.J. 407, Autumn 1994, p. 411.

[4] *Id*, p. 412.

[5] Supra note 5, p. 7.

[6] Supra note 126.

[7] Supra note 5, p. 7.

[8] Supra note 555, p. 412.

[9] *Ibid.*

[10] "The Atomic Energy Act of 1946", 42 U.S.C. 2011-2396 (1988 & Supp. 1992).

[11] Supra note 555, p. 412.

feeling inferior, was readier to support such an initiative. The purpose of the "Atoms for Peace" initiative was to increase the level of cooperation among three nuclear states in a bid to prevent further proliferation of nuclear weapons without infringing upon the right of states to produce nuclear energy for peaceful purposes.[12] A characteristic element of this initiative was the proposal for the creation of a nuclear energy bank which would be managed by the IAEA and which would be used by states to deposit and secure nuclear materials provided by nuclear states. This bank would be used to sell nuclear energy to those states requiring it for peaceful purposes.[13] However this proposal would never come into reality.[14]

The "Atoms for Peace" initiative started to yield results in the following years. As a result of its work, the states managed to adopt and sign some important treaties for controlling nuclear proliferation.[15] This period saw an increase in international cooperation among the GA members which managed to approve two resolutions. One called on states on the prevention of the use of nuclear weapons, while others called for the prevention of the deployment of nuclear weapons in space.[16] From the legal point of view, these resolutions did not have any binding effect because of the GA powers only to make recommendations.[17] However, in time, Resolution 1653 (XVI) would increase its significance as it would

[12] *Id*, p. 412-413.

[13] "Atoms for Peace" President Eisenhower's Speech at UN GA, 8 December 1953, Atomic Archive, Historical Documents, Arms Control, Deterrence and Nuclear Non-Proliferation, visited on 20 January 2012, http:/www.atomicarchive.com/Docs/Deterrence/Atomsforpeace.shtml.

[14] The former IAEA director 1997-2009, Mohamed El Baradai, called in 2005 for creation of a nuclear fule bank which would supply states with nuclear energy for peaceful use, see "IAEA Chief Calls for International Nuclear Fuel Bank", *Voice of America*, 7 November 2005, http://www.voanews.com/english/news/a-13-2005-11-07-voa46-66368037.html?moddate=2005-11-07.

[15] Among these treaties are: The Antarctic Treaty, 402 U.N.T.S. 71, 1 December 1959; The Treaty Banning Nuclear Weapons Tests in the Atmosphere, in Outer Space and Under Water, 480 U.N.T.S. 43, 5 August 1963; Treaty on Principles Governing the Activities of States in the Exploration and Use of Outer Space, including the Moon and other Celestial Bodies, 610 U.N.T.S. 205, 19 December 1966 and other treaties which would establish nuclear free zones which are analyzed below.

[16] See, "Declaration on the Prohibition of the Use of Nuclear and Thermo-Nuclear Weapons", General Assembly Resolution 1653, Un. Doc. Aë5100 (1961), 8 November 1961, and also "Question of General and Complete Disarmament", General Assembly Resolution 1884, Un. Doc. A/5515 (1963), 17 October 1963.

[17] Supra note 121, Art. 10 on the powers and functions of the GA: *"The General Assembly may discuss any questions or any matters within the scope of the present Charter or relating to the powers and functions of any organs provided for in the present Charter, and, except as provided in Article 12, may make recommendations to the Members of the United Nations or to the Security Council or to both on any such questions or matters".*

be reiterated frequently by states positioning themselves on the side of states wanting to delegitimize nuclear weapons.[18]

In the meantime, five nuclear states started to negotiate for the adoption of a comprehensive treaty for controlling the proliferation of nuclear energy which resulted with the adoption of the NPT. This treaty was opened for signing in 1968 and came into force on 5 May 1970 after 62 states deposited their instruments of ratification.[19] The NPT makes a distinction between states which produced and detonated nuclear weapons before 1 January 1967 as the nuclear states and other states which did not do it as the non-nuclear states.[20]

The NPT is composed of eleven articles where the first six articles present the main principles of controlling nuclear energy. Article I refers to nuclear states requiring them to undertake obligations not to transfer nuclear weapons or other similar means or the technology for the production of such weapons. According to this article *"Each nuclear-weapon State Party to the Treaty undertakes not to transfer to any recipient whatsoever nuclear weapons or other nuclear explosive devices or control over such weapons or explosive devices directly, or indirectly; and not in any way to assist, encourage, or induce any non-nuclear weapon State to manufacture or otherwise acquire nuclear weapons or other nuclear explosive devices, or control over such weapons or explosive devices"*.[21] As it may be seen, this article uses the wording *"any recipient whatsoever"*, avoiding the use of the word, "state". This formulation attempted to avoid the possibility of nuclear weapons and technology passing into the hands of a non-state actor. Article II has to do with the same provision but referring to the non-nuclear states.[22] When talking about nuclear energy we have to keep our mind on the benefits we have if we use it for peaceful purposes, such as the production of electricity,[23] so the world would not have any understanding had it been designed for the total prohibition of nuclear en-

[18] In their statements filed in ICJ on the legality of threat or use of nuclear weapons states like Egyp and Mexico alleged that this resolution has now become part of a general customary law with binding character.

[19] Supra note 555, pp. 413-414.

[20] Supra note 397, neni IX para. 3.

[21] *Id*, Art. I.

[22] *Id*, Art. II.

[23] For more on this issue see Chapter II.

ergy[24]. So, according to the above mentioned Articles, the states which possess nuclear energy and production technology undertake to support other states in securing nuclear energy for peaceful purposes. It does not mention how to do this.[25]

The relation between Article I and II on the one hand, and Article IV on the other, present the main complexity in controlling the use of nuclear energy. The issue becomes more complex in cases where a state possesses its own technology for the production of nuclear energy. A state which possesses such technology may make it available for military requirements.[26] To monitor this process, the NPT, according to Article III, authorizes the IAEA to verify obligations of states taken by this treaty. To realize this, this article requires each state to enter into a safeguard agreement with the IAEA.[27] The safeguard agreement deals specifically with the: 1) specific sources or fission material; and 2) devices or specifically designed materials or prepared for processing, use or production of fission materials in specific.[28] According to Article V, all states which benefit from technological achievements for the production of nuclear energy undertake to make it available to other states. The transfer of these benefits should be facilitated by special international agreements through an adequate international body.[29] Article VI

[24] Supra note 397, Art. IV, para. 1 *"Nothing in this Treaty shall be interpreted as affecting the inalienable right of all the Parties to the Treaty to develop research, production and use of nuclear energy for peaceful purposes without discrimination and in conformity with articles I and II of this Treaty."*

[25] *Id*, Art. IV, para. 2 "*All the Parties to the Treaty undertake to facilitate, and have the right to participate in, the fullest possible exchange of equipment, materials and scientific and technological information for the peaceful uses of nuclear energy. Parties to the Treaty in a position to do so shall also cooperate in contributing alone or together with other States or international organizations to the further development of the applications of nuclear energy for peaceful purposes, especially in the territories of non-nuclear-weapon States Party to the Treaty, with due consideration for the needs of the developing areas of the world."*

[26] For more see Chapter II.

[27] Id, Art.III, para. 1 *"Each non-nuclear-weapon State Party to the Treaty undertakes to accept safeguards, as set forth in an agreement to be negotiated and concluded with the International Atomic Energy Agency in accordance with the Statute of the International Atomic Energy Agency and the Agencys safeguards system, for the exclusive purpose of verification of the fulfillment of its obligations assumed under this Treaty with a view to preventing diversion of nuclear energy from peaceful uses to nuclear weapons or other nuclear explosive devices."*

[28] *Id*, Art. III, para. 2.

[29] *Id*, Art. V, *"Each party to the Treaty undertakes to take appropriate measures to ensure that, in accordance with this Treaty, under appropriate international observation and through appropriate international procedures, potential benefits from any peaceful applications of nuclear explosions will be made available to non-nuclear-weapon States Party to the Treaty on a nondiscriminatory basis and that the charge to such Parties for the explosive de-*

requires nuclear states in good-faith to stop the arms race and to design a treaty on general nuclear disarmament.[30] The main purpose of Articles III-VI is to offer incentives to states to become parties to the treaty. According to this, states which become parties to the treaty gain the right to request from nuclear states the transfer of nuclear energy at a lower price or technology for the production of nuclear energy. The second aspect is more problematic, because the state which acquires technology for the production of nuclear energy might opt to use it also for military purposes. In this way, nuclear states are much more willing to go for the first option the transfer of nuclear technology to other states. Nuclear states would rather do this even if it meant selling the nuclear energy at a lower price. However, the NPT does not make any difference between these two options and it does not give any advantage to any one of them.

The NPT requires universal membership and is open to all states because nuclear weapons and the control of nuclear energy and the production technology remains a worldwide concern and only with a universal/general membership may it be possible to realize its objectives and purposes. Aside from this, the *bona fide* aspect and full cooperation with the IAEA remain the key preconditions to stop further proliferation. The importance of being a party to the treaty, in particular of those states which already possess nuclear weapons and production technology, lies in becoming part of a multilateral control mechanism where a state member may request accountability from another state in cases when that particular state has crossed the limits of the treaty by any of its actions.[31] Outside of this mechanism, there would not be any concrete parameters to require accountability from a states but only the utilization of diplomatic means in which case power politics play a ma-

vices used will be as low as possible and exclude any charge for research and development. Non-nuclear-weapon States Party to the Treaty shall be able to obtain such benefits, pursuant to a special international agreement or agreements, through an appropriate international body with adequate representation of non-nuclear-weapon States. Negotiations on this subject shall commence as soon as possible after the Treaty enters into force. Non-nuclear-weapon States Party to the Treaty so desiring may also obtain such benefits pursuant to bilateral agreements".

[30] *Id*, Art. VI "*Each of the Parties to the Treaty undertakes to pursue negotiations in good faith on effective measures relating to cessation of the nuclear arms race at an early date and to nuclear disarmament, and on a Treaty on general and complete disarmament under strict and effective international control*".

[31] Supra note 553, p. 213.

jor role.[32] In event of failure to gain a general membership, then it would be highly desirable to have all nuclear states on board. This would mean that, in an ideal case, it would increase the effect of control and possible transfer of nuclear energy and production technology to another state. This would not guarantee the absolute non-proliferation but it would place huge obstacles in place to states wanting to do so.

However, even a general membership would not present an absolute guarantee for non-proliferation because the NPT allows states to withdraw from the regime with three months prior notice.[33] This right was used by North Korea in 2003 which gave notice of withdrawal. The withdrawal of this state marked, perhaps, the biggest blow to the regime because it demotivated other states to accept becoming a party to the treaty or for members to stay in the regime.[34] Article X refers to the extraordinary circumstances which a state may refer, to withdraw but it still remains unclear what such circumstances are and who determines the existence of that. In this way, this article allows a withdrawal state to determine these circumstances on its own. A state may at any time refer to requirements of national security in deciding to withdraw.[35] However, Article X requires the withdrawing states to notify the SC which may use its competence to discuss the eventual consequences on international peace and security by that withdrawal. This implies that, in cases when the SC determines that the withdrawing state endangers international peace and security, it may stop that state from withdrawing.[36]

In cases of the lack of specific provisions for withdrawal from a treaty, we refer to the provisions of the Vienna Convention on the Law of Treaties (VCLT) according to which the withdrawal of a state from an indefinite treaty in time, as is the case with the NPT, should be in compliance with it. According to this, the reasons for withdrawal from such a treaty should be along the lines of: 1) material breach of a treaty by one of the parties entitled and 2) by *rebus sic standibus* clause which

[32] *Ibid.*

[33] Supra note 297, Art. X, para. 1 *"Each Party shall in exercising its national sovereignty have the right to withdraw from the Treaty if it decides that extraordinary events, related to the subject matter of this Treaty, have jeopardized the supreme interests of its country".*

[34] Supra note 553, p. 222.

[35] Supra note 555, p. 426-427.

[36] Antonio F. Perez, "Survival of Rights Under the Nuclear Non-Proliferation Treaty: Withdrawal and the Continuing Right of International Atomic Energy Agency Safeguards", *Virginia Journal of Internaitona Law*, 34 Va. J. Int'l L. 749, 1994, pp. 770-780.

has to do with a fundamental change of circumstances which make the treaty unviable.[37] With regards to the first element, a state wishing to withdraw from a treaty should show that by breaching the provision/s of the treaty, the other party caused a major impact on its position related to the fulfilment of the treaty obligations.[38] While with regards to the *rebus sic standibus* doctrine the issue becomes simpler, because this has to do with unforeseen future events which establish a new circumstance for a state party making it impossible for the fulfilment of the agreement. The test for the existence of *rebus sic standibus*, according to the VCLT, is done using the objective standard avoiding the possibility of using this doctrine by a particular state in cases when that state contributed in the establishment of the new circumstance.[39]

The technical procedure, so feasible for withdrawal from the NPT, presents a problem for states wishing to come within the terms of the treaty and set aside their attempts to acquire nuclear energy for military purposes. For this reason, some states may develop an unfaithful view against the treaty arrangements because a state may intentionally choose to remain part of the treaty only for the purpose of benefiting from a more feasible access to nuclear energy and the possibility of acquiring technology for the production of nuclear energy.[40] In the same manner, many states from the Middle and Near East expressed their concerns over Israel, still remaining outside the treaty while other states of the region became part of the treaty undertaking not to contribute in proliferation.[41] Today 185 states are members of the NPT but still some states with nuclear capabilities remain outside the regime, mainly Israel, India, Pakistan and North Korea.[42]

The NPT lacks an administrative body to help states in the implementation of its provisions.[43] The treaty gives importance to the role of the IAEA however the latter does not present any adequate admin-

---

[37] The Vienna Convention on the Law of Treaties, 1155 U.N.T.S. 331, 22 May 1969, Art. 60, para. 1.

[38] Supra note 588, p. 788.

[39] Id, pp. 789-791.

[40] Supra note 46, p. 63.

[41] *Id*, p. 64.

[42] See "Vendet Nënshkruese dhe Palët e Traktatit për Mos-Përhapje të Armëve Bërthamore", Federation of Nuclear Scientists, visited on 23 January 2012, http://www.fas.org/nuke/control/npt/text/npt3.htm

[43] Supra note 592, p. 63.

istrative body, while three depository states (the US, Great Britain and Russia) have only a formal role of convening conferences. The treaty, also, does not have provisions which foresee consultations or special meetings among parties to discuss cases dealing with states which avoid their obligations or in cases of withdrawal of a state.[44]

Another very serious point relates to the non-fulfilment of obligations by Member States such as Iran. Iran had been developing its nuclear programme for many years before it was discovered in 2005.[45] In official declarations of Iran, it continuously states that its nuclear programme is for peaceful purposes only and that is hardly received as a true statement by many states. This is confirmed by many IAEA reports which continuously reported that Iran is breaching its commitments taken under the NPT.[46] In the report issued by the IAEA in November of 2011, Iran was accused of not cooperating with the agency and not respecting earlier resolutions regarding its nuclear programmes dealing with the facilities for the enrichment of Uranium and the Uranium enrichment process.[47] Such cases may have a negative impact on the will and stance of Member States to fulfil their obligaions. It may be a slap in the face to the objective of general membership.

Another important issue is what to do with the state with nuclear capabilities which one day may decide to become part of the treaty. The NPT accepted five nuclear states as such but should the same privileges be given to other states with nuclear capabilities in order for them to become members. In favour of this, the argument is that in this way these states and their nuclear programmes would be put under control of the NPT. But on the other side if such states are admitted to the regime it would go against the objective of the treaty because other states, even those within the regime, would leave the regime, work on their nuclear programmes for military purposes and re- enter the regime later on. This would be a paradise for states which would use their membership

[44] Canada and Ireland proposed for the creation of a Bureau or Executive Committee but failed to receive necessary support, see, *Id*, p. 64.

[45] For more see supra note 397, Chapter VII.

[46] Gustavo R. Slauvienen, "Nuclear Non-proliferation and Unique Issues of Compliance", *ILSA Journal of International & Comparative Law*, 12 ILSA J Int'l & Comp L 593, 2005, p. 596-597, see also supra note 592, p. 69.

[47] For an overall view on this issues see Implementation of the NPT Safeguards Agreement and relevant Provisions of Security Council Resolutions in the Islamic Republic of Iran, Report of the Director General, IAEA Doc. GOV/2011/65, 8 November 2011.

in the first place to possibly acquire technology for the production of nuclear energy. Anyhow, the NPT does not have an expressive provision which would regulate this issue, but it should be implied that only the five nuclear states and members of the NPT ought to be accepted as such with the aim of reaching a completed nuclear disarmament sometimes in the future.

The NPT marked an important step in efforts to control nuclear energy, despite all difficulties in the realization of its objectives and purposes. These difficulties may come from the lack of a mechanism with adequate extensive competences through which a much easier and stricter control would be placed upon states. Nuclear states should take the leadership role and act as a model by reducing their nuclear arsenals and make available nuclear energy and technology for all those states requiring them for peaceful purposes only. In this direction, bilateral/multilateral agreements and also a unilateral commitment by states to reduce and eliminate nuclear weapons present good ground for building trust amongst the NPT Member States but also towards other states outside it. At the same time, all states, particularly the SC, should work better and in a more efficient manner to deal with security issues and leave no justification for states who may consider that because of this they opt for nuclear weapons to protect their national security.

The real challenge remains the cooperation with the IAEA which could cease if there is a lack of good-faith and sincerity, whereby a state may very easily be capable of quibbling with the IAEA while going ahead with their intentions until the creation of a *fait accompli* situation compelling other states to accept a new reality. If a state wants to work on its peaceful programmes then it is not understandable why a state would do so outside the NPT framework instead of using their right as members to secure nuclear energy or technology to produce it by obliging other states to facilitate it. In cases of quarrels and a lack of proper cooperation with the IAEA, suspicion may immediately rise as to the true purpose of their intention. The safeguard agreements play an important role in increasing cooperation and trust among states in controlling nuclear energy.

V.2 THE SAFEGUARD GUARANTEES AND THE ROLE OF THE INTERNATIONAL ATOMIC ENERGY AGENCY (IAEA)

The NPT gives a crucial role to the IAEA in monitoring the fulfilment of commitments taken by the NPT state parties.[48] The NPT takes into consideration a possible problem which may arise from non-member states which, by not being a Member State, may consider they have a free hand with non-proliferation obligations. To address this issue Article II para. 2 of the treaty uses general language which also stretches to the non-Member States. According to this provision fission materials should be safeguarded by a Member State no matter its destination.[49] Accordingly if a state party exports fission materials to a non-Member State, that material should continue to remain within the same safeguard regime as determined by the NPT or other related agreements. This formulation obliged non-Member States to enter into a specific arrangement with the IAEA in order for them to be able to receive the fission material from a Member State.[50]

The need for safeguard agreements with non-nuclear states becomes evident when taking into consideration that the NPT presents a characteristic regime creating, among others, a balance between nuclear and non-nuclear states in order to prevent the proliferation of nuclear weapons by these states which in turn benefit with access to securing nuclear energy for peaceful use or the technology for the production of that energy.[51] The safeguards agreements are designed to catch the eventual diversion of a considerable volume of nuclear material towards its use for military purposes. According to IAEA a considerable amount of nuclear material is diverted and it is that which is necessary to produce any kind of explosive device. If we make a comparison with HEU, then this amount may be equal to 25 kg of that Uranium or 8 kg of Plutonium.[52]

---

[48] Supra note 397, Art. III.

[49] *Id*, para. 2.

[50] Michael Spies, "Iran and the Limits of the Nuclear Non-Proliferation Regime, Symposium on the Nuclear Non-Proliferation Treaty: A Legal Framework in Crisis?", *American University of International Law Review*, 22 Am. U. Int'l L. Rev. 401, 2007, pp. 414-415

[51] Supra note 397, Art. IV.

[52] See The Structure and Content of Agreements between the agency and States Required in Connection with the Treaty on the non-Proliferation of Nuclear weapons, IAEA Doc. INFCIRC/15, 3 June 1972.

To discharge its duties assigned by the NPT and its Statute, the IAEA is supposed to develop various activities which would enable it to gather necessary and reliable information related to nuclear activities of a particular state. This would be impossible without having prior admission from adequate authorities of a particular state in an international system where states are sovereign and only they may allow international mechanisms to develop any activity inside its territory. For this purpose, the IAEA has entered into bilateral safeguard agreements with the NPT Member States which would enable it to exercise its function. A key role in reaching such agreements was played by the five nuclear states which offered their guarantees for the non-use of nuclear weapons against any of those states entering safeguard agreements. The IAEA was authorized by its statute to negotiate and execute specific safeguard agreements "w*ith a veiw to preventing diversion of nuclear energy from peaceful uses to nuclear weapons or their nuclear explosive devices"*[53] creating in this way a complex security system of controlling nuclear energy.

The NPT safeguard system takes it authority from three main sources: 1) Article II of the NPT; 2) the IAEA Statute; and 3) protocol agreements signed between the IAEA and the NPT Member States.[54] According to the safeguard agreements, the compliance verification mechanism comprises of two components: 1) initiating provisions according to Article 19 of the safeguard agreement; 2) reporting provisions according to Article XX.C of the IAEA statute.[55] The first provision sets the criteria based on which a conclusion may come on the (non)compliance of a state with the commitments taken. The second provision sets the procedure for taking measures against a state which does not comply with its commitments and also defines which organs should deal with the situation and whether the issue is supposed to go to the SC if a specific case endangers international peace.[56]

The IAEA applies different measures in exercising its duties where one has to do with the so called conventional measures used to verify nuclear materials through direct monitoring in factories and other

[53] Supra note 397, Art. III, para. 4.

[54] Supra note 602, p. 412.

[55] Compare Model Safeguard Agreement IAEA Doc. INFCIRC/26, Art. 19 with The Statute of the IAEA, 276 U.N.T.S. 3, 26 October 1956, Art. XII.C.

[56] *Ibid.*

facilities in states which have declared the presence of nuclear materials according to the safeguard agreement.[57] Other measures are applied to support conventional measures which have come into practice from 1992. These measures may be divided into two categories: 1) implementing measures according to the safeguard agreement; and 2) implementing measures according to the additional protocol.[58] From 1998, the integrated implementation measures came into action which basically was a combination of all measures that the IAEA had in its hands to control the implementation of the NPT. After collection and processing of data collected the IAEA drafts a periodic report for each state.[59]

The safeguard system relies on the fulfilment of obligations by both parties which implies the state reporting on its nuclear programmes from one side and the official site visits by the IAEA inspector in that state.[60] States are obliged to submit a report to the IAEA explaining among other things: changes in the inventory; the list of physical inventory; the nuclear material balance.[61] States which are considered not to be in compliance with the provision of NPT are reported to the Board of Governors. The Board of Governors, according to the IAEA statute, may take the following measures: direct curtailment or suspension of assistance for that state; call for the return of equipment and materials made available; suspension from IAEA membership; and as a last resort, reporting the case to the SC and GA for noncompliance of that state with the NPT provisions.[62]

So far, the IAEA has signed 178 safeguard agreements representing agreements with all non-nuclear Member States. In addition, it has signed 111 additional protocols providing for application of additional measures in verifying nuclear programmes. As a result, today more than 1100 facilities are under the regime and monitored on a regular basis.[63] The scope of the security system is confined within nuclear potential materials, which are automatically put outside the scrutiny of

[57] "About Safeguards, What do we do", IAEA, visited on, 24 January 2012, http://www.iaea.org/OurWork/SV/Safeguards/what.html.

[58] *Ibid.*

[59] *Ibid.*

[60] Supra note 588, pp. 757-758.

[61] Report Forms and Explanations for their Use, IAEA, Departmet of Safeguard, Agency No. SG-FM-1171, version date: 02-11-2011.

[62] The Statute of the IAEA, 276 U.N.T.S. 3, 26 October 1956, Art. XII, para c.

[63] Supra note 609.

non-nuclear components of a weapon which may become a potential nuclear device by small modifications.[64] Here for example are included chemical packaging with a high destruction capacity which is used in all nuclear weapons for detonation and also delivery systems such as the ballistic missiles.[65]According to Article II para. 1 of the NPT, the specific procedures set with the safeguard agreement should be respected by all parties representing a legal compulsory language. However, it is important to reiterate that this regime is based upon voluntary agreements giving it another element of security in the fulfilment of obligations.

The relation between the NPT Articles II[66] and II[67] is very complex, in particular when we put it into practice. A state may be in non-compliance with Article III while still remaining within the requirements of Article II.[68] A particular state under a safeguard agreement may intentionally or not, for one reason or another, not report in the proper way, the way it was supposed to according to the agreement. Such a move makes that particular state not conforming with the requirements of Article III but this still does not mean that that state has taken steps to divert its nuclear programme for military purpose. To verify noncompliance with Article II, which in fact represents the object and purpose of the NPT, other proofs should be put beforehand. As a typical case may be found with Iran which, up to now, according to the IAEA has many times failed to satisfactorily cooperate with the IAEA but, still, it could not be concluded that Iran had diverted it nuclear material and

---

[64] Supra note 602, p. 413.

[65] *Id*, p. 414.

[66] Supra note 397, Art. II *"Each non-nuclear-weapon State Party to the Treaty undertakes not to receive the transfer from any transferor whatsoever of nuclear weapons or other nuclear explosive devices or of control over such weapons or explosive devices directly, or indirectly; not to manufacture or otherëise acquire nuclear weapons or other nuclear explosive devices; and not to seek or receive any assistance in the manufacture of nuclear weapons or other nuclear explosive devices".*

[67] *Id*, Art. III, para. 1 *"Each non-nuclear-weapon State Party to the Treaty undertakes to accept safeguards, as set forth in an agreement to be negotiated and concluded with the International Atomic Energy Agency in accordance ëith the Statute of the International Atomic Energy Agency and the Agency's safeguards system, for the exclusive purpose of verification of the fulfilment of its obligations assumed under this Treaty with a view to preventing diversion of nuclear energy from peaceful uses to nuclear weapons or other nuclear explosive devices. Procedures for the safeguards required by this Article shall be followed with respect to source or special fissionable material whether it is being produced, processed or used in any principal nuclear facility or is outside any such facility. The safeguards required by this Article shall be applied on all source or special fissionable material in all peaceful nuclear activities within the territory of such State, under its jurisdiction, or carried out under its control anywhere".*

[68] Supra note 602, pp. 417-418.

violated Article II. Thus there are still no verified data that Iran has produced nuclear energy for military purpose.[69]

In such cases, the IAEA may require additional information related to a particular nuclear programme and also may send its inspector on a visit to verify specific facilities where nuclear energy is produced. These visits may arise on an *ad hoc* basis in order to verify the preliminary report according to the safeguard agreement. The routine inspections are the most frequent visits which are done based on a pre-set agenda in cooperation with a state to be inspected. The special inspections, which may be taken under a specific mandate, are usually taken in cases where there is disharmony between the information presented in the state's report with information taken after the visit had been carried out. The safeguard visits deal with the verification of the reporting model of the particular state. In this way parties may come to the conclusion that the safeguard agreement or the additional protocol should be changed on particular technical points to comply with timing and current developments of a particular state. As a last measure, the IAEA may send a report to the SC or the GA reporting eventual non-compliance of a particular state with the safeguard agreement.[70]

The situation becomes more complicated in cases when a state does not declare all the locations in use for its nuclear programmes. By the mere fact that, that state did not declare all its nuclear facilities, makes it less cooperative with the IAEA and thus to report the required data. It becomes a hot issue when that state has developed its own capacities for the production of nuclear energy because in cases of transfer of nuclear energy from one state it would be much easier to follow its destination. According to the initial safeguard agreement, the IAEA had some constraints in its mandate to verify the presence of facilities not reported by a state. But with the additional protocol[71], approved by the IAEA Board of Governors in 1997, it was given the instruments to take environmental samples from any suspected location in the territory

---

[69] For more see Chapter VII of this work..

[70] For more see "Safeguards Overview" IAEA, Publications, Factsheet, visited on 25 January 2012, http://www.iaea.org/Publications/Factsheets/English/sg_overview.html.

[71] The need for drafting an additional protocol came after the revelation of Iraqi clandestine programme for production of nuclear energy in 1993, see, "Safeguards to Implement Nuclear Proliferation", World Nuclear Association, updated in September 2011, http://world-nuclear.org/info/inf12.html.

of a state disregarding the protocol whether that state had reported the existence of the location or not.[72] According to this protocol, the IAEA is allowed to use modern communication instruments including satellites to gather the necessary information. To realize its duty in the field, the IAEA may require states to allow long term visits by its inspectors, giving them enough time to visit and verify all suspected locations.[73] The realization of this may be done with only 2 hours prior notice in a bid to prevent a state from taking measures to conceal its programmes and to come clean while possibly hiding something.[74]

With available measures, the IAEA can verify to a certain extent that there are no undeclared activities at any eventual facility. If it finds indications of the existence of an undeclared facility then it takes further much stricter action by sending its inspectors to verify the information.[75] After verification, the IAEA may issue a report in the end, declaring that that particular state has no undeclared facilities for the production of nuclear material.[76] The issuance of such a report is a sort of certificate which sometimes may take time to be produced and depends on the IAEA activities and cooperation offered by that particular state under scrutiny.[77] Receiving such a certificate has a great impact on the relaxation of international relations in cases when there is tension regarding nuclear programmes of a particular state.

The NPT lacks a permanent mechanism available in its hands in charge of executing penalties against states which do not comply with its provisions.[78] Article IV of the NPT allows states to develop technology for the production of nuclear energy in compliance with Articles I and II.[79] This implies that if a state infringes this provision it should be penalised in a way by the NPT which lacks that permanent mechanism.[80] According to its statute, the IAEA may apply some measures against non-cooperating

---

[72] See Additional Model Protocol, neni 5, IAEA Doc. INFCIRC/540(corrected), September 2007. See also supra note, p. 419.

[73] Supra note 622.

[74] Supra note 623.

[75] Supra note 602, p. 419.

[76] *Ibid.*

[77] In the case of North Korea, the Additional Protocol entered into force in 1993 but the IAEA was only in 2003 was able to issue a report that this state does not possess any undeclared facilities for fission materials, see IAEA Annual Report, IAEA Doc. GC (48)/3 (2004), p. 53.

[78] Supra note 602, pp. 419-420.

[79] Supra note 397, Art. 4.

[80] Supra note 602, p. 420.

states as stipulated by the safeguard agreement or additional protocols. The means available to the IAEA are to order the halt of cooperation and support to that state by the IAEA or other states and as a final measure to suspend the membership of that particular state.[81] However, such measures may be ineffective in cases were a state has managed to produce nuclear material independently and thus does not depend on the IAEA or any other state to secure those materials. In such circumstances the best way to address the issue is to refer it to the SC[82] through the Board of Governors which is a decision making body regarding state activities and commitments towards the NPT and the safeguard agreement.[83]

There may be cases when problems may arise in connection to the interpretation of the safeguard agreement provisions. For this reason, Article 22 of the agreement defines that in cases when states cannot solve a dispute with the IAEA through diplomatic means, any party[84] may refer that disagreement to arbitration the decision of which should be binding to both parties.[85] Neither the NPT nor the IAEA statutes require such a procedure, however during negotiations of safeguard agreements with states, the IAEA managed to impose such a provision.[86] The selection of arbitrator, according to this provision, should be done in such a way that the two arbitrators are selected by the IAEA and a state in dispute respectively while the third one is selected by the first two elected arbitrators.[87] The decision is taken by majority where, obviously, at least two arbitrators should vote in favour of a decision.[88] All safeguard agreements contain this provision.[89]

Parties cannot use arbitration to solve their disputes related to the findings of the Board of Governors according to Article 19; "...

---

[81] Supra note 614, Art. XII para. C.

[82] *Ibid.*

[83] *Ibid.*

[84] This can be done by the Board of Governors in the name of IAEA which is the only executive and decision making organ of this agency, see supra note 614, Art. VI on the responsibilities of this organ.

[85] Model Safeguards Agreement, Art. 22, IAEA Doc. INFCIRC/26, 30 March 1961.

[86] James D. Fry, "Arbitrating Arms Control Disputes", *Stanford Journal of International Law*, 44 Stan. J. Int'l L. 359, verë 2008, pp. 379-380.

[87] In cases when oen party failes to present its arbiter, the ICJ propose one for that state. The same applies with regards to the selection of the third arbiter if parties fail to do find a common solution, see supra note 637, Art. 22.

[88] Supra note 637, Art. 22.

[89] See ANEA official webpage, www.iaea.com.

except a dispute with regard to a finding by the Board under Article 19 or an action taken by the Board pursuant of such finding... ".[90] Article 19 deals with situations when the Board is unable to verify whether or not there was any diversion of nuclear material for military purposes or other explosive devices.[91] This provision is criticized because it may be misused in certain circumstance by preventing in this way the referral of a dispute for arbitration which might present an adequate body to solve it.[92] To avoid such a circumstance a state would have to request the dispute be referred for arbitration, before the finding of the Board is issued. Such a request for arbitration should refer to the actions of inspectors or the Director General of the IAEA which in a concrete case may be of the opinion that a state is not complying with the safeguard guarantees.[93] With regards to cases related to the quality of nuclear material which is used for peaceful purposes determined as such by the importing and exporting states, which does not have to do directly with compliance with the NPT, parties may, in cases of disputes, refer it directly for arbitration.[94]

The standard language used in most of the cases in the test of a safeguard agreement, suffered some changes in particular cases. This was enabled for it to be accommodated as much as possible to the needs of different states as an incentive to enter into that agreement. The most visible change relates to the precluding provision. In this aspect for example the safeguard agreement between the IAEA and India contains such a provision.[95] In this way, India made sure that it can refer to arbitration all disagreements related to any provision of the agreement. The same approach was taken by other states wanting to tailor the agreement to their needs.[96] The IAEA inspections are also used to verify that

---

[90] Supra note 637, Art. 22.

[91] *Id*, Art. 19.

[92] Supra note 638, p. 382.

[93] *Ibid.*

[94] *Ibid.*

[95] *Ibid.*

[96] See Agreement of 13 December 1991 between the Republic of Argentina, the Federative Republic of Brazil, the Brazilian-Argentine Agency for Accounting and Control of Nuclear Materials and the International Atomic Energy Agency for the Application of Safeguards, March 1994, neni 22, IAEA Doc. INFCIRC/435, March. 1994; The Text of the Agreement between Belgium, Denmark, the Federal Republic of Germany, Ireland, Italy, Luxembourg, the Netherlands, the European Atomic Energy Community and the Agency in Connection with the Treaty on the Non-Proliferation of Nuclear Weapons, neni 22, IAEA Doc. INFCIRC/193, 14 September 1973 (Austria, Finland, Greece, Portugal, Spain, Sweden, Poland, Slovenia and Slovakia would become later part of the agreement).

sates comply with agreements establishing nuclear free zones in Latin America, the South Pacific, Africa and Asia.[97]

In the contemporary world when different terrorist organisations show no hesitation in the use of every available means to achieve their objectives, some loopholes to the safeguard agreement are revealed. The possibility that terrorists might come into possession of nuclear material seems very challenging.[98] The 9/11 attacks showed that such organisations as *Al Qaeda* are capable of organizing a large scale attack. According to the current safeguard agreement there is no guarantee that nuclear material is not stolen by structures within a state or terrorist organisations. This is so because the agreement states the purpose of it is the "*timely detection of significant nuclear material*" while according to the additional protocol it comprises also the *"detection of undeclared nuclear activities"*. So, the system may be vulnerable in cases involving the diversion of very small amounts of nuclear material taking place during an undetected period of of time by individuals or organisations involved in a state system. The same may be said of intentional diversion of small quantities by the state itself.[99]

This is significant when not all of the nuclear material is in the states hand and under safeguard monitoring. Outside of the safeguard agreement still remain military nuclear programmes. This increases the need to review these agreements in a bid to design techniques and structures which would follow a potential leak of even tiny amounts of nuclear material but also to include the monitoring of military nuclear material.[100]

The NPT regime together with the IAEA statute and the safeguard agreement have not yet achieved its objective for a general inclusion of all states and reduction and elimination of all nuclear weapons however idealistic that may sound. Out of 193 UN Member States, 8 are still outside of the regime among them states with nuclear capabilities. Apart from this, there are states such as Kosovo for example, which is

---

[97] James Tape and Joseph Pilat, "Nuclear Safeguards and the Security of Nuclear Materials" në *Nuclear Safeguards, Security and Non-Proliferaiton*, ed. James E. Doyle (Butteworth Heinemann, Massachusetts, USA, 2008), p. 27.

[98] For more see Chapter VII of this worki.

[99] Siegfried S. Hecker, "Why we need a Comprehensive Safeguards System to Keep Fissile Materials out of the Hands of Terrorists", në *Nuclear Safeguards, Security and Non-Proliferation*, ed. James E. Doyle (Butteworth Heinemann, Massachusetts, USA, 2008), p. 403-415.

[100] *Ibid.*

still not a UN member state and at the same time out of the NPT regime.[101] The NPT regime would benefit a great deal if it were made available to states such as Kosovo to become part of the regime. In the future we might expect cases of new-born states, disputed territories etc. which may create possible control vacuums outside of the control of the IAEA thus the NPT regime should design specific provision dealing with such situations before endangering international peace and security in this regard.

Outside of the NPT regime, states have established nuclear free zones which are extraordinarily helpful for the regime, thus solidifying large tracts of territory where nuclear weapons are outlawed. What could not be achieved by the NPT was achieved by these regimes which so far seem to work well.

V.3 NUCLEAR FREE ZONES AS A MODEL TOWARDS THE CREATION OF A UNIVERSAL ZONE FREE OF NUCLEAR WEAPONS

The main objective of the NPT is to prevent the further proliferation of nuclear weapons outside the five nuclear Member States. This objective has not yet been met since some states remaining outside the regime have developed their nuclear programmes for military purposes with the most notable event when North Korea withdrew from the treaty only to carry out its first nuclear test later in 2006. In the case of Iran, it still cannot be concluded that Iran has developed any nuclear military programmes while the IAEA has accused it in several cases of violation of the safeguard agreement regarding its nuclear programmes which according to Iran is only for peaceful purposes. On the other hand, states like South Africa, Libya and Brazil have stopped their nuclear programmes. Still, a problematic issue remains of what to with states outside the NPT regime, in particular with those states which have nuclear military capabilities for military use such as India,

[101] Kosovo has been recognizes by more than 100 states thus far, see official webpage of Kosovo Ministry of Foreign Affairs, www.mfa-ks.net.

Pakistan, Israel and North Korea. The situation becomes obscure by the relative easy way of withdrawal from the NPT regime by any state, in particular, those who have already benefitted from various cooperation agreements while being a member of it.

Nuclear free zones present one of the most important developments towards the prevention of nuclear proliferation. This regime has a direct impact in laying foundations towards a world free of nuclear weapons.[102] These zones require that certain regions put a halt to production, acquiring, testing or possession of nuclear weapons and material for military purposes.[103] While the NPT is based on a discriminatory principle among nuclear and non-nuclear states, these zones are based on the principle of non-discrimination and equality by placing requirements on all Member States. The establishment of these zones is in compliance with Article VII of the NPT according to which: "*Nothing in this Treaty affects the right of any group of States to conclude regional treaties in order to assure the total absence of nuclear weapons in their respective territories*".[104] From the language used in this article, it may be seen that the NPT acknowledges the complexity of nuclear energy at the global level to become free of nuclear weapons and open the way to achieve this on a regional basis which has proved to more efficient. In this way it would enable the increase in the number of states and amount of territory protected from nuclear weapons or any other related activity.

The establishment of these zones did not go ahead without criticism mainly based on realist theories.[105] They start from the anarchic international system and the security dilemma as the main element of this theory. Accordingly if all states possess a nuclear weapon then they would not feel insecure and in this way they would not attack other states for their own security.[106] However, even if this argument were sound, the proliferation of nuclear weapons would not be related to state actors only. The proliferation of nuclear weapons would create more opportunities for non-state actors to get them in their hands or

[102] Winston P. Naga, "Nuclear Arsenals, International lawyers, and the Challenge of the Millennium", *The Yale Journal of International Law*, 24 Yale J. Int'l L. 485, summer, p. 506.

[103] Peter Crail and Dariyl G. Kimbal, "Nuclear Weapons Free-Zones at a Glance", Arms Control Association, 30 January 2012, http://www.armscontrol.org/factsheets/nwfz.

[104] Supra note 397, Art. VII.

[105] For more on this concept see Kenneth Waltz, "The Spread of Nuclear Weapons: More May Be Better", *Adelphi Papers, International Institute of Stategic Studies*, No. 171, summer 1981.

[106] *Ibid.*

nuclear material to produce such weapons and in this way threatening states for the realization of their objectives and endanger international peace and security. Not all states have capacities to safeguard nuclear material, thus peace and security would be much more likely to be preserved without nuclear material and within a multilateral security and control system of nuclear programmes around the world.[107]

Fidelity among states and the verification of the eventual elimination of all nuclear weapons or technological capacities to produce them is at the core of sustainability of these zones.[108] We can never be secure enough that a state would not eventually hide a nuclear weapon or material for military purposes with the intention of using it or as a negotiating lever at a particular event in the future against another state/s in a kind of conflict of disagreement.[109] This concept also relates to realism and the aggressive nature of states, the main purpose of which is to increase its relative strength against other states defined in force.[110] The opponents of this concept however believe that today there is adequate technology available for accurate verification and detection of nuclear weapons programmes even in cases when a state is reluctant to cooperate and declare them. This may be done by the use of satellites or by detection of radioactivity in the air. At the same time, states are aware of possible consequences which may arise from reactions by other states in cases of a state trying to hide its nuclear programmes contrary to its obligations taken by a particular agreement therefore in most cases they would opt to cooperate than lose faith of other states.[111] In this case the determination of other states to compel a state to return to the previous situation without verified nuclear programmes or weapons is a very important factor in preventing a state from concealing its programmes.

By establishing nuclear free zones, states have embraced the concept that the world would be better off without nuclear weapons. According the Canberra Commission on the elimination of nuclear

---

[107] Compare supra note 5, p. 50; Scott D. Sagan, *The Limits of Safety: Organizations, Accidents, and Nuclear Weapons* (Princeton University Press, 1993).

[108] Agreement ought to be respected based on the principle *pacta sunt servanta* and with *bona fides,* supra note 589, Art. 26.

[109] Supra note 5, p. 50.

[110] For more on classical realism see Hangs Morgenthau, *Politics Among Nations* (Knopf, New York, 1948).

[111] Supra note 5, p. 50.

weapons,[112] only the total and general elimination of all nuclear weapons is a crucial factor to guarantee international peace and security.[113] Today there are five nuclear free zones established by specific treaties: The Treaty for the Prohibition of Nuclear Weapons in Latin America and the Caribbean (the Tlatelolco Treaty);[114] The South Pacific Nuclear Free Zone Treaty (the Rarotonga Treaty);[115] The Treaty on the South East Asia Nuclear Free Zone (the Bangkok Treaty);[116] the African Nuclear Weapon Free Zone Treaty (the Pelindaba Treaty);[117] and the Treaty on a Nuclear Weapon Free Zone in Central Asia.[118] These regional regimes

[112] This commission was established in Australia in 1995 with a task of proposing practical steps toward creation of a world free of nuclear weapons including other proposals for preservation of international stability and security, for more see in general "Report of the Canberra Commission on the Elimination of Nuclear Weapons", Australian Government, Department of Foreign Affairs and Trade, August 1996.

[113] *Id,* p. 10.

[114] Treaty for the Prohibition of Nuclear Weapons in Latin America and the Caribbean, 634 U.N.T.S. 326, was opened for signature on 14 February 1967 and entered into force on 23 October 2002. All Latin American and Caribbean states have ratified the treaty: Antigua and Barbuda, Argentina, Bahamas, Barbados, Belise, Bolivia, Chile, Colombia, Costa Rica, Cuba, Dominica, Ecuador, El Salvador, Grenada, Guatemala, Guyana, Haiti, Honduras, Jamaica, Mexico, Nicaragua, Panama, Paraguay, Peru, Saint Kitts and Nevis, Saint Lucia, Saint Vincent and Grenadines, Suriname, Trinidad and Tobago, Uruguay, and Venezuela, for more on this regime see United Nations Office for Disaramament Affairs, visited on10 January 2012, http://disarmament.un.org/treaties/t/tlatelolco.

[115] South Pacific Nuclear Free Zone Treaty, 24 I.L.M. 1442, was opened for signatures on 6 August 1985 and entered into force on 27 March 1997. 13 states have ratified the treaty: Australia, Cook Islands, Fiji, Kiribati, Nauru, New Zealand, Niue, Papua New Guinea, Samoa, Solomon Islands, Tonga, Tuvalu, and Vanuatu, for more on this regime see United Nations Office for Disaramament Affairs, visited on10 January 2012, http://disarmament.un.org/treaties/t/rarotonga.

[116] Treaty on the South East Asia Nuclear Weapon-Free Zone, 35 I.L.M. 635, was opened for signatures on 15 December 1995 and entered into force on 27 March 1997. 10 states have ratified the treaty: Brunei Darussalam, Cambodia, Indonesia, Laos, Malaysia, Myanmar, Philippines, Singapore, Thailand, and Vietnam, for more on this regime see United Nations Office for Disaramament Affairs, visited on10 January 2012, http://disarmament.un.org/treaties/t/bangkok.

[117] African Nuclear Weapon-Free Zone Treaty, 35 I.L.M. 698, was opened for signature on 11 April 1996 and entered into force on 15 July 2009. 28 states have ratified the treaty: Algeria, Benin, Botswana, Burkina Faso, Burundi, Cote d'Ivoire, Equatorial Guinea, Ethiopia, Gabon, Gambia, Guinea, Kenya, Lesotho, Libyan Arab Jamahiriya, Madagascar, Malawi, Mali, Mauritania, Mauritius, Mozambique, Nigeria, Rwanda, Senegal, South Africa, Swaziland, Togo, United Republic of Tanzania, and Zimbabwe. Signatories that have not ratified the treaty are: Angola, Cameroon, Central African Republic, Cape Verde, Chad, Comoros, Congo, Djibouti, Democratic Republic of Congo, Egypt, Eritrea, Ghana, Guinea-Bissau, Liberia, Niger, Seychelles, Sierra Leone, Somalia, Sao Tome & Principe, Sudan, Tunisia, Uganda and Zambia, including the territory known as the Sahrawi Arab Democratic Republic, for more on this regime see United Nations Office for Disaramament Affairs , visited on10 January 2012, http://disarmament.un.org/treaties/t/pelindaba.

[118] Treaty on a Nuclear-Weapon-Free Zone in Central Asia, Un. Res. 51/45, was opened for signature on 8 September 2006 and entered into force on 21 March 2009. 5 state have ratified the treaty: Kazakstan, Kyrgystan, Tajikistan, Turkmenistan and Uzbekistan, for more on this regime see United Nations Office for Disaramament Affairs, visited on10 January 2012, http://disarmament.un.org/treaties/t/canwfz.

encompass huge geographic zones which also represent a large part of the population of different civilizations, cultures and economic development. A common language of these agreements is that states commit to put to a halt to all direct and indirect activities related to testing, use, acquisition, production, possession or control of any nuclear weapon.[119]

In the same token, there are cases when a state unilaterally declared itself free of nuclear weapons[120] such as Austria[121] and Mongolia[122] which enacted specific legislation halting their activities related to the production, deposition, transport or testing of nuclear weapons inside their territories. These zones as such, however, lack any formal international agreement with nuclear states formally acknowledging their status at international level.[123]

Nuclear free zones represent a large number of the world's population who expressed their determination to eliminate nuclear weapons. Agreements establishing these zones represent a clear political stance to achieve this end. They bear a very important element in the development of the law starting, in the first instance, towards the creation of a principle, still without any universal support.[124] This is about the possibility of the creation of a general international customary law for the prohibition of nuclear weapons. Also, these agreements strongly reaffirm the right to each individual state to use or produce nuclear energy for peaceful use.

Several factors played their role in establishing and expanding these zones which are related to global political changes but also with inter-state movements in the way they started to portray nuclear weapons. In this aspect for example the establishment of the nuclear free zone in central Asia would have been impossible without the prior dissolution of the USSR. All Member States of this zone would still be members of the USSR. In establishing a nuclear free zone in Africa a crucial part was played by the political changes in South Africa after the removal of the apartheid regime.[125] The same lines may be drawn

[119] See Art. 1(2) of Tlatelolco Treaty, Art. 3 of Rarotonga Treaty and Art 3 of Pelindaba Traty.

[120] "Nuclear Weapons Free Zones", Project of the Nuclear Peace Foundation, visited on 31 January 2012, http://www.nuclearfiles.org/menu/library/treaties/nuclear-free-zones/trty_nuclear-free-zone-index.htm.

[121] See Federal Constitutional Act concerning a Nuclear Free Austria, MGBL/OS/199990813/1/0149, 1 July 1999.

[122] See Law of Mongolia on its Nuclear-Weapon-Free Status, 3 February 2000.

[123] Supra note 627.

[124] Supra note 654, p. 507.

[125] South Afrika had a real potential to develop nuclear weapons but it wilfully pulled

in analysing the establishment of these zones in Latin America and the Caribbean and the role played by Brazil and Argentina in halting their nuclear military programmes on a voluntary basis.[126]

In essence, the agreements establishing nuclear free zones have similar provisions because they attempt to achieve the same objective and purpose. All of these agreements were reached to cover an indefinite period of time[127] and have provisions expressly prohibiting placing reservations on any of their provisions.[128] Agreements require states to enter into the safeguard agreements with the IAEA giving in this way a central role to their agency in the monitoring of all activities related to nuclear material for peaceful purposes.[129] In addition to that the Central Asia Nuclear Free Zone Treaty requires states to sign the additional safeguard protocol as well thus enabling the IAEA inspectors to extend their activities around undeclared activities.[130] These agreements have territorial applications against all states in land, internal waters and archipelagos and space above that territory.[131]

The Latin American and Caribbean states have tried to push the boundaries of territorial application deep into the Pacific Ocean but without success after failing to gain the consent of nuclear states which, by referring to the principle of free ocean, are reluctant to limit their activities by applying such an agreement. In particular this related to the transportation of nuclear weapons on the high seas which could also be used for the production of nuclear weapons.[132] The same stance by nuclear states is shown in the case of the Chagos archipelago in Africa. The US has established a military base on this archipelago which is still in existence and thus refuses to accept the application of the Pelindaba Treaty over this territory.[133]

out of such programmes, see, supra note 5, pp. 46-48.

[126] See "Country Profiles, Argentina and Brazil", Global Security Initiative, Disarmament and Peace Education, visited on 30 September 2012, http://www.gsinstitute.org/dpe/countries/argentina_brazil.html.

[127] Compare ARtl 31 of Tlatelolco Treaty, Art. 15 of Central Asia Nuclear Free Zone Treaty, Art. 16 of Pelindaba Treaty, Art. 22 of Bangkok Treaty and Art. 13 of Rarotonga Traety.

[128] Compare Art. 28 of Tlatelolco Treaty, Art. 16 of Pelindaba Treaty, Art. 17 of Bangkok Treaty, Art. 14 of Rarotonga Treaty and Art. 13 of Central Asia Nuclear Free Zone Treaty.

[129] Compare Art. 13 of Tlatelolco Treaty, Art. 5 of Bangkok Treaty, Art. 9(b) of Pelinaba Treaty, Art. 8 of Rarotonga Traety and Art. 8 of Central Asia Nuclear Free Zone Treaty.

[130] See Art. 8(b) of Central Asia Nuclear Free Zone Treaty.

[131] Compare Art. 3 and 4 of Tlatelolco Treaty, Art. 2 of Bangkok Traety, Art. 2 of Pelindaba Treaty, Art. 2 of Rarotonga Traty and Art. 2 of Central Asia Nuclear Free Zone Trearty.

[132] Supra note 655.

[133] *Ibid.*

The establishment of nuclear free zones was seen as a good step by nuclear states which entered into specific agreements with those states committing themselves to respect the principles of those zones and that they would not use or threaten to use nuclear weapons against any Member States nuclear free zones Member States.[134] In the case of Africa and the South Pacific, the Member States have adopted an additional protocol which expressly prohibits the testing of nuclear weapons within its territory.[135] Even though other zones do not have such a protocol, nevertheless it would be implied that such an activity would go against the object and purpose of the obligations taken by the five nuclear states to respect the principles of the nuclear free zones.

But, not all nuclear free zones managed to secure guarantees from nuclear states such as for example the Central Asian Zone and that of south-east Asia which do not have such guarantees from any of the nuclear states.[136] This is because of high political interests around these zones where military activities are a permanent feature including the re-deployment of nuclear weapons.[137] In other cases, aside from the Tlatelolco Treaty, not all nuclear states have ratified the additional protocol. The US did not sign protocols II and III of the Rarortonga Treaty and neither protocols I and II of the Pelindaba Treaty. Other nuclear states have signed all additional protocols.[138] Additional protocols do not contain express provisions prohibiting the transit of nuclear weapons through their territories. But on the other side, there is a practice established by the nuclear states to not declare whether their ship's cargo contains any nuclear weapons while they transit one of the treaty Member States territory and in this way showing at least some respect for the zone with Member States not questioning it, in a sort of "don't ask don't tell policy".[139]

---

[134] Compare Protocol II of Tlatelolco Treaty, Protocol II of Rarotogna Treaty and Protocol I of Pelindaba Treaty.

[135] Compare Protocol III of Rarotonga Traty and Protocol II of Pelindaba.

[136] "Nuclear Weapons Free Zones", Arms Control Association, visited on 1 February 2012, http://www.armscontrol.org/factsheets/nwfz.

[137] The conflict between North and South Korea, the issue revolving around and possession of nuclea weapons by states outside of the NPT regime such as India and Pakistan have impacted the decision of nuclear states to give similar safeguards as with other regimes, see Ian Bellany, *Curbing the Spread of Nuclear Weapons* (Manchester University Press, Manchester 2005), pp. 116-120.

[138] Supra note 688. The US have signed the Protocol I of Pelindaba Treaty in April 1996 but has not ratified it yet.

[139] Supra note 688.

Besides the establishment of nuclear free zones there are other regimes established by states which directly or indirectly prohibit nuclear weapons. This is the case with the Antarctic Treaty (1959)[140]; The Treaty on Principles Governing the Activities of States in the Exploration and Use of Outer Space, Including the Moon and other Celestial Bodies (1967)[141]; the Treaty on the Prohibition of the Emplacement of Nuclear Weapons and other Weapons of Mass Destruction on the Seabed and the Ocean Floor and in Subsoil Thereof (1971). The first treaty prohibits indirectly the activities which relate to nuclear weapons and materials for non- peaceful use, while the other two treaties have expressive provisions prohibiting them or in a form of the purpose and object of the Treaty. The first two treaties allow for the use of military personnel and means for peaceful purposes.[142] On this issue the third treaty is silent but at the same time it is also silent with regards to the deployment of other conventional weapons. This may be implied that the deployment and use of such weapons in places under the regime of this treaty is allowed in compliance with the principle of international law that states are allowed to do anything which is expressly not prohibited, even though according to the ICJ opinion on the legality of use or threat to use nuclear weapons, this principle should be interpreted in harmony with actual circumstances.[143]

The Atlantic Treaty attempts to protect this part of the world uninhabited by people. The treaty requires states to conduct their activities only for peaceful purposes and it prohibits the construction of military bases and fortifications, military exercises or testing of any weapons. [144] The Treaty on Principles Governing the Activities of States in the Exploration and Use of Outer Space, Including the Moon and other Ce-

[140] Antarctic Treaty, 402 UNTS 71, entered into force on 23 June 1961 and is signed by following states: Argentina, Australia, Belgium, Chile, France, Japan, New Zealan, Norway, South Africa, USSR, United Kingdom and the US.

[141] Treaty on the Prohibition of the Emplacement of Nuclear Weapons and other Weapons of Mass Destruction on the Sea-Bed and the Ocean Floor and in the Subsoil Thereof, 955 UNTS 115, entered into force on 18 May 1972 so far it is ratified by 100 shtete, for more on this regime see United Nations Office for Outer Space Affairs, visited on11 November 2012, http://www.oosa.unvienna.org/oosa/SpaceLaw/outerspt.html.

[142] Compare Art. 2 of Antarctic Treaty and Art. 4(2) of Treaty on Principles Governing the Activities of States in the Exploration and Use of Outer Space, including the Moon and other Celestial Bodies (1969).

[143] For more see Chapter III.

[144] Supra note 692 Art. 1 para. 1. Art. 2 of this treaty allows for the use of military personnel and means for peaceful purposes only.

lestial Bodies attempt to establish a regime on the use and exploration of outer space in a way that would lead to the benefit of all mankind considering it a common good.[145] According to this treaty *"States Parties to the Treaty undertake not to place in orbit around the Earth any object carrying nuclear weapons or any other kind of weapons of mass destruction, install such weapons on celestial bodies, or station such weapons in outer space in any other manner"*[146]. While according to the second paragraph of this article, it prohibits the use of outer space for military purposes including the establishment of military bases and testing of any weapons.[147] With regards to the third treaty, it may be seen that the object and purpose of it is to expressly forbid nuclear weapons and other weapons of mass destructions on the sea-bed, ocean floor and its subsoil. This treaty was signed at the height of the Cold War and the weapons race, at a time when there was not a lack of effort to develop new means and methods to create an advantage over the enemy in which case states also used the ocean to test their achievements in this direction. This treaty has three clear and brief points. According to the first one "*Parties undertake not to place on the sea-bed, on the ocean floor or in the subsoil thereof, nuclear weapons or other weapons of mass destruction, or structures for launching, storing, testing or using such weapons"*.[148] While the second set the extent of outer limits of the sea bed of 12 miles in compliance with the Convention on the Territorial Sea and Contiguous Zone.[149]

The nuclear free zones are very present and a very important development because they attempt to create safe environments. A large percentage of mankind seems to be under the protection of these regimes. These present good examples on how states may cooperate and build mutual trust for a total refusal of nuclear weapons. However, the volatility of these zones may come into the attention of a potential lack of cooperation by nuclear Member States which may in cases involving high national interests as may be perceived by them, not to respect the regimes of these zones such as it is the case with the nuclear free zones in Central and South-east Asia. This

[145] *Id*, Preamble and Art. 1.

[146] *Id*, Art. 4 para. 1.

[147] Treaty on Principles Governing the Activities of States in the Exploration and Use of Outer Space, including the Moon and other Celestial Bodies, 19 December 1966, 610 U.N.T.S. 205, Art. 4.

[148] Supra note 693, para. (a).

[149] *Id*, para. (b).

may influence the failure of these particular zones and further on other zones and ultimately damage the whole attempt to prohibit nuclear weapons.

If states at the global level could not agree on the general prohibition of nuclear weapons they managed to on banning a particular feature related to them, very important in the development of nuclear weapons, which has to do with testing. In the first place this has an impact on the protection of the environment but also may impact on the decrease of pace, if not, further proliferation of nuclear weapons because for a weapon to be operational it should be tested.

V.4 NUCLEAR TEST BAN

The testing of nuclear weapons followed the development of such weapons as an important part of it. Tests in the field of nuclear weapon development as much as in other scientific developments, is an important element because in this way one can analyse the effect of a product such as the explosion effect. Aside from this, nuclear weapon testing is carried out for design purposes of nuclear warheads to increase its efficacy.[150] Up to now no states with nuclear military capabilities has conducted more than 2000 nuclear tests out of which the US and the USSR are absolute leaders. These tests are carried out in different parts of the world such as the US, China, Russia, Algeria, the South Pacific, the South Atlantic, Kazakhstan etc. A large number, over 500, of the tests were done in the atmosphere.[151] The first tests were done by the US followed by the USSR, the United Kingdom, France, India, China and Pakistan.[152]

The destruction capacity of nuclear weapons under test is the same as those which are produced for an eventual attack against a state.

[150] O. Dahlman, S. Mykkeltveit, H. Haak, *Nuclear Test Ban: Converting Political Visions to Reality* (Springer, 2009), p. 9.

[151] "Nuclear Testing Tall", Arms Control Association, 2 February 2012, http://www.armscontrol.org/factsheets/nucleartesttally.

[152] Supra note 5, pp. 10-11.

The difference here is that in the first case states try to take safety precautions to avoid human injury in the first place and minimalize as much as possible other damage. But still, the issue is not about the immediate effect of a nuclear weapon but it also entails the long term effect related to radioactive leak with the risk effects on humans and other living creatures, both flora and fauna. During testing, the radioactivity is dispersed in air, water and land causing long-term effects and direct and indirect damage to humans in contact with such contaminated places or eating contaminated food. It was exactly such a case which awakened US public opinion against the testing of nuclear weapons. In the US, in the late 1950s, health officials detected the presence of radioactivity in cow's milk in New York as a result of nuclear testing in Nevada which represents a relatively great geographic distance.[153] It became clear that no region may easily escape nuclear testing because the effects may not be confined within a certain a geographic area and time.

The first attempts to limit nuclear tests were done by the UN Commission on Disarmament in May of 1955. During discussions within the commission, among others, fundamental issues were raised related to the verification capabilities of a nuclear test ban, which according to the technological development of the time seem to be very hard. This lead to the break-down of further discussions and negotiations.[154] Another important moment to initiate such negotiations was found after the Cuban Crisis by the then two main foes, the US and the USSR, which at the time were on the brink of a nuclear war.[155] During this crisis, the two main world powers conducted nuclear tests in space to show their determination and power despite the fact that their action may be misunderstood by the other party for initiating an eventual nuclear attack.[156] Seeing such a risk, the US, the USSR and the United Kingdom, at the beginning of the 1960s used the Geneva Eighteen Member Commission on Disarmament to negotiate the Treaty Banning Nuclear Weapons Tests in the Atmosphere, in Outer Space and Under Water known as the Limited Test Ban Treaty (LTBT).[157] The agreement

[153] *Ibid.*

[154] Keith A. Hansen, *The Comprehensive Nuclear Test Ban Treaty: An Insider's Perspective* (Stanford University Press, California, 2006), p. 6.

[155] For more see Chapter II of this work.

[156] Supra note 5, p. 11.

[157] Treaty Banning Nuclear Weapons Tests in the Atmosphere, in Outer Space and Under Water, 480 U.N.T.S. 43, 5 August 1963, entered into force on 10 October 1963. For more

was reached in 1963 and was signed by the three powers stated above and was opened for signature by other states.[158] According to this treaty, every state undertakes to *"prohibit, to prevent, and not to carry out any nuclear weapon test explosion, or any other nuclear explosion, at any place under its jurisdiction or control: (a) in the atmosphere; beyond its limits, including outer space; or under water, including territorial waters or high seas; or (b) in any other environment if such explosion causes radioactive debris to be present outside the territorial limits of the State under whose jurisdiction or control such explosion is conducted"*.[159] The second paragraph of this article further specifies that states should constrain themselves from taking any action which may cause or incite in any other way nuclear testing in the specified places determined in point 'a' and 'b' of the first paragraph.[160]

By expressly specifying places where nuclear testing is prohibited, this agreement leaves it open to states do decide the possibility of conducting underground nuclear tests.[161] States were not ready to limit all of their opportunities to conduct nuclear tests[162] but LTBT deals also with this aspect in a way. According to it, the underground tests are banned in cases when the impact of radioactive particles extend outside the territory of a stated area when conducting the test[163] Maybe the scientific development of the time was not capable of understanding of potential damage caused by underground testing.[164] In the contemporary world science has proved that even underground nuclear testing may leak radioisotopes into the environment.[165] These radioisotopes cannot be contained underground forever because in time they may spread their effect outside the place it took place and also outside the borders of that state.[166]

on this regime see United Nations Office for Outer Space Affairs, visited on11 November 2012, http://disarmament.un.org/treaties/t/test_ban.

[158] Supra note 706, p. 6.

[159] Supra note 709, Art. 1 para. 1.

[160] *Id*, Art. 1 para 2.

[161] The treaty leaves a door open for a possibility of banning all nuclear tests in the future including underground testing, *Id,* Art. 1 (1) para 2.

[162] Supra note 706, p. 6.

[163] Supra note 706, Art. 1.

[164] Grant Guthrie, "Nuclear Testing Rocks the Sub-Continent: Can International Law Halt the Imenpding Nuclear Conflict Between India and Pakistan?", *Hasting International and Comparative Law Review*, 23 Hastings Int'l & Comp. L. Rev. 495, spring/summer pp. 506-507.

[165] "Nuclear Weapons Testing", WHO Report, WHO/69-12, September 1995.

[166] *Ibid.*

To limit nuclear testing further, the US and USSR managed to achieve an agreement to limit the exploding capacity of underground nuclear tests. Through the Treaty on Nuclear Testing Threshold, it put a maximum capacity of 150 metric kilotons allowance for a single underground test.[167] To make sure that also nuclear tests for scientific purposes are under control these two states reached another agreement called the Treaty on Scientific Nuclear Explosions which covered all underground testing outside of the location used for military tests putting identical limitations as that of the Treaty on Nuclear Testing Threshold.[168] This treaty also reminds states of their obligations undertaken by the NPT the provisions of which should be observed at any time during testing.[169]

All agreements mentioned above related to nuclear weapons testing and made huge steps forward nevertheless the requirement came forward for a general ban on nuclear testing. This requirement came first of all from nuclear states.[170] In the Hatfield-Exon-Mitchel Amendment, during the Bill Clinton administration, in July of 1993, President Clinton required from Congress to announce a moratorium on testing nuclear weapons stating that it would have a positive impact in preventing nuclear proliferation and that *"the price we would pay in conducting those tests now by undercutting our own non-proliferation goals and ensuring that other nations would resume testing outweighs these benefits"*.[171]

The end of the Cold War created a new momentum between the two foes on a very important issue. At that time, the need for further improvement and development of nuclear weapons decreased and at the same time it increased the pressure to come to an agreement for a general test ban treaty.[172] In 1990, the USSR announced its moratorium on nuclear testing and France did the same in 1992. In 1992 the US

[167] Treaty Between The United States of America and The Union of Soviet Socialist Republics on the Limitation of Underground Nuclear Weapon Tests, 13 I.L.M. 906, 3 July 1974, Art. 1.

[168] Treaty Between the United States of America and the Union of Soviet Socialist Republics on Underground Nuclear Explosions for Peaceful Purposes, 15 I.L.M. 891, 28 May 1976, Art. III.

[169] Id, Art. VII.

[170] Supra note 5, p. 44-45.

[171] "Special Briefing on the Nuclear Posture Review", U.S. Department of Defence, News Transcript, 9 January 2002,
http://www.defencelink.mil/transcripts/2002/t01092002_t0109npr.html.

[172] Jonathan Medalia, *Comprehensive Nuclear Test-Ban Treaty: Background and Current Developments* (Congressional Research Service, Report For Congress, 28 January 2009), p. 1.

Congress voted to announce the moratorium on same issue.[173] In these circumstances, nuclear powers negotiated and managed to adopt a text on Comprehensive Test Ban Treaty in Geneva in 1996. The treaty was placed in the GA agenda for approval which was put through on 10 September 1996.[174]

However, from the time of its approval by the GA, the treaty never came into force because of the procedures needed for this. 183 states signed the treaty while 159 of them have ratified it. States which are needed to ratify in order for it to come into force, according to the second annex of the treaty, and which did not do so are China, Egypt, Iran, Israel, and the US. India, Pakistan and North Korea did not bother to sign the treaty.[175] In compliance with Article XIV paragraph 3, from 1999 conferences were held every year to facilitate the entry into force of the treaty but it still remains at the will of the remaining states to ratify it.[176] This conference brings together states that signed the treaty in a body called the Preparatory Commission of the CTBT.[177] At its last conference held in New York on 23 September 2011, it approved a final declaration calling on all states, especially those included in annex 2 to sign and ratify.[178]

The CTBT requires a ban on nuclear tests once and for all. Article 1 uses a compulsory language placing a general ban stating that *"Each State Party undertakes not to carry out any nuclear weapon test explosion or any other nuclear explosion, and to prohibit and prevent any such nuclear explosion at any place under its jurisdiction or control"*.[179] The second paragraph of this article requires states to refrain from causing, encouraging or in any way participating in carrying out any nuclear weapon test or any other nuclear explosion.[180] To achieve

---

[173] *Ibid.*

[174] Supra note 5, p.45.

[175] "Status of Signature and Ratification", CTBTO, 6 February 2012, http://www.ctbto.org/the-treaty/status-of-signature-and-ratification/ .

[176] Supra note 727, Art. XIV, para 3.

[177] "Establishment of Preparation Commission", CTBTO, visited on 6 February 2012, http://www.ctbto.org/the-treaty/developments-after-1996/1996-97creating-actbto-preparatory-commission/page-1-1996-97-creating-the-ctbto/.

[178] Final Declaration and the Measures to Promote the Entry into Force of the Comprehensive Nuclear-Test-Ban Treaty, New York, CTBTO, 23 September 2011, http://www.ctbto.org/fileadmin/user_upload/Art_14_2011/23-09-11/Final_Declaration.pdf.

[179] Supra note 727, Art. 1 para 1.

[180] *Id*, Art. 1 para 2.

this end, the treaty has foreseen some important measures to verify circumstances. Technical activities for verification are supposed to be headed by the technical secretary[181] while the final monitoring is under the umbrella of the CBTB Organisation composed of all states which had signed and ratified the treaty.[182] The measures foreseen for verification activities may be placed in four groups: 1) seismic; 2) hydro acoustic; 3) infrasound; and 4) radionuclide.[183]

Seismic monitoring attempts to detect and localize underground nuclear explosions including the magnitude of that explosion through studying the body and superficial waves which are caused in the event of a nuclear explosion. This measure faces challenges in distinguishing waves which are caused by earthquakes or any other natural event from those which are caused by a nuclear explosion. To do so it requires field experts to support it with expertise to analyse each wave caught in the process of monitoring.[184]

The acoustic measures try to study sound waves to detect, localize and establish the magnitude of a nuclear explosion. This measure is used for nuclear tests conducted in water, atmosphere close to the oceans or underground tests close to ocean bed. This measure offers a high precision result because it can detect even very small sound signals due to high conduction capacity of the water waves. This measure is capable of distinguishing waves created by a nuclear explosion from those created by other human activities or different water animals and other natural events.[185]

---

[181] The Secretariat together iwth the Conference of Member States and the Executive Council were established in compliance with the Art II para. 4 and present the main organs of the CTBTO, see *Id,* Art. II.

[182] Thie headquarters of this organization are located in Vienna, *Id*, Art. 2.

[183] Compare the CTBT Protocol on the Monitoring Systems and Functionin of International Data Center, para 2 with annex II para. 2-5 of the CTBTO on the List of Characterisation Parametres for International Data Center Standard Event Screening.

[184] "Seismic Monitoring", CTBTO, visited on 6 February 2012, http://www.ctbto.org/verification-regime/monitoring-technologies-how-they-work/seismic-monitoring/page-2/. The treaty foresees for the installation of around 50 primary stations and 120 auxilliary ones in the world to monitor these waves, see Table 1-A e CTBT on the List of Seismological Stations Comprising the Primary Network and Table 1-B on the Liar od Seismological Stations Comprising the Auxiliary Network, p. 159 and 163.

[185] "Hydroaccoustic Monitoring", CTBTO, visited on 6 February 2012, http://www.ctbto.org/verification-regime/monitoring-technologies-how-they-work/hydroacoustic-monitoring/page-2/. The treaty foresees for the installation of 11 hydroaccoustic stations in the world, see Table 3 Tabela 3 of the Traty on the List of Hydroaccoustic Stations, p. 80.

The ultrasound measure is used to detect sound with a very low frequency. Nuclear tests in air and shallow water may cause sounds of very low waves which may be detected using this measure. The main focus of this measure is atmospheric nuclear tests and localizing them. This measure is used, also, in conjunction with the seismic measure to gather more data for a more accurate detection of any underground nuclear activity.[186]

The objective of radionuclide monitoring is to detect the abundance of radioactive particles or noble gas even with minute measurements. After a nuclear explosion radioactive particles such as the xenon isotopes, are released and which may be detected from thousands of miles away. This technology is used as a complementary measure to confirm a nuclear explosion detected by other measures.[187]

Besides the measures mentioned, the treaty foresees the application of other verification measures such as consultations, on the spot inspections and other measures to increase credibility in which case a crucial role is played by the Executive Council of the CTBT Conference which should prepare reports regarding particular findings in specific cases.[188]

If the monitoring shows that a state has violated the CTBT rules, the Executive Council may give specific recommendations to improve the situation. If that state does not comply with the recommendation then the CTBT Conference may decide to limit the rights or suspend that state from the treaty.[189] In cases when a state has gone against the objective and purpose of the CTBT then the conference may recommend to Member States for *"collective measures which are in conformi-*

---

[186] "Infrasound Monitoring", CTBTO, visited on 6 February 2012, http://www.ctbto.org/verification-regime/monitoring-technologies-how-they-work/infrasound-monitoring/page-2/. The treaty foresses for the installation of 60 infrasound stations in the world, see Table 4 of the Treaty, p. 82.

[187] "Radionuclide Monitoring", CTBTO, visited on 6 February 2012, http://www.ctbto.org/verification-regime/monitoring-technologies-how-they-work/radionuclide-monitoring/page-3/. The Treaty foresees for the installation of 80 radionuclide stations in the world, mainly around the earths' ecuator for better detection capabilities. Also it is foreseen for the installation of 16 laboratories, see Table 1-A on the List of Radionuclide Stations and Table 2-B on the List of Radionuclide Laboratories, pp. 174 and 178.

[188] Supra note 727, Art. 4.

[189] *Id*, Art. V, para. 2.

ty with international law".[190] The treaty does not specify what is meant with collective measures but it may be implied that they are about the measures which are used to preserve international peace and security. Such a situation would arise when a state has tested nuclear weapons or supported another state to do so, encouraged or took part in a certain way in testing nuclear weapons. The testing of nuclear weapons is considered a threat to international peace and security. In this aspect, this provision refers to measures including the use of force. Further it leads to the question of who should decide about these collective measures. The UN SC is the only competent organ under Chapter VII of the Charter.[191] This should be read in conjunction with Article V of the CTBT, according to which in emergency cases, the Conference or the Executive Council may refer a case to the UN.[192] According to Article XV, reserves are not permitted against articles and annexes of the CTBT but they are allowed against the provision of the protocol and its annexes which do not go against the object and purpose of the treaty.[193]

The CTBT has not come into force yet but having the signatures and ratifications of 153 states presents a fact that the majority of states are against nuclear testing. The treaty supporters consider that this treaty would play a crucial role in the global endeavour for the prevention of nuclear weapons proliferation including the states with nuclear capabilities.[194] The states with nuclear capabilities would find it difficult to further improve their nuclear capabilities and technology because they would need real testing to measure their effect while states without nuclear capabilities would be faced with additional difficulties since they do not have any such capability thus eventually having a comprehensive preventive effect of nuclear proliferation on these states. Nuclear tests are very important in the initial development of nuclear weapons.[195]

There are important states such as the US which have not yet ratified the CTBT. According to the former senior adviser of the Bush Presidency, Stephen Rademaker, the reasons for refusing to ratify this treaty are the following: the ratification by the US would not indicate entry into

---

[190] *Id.* Art. V, para 3.
[191] Chapter VII of the charter deals with implementation measures, see supra note 121.
[192] Supra note 727, Art. V.
[193] *Id*, Art. XV.
[194] Supra note 5, p.45.
[195] *Ibid.*

force of the treaty because other states should also ratify it; the treaty is still non verifiable; the US would have to further test its nuclear arsenal to modernize them; there is no definition of "ground zero" nuclear testing; and that Russia and China are not on board on their terms of definition of the "ground zero" effect.[196] The last point regarding the testing of "ground zero" presents the main concern because these tests may avoid verification measures due to their very low effect thus allowing states to continue improving their nuclear weapons.[197] Other critics, trying to minimize American concerns, think that as a result of technological developments, states may no longer need to carry out nuclear tests because instead they can use computer simulations to precisely determine the results related to the effect, power and nuclear technology.[198]

A major blow to the CTBT is presented by the case of India and Pakistan which have not yet signed the treaty. Furthermore, these two states conducted their nuclear tests after the opening of this treaty for signature. In May of 1998 India conducted two underground nuclear tests, declaring openly that they were military related tests.[199] On the other side, Pakistan reacted with two such explosions as a countermeasure.[200] Following these tests both parties declared a moratorium on nuclear tests. In October of 2006 another nuclear test was conducted by North Korea which has not signed the CTBT and which was repeated again in May of 2009.[201]

The critics of the American stance think that the lack of ratification by the US negatively influences the international struggle to

---

[196] The speech of former senior advisor rademaker was hold at the East/West Institute during a seminar called"The Comprehensive Test Ban Treaty: New Technology, New Prospects?", see Alicia Godsberg, "CTBT Ratification and fact-twisting argument", Federation of American Scientists, visited on 7 February 2012, http://www.fas.org/blog/ssp/2010/03/ctbt-ratification-and-fact-twisting-arguments.php . The notion "zero power" refers to testings conducted with explosive devices with very little capacities which man not be detected by monitoring systems and technology available today, see "CTBT ratification and fact-twisting arguments", Federation of American Scientists, 7 February 2012, http://www.fas.org/blog/ssp/2010/03/ctbt-ratification-and-fact-twisting-arguments.php.

[197] *Ibid.*

[198] Daryl G. Kimball, "Why We Don't Need to Resume Nuclear Testing", Arms Control Association, Arms Control Today, November 2009, visited on 15 September 2012, http://www.armscontrol.org/act/2009_11/focus.

[199] After nuclear testing in 1974, India declared that the nature of its nuclear testing was for peaceful purposes, see "Nuclear Testing", CTBTO, 1949-2009, visited on 15 September 2012, http://www.ctbto.org/nuclear-testing/history-of-nuclear-testing/nuclear-testing-1945-2009/page-7-nuclear-testing-1945-2009/.

[200] *Ibid.*

[201] *Ibid.*

put India and Pakistan as well as North Korea under the treaty regime the signatures of which are important for the treaty to come into force. Eventual entry in force of the treaty would put in function foreseen measures to verify nuclear tests. Furthermore, this would enable the use of legal mechanisms to solve eventual disputes among Member States and also in taking adequate measures to improve credibility between states. This would have a great impact on the relaxation of international relations and in the eventual prevention of a nuclear arms race coming out of attempts by states to develop or improve their nuclear weapons.

CHAPTER VI

THE PROLIFERATION OF NUCLEAR WEAPONS AND TECHNOLOGY IN CONTEMPORARY CASES AND ISSUES REVOLVING AROUND THEM

VI.1 THE ROLE OF AN INDIVIDUAL AND THE NEED FOR IMPROVEMENT OF MEASURES AND INTERNATIONAL COOPERATION IN REGULATING INDIVIDUAL ACTIVITIES: THE CASE OF A.Q.KHAN

The proliferation risk of nuclear material and its technology is one of the main concerns in our minds. Besides the state, the role of an individual acting in a private capacity may be very important and an essential factor. Taking practical examples on the role of an individual in proliferation, this subject is analysed at the beginning of this chapter. A great deal of attention has been directed, at international level, to the case of Abdul Qadeer Khan (A.Q. Khan),[1]who is known as the father of the Pakistani nuclear bomb. A.Q. Khan managed to control an international supply network through which he attempted to sell technology for the production of nuclear energy for military use to states like Iran, Iraq and North Korea.[2] He did this during the years of 1987-2003 using to a large extent his privileged position as one of the leaders of one of the main nuclear research organisations in Pakistan.[3]

A.Q. Khan was born in the city of Bhopal in India in 1936 and moved to Pakistan in 1952. In 1961 he went to Western Europe studying at the Technical University in West Berlin and the Technical University in Delft, Holland. In Delft, he met one of the most renowned

[1] On the chronology of Abdul Qaderr Khan activities see "A. Q. Khan Nuclear Chronology", *Carnegie Endowment for International Peace*, Vol. VIII. No. 8, 7 September 2005.

[2] Christopher O. Clary *"The A.Q. Khan Network: Causes and Implications"* (Master Thesis, Naval Postgraduate School, California, December 2005), pp. 21-25.

[3] *Ibid.*

physicians, W.G. Burgers who later would become his mentor in his Master thesis which earned him a Master of Engineering Sciences degree.[4] He continued with his doctoral studies in Belgium at the Catholic University of Leuven focusing on the field of the elasticity of mixed materials.[5] Attending some of the best European universities and in co-operation with different renowned scientists enabled him to gain access to European laboratories dealing with the design and methodology of centrifuge production for enriching Uranium. A.Q. Khan succeeded in getting a working contract at the laboratory for dynamic physics research which was a subcontractor for developing such centrifuges for the Urenco company branch[6] named Ultra-Centrifuges Holland. Because of the sensitivity of the work at the laboratory it could also be considered as a potential risk to national security, he managed to get clearance also from the Dutch security service.[7]

From that time, A.Q. Kahn gained direct access to highly sensitive information which he started to gradually retrieve for other purposes over the following years. He intensified this activity at the time when he was put in charge of translating documents containing information about nuclear technology from German to the Dutch language for laboratory needs.[8] Information gathered during this process laid the main foundation in building his abilities and knowledge in the construction of centrifuges for Uranium enrichment to be used later for the development of the Pakistani nuclear programmes.[9]

After 1975, A.Q. Khan returns to Pakistan where he took charge of the Pakistani Engineering Research Laboratory (ERL).[10] Here, he used his earlier contacts with the technician Frits Veerman, to whom

[4] Joop Boer, Henk van der Keur, Karel Koster and Frank Slijper, "A.Q. Khan, Urenco and the Proliferation of Nuclear Weapons technology: The Symbiotic relation between nuclear energy and nuclear weapons", Report Commissioned by Greenpeace International, May 2004, p. 9.

[5] *Ibid.*

[6] Urenco LTd is a consortium of British INFL company, Duch UCN BV and a German company called German Uranit. Its work is focused on production of ultra centrifuge technology which is used in Uranium enrichment. For more see Urenco official web page, visited on15 June 2012, http://www.urenco.com/custom/1/homepage/default.aspx.

[7] Supra note 758, p. 9.

[8] David Albright & Mark Hibbs, "Pakistan's Bomb: Out of the Closet", *The Bulleting of the Atomic Scientists*, Vol. 48. No. 6 July-August 1992, p. 40.

[9] This was confirmed by a Dutch intelligence report and later in 1991 by the IAEA, see *Id*, pp. 39-40.

[10] "Khan Research Laboratories", Global Security, visited on 9 February 2012, http://www.globalsecurity.org/wmd/world/pakistan/kahuta.htm

he sent a letter in the summer of 1976 requesting *"in great confidence"* to help them.[11] Concretely, he requested from him to be provided with the technical specifications, types of membranes and pivots and also the negatives to see what they looked like, emphasising that *"this is absolutely urgent since the entire project has been halted"*.[12] From later revelations of A.Q. Khan's activities problems were identified in relations to the development of his programme.[13] In 1986, his laboratory reported the installation of 14,000 centrifuges for Uranium enrichment but according to the US official data, not more that 1,000 of them were functional.[14] A big help for fulfilling his shortcomings and improve results came from China. Different Chinese experts of nuclear technology visited his laboratory during the 1980s.[15] In this way, gradually during the 1990s, Pakistan also started to develop the technology for Uranium waste reprocessing.[16]

A.Q. Khan benefited from the unreserved support of Pakistani authorities in his activities. At the same time, Pakistan created another laboratory, in a way rivalling A.Q. Khan's activities named the Pakistani Commission for Atomic Energy. This rivalry seemed to be very strong and might have influenced A.Q. Khan to accelerate his activities to achieve concrete results.[17] However, in the midst of rivalry, the ERL laboratory was placed at a more advantageous situation because its work was outside the government umbrella and its direct supervision. This enabled Khan to avoid security procedures and other regulations when conducting his activities. In particular, this reflected in the procurement procedures giving him more privacy in purchasing different materials.[18]

[11] He met with Frits Veerman while working for Urenco laboratory, see "The Letters of Abdul Khan", *Bulletin of the Atomic Scientists*, Vol. 48. No. 6 July-August 1992, p. 40.

[12] This letter would be used later against him at a Dutch Court because Frits Verman, being suspicious of the letter, showed it to the LHI management. Ini 1993 Khan was sentenced in absentia by a Dutch Court for theft attempt in relation to secret documents on Uranium enrichment but htis sentence was quashed after two years by an appeals Court because subpoena and other case materials were not haned duly to him during the court process, see *Ibid.*

[13] In a letter addressed to Abdul Aziz Khan, an electrical engineer in Canada, Khan stated that the US and UK embargo was having its effect. According to him, the british companies are withholding exports even of needls and bolts, see *Id*, p. 41.

[14] Supra note 762, pp. 39-40.

[15] Michael Quinlan, *Thinking About Nuclear Weapons: Principles, Problems, Prospects* (Oxfort University Press, Oxford, 2009), pp. 133-134.

[16] Supra note 762, p. 42.

[17] "Nuclear Black Markets: Pakistan, A.Q. Khan and the rise of proliferation network: A Net Assessment", *The International Institute for Strategic Studies*, 2007, p. 65.

[18] *Id*, pp. 65-66.

His activities for purchasing different materials avoided controls by the Pakistani government thus enabling him complete secrecy with a government resolution to protect his activities.[19]

The Pakistani government was highly interested in having in its possession a nuclear weapon, now that India was ahead in this aspect.[20] In 1987, A.Q. Khan, during an interview, confirmed that Pakistan had achieved enriching Uranium to a high level which may be used for military purposes. At the same time he expressed that: *"nobody can undo Pakistan or take us for granted. We are here to stay and let it be clear that we shall use the bomb if our existence is threatened"*.[21]

A.Q. Khan, gradually, managed to create a network of brokers, financiers and other companies to the benefit of his activities and programmes.[22] The same structures would play a crucial role in the proliferation of nuclear programmes in other states. The father of the Pakistani nuclear bomb would become *"the mother of all nuclear nightmares, selling weapon designs, centrifuges, and who knows what else to interested buyers"*.[23] The clandestine network of A.Q. Khan would be used as a supermarket where states would be supplied with the technology for Uranium enrichment.[24] Even though the world would less reluctantly accept the fact that Pakistan became a member of the nuclear states club, the evidence which started to mount related to his activities of nuclear technology proliferation from A.Q. Khan increased heavily the concern of world leaders afraid of a potential nuclear arms race in the Middle East and East Asia. Henry Kissinger expressed this concern in his words stating that *"The world is faced with the nightmarish pros-*

[19] *Ibid.*

[20] The Pakistani determination is marked on the words of its President Zulfiqar Ali Bhutto saying that Pakistani will acquire a nuclear weaon *"even if we have to eat grass."*, Michael Krepon, Better Safe than Sorry: *The Ironies of Living with the Bomb* (Stanford Security Studies, Stanford University Press, California, 2009), pp. 96-97.

[21] These declarations were denied later byKhan but nevertheless it seems that they were don on purpose of sendin a message for India implying that now Pakistani has enough capabilities to produce nuclear weapons, Mario Esteban Carranza, *South Asian Security and International Nuclear Order: Creating a Robust Indo-Pakistani Nuclear Arms Control Regime* (Ashgate, Burlington US, 2009), pp. 31-32.

[22] Supra note 771, pp. 66-67.

[23] Supra note 774, p. 96.

[24] Walmart is one of the biggest chain retailers in the US and this term was used by former IAEA chief, Mohammed ElBaradei, see Mathew Fuhrmann, "Spreading Temptation: Proliferation and Peaceful Nuclear Cooperation Agreements", *International Security* Vol. 34 no. 1, summer 2009.

pect that nuclear weapons will become a standard part of national armament and wind up in terrorist hands. The negotiations on Korean and Iranian nuclear proliferation mark a watershed".[25]

The main activities of A.Q. Khan in selling his technology for production of centrifuges were carried out at a period of political turmoil in Pakistan following and due to the death of President Zia in 1988 and upon the arrival of President Pervez Musharraf in 1999.[26] The political vacuum created at this time, enabled him to a large extent to work freely. However, the first contact with another government to sell his technology was made at the beginning of the 1980s with Iran appearing to be his first targeted country.[27] The potential motivation to help Iran is one of the most controversial issues to be studied because Pakistan has, almost, never had good relations with Iran with specific turbulences at specific times.[28] The first concrete offer to Iran was made in 1987 when the A.Q. Khan network handed Iranian agents a handwritten list with items which may be available for Iran to purchase from him.[29]

However, it seems that A.Q. Khan did not become rich enough as he had first thought he would, because the Iranian agents ordered and purchased a few items regarded as necessary but on the other side they focused their efforts on securing other items, based on the initial list of items from A.Q. Khan, from other suppliers offering them at a lower price.[30] The cooperation would continue further and as a result, Iran received a copy of a design set for the construction of P1 centrifuges together with 500 spare parts for those centrifuges between 1994 and 1996. In the same period, Iran also received the design for the more

[25] Patrick M. Cronin, ed. *Double Trouble: Iran and North Korea as Challenges to International Security* (Praeger Security International, London, 2008), Introduction, p. 3.

[26] Supra note 771, p. 66.

[27] *Id*, p. 67.

[28] Supra note 756, pp. 38-39.

[29] The list included a sample of disassembled P-1 centrigue; figures, explanations, specifications and calculation for building a factory; materials for 2,000 centrifuges and vacumme and electrical materials which are used for this purpose. This list would be later offered to IAEA by Iran in 2005, but after IAEA inspectors requested it to be sent to Vienna for further examination to determine the origin of the letter, Iran refused the request, see supra note 771, p. 69.

[30] The A.Q. Khan offer included articles which had trade value of hundreds of millions of dollar but Iran limited its procurement by a contract focusing on purchasing specific items which is supposed to have reached a value of around 3 million dollars. Other suppliers from China, Russia or Europe would offer the sam items for less money. Ultimately in list of purchased items from A.Q. Khan were centrigue designes and technology, see supra note 756, pp. 38-40.

advanced centrifuges P2.[31] This cooperation continued until 1999 to be broken possibly after the worsening bilateral relations between Pakistan and Iran.[32]

The A.Q. Khan network played a crucial role in the development of the North Korean nuclear programme. Compared to Iran, it seems that here this activity proved beneficial also for the Pakistani state as well because while North Korea gained technology for the production of centrifuges for Uranium enrichment, in turn, Pakistan benefited from the technology for the production of ballistic missiles.[33] This transaction places a big question mark on the official Pakistani declarations regarding the role of Pakistan in the proliferation of nuclear weapons denying that they knew or were involved in such activities. A.Q. Khan was caught being present on one of Pakistan's official visits to North Korea while accompanying high military and civil Pakistani officials, the purpose of which was to procure the technology for the production of ballistic missiles.[34]

North Korea managed to benefit by securing centrifuge designs and a small number of complete centrifuges accompanied with a list of items needed to build such centrifuges.[35] A.Q. Kahn made around 13 visits to North Korea while between 1997 and 1998 North Korea ordered P-1 centrifuges and received technical assistance from the A.Q. Khan network between 1998 and 2000. In 2000, the Pakistani intelligent service raided an airplane ordered by the A.Q. Khan laboratory but they failed to find anything illegal.[36] Later, in 2003, a cargo ship was stopped in the Suez Canal transporting pipes which may be potentially used for rinsing centrifuges P-2. In 2005 the Pakistani President

---

[31] *Id*, pp. 40-41.

[32] Supra note 771, p. 71.

[33] Balistic missiles are important for delivering of nuclear warheads. In fact, these are to necessary elements for a military nuclear programme: possession of HEU and nuclear warheads which can be delivered by ballistics missiles, see supra note 756, p. 40-41.

[34] According to Pakistani Presidents from Benazir Bhuta, the agreements with North Korea for production of ballistic missiles are based exlclusively on contracs with cash and not on any other exchange basis such as Uranium enrichment technology in exchange for ballistic missiles, compare supra note 771, p. 75 and "Weapons of Mass Destruction: AQ Khan Network", Global Security, visited on 11 February 2012, http://www.globalsecurity.org//md//orld/dprk/khan-dprk.htm.

[35] "Weapons of Mass Destruction: AQ Khan Network", Global Security, visited on 11 February 2012.

[36] In this process A.Q. Khan was warned on eventual nuclear proliferation, see *Ibid.*

Musharraf admitted that A.Q. Khan transferred centrifuges and spare parts together with their designs to North Korea.[37]

At the end of 1990 and the beginning of the new millennium, the A.Q. Khan network expanded their activities outside of Pakistan and succeeded in even constructing factories for the production of different parts in countries such as Malaysia.[38] He started to recruit people who earlier worked for nuclear programmes in South Africa together with other activities conducted in different countries where they concluded contracts such as with Turkey and Saudi Arabia amongst others.[39] This enabled him to focus on a more ambitious plan such as the cooperation with Libya between the years 1999 and 2003. Regarding cooperation with Libya the situation is much clearer because, in 2003 the Libyan leader Gaddafi agreed to open all documents related to their nuclear programmes. Gaddafi agreed to cooperate with the international community when a cargo ship registered in Germany under the name "BBC China" was caught carrying centrifuges with Libya as its final destination.[40] Libya managed to secure 20 complete P-1centrigues and spare parts for the construction of another 200 such centrifuges. At the beginning of 2000, Libya ordered 10,000 P-2 centrifuges with the first order received in December 2002.[41] The ambitious programme for supplying 10,000 centrifuges failed after the capture of the cargo ship in 2003 and followed by the Gaddafi decision to halt its nuclear programme.[42]

The A.Q. Khan network also developed contacts with Iraq and Syria at different times but it seems without any concrete result. During the 1980s, it seems that Iraq started to develop a secret programme for the production of nuclear weapons, the details of which would be revealed after the Gulf War and the involvement of the IAEA inspec-

[37] David E. Sanger, "Pakistan Leader Confirms Nuclear Exports", *New York Times*, 13 September 2005, visited on 13 March 2013, http://www.nytimes.com/2005/09/13/international/asia/13musharraf.html.

[38] A fabric constructed in Malaysica in 2001 hired 20 workers under the management of Scomi Precission Engineering as a brach of Scomi Group Berhad which was involved in oil and gas business, see supra note 756, p. 75.

[39] *Id*, pp. 78-79.

[40] Supra note 771, p. 76.

[41] Supra note 756, p. 75.

[42] For more on thi issue see "Chronology of Libya's Disarmament and Relations with the United States", Arms Control Association, visited on 11 February 2012, http://www.armscontrol.org/factsheets/LibyaChronology.

tors and those of the UN Special Commission for Iraq.[43] Traces of contacts between Iraq and A.Q. Khan were found after Saddam Hussein's nephew deserted and revealed important information to the UN Special Commission on the existence of a farm containing information about weapons of mass destruction programmes in Iraq which included nuclear, biological and chemical weapons programmes. Documents later to be found by the commission revealed contacts between A.Q. Khan and Iraq brokered by a person code named *"Malik"*. The code name of this process was A-B which according to the IAEA has reference to the atomic bomb.[44] Nothing more could be revealed related to these relations. With regards to Syria, there are indications that the A.Q. Khan network made offers to this state but were refused for no particular reason.[45]

The level of the official Pakistani involvement still remains a controversial issue and one which has never been confirmed, but there may be indications that at least, indirectly the Government of Pakistan may have had knowledge about the activities of A.Q. Khan. The strongest indication is the official visit made to North Korea as a result of which Pakistan gained technology for the production of ballistic missiles while North Korea gained technology for the production of centrifuges for Uranium enrichment. When Pakistan carried out its nuclear tests a 20 member North Korea delegation took part in the event which did not seem to be only for ceremonial purposes.[46]

International legislation regulating the transfer of technology and nuclear material foresees obligations for states but it does not regulate the actions of individuals towards the international community. The case of A.Q. Khan serves as a concrete case showing the need to determine the responsibility of individuals and such networks towards the international community as well as towards an individual state. The actions of an individual in the proliferation of nuclear material and technology or knowhow for the production of nuclear weapons would be regarded as actions with *erga omnes* effect against the international

[43] Supra note 771, p. 71.

[44] *Id*, p. 72.

[45] Kamrahn Khan, "Pakistanis Exploited Nuclear Network", *The Washington Post*, 28 January 2004, visited on 15 March 2013, http://www.washingtonpost.com/wp-dyn/articles/A54334-2004Jan27.html.

[46] Compare supra note 758, pp. 13-14 and Paul Watson and Mubashir Zaidi, "Death of N. Korean Woman Offers Clues to Pakistani Nuclear Deals", *Los Angeles Times*, 01 March 2004, visited on 15 March 2013, http://articles.latimes.com/2004/mar/01/world/fg-murder1.

community and should be prosecuted in the same manner at international and local level by all states under the universal jurisdiction competence. The International Criminal Court would present a competent forum with objective and professional judges for adjudicating individuals engaged in such activities and at the same time it would avoid potential quarrels between states regarding jurisdiction to adjudicate a particular individual or organisation. Regulation of individual acts at international level is done in the field of international humanitarian law, but seeing the seriousness of acts involving nuclear material, which may fall into the hands of criminal and/or terrorist organisations, states should work more on designing specific norms for international prosecution of such crimes. Also, internal legislation of states should foresee specific norms and authorisation for public authorities to fight such negative features. Better international cooperation may have a positive impact in removing legal and political barriers in this endeavour.

VI.2 NUCLEAR PROGRAMMES FOR PEACEFUL USE OR MORE PRECISELY: THE CASE OF IRAN

The case of Iran emphasises the best issues and dilemmas related to the NPT provisions and limitations and the safeguard guarantees concerning the independence of states to produce nuclear energy for peaceful use on one hand and international obligations on the other. The precise fulfilment with good-faith of the NPT provisions, close cooperation with the IAEA and transparency over the development of nuclear energy and technology are essential should a state desire to enter the club of states which produce nuclear energy for peaceful use. Any establishment of a distrustful situation within this relationship may lead to raise tension even in cases when a state did not have any intention to develop technology or produce nuclear energy for military purposes which is the main concern of the NPT. A state is a sovereign entity and exercises its control over its territory with open and transparent cooperation with the IAEA inspectors in compliance with the safeguard agreement and is essential for building trust and avoiding any misunderstandings.

Iran now has an advanced programme for Uranium enrichment. The biggest dilemma related to the Iranian nuclear programme come from the fact that this state for a long time had kept its programme totally secret. The Iranian nuclear programme was made public only in August 2002 by the Iranian opposition in exile, revealing that Iran possesses scientific facilities for Uranium enrichment in Natanz and also a factory for the production of heavy water in Arak.[47] Some states however, seem to have had intelligence on such activities much earlier. In his state of the union address to the Congress in 2002, American President George Bush used the notion of "axis of evil" referring to Iran, North Korea and Iraq and hinting that these states might be in the process of developing nuclear programmes for military use.[48] The US together with other states mainly from the Western Europe was committed to halting any eventual Iranian programmes for Uranium enrichment for military use.[49] The issue becomes more complicated considering the international relations in the Middle East and the role of Iran in this part of the world in particular its relations with Israel. One of the reasons for development of nuclear programmes and eventually the construction of a nuclear weapon would be the deterrence of Israel which is considered an enemy with nuclear weapons capability by Iran. President Ahmadinejad had hinted that Israel should be wiped off the map in the support he gave to the Iranian supreme leader Ruhollah Mostafavi Musavi Khomeini (Khomeini) declaration.[50] Such a declaration was a huge blow to the peace and security in the region and obviously no normal state in the world would like to see a regime like that become a nuclear military power.

From the Iranian viewpoint the secrecy over the development of its nuclear programme was necessary because other states would cut cooperation with it and thus limiting to the maximum level possible, the

---

[47] Patrick M. Cronin, "The Trouble with Iran" në *Double Trouble: Iran and North Korea as Challenges to Interantional Security*, ed. Patrick M. Cronin (Praeger Security International, London, 2008), p. 14.

[48] See The President's State of the Union Address, 29 January 2002, The White House, visited on 28 June 2012, http://georgewbush-whitehouse.archives.gov/news/releases/2002/01/20020129-11.html.

[49] Steven E. Miller, "Proliferation gamesmanship: Iran and the Politics of Nuclear Confrontation", *Syracuse Law Review, 57 Syracuse L. Rev.* 551, summer 2008, p. 557-558.

[50] Ahmedinejad made this statement during his lecture titled "The World Without Zionism", see Nazila Fathi, "Wipe Isreal 'off the map' Iranian says", *The New York Times*, 27 October 2005, visited on 15 March 2012 http://www.nytimes.com/2005/10/26/world/africa/26iht-iran.html.

development of its programmes. According to the Iranian permanent representative at the UN, Ambassador Javad Zarif "*had we declared it we would not have been able to do it. We would have been denied the necessary imports. The very meagre resources that we had outside of the country to acquire the needs of the programmes were blocked*".[51] According to him, the Iranian nuclear programme is connected with misunderstandings stemming from issues going back to the 1979 Islamic revolution in Iran, the hostage crisis and the Iraq-Iran war.[52] The west, *inter alia* the US, are obsessed with Iran due to the influence that Iran, an Islamic state of Shia denomination, might establish in the region. In this way, through religion, Iran may control Iraq or even Libya for example.[53] Referring to critics who say that Iran does not need to produce nuclear energy for peaceful use because it has enough natural resources of oil and gas, the Ambassador stated that these resources are limited and that in a few decades Iran would have to import oil to fulfil its needs for electricity but also it wants to develop this important technology as a sign of technological achievement and state prestige.[54]

The Iranian ambitions for the production of nuclear energy did not start after the Islamic revolution. These ambitions are related to the government of Iranian Shah Mohammad Reza Pahlavi who made public the intention of Iran to develop a programme for the production of nuclear energy. To do so, he established the Iranian Atomic Energy Organisation (IAEO) in 1974.[55] In 1969, Iran signed the NPT and as a result it managed to benefit from international cooperation, in particular from the US, in the development of nuclear technology for peaceful use. At that time, it was in the US interest to strengthen Iran as a reliable partner in the region while the US was involved in the Vietnam War.[56]

Earlier, in 1957, Iran and the US had signed an agreement within the framework of the US "Atoms for Peace" programme according

[51] The Speech of Permanent Representative of the Islamic Republic of Iran in the UN, Ambasador Javad Zarif at the conference organized by The Liechtenstein Colloquium on European and International Affairs titled "Iran's Security Challenges and the Region", Lichtenstein Colloquium Report Vol 1, pp. 28-35, Princeton, August 2005.

[52] *Ibid.*

[53] *Id*, p. 29.

[54] *Id*, p. 30.

[55] Saira Khan, *Iran and Nuclear Weapons: Protracted Conflict and Proliferation* (Routledge, New York, 2010) p. 11.

[56] Supra note 779, pp. 13-14.

to which Iran was provided with a nuclear reactor of 5 MW sent for the purposes of the Teheran Centre for Nuclear Research. This technology was transferred in 1967.[57] The US had never intended to transfer any technology which might be used for other purposes thus they also convinced their European partners not to transfer any technology which might be used for military purposes.[58] In the year 1974, Iran entered the safeguard regime and in this way took on specific obligations and establishing trust related to its ambitions. In this way, the IAEO in 1974 started to design specific plans which foresaw Iran producing 23,000 MW of nuclear energy in the following 20 years and also to obtain the total cycle of nuclear fuel including the means for Uranium enrichment, fuel fabrication and also for the processing of nuclear waste to gain Plutonium which should also be used for peaceful purposes. To realize the plan, Iran signed specific agreements with France, Germany and the US. [59] These agreements would help Iran to obtain 22 nuclear reactors for the production of 23,000 MW of nuclear energy. In 1976 Iran signed an agreement with South Africa to the value of $700 million for the supply of the "yellow cake" by the latter.[60] Iran also has large reserves of Uranium ore in various regions of the country.[61]

The US believed that Iran was capable of producing nuclear energy for military purposes from the 1970s and that it would not hesitate to do so if deemed necessary by Iran.[62] Concern grew when India carried out its first nuclear test in 1974 triggering fears in Iran, for Iran to go ahead with such steps. However, signing the NPT and subsequently the safeguard agreement relaxed to a certain extent the fears of the western world.[63]

The Iranian plans suffered a breakdown after the Islamic revolution of 1979 when Khomeini became the head of state. The construction of new nuclear reactors was put on hold while the reactor in Bushehr was bombed during the war with Iraq while other reactors under construction were damaged to a large extent. A large number of nuclear

[57] Supra note 809, p. 47.
[58] Krahaso Supra note 779, pp. 13-14 and supra note 9, pp. 99-100.
[59] Supra note 809, pp. 47-48.
[60] *Ibid.*
[61] For more see supra note 59.
[62] Supra note 809, pp. 49-50.
[63] *Ibid.*

scientists fled the country.[64] After coming to power, Khomeini would not defer from the development of nuclear programmes but in new circumstances where it broke relations with the US, he attempted to reach agreements with other states to continue with nuclear development. Negotiations were held with France, West Germany, China, Russia etc. for this purpose. [65]

Of particular concern for the world was an argument stating the right of the Islamic people to have a nuclear weapon.[66] On 23 October 1991, the Iranian vice president Mohajerani when referring to Israel, declared that *"because the enemy has nuclear facilities, the Muslim states should be equipped with the same capacity"*.[67] In the meantime, many of the scientists who had fled the country after the Islamic revolution started to return to Iran while the IAEA report at the beginning of 1992 would not show any Iranian nuclear activity outside of the NPT framework.[68]

Revelations of the nuclear programme by the government in exile and the blow to the A.Q. Khan network in 2003[69], pushed Iran to admit openly its nuclear programme. This might also have come as a result of EU involvement in discussions and negotiations with Iran during 2002-2003.[70] Besides admission of the existence of nuclear programmes, Iran declared that it was ready to sign the additional protocol of the Safeguard Agreement which would enable greater access to the IAEA inspectors and that the protocol would enter into force on the day of placing the signature.[71] Ultimately, within this development, Iran

[64] Supra note 9, p. 100.

[65] *Ibid.*

[66] *Ibid.*

[67] *Ibid.*

[68] The reports were regardes as not objective from the US because the IAEA was not able to inspect all facilities but only those which were permitted by Iran. This, according to the US, would mean that Iran is conducting secret activities especially taking under consideration that Iran had made earlier contacts with the A.Q. Khan network for acquiring Uranium enrichment technology, see also supra note 9, p. 101.

[69] See subchapter above on Iranian nuclear programme and A.Q. Khan activities.

[70] On 21 October 2003, the Iranian Foreign Ministry issued a declaration negotiated with the EU3 according to whih it has decided to fully cooperate with the IAEA to solve all pending issues through a tranpared process with the IAEA, see Statement by the Iranian Government and Visiting EU Foreign Ministers, 21 October 2003, para 2.a, IAEA, visited on20 June 2012, http://www.iaea.org/newscenter/focus/iaeairan/statement_iran21102003.shtml. See also supra note 803, p. 554.

[71] The promise to enact the Protocol into force upon signing it presented a significant element because it avoided ratification procedures from the Iranian Parliament (Majlis), where the ratification could be fail, see *Id.* para 2.b.i.

promised to halve *"all Uranium enrichment and reprocessing activities as defined by IAEA"*.[72]

Reaching this agreement was very important as it would potentially increase trust for a long term solution of the Iranian nuclear programme issue. But soon, these negotiations would go through turmoil with many difficulties. During 2004, Iran cooperated to a certain extent with the IAEA but not at the desired level thus pushing the latter to criticize Iran for failing to fully cooperate with the IAEA in matters such as the lack of transparency in the development of nuclear programmes and the purchase of different magnetic parts.[73] On the issues related to Uranium enrichment further issues would arise later after Iran failed to fulfil all the requirements of the IAEA Board of Governors resolution to suspend its enrichment activities.[74] Another round of negotiations started during 2004 yielding in the end the so called Paris Agreement on 15 November 2003 focusing specifically on enrichment activities. Once more, divergences in interpretation of the agreement impacted on continuing further negotiations.[75] The Paris Agreement, in the first place, was not a treaty in the strict sense with binding imperative provisions, and in the second place the language used was weak and general allowing for different interpretations. This agreement was more of a memorandum of understanding and eventual non-compliance would not present a violation from the legal point of view but eventually only the break of negotiations.[76]

In September of 2005, the IAEA drafted a resolution on the Iranian activities which found it in breach in many aspects of fulfilling its obligations within the safeguard regime related to the reporting of nuclear material, processing and its use and also the declaration of facilities used for the processing and stockpiling of nuclear material.[77] The

[72] *Id*, para 2.b.ii.

[73] Implementation of the NPT Safeguards Agreement in the Islamic Republic of Iran, Report by the Board of Governors, IAEA Doc. GOV/2004/34, 1 June 2004.

[74] *Ibid.* According to Iranian stance, the suspension of Uranium enrichmet activities had to do with activities related to the pilot project for Uranium enrichment in Natanz and it did not cover activities in Esfahan, while for the Europeans it meant for the suspension of activities at all facilities, see supra note 803, p. 555.

[75] Supra note 803, p. 556.

[76] Supra note 602, p. 440.

[77] For more see Implementation of NPT Safeguards Agreement in the Islamic Republic of Iran, Report of the Board of Governors, IAEA Doc. GOV/2005/67, 24 September 2005.

language used by the IAEA in this resolution was not in compliance with the IAEA statute on the failure to fulfil the provision of the treaty mentioned in Article XII.C.[78] The resolution in point mentions that Iran failed to fulfil its obligations related to the diversion of nuclear material for military purposes, infringement of health or security or other conditions.[79] Also, the resolution did not find any violation of the safeguard agreement thus there were not enough arguments for the issue to be referred to the SC.[80]

It seems that the IAEA used this language due to the background of the development of Iranian nuclear programmes having been kept secret for many years, thus criticizing it even though any diversion of nuclear material had not been proven. In this way, the resolution might have a preventive effect and to bring into supervision as soon as possible all activities related to the Iranian nuclear programmes which would also bring back the trust.[81] This resolution marks and important moment because it would define future relations between the IAEA and Iran on the one hand and also Iranian commitment towards other states on the other. In particular, an open issue would remain the production of Uranium metallic hemispheres which are used only for the purposes of nuclear programmes for military purposes.[82] This was pointed out in a declaration of the SC President in calling Iran to respect the requirements stemming from the resolution of the Board of Governors of 4 February 2006 and also requested a report to be drafted by the Director General of the IAEA regarding this issue within a period of 30 days.[83] The report of the Director General showed that there is still a lack of transparency, including also the lack of explanation regarding the role of the military in the nuclear programmes, access to different documents, the use of multipurpose tools etc.[84] This report influenced the SC to approve the

[78] Supra note 602, pp. 425-426.

[79] Supra note 614, Art. XII.C.

[80] Supra note 602, p. 427.

[81] The resolution required for the suspension of all activities of Uranium enrichment and other related activities, see Implementation of NPT Safeguards Agreement in the Islamic Republic of Iran, Report of the Board of Governors, IAEA Doc. GOV/2006/14, 04 February 2006, para 1.

[82] *Id,* para. 3.

[83] Statement by the President of the Security Council, UN. Doc. S/PRST/2006/15, 29 March 2006.

[84] The resport marked the cooperation by Iran in allowing control at some military objects, see Implementation of the NPT Safeguards Agreement in the Islamic Repubilc of Iran, Report of the Board of Governors, IAEA Doc. GOV/2006/27, 12 June 2006.

first resolution regarding the Iranian nuclear programmes expressing concerns stemming from the IAEA reports and resolutions requesting Iran to suspend all its activities for enriching, reprocessing including research and development under the IAEA verification.[85]

Iran would still be violating the IAEA resolutions and now also in violation of the SC Resolution.[86] In the meantime, because of mounting critic from the IAEA, Iran suspended the application of the additional protocol, even though it had never ratified it in the Iranian assembly but nonetheless the government observed it unilaterally.[87] For this reason, the SC, in an emergency meeting, approved another resolution which, compared to the previous one, used a stronger language requesting that Iran *"shall without further delay suspend the following proliferation sensitive nuclear activities"*.[88] These include activities related to enrichment and reprocessing and also the on-going work on all heavy water projects.[89] At the same time, this resolution for the first time orders sanctions against Iran requesting states to *"take the necessary measures to prevent the supply, sale or transfer directly or indirectly from their territories, or by their nationals or using their flag vessels or aircraft to, or for the use in or benefit of, Iran, and whether or not originating in their territories, of all items, materials, equipment, goods and technology which could contribute to Iran's enrichment-related, reprocessing or heavy water-related activities, or to the development of nuclear weapon delivery systems"*[90]

Based on the reports of the IAEA Board of Governors on Obstacles and lack of cooperation by Iran related to the above mentioned issues, the SC, on 24 March 2007, would approve another set of sanctions against Iran calling of all states and financial institutions not to sign any agreements related to grants, financial assistance or conces-

---

[85] See Security Council Resolution 1969, UN. Doc. S/RES/1969/2006, 31 July 2006.

[86] For mor see Raports of the IAEA Board of Governors on the Implementation of Safeguard Agreement by Iran: IAEA Doc. GOV/2006/27, 12 June 2006; IAEA Doc. GOV/2006/38, 12 June 2006; IAEA Doc. GOV/2006/53, 14 September 2006; dhe IAEA Doc. GOV/2006/64, 14 November 2006.

[87] Supra note 602, pp. 433-435.

[88] Security Council Resolution 1737, UN. Doc. S/RES/1737/2006, 27 Djetor 2006, para. 2.

[89] *Ibid.*

[90] *Id*, para. 3.

sional loans aside from those agreements for humanitarian purposes.[91] These measures seem to gradually have had results by the end of 2007 and beginning of 2008 when IAEA and Iranian officials met several times within Iran giving explanations regarding many issues revolving around its nuclear programmes. This step was welcomed by the SC.[92]

But, this cooperation did not last long with Iran finding itself on an opposite side of cooperation. The last SC resolution on Iran with 38 points contains specific obligations and requests for Iran to fulfil and also for other states and organisations. The first point of this resolution emphasises that Iran had failed to reach the requirements of the IAEA Board of Governors and the SC Resolutions.[93] The Board of Governor's resolution of 2011, states that Iran is still not complying with the IAEA and the SC resolutions.[94] The SC resolutions supported by sanctions appears to have been unable to achieve their objective, to put a halt to enrichment activities and work related to heavy water. This may be attributed to a not adequate language used in these resolutions due to objections by Russia and China who were for a softer and general language.[95] It seems that the problem around the Iranian nuclear programmes is not easy to be solved due to many controversial and complex issues which may have a direct impact on regional peace and security. To achieve this all parties should be engaged at the legal and political level taking into consideration the geopolitical aspect of the region and their concerns and requirements.[96] If Iran did not have any intention to develop nuclear programmes for military purposes it should not be hard for it to be more open and transparent on all aspects of its nuclear programmes. The case of Iran shows the importance of trust in a very sensitive international issue and how hard it is to re-establish it when lost. The only way to do it is for all sides to show a direct approach, sincere and open negotiating and discussing all controversial

[91] *Id*, para. 7.

[92] Security Council Resolution 1804, UN. Doc. S/RES/1804/2008, 03 March 2008.

[93] Security Council Resolution 1929, UN. Doc. S/RES/1929/2010, 09 June 2010, para., 1.

[94] Implementation of the NPT safeguards agreement and relevant provisions of United Nations Security Council resolutions in the Islamic Republic of Iran, IAEA Board of Governors Resolution, IAEA GOV/2011/69, 18 November 2011, para. 1-3.

[95] For more on the result of sanctions against Iran or other states related to their nuclear activities see Cody Coombs, "Blue Morning-Glories in the Sky: Correcting Sanctions to Enforce Nuclear Nonproliferation Iran", *Indiana International & Comparative Law Review*, 19 Ind. Int'l & Comp. L. Rev. 419, 2009.

[96] Supra note 779, p. 74.

issues. Iran has the right to develop its nuclear programmes for peaceful use but it must cooperate with the international community within the NPT regime no matter what its intentions are.

Another case has to do with a state with direct intention to produce nuclear material for military use. North Korea sees its nuclear programmes as essential to protect its territorial integrity and sovereignty which also serves as a survival tool for the regime. The case of this state at the same time may be regarded as the only case where the withdrawal from the NPT regime involved opening different issues related to the right of states to withdrawal from the regime and its subsequent obligations.

VI.3 A BLOW FROM INSIDE AGAINST THE NON-PROLIFERATION TREATY: THE CASE OF THE DEMOCRATIC PEOPLE'S REPUBLIC OF KOREA

The programme of the Democratic People's Republic of Korea (DPRK or North Korea) originates from 1950 when this sate signed an agreement with the former USSR (1956) and China (1959), according to which the USSR would offer support in the establishment of a nuclear research centre in the city of Yongbyon, while China would give its support mainly in the field of Uranium ore research in North Korea.[97] As a result, North Korea managed to build its first nuclear reactor for scientific purposes in 1956 in Yongbyon. The second similar reactor would be built later with its own resources in 1976.[98] In 1987, North Korea built one of its two radiochemical labs with a relatively high level of reprocessing capacities. The revelation of these reactors increased international concerns and with Russian help and pressure coming from the US North Korea was pushed to enter the safeguard regime with the IAEA enabling international inspectors to verify its activities.[99]

---

[97] Supra note 9, pp. 82-83.

[98] To fulfil its needs for raw material North Korea opened a Uranium mine, see supra note 553, p. 231.

[99] Activities of the raciochemical lab were discovered by the US intelligence service at the beginning of 1990s, see *Id,* pp. 231-232.

The safeguard agreement was signed in 1992 according to which "*The Democratic People's Republic of Korea undertakes, pursuant to paragraph 1 of Article III of the Treaty, to accept safeguards, in accordance with the terms of this Agreement, on all source or special fissionable material in all peaceful nuclear activities within its territory, under its Jurisdiction or carried out under its control anywhere, for the exclusive purpose of verifying that such material is not diverted to nuclear weapons or other nuclear explosive devices*".[100] North Korea agreed to enter the regime after the US gave their guarantees not to use their nuclear weapons against North Korea and that such weapons would not be put into the hands of the Republic of Korea (RK or South Korea).[101] Earlier, on 12 December 1985, North Korea became party to the NPT, 8 years after signing it on 20 July 1977, which enabled it to benefit from an agreement with the former USSR in the building a nuclear reactor with a capacity of 440 MW(e), in the city of Sinpo.[102]

The existence of nuclear programmes on the Korean peninsula is a highly sensitive issue, taking into consideration the critical relations between North and South Korea, from their division by parallel 38 in 1954.[103] Possession of a nuclear programme by one side and the possibility of using it for military purposes followed by a big mistrust between these two states may very easily lead to an arms race between them. To prevent this, before agreeing to the safeguard agreement, these two states on 20 January 1992, signed a "Joint Declaration of South and North Korea on the Denuclearisation of the Korean Peninsula."[104] This declaration prohibited the testing, production, receiving, possession, deposition, deployment or the use of nuclear weapons and that the nuclear energy would be used only for peaceful purposes.[105] This declaration expressly prohibited these states from possessing any nu-

[100] Agreement of 30 January 1992 between the Government of the Democratic People's Republic of Korea and the International Atomic Energy Agency for the Application of Safeguards in Connection with the Treaty on the Non-Proliferation of Nuclear Weapons, IAEA Doc. INFCIRC/403, May 1992.

[101] Raven Winters, "Preventing Repeat Offenders: North Korea's Withdrawal and the Need for Revision to the Nuclear Non-Proliferation Treaty", *Vanderbilt Journal of Transnational Law*, 38 Vand. J. Transnat'l L. 1499, November 2005, pp. 1508-1509.

[102] Supra note 9, pp. 82-83.

[103] For more see David Edwin Mathews, *The Division of Korea: How it Came to Be and the Possibility of Unification* (University of Adelaide, Department of Politics, Australia, 1998).

[104] Joint Declaration of South and North Korea on the Denuclearization of the Korean Peninsula, 19 February 1992, publikuar n/ http://cns.miis.edu/inventory/pdfs/aptkoreanuc.pdf.

[105] *Id*, para 1 and 2.

clear enrichment activity, they *"shall not possess nuclear reprocessing and Uranium enrichment facilities."* [106] According to this provision, this agreement went beyond the NPT regime which does not foresee the prohibition of possessing facilities for nuclear reprocessing and Uranium enrichment.[107] To verify these obligations, a joint nuclear control commission was established with a territorial mandate over the whole Korean peninsula.[108] Unfortunately, this agreement never materialized being dragged over never ending negotiations dealing with its interpretation and implementation without any common solution.[109]

When the IAEA started with its inspections, they immediately revealed sensitive issues related to the North Korean nuclear programmes regarding the declaration of Plutonium and the issue of nuclear waste which did not match the IAEA analysis. According to the analyses by the IAEA inspectors, North Korea was in possession of undeclared Plutonium which led them to ask for permission to access other undeclared facilities which may have been used to store nuclear waste. In order to solve these issues, the Board of Governors requested North Korea to give permission for a special inspection but was refused by the latter.[110]

The notification for withdrawal from the NPT regime pushed the IAEA to conclude that North Korea is not respecting the safeguard agreement and Article XII.C of its Statute. In the report of the IAEA General Director on behalf of the Board of Governors, North Korea was found to be "*in non-compliance with its obligations under its Safeguards Agreement with the Agency*".[111] However, the IAEA, still, was

[106] *Id*, para. 3.

[107] Supra note 397, Art. II. This article bans diversion of fission materials but not possession of facilities use for resprocessing Uranium, shih also Geoffrey S. Carslo, "An offer They Can't Refuse? The Security Council Tells North Korea to Re-Sign the Nuclear Non-Proliferation Treaty", *Columbia Journal of Transnational Law*, 46 Colum. J. Transat'l L. 420, 2008, pp. 433-434.

[108] Supra note 857, pika 4.

[109] Geoffrey S. Carslo, "An offer They Can't Refuse? The Security Council Tells North Korea to Re-Sign the Nuclear Non-Proliferation Treaty", *Columbia Journal of Transnational Law*, 46 Colum. J. Transat'l L. 420, 2008, pp. 433-434.

[110] *Ibid.*

[111] Compare The Non-Compliance of the Democratic People's Republic of Korea with the Agreement Between the IAEA and the Democratic People's Republic of Korea for the Application of Safeguards in Connection with the Treaty on the Non-Proliferation of Nuclear Weapons, Report by the Director General of the IAEA on Behalf of the Board of Governors to all Members of the Agency, IAEA Doc. INFCIRC/419, 8 April 1993 and The Agency's inability to verify the Non-Diversion of Material Required to be Safeguarded, Report by the Director

not able to conclude that there is any diversion of the nuclear material. At the same time the Board of Governors decided that the issue should be sent to the SC for discussion.[112]

North Korea considered the IAEA report as threatening and announced its withdrawal effectively from January 1993 and also notified the SC.[113]The SC, condemning the decision to withdraw, found it to be in noncompliance with the NPT.[114] Such an action moved the world diplomacy, in particular the US, which at that time had run into a very constrained relationship with North Korea and at certain moments it seemed that military confrontation among the US and North Korea is immediate.[115] As a result of negotiations between the US and North Korea, on 21 October 1994, a framework agreement was achieved foreseeing specific provisions addressing both states.[116] According to this agreement, the US would help to finance and supply a project to build a light water reactor[117] and at the same time, these two states would be engaging in reaching bilateral agreements for cooperation in nuclear programmes for peaceful use.[118] On the other side, North Korea was obliged to give guarantees to halt its activities with graffite moderated reactors and that in future it would demolish other facilities related to it.[119] In the end, the US gave guarantees to North Korea for the non-use of nuclear weapons which was very crucial in establishing trust between them.[120] Signing this agreement seemed to have relaxed the relations between these two parties inciting a cooperation lasting until the beginnings of 2000.[121] In the meantime, during the 1990s, North Korea

General of the IAEA on Behalf of the Board of Governors to all Members of the Agency, IAEA Doc. INFCIRC/419, 8 April 1993, para. 2 operational paragraph 1.

[112] *Id*, para. 1 operational paragraph 2 and 3.

[113] Supra note 855, p. 1509.

[114] Security Council Resolution 825, UN. Doc. S/RES/825, 11 May 1993, pika 1 dhe 2. The resolution call on Norht Korea to review its announcement for withdrawal and to abide by the NPT.

[115] Supra note 855, p. 1510.

[116] See Agreed Framework of 21 October 1994 between the United States of America and the Democratic People's Republic of Korea, IAEA Doc. INFCIRC/457, 2 November 1994.

[117] *Id*, Art. I (1) para. 1.

[118] *Id*, Art. I (1) para. 3. According to Art. I (2) para. 1 and 2, the US will supply North Korea with heating and energy fuel a the measure of 500,000 metric tons per year until this state construct its light water reactor.

[119] *Id*, Art. I (3) para 1-3.

[120] *Id*, neni III (1).

[121] According to this agreement the US established a commission called the Organization for Energy Development of Korean Penninsula. Up to 31 July 2000 6 units of nuclear facilities within the Korean standard were operational or under construction, see Eric Yong-Joong

managed to benefit from the A.Q. Khan network which supplied it with gas centrifuges for Uranium enrichment, other necessary materials and technical support.[122]

In 2001, the situation took another direction. At the end of that year there were reports coming out of the American Intelligent Service stating that North Korea had secretly started its activities in the construction of a facility for Uranium enrichment.[123] After this revelation, President George Bush decided to suspend deliveries of energy fuel to produce energy and for heating accusing North Korea of violation of the framework agreement.[124] In 2002, North Korea admitted the existence of its nuclear enrichment programme and by the end of this year it withdrew from the policy of freezing its nuclear activities.[125]

On 29 November 2002, the IAEA Board of Governors approved a resolution calling on North Korea to cooperate and to explain its Uranium enrichment programmes.[126] The resolution "*Deplores the DPRK's repeated public statements that it is entitled to possess nuclear weapons, which runs contrary to its obligations under the NPT not to develop or possess nuclear weapons*".[127] As a response, North Korea accused the IAEA of a biased and unjust stance with a formal notification of its decision to withdraw from its policy of freezing nuclear activities because of US suspension in delivering fuel to North Korea foreseen in the framework agreement.[128]

In the midst of an escalating situation, North Korea officially announced its withdrawal from the NPT regime emphasising that it "*no*

Lee, "The Six-Party Talks and the North Korean Nuclear Dispute Resolution Under the IAEA Safeguards Regime", *University of Hawaii Asian-pacific Law & Policy Journal*, 5 Asian-Pacific L. & Pol'y J. 101, 2004, pp. 110-114.

[122] Supra note 771, p. 72.

[123] Supra note 553, p. 232.

[124] Supra note 849, p. 430. While addressin the Congress, President Bush put an emphasis on Norht Korea as part of the axis of evil, see The President's State of the Union Address, 29 January 2002, The White House.

[125] "DPRK Factsheet", IAEA, visited on 30 February 2012 http://www.iaea.org/newscenter/focus/iaeadprk/fact_sheet_may2003.shtml.

[126] This followed an earlier request for negotiations to explain developments in North Korea without any response, see The implementation of IAEA safeguards in the Democratic People's Republic of Korea (DPRK), Resolution of the Board of Governors, IAEA UN. Doc. GOV/2002/60, 29 November 2002.

[127] *Id*, para. 11.

[128] Supra note 878.

longer remains bound by the NPT, allowing country's security and the dignity of our nation to be infringed upon."[129] At the same time, it announced its withdrawal from the safeguard agreement with the IAEA and expelled its inspectors who were, at the time, present in the state on their verification mission.[130] According to Article X of the NPT, a state should refer to extraordinary situations for withdrawal for which North Korea brought as justification its self-defence from the USA, giving guarantees at the same time that it has no plans to produce any nuclear weapons.[131] On 9 June 2003, it declared that if the US continued with their policy of threat to use nuclear weapons against North Korea, it would be left no other option than to build its deterring nuclear power.[132] In the meantime, the US were accused of inciting on purpose the special inspection on the Korean peninsula while deploying weapons with depleted Uranium in the same territory which are prohibited by international law.[133] North Korea also accused the US of violation of the framework agreement in the provisions specifying the supply of fuel and opposed to the American concept of preventive strikes which may eventually be used against North Korea.[134]

At the Board of Governors meeting held on 12 February 2003, a resolution was adopted which once more declared that North Korea continues to be in violation of the NPT and referred the issue for discussion in the SC.[135] In other resolutions, this organ, continuously, requested North Korea to stop its nuclear programmes activities.[136]

To manage the situation, the world diplomacy moved in, in the form of six party talks.[137] In August of 2003, the six states came together, the US, North Korea, China, Russia, Japan and North Korea, in a

[129] Supra note 855, p. 1510.

[130] Supra note 553, p. 232.

[131] Supra note 855, p. 1510.

[132] Charles J. Moxcley, Jr. "The Sword in the Mirror: The Lawfulness of North Korea's use and Threat of Use of Nuclear Weapons Based on the United States Legitimization of Nuclear Weapons", *Fordham International Law Journal*, 27 Fordham Int'l L. J. 1379, April 2004, p. 1388.

[133] Supra note 855, p. 1510.

[134] *Ibid.*

[135] See, IAEA Board of Governors Adopts Resolution on Safeguards in North Korea, IAEA Media Advisory, 2003/48, 12 February 2003.

[136] See IAEA Resolutions, IAEA Doc. GC(48)/RES/15, September 2004; and IAEA Doc. GC(49)/Res/14, September 2005.

[137] Initially, in April 2003 they started three party talk between the US, North Korea and China with later involvement of South Korea, Russia and Japan, see supra note 875, p. 118.

bid to solve the issue of North Korea's nuclear programmes. This came at a convenient time when North Korea was seeking to normalize its relations with the US for economic gains.[138] The negotiations at this level continue still and in the fourth round held in two sittings during the months of July and September of 2005 they managed to issue a joint declaration.[139] In this declaration, North Korea was committed to abandon all its nuclear programmes and would return to the NPT and IAEA in a short time.[140] On the other side, the US committed themselves to the fact that there would not be any nuclear weapon in the Korean peninsula and that they do not have any intention of attacking North Korea with nuclear or conventional weapons.[141]

The purpose of the declaration was well founded, but the language used was not a legal one while the agreement was drafted in the form of a declaration. North Korea took "commitments" to halt all nuclear programmes, which meant that it would still depend on its will and readiness as to when and how this would be achieved. On the other side, the US left many open issues related to economic incentives to be made available for North Korea when fulfilling its commitments. According to this declaration, North Korea "may" benefit economically in the field of energy, trade and bilateral or multilateral investments.[142]

Despite these achievements, during 2006 North Korea would test its ballistic missile and what is more important, would conduct its first and second nuclear test on 5 July 2006 and 9 October 2006 respectively.[143] These actions would set immediately into motion the SC which would approve two resolutions to respond to the new circumstances. With the resolution 1695 adopted in 5 July 2006, the SC condemns the launch of ballistic missiles and requests North Korea to halt its ballistic missiles programmes and to go back to six party talks.[144] The nuclear tests impacted more on the minds of the SC members which approved a resolution with a firmer and stricter language

---

[138] *Ibid.*

[139] Daniel A. Piknktson, "North Korea's Nuclear Weapons Programmes and the Sixth-Party Talks", Nuclear Threat Initiative, 1 April 2006, http://www.nti.org/analysis/articles/north-koreas-nuclear-weapons/

[140] *Ibid.*

[141] *Ibid.*

[142] *Ibid.*

[143] Supra note 878.

[144] Security Council Resolution 1695, UN. Doc. S/RES/1695 (2006), 15 July 2006, para. 1, 2 and 6.

including also the approval of international sanctions on 14 October 2006.[145] The Resolution 1718 affirmed that nuclear weapons proliferation presents a risk to international peace and security and that North Korea *"cannot have the status of a nuclear-weapon state in accordance with the Treaty on the Non-Proliferation of Nuclear Weapons."*[146] This would mean that even if this state comes back to the NPT regime as a member, it would not be accepted as a nuclear state because it would be considered as an NPT violator.[147] In compliance with this, the SC decides that *"DPRK shall suspend all activities related to its ballistic missile programme and in this context re-establish its pre-existing commitments to a moratorium on missile launching"*.[148] Also, the resolution requests that North Korea *"shall abandon all nuclear weapons and existing nuclear programmes in a complete, verifiable and irreversible manner"*, including all other existing material for mass destruction and ballistic missiles.[149] According to this point, the resolution goes beyond the NPT by referring to all other weapons of mass destruction. Such language is very rare for the SC, because never before had the SC, acting under Chapter VII of the Charter, attempted to compel a state to become party to a treaty.[150]

Furthermore, Resolution 1718 foresaw the establishment of sanctions against North Korea asking all Member States to prevent direct or indirect supply of heavy weapons, including artillery, helicopters and rockets, and some other items which may be used for the development of nuclear, ballistic or weapons of mass destruction programmes.[151]

This strong reaction from the SC, brought North Korea back to six party talks which, during negotiations in February 2007, managed to have North Korea agree to stop and put the verification seal and eventually to abandon its nuclear facility in Yongbyon, including the reprocessing facility.[152] In compliance with this, North Korea, in July 2007, shut down its five nuclear facilities in Yongbyon, on which the IAEA inspector put the verification seals and installed adequate mon-

---

[145] Security Council Resolution 1718, UN. Doc. S/RES/1718 (2006), 14 October 2006.

[146] *Ibid.*

[147] Supra note 863, p. 439.

[148] Supra note 899, para. 5.

[149] *Id*, para. 6.

[150] Supra note 863, p. 440.

[151] Supra note 899 para. 8. The resolution enforced sanctions on *"luxury goods"* in an attempt to attack Northe Korean political elite and a placed a travel and asset ban on high ranking North Korean officials.

[152] Supra note 878.

itoring cameras.[153] However, a report by the Director General in June 2008 roused some concerns related to North Korean activities, which were deemed to be unjust by the latter leading it to request the removal of the verification seals and monitoring cameras. At the same time, it requested the removal of inspectors which occurred on 15 April 2009 after the withdrawal of verification seals and monitoring cameras.[154]

The death of Kim Jong Il in December 2011[155], may have increased the hopes that his successor/son Kim Jon Un would change his nuclear policy and the stance of this state against the west. At the end of February 2012, the new president accepted suspending all its nuclear testing and nuclear enrichment and for the permission of international inspectors to monitor and verify activities at its main nuclear reactor. In exchange the US promised to help North Korea to overcome food shortages.[156] However, it seems that this was also a diplomatic move because very soon, North Korea would enter into a new adventure of ballistic missile testing against international pressure not to do so.[157]

At a certain level it seems that North Korea uses its nuclear programmes to achieve its political aims to the benefit of the political party in power, to preserve the reign of its elite and threat to other states against a possible attack. North Korea, remains today one of the most isolated states in the world and cooperation with it is still problematic. However, in certain circumstances when North Korea faces difficulties such as food shortages, it becomes more cooperative in a bid to overcome its problems in return for talks. It seems that despite guarantees offered by the US and South Korea for non-intervention in North Korea, the latter shows a lack of trust because in this way it also keeps the current political elite undisturbed and in power.

---

[153] *Ibid.*

[154] *Ibid.*

[155] "North Korean Leader Kim Jong Il Dead, state TV report", *CNN*, 18 December 2011, visited on 20 February 2012, http://articles.cnn.com/2011-12-18/asia/world_asia_north-korea-leader-dead_1_state-tv-reports-north-korean-leader-kim-jong?_s=PM:ASIA.

[156] "North Korea Agrees to Freeze Nuclear Work: US to Give Aid", *The New York Times*, 29 February 2012, visited on 30 March 2012, http://www.nytimes.com/2012/03/01/world/asia/us-says-north-korea-agrees-to-curb-nuclear-work.html?_r=1&hp=&pagewanted=print.

[157] The test was a failure but it showed the determination of this state *vis a vis* it obligations toward international community, see Choe Sang-Hun, "North Korean Rocket Fails Moment after Liftoff", *The New York Times*, 12 April 2012, visited on11 June 2012, http://www.nytimes.com/2012/04/13/world/asia/north-korea-launches-rocket-defying-world-warnings.html?_r=1&hp.

Cases previously mentioned in this chapter present concrete problems in the proliferation of nuclear energy and technology but a very serious issue revolves around the states which suffer from internal struggles and on the verge of collapse and known as weak states. The problem multiplies when such states have nuclear capabilities. States facing problems with a lack of adequate state authority in the economic and political aspect are necessarily affected in other fields, such as military as a primary concern. Here, the issue develops on how to save the leak of sensitive information and fission materials from a state with no adequate political control. The case of Pakistan and Russia during the 1990s reflects, perhaps in the best way, this issue.

VI.4 THE RISK OF PROLIFERATION FROM WEAK STATES

Nothing, perhaps, presents more concern for nuclear proliferation than that of weak states in possession of nuclear material and weapons undergoing internal crisis and struggle, related to internal and external politics, such as the case of Russia after the collapse of the former USSR and Pakistan today. In the case of Russia, the problem appeared after the former USSR broke into several independent states followed by an internal political and economic struggle during transitioning phase. In the case of Pakistan, it is about a political struggle coming from a lack of political cohesion and also the reflection of the crisis in Afghanistan.

The good think, if we dare to say so, that of the activities of A.Q. Khan was that this network cooperated only with state actors, at least as far as we are aware today. In the case of weak states, nuclear materials may fall into the hands of different criminal and terrorist organisations with the intention of using them to achieve their political aims. This is the worst nightmare of every individual and presents a threat to international peace and security. If in the possession of nuclear materials, criminal and terrorist organisations may easily construct an improvised nuclear bomb capable of causing huge human and material damage.[158]

The problem revolving around the weak states and illegal activities related to nuclear materials became visible during the 1990s. The vulnerability of personnel and nuclear material created great opportunities for various criminal organisations which showed willingness and determination to get hold of nuclear material. To trace such activities, the IAEA established in 1995 a data base for illegal trafficking and other unauthorized activities related to fission materials not under regular control.[159] From January 1993 to December 2011 this database reported 2164 incidents out of which 399 cases had to do with unauthorized possession and other criminal activities with fission materials. This includes 16 cases involving HEA or Plutonium. In 2011 alone it reported 147 different incidents of this nature.[160] The total amount of confiscated HEU and Plutonium during 1991 to 2006 reached the level of 38 kg.[161]

Securing fission materials from different clandestine activities requires international cooperation. To secure such material, states agreed to design specific legal measures which set the standard and level on security such as: the Convention on Physical Protection of Nuclear Material and its amendments; the International Convention for the Suppression of Acts of Nuclear Terrorism; the Safeguards Guarantees and its protocols; the SC Resolution 1540 (2004), 1673 (2006) and 1373 (2001). Also, this legal framework includes another instrument, although not binding from the strict legal viewpoint, but very important: the Code of Conduct on the Safety and Security of Radioactive Sources and Supplementary Guidance on the Import and Export of Radioactive Sources.[162]

Having regard for these international agreements, one has to bear in mind that in the end the state is at the core of international relations and responsible to discharge its duties stemming from such

[158] Nuclear Security Report 2007: Meassures to Protect Against Nuclear Terrorism, The IAEA Board of Governors General Conference, pika 10, IAEA Doc. GOV/2007/43-GC (51)15, 15 August 2007.

[159] This data base includes data related to incidens with unauthorised dealing with nuclear radioactive materials, their supply, possession, use, transfer or disposal, see, "Illicit Trafficing Database", IAEA visited on15 December 2012 http://www-ns.iaea.org/security/itdb.asp. From 31 December 2011, 113 states take part in following activities with thise data base.

[160] *Ibid.*

[161] Supra note 771, pp. 125-126.

[162] Supra note 912, para. 13-14.

agreements. A state should possess at any time, adequate mechanisms for its proper functioning and implementing international agreements. This means that if a state party to a treaty, may reach a situation that due to its internal problems it is not possible to implement international agreements. The issue becomes more complex in cases when internal political and economic systems lead to social disturbances and weakening of state structures. The case of Russia during the 1990s and Pakistan may be within this meaning.

The problem of large stockpiles of fission material and its security in Russia started with the collapse of the USSR. The USSR was the main foe of the US and its allies which created an international system known as the bipolar world. During this period, the two blocks entered into an arms race leading to the creation of huge nuclear weapons and material stockpiles on the two sides in a bid to create the so called nuclear deterrence by threatening the enemy with huge retaliation in case it threatens or uses nuclear weapons.[163] In December of 1991, the USSR collapsed marking at the same time the end of the Cold War which was greeted with huge enthusiasm all around the world and the hope that with this, the threat to world devastation by nuclear weapons had come to an end.[164] At that time the USSR was in possession of around 30,000 nuclear warheads dispersed around its territory, included here territories which became independent after the collapse[165] and with it around 603 metric tons of HEU and Plutonium.[166]

After the collapse of the former USSR, Russia and the newly created independent states entered into a difficult phase of radical social, political, economic and legal transformation.[167] Luckily, all these states acknowledged the premise to get rid of the nuclear weapons remaining in their territories,

---

[163] For more on bipolar relationship and nuclear deterrence see Robert Powell, *Nuclear Deterrence: Theory: The Search for Credibility* (Cambridge University Press, USA, 1990).

[164] Wendy L. Mirsky, "The Link Between Russian Organized Crime and Nuclear-Weapons Proliferation: Fighting Crime and Ensuring International Security", *University of Pensylvania Journal of Internationl Business Law*, 16. U. Pa. J. Int'l Bus. L. 749, 1995, p. 750.

[165] *Ibid.*

[166] Nuclear Non-Proliferation: Security of Russia's Nuclear Material Improving; Further Enhancements Needed, United States General Accounting Office, Report to Congressional Requester, February 2011, p. 1. For construction of a nuclear weapon it is needed around 25 kg Uranium or 8 kg. Plutonium.

[167] After dissolution of the USSR 16 new states were created: Armenia, Azerbaijan, Belarus, Estonia, Georgia, Kazakhstan, Kyrgistan, Latvia, Lithuania, Modlavia, Russia, Tajigista, Turkmenistan, Ukraine and Uzbekistan, see supra note 918, p. 750.

thus making Russia the only successor of all former nuclear weapons and materials.[168] The social, political, economic and legal vacuum left in Russia created a lot of space for different groups to benefit from the situation in advancing their interests. Amongst them, organized crime emerged in Russia as the most dangerous feature in Russia during the 1990s.[169] The vulnerability of fission materials came at the centre of attention while organized crime was ready to find all trade roots and potential buyers on the European black market for financial profit.[170] Difficult economic conditions, the late payment of salaries for employees in different nuclear programmes increased their vulnerability and the risk of them being the source of supply of nuclear material and other sources for criminal organisations.[171]

Amongst the attractive fission material for organized crime were materials situated in different nuclear weapons laboratories, civilian scientific centres and Russian marine fuel stocks.[172] Material situated in these places was not very radioactive meaning that persons involved in this crime did not need special instruments to commit their acts and also these materials could be carried easily in different containers or as components of dismantled weapons.[173]

One of the most noticeable incidents was that of 10 May 1994 when the German police arrested a businessman in Berlin Tegel Airport with 6 grams of 99.7 % pure Plutonium content which may be used for military purposes.[174] A few months earlier the German police had arrested a Columbian and three Spanish citizens at the Munich airport carrying with them a few hundred grams of Litium-6 and 400 grams of 87% pure

[168] Up to the year 1992 all of the strategic nuclear arsenal was withdrawn from states formerly belonging to USSR including the withdrawal of nuclea weapons from Mongolia, see Owen R. Cote, Jr. "The Russian Nuclear Achipelago", n/ *Avoiding Russian Anarchy: Containing the Threat of Russian Loose Nuclear Weapons and Fissile Material* ed. Graham T. Allison, Owen R. Cote, Jr., Richard A. Falkenrath, Steven E. Miller (Center for Science and International Affairs, Harvard, Massachusetts, 1999), p. 179.

[169] Supra note 918, p. 752.

[170] *Id*, p. 753.

[171] Supra note 920, p. 5.

[172] *Ibid.*

[173] *Ibid.*

[174] Barry Kellman & David S. Gualtieri, "Barricading the Nuclear Window: A legal Regime to Curtail Nuclear Smuggling", *The University of Illinois Law Reviews*, 1996 U. Ill. L. Rev. 667, 1996, p. 672. The high purity of Plutonium indicated that this material may originated from a scientific lab. Further investigation by police came with a conclusion that this person had connections with trade organizations in Bulgaria suspected of conducting illegal narcotics and arms trade and that a possible buyer migh have been an Iraqi person.

Plutonium and according to American sources this material may have come from a Physics laboratory in Moscow.[175] In another action in December 1994, the Czech police in Prague arrested three former nuclear employees from the Czech Republic, Belarus and the Ukraine who were carrying with them 3 kg of HEU with 88% purity and suspected of originating from the Russian Navy because it was carried in a container with labels of the USSR Black Sea Fleet in Odessa.[176] In another incident in the Ukraine, the police stopped two Russians with around 6 kg of Uranium U-235 and made some other confiscations at different times and places.[177]

Below are listed some of the most noticeable incidents involving nuclear material during the 1990s;

- 1992- in Podolsk a technician stole 1.5 kg HEU
- 1993-in Murmansk, a Russian navy official stole 4.5 kg HEU
- 1993-according to the German magazine Stern, a Russian counterintelligence officer stated that North Korea smuggled 56 kg of Plutonium from Russia, but it was never verified.
- 1993-a thief stole 1.8 kg of HEU from a navy facility in Russia.
- 1994-a small quantity of Plutonium produced in Russia was confiscated at the Munich airport.
- 1994-the police in Prague confiscated 2.7 kg of HEU produced in Russia
- 1998-Russian Foreign Intelligence Service traced down and prevented an attack in Chelyabinsk, one of the most important Russian laboratories. According to Russian sources the aim was to grab 18.5 kg HEU from that laboratory.[178]

---

[175] *Id*, p. 673, German agents offered 250 million dollars for purchasing of that materials but they could not managed to verify the origin of tha material.

[176] *Ibid.*

[177] *Id*, pp. 673-674.

[178] Jack Carravelli, *Nuclear Insecurity: Understanding the Threat from Rouge Nations and Terrorists* (Praeger Security International, USA, 2008), p. 17.

These cases show that during the 1990s the security level of nuclear material was very low. But, what increased the level of vulnerability of these materials was the fact that employees in different nuclear facilities became part of this crime. Another important question one may ask is how much is the quantity and quality of nuclear material stolen. Maybe what we know today is only the tip of an iceberg. How true may be the report of the Russian Foreign Intelligence Service about the smuggling of 54 kg of Plutonium to North Korea but never documented.[179] The process of accurate accounting of produced fission material and that which is in the possession of a state is very important. In cases when a state possesses large quantities of fission material, only a small margin of error may lead to major consequences. During the US assistance to Kazakhstan, during the recuperation of HEU in a project called Sapphire, they discovered 104% of the fission material declared in the country, which is 4% more than what official documents had said initially.[180] If one makes such a comparison with a 4% margin of error in the case of Russia for example may be translated into an unaccounted quantity of fission material which may be used for the production of around 4,000 nuclear weapons.[181]

With regards to the potential destination of smuggled nuclear material, very little is known, but it is supposed that potential buyers may be state actors, terrorist organisations, secessionist movements and different extreme religious organisations. Up to now, the destination of such material could not be determined.[182]

Having regard to this problem and the seriousness related to the fission material in Russia but also in other countries, the US from the beginning of the 1990s established programmes implemented by the Department of Defence[183], Department of Energy, the National Nu-

---

[179] Graham T. Allison, Owen R. Cote, Jr., Richard A. Falkenrath, Steven E. Miller, *Avoiding Russian Anarchy: Containing the Threat of Russian Loose Nuclear Weapons and Fisile Material* (Center for Science and International Affairs, Harvard, Masachusets, 1999), p. 38.

[180] *Ibid.*

[181] *Ibid.*

[182] Supra note 771, p. 134.

[183] The Department of Defence established a programme Cooperative Threat Reduction in 1991 to help Russia and other newly independent states formely belonging to USSR, while in 1992 the US and Russia have sigend a so called "rainbow agreement" called Agreement Between the USA a the Russina Federation concerging the Safe and Secure Transportation, Storage and Destruction of Weapons and the Prevention of Weapons Prolifeartion of June17, 1992, see. Nuclear Nonproliferation: Comprehensive U.S. Planning and Better Foreign Cooperation

clear Safety and the State Department to help these states secure their nuclear stockpile.[184] These programmes showed good results and today it is believed that the level of security of nuclear material and weapons in Russia is at a high level.[185] From the American viewpoint, it is still considered that, at least, some programmes should continue their work until 2020 in order to achieve their aim.[186]

While, today, Russia is seen as a state with adequate security measures safeguarding their nuclear materials and weapons, attention has shifted to other countries undergoing similar political, social and economic crises such as Pakistan today. The case of Russia tells us how risky an internal struggle of a state may be and that immediate measures should be taken in order to prevent crimes related to illegal trafficking of fission materials. This is confirmed by the A.Q. Khan network, the intensity of which reached its peak during the 1990s when Pakistan was at the height of its internal struggle. After coming to power, President Pervez Musharraf managed to somehow consolidate the state impacting also the risk of nuclear material or weapons flowing into non-state actors. However, Pakistan, still facing difficult political, economic and social problems, the war in Afghanistan and the impact of the global war on terrorism, stands in a difficult position which may put its nuclear material and weapons in a vulnerable position.[187]

According to a report, Pakistan is an unsustainable state facing violence and it is also the centre of "global jihad".[188] The Pakistani government is faced with problems to stretch its authority over its total territory while the military services and intelligence services are faced with problems of infiltration from certain jihadi elements and other such organisations operating in this state.[189] The situation in Pakistan presents risks in three different dimensions: the risk of stealing from the military nuclear arsenal by terrorist organisations; potential transfer of a nuclear

---

Needed to Secure Vulnerable Nuclear Materials Worldwide, US Governmental Accountability Office, Report to the Chairmen and Ranking Member, Subcommittee on Energy and Water Development, Committee on Appropriations, House of Representatives, December 2010, p. 5.

[184] *Id*, pp. 3-4.

[185] *Id*, p. 20.

[186] *Id*, pp. 20-24.

[187] Supra note 771, pp. 65-92.

[188] Jeffrey Goldberg & Marc Ambinder, "The Ally from Hell", *The Atlantic Magazine*, December 2011, http://www.theatlantic.com/magazine/archive/2011/12/the-ally-from-hell/308730/.

[189] *Ibid.*

weapon to Iran; getting hold of a nuclear weapon from groups within the military structures during political struggles.[190] During an interview, President Musharraf let it be understood that the Pakistani military arsenal may be vulnerable if radical Islamic forces were to come to power.[191] This may be a political statement but should be taken with great concern.

The vulnerability of nuclear material is increased when taking into consideration that most facilities used for the production of nuclear material and weapons are located in the western side of the state, where different terrorist organisations are present and active.[192] The Pakistani policy for constant redeployment of nuclear weapons is of great concern because in many cases they are placed in inadequate storage. This policy is a result of concerns of attack by the US as regarded by Pakistan. Also, it is a result of a fear from the Indian threat in particular after an eventual terrorist attack in India in which case India may retaliate eventually against the Pakistani nuclear weapons stockpile.[193] In certain cases there was information stating that the redeployment of such weapons was carried out by an inadequate and unsafe vehicles by using vehicles designed for civil use.[194] Such a policy is of great concern due to the fact that terrorist organisations may improvise an attack against such nuclear stockpiles with the aim of getting them on the move for redeployment and in which case they could organize an ambush against military convoys carrying those nuclear weapons and put such a weapon into their hands.[195] Up to now, there is no information or data of possible leaks of nuclear materials or weapons from Pakistan into the hands of clandestine organisations, however much remains to be done by Pakistanis to take security measures to assure the world that their nuclear material and weapons are secure enough.

The case of weak states is of great concern for the international community which should cooperate more at the international level to

---

[190] *Ibid.*

[191] "Pervez Muhsaraf on Pakistan Nuclear Weapons" interview with, Fareed Zakaria, *CNN GPS*, 04 November 2011, visited on 10 June 2012, http://globalpublicsquare.blogs.cnn.com/2011/11/05/this-week-on-gps-pervez-musharraf-on-pakistani-nuclear-weapons-plus-bill-gates-and-arne-duncan-on-education/.

[192] Pakistan's Nuclear Weapons Arsenal Safety Endangered, Report by Dr. Subhash Kapila for South Asia Analysis Group, 25 May 2011.

[193] *Ibid.*

[194] Supra note 942.

[195] Supra note 946.

design specific programmes and protection for their nuclear material. These programmes should not only relate to the physical protection of nuclear material but in the management of knowhow and knowledge which exists in the minds of many individuals engaged in nuclear programmes. A state with nuclear capabilities which may be highly vulnerable to internal struggles in cases of regime change in the future is North Korea. Maybe this is the main reason why the US and other states are not greatly interested in a radical change of the regime in this state, which in turn uses this situation to retain power. Concrete programmes should be designed in order to manage future uncertainties and this should be a global endeavour and should not be supported actively by only a few states, because these issues present problems with global character. An essential role should be always played by the IAEA.

CHAPTER VII

NUCLEAR TERRORISM: PREVENTION AND THE FIGHT AGAINST IT

VII.1 NUCLEAR TERRORISM AS A REAL INTERNATIONAL CONCERN IN THE CONTEMPORARY WORLD

The most dangerous case scenario would perhaps be the one when a terrorist organisation succeeded in getting hold of enough nuclear material to enable it to build an improvised nuclear devise and to use it to achieve its aims. Such a device may be dropped on big cities crowded with people by persons without a known identity making it very difficult for state agents to react and catch the persons responsible.[1] This scenario draws huge concerns because non-state agents arc involved as opposed to state agents who are indefinable and have specific and open policies.[2] In a joint US-Russian report on the evaluation of nuclear terror risk, this feature is considered to be very real and calls on all states to change their stance against terrorists because "*If current approaches toward eliminating the threat are not replaced with a sense of urgency and resolve, the question will become not if but when, and on what scale, the first act of nuclear terrorism occurs.*"[3] This risk increases proportionally with the increase in the number of states possessing nuclear weapons or material.[4]

History has shown that states may be deterred from one another because they are placed in an equal overall condition and are identifi-

[1] James C. Kraska, "Adverting Nuclear Terrorism: Building a Global Regime of Co-operative Threat Reduction", *American University International Law Review*, 20 Am. U. Int'l L. Rev. 703, 2005, p. 725.

[2] *Ibid.*

[3] For more see The US-Russia Joint Threat Assessment of Nuclear Terrorism, Report by Belfer Center for Science and International Affairs, Harvard Kennedy School and Institute for US and Canadian Studies, May 2011.

[4] 98-99 % of HEU is located in storgages with a substantial level of security, mainly this includes military facilities, see *Id*, p. 39.

able. The whole concept of nuclear deterrence revolves around intimidation with massive counter action against a possible attacking state which is also known as *Mutually Assured Destruction (MAD)*[5]. In the fight against non-state actors, the concept of deterrence becomes very complicated if not to say it does not exist at all because we have to do with a so called Asymetrix war. In such wars, between state and non-state actors, the prevention of a possible nuclear attack becomes very complex.[6]

A *prima facie* problem in this situation is related to the definition of terrorism for which there is still no international consensus to defining it. This is so because in itself terrorism entails political and emotional elements.[7] Many states label different actions by an opposition as terrorists while many extremists pretend to be victims of state terror.[8] Ordinary criminal organisations may commit a terrorist act such as mafia actions in Italy or actions by drug lords in Columbia, while terrorist organisations may have persons with mental disorders among their ranks who are not able to evaluate their own and organisation's deeds.[9] In certain cases, a person responsible for committing a crime without being identified is considered to be a terrorist or committing a terrorist act such as was the case in 2001 when an unidentified person sent letters containing anthrax addressed to public officials and media personalities in the US.[10] Can such an act be considered as terrorism when the person is not identified yet and thus without being able to determine the purpose of action as one of the main elements of committing such a crime. Unveiling the motive of an identified person is impossible. The motives for taking such actions considered to be terrorist deeds come from different elements such as liberating wars as is

---

[5] For more on this concept see Henry D. Sokolski, *Getting Mad: Nuclear Mutual Assured Destruction, its Origins and Practice* (Strategic Studies Institute, November 2004).

[6] For more on asymmetric war against international terrorism see Ivan Sascha Sheehan, *When Terrorism and Counterterrorism Clash: The War on Terror and the Transformation of Terrorist Activity* (Cambria Press, New Jork, 2007).

[7] Angus Martyn, *The Right of Self-Defence under International Law: The Response to the Terrorist Attacks of 11 September* (Department of the Parliamentary Library, Canberra, 2001).

[8] Robert W. Marrs, *Nuclear Terrorism: Rethinking the Unthinkable* (University Press of the Pacific, 2004, Hawaii), p. 18

[9] Brian Michael Jenkins, *Will Terrorists Go Nuclear?* (Prometheus Books, New York, 2008), p. 65. A person nicknamed "unabomber" with a 17 years history of dropping bombs was later considered to be retarded but was labelled as a terrorist. But it is very hard to establish the subjective element of motive and purpose from a retarted person.

[10] *Id*, p. 66.

the case of Chechnya. The Chechen rebels, in their fight against Russian control, in many cases attempted to put their hands on nuclear material to build improvised nuclear devices or by sabotaging nuclear reactors in peaceful use so as to cause huge damage to Russia and compel them to withdraw their forces from Chechnya which would become an independent state afterwards.[11]

A general definition of terrorism is defined by an English dictionary as *"the systematic use of terror, violence and intimidation to achieve the end"*.[12] The International Convention on the Suppression of Acts of Nuclear Terrorism defines the act of nuclear terrorism when a person possesses or uses radioactive material or produces or possesses devices with the purpose of causing death or bodily injury or material damage or if uses them.[13] International terrorist organisations are very hard to control or to fight against, as is the case with Al Qaeda which does not have any centralized structure or organisation and action with its presence in all continents.[14] Such organisations are very hard to be traced because in many cases the communication between their members is very rare which avoids them being intercepted. Al Qaeda is based on a highly decentralised system of communication with its cells spread all around the world and which can function from highly independent bases without having to hold constant communication links with its centre leaders.[15]

The 9/11 attack in the US showed that organisations like Al Qaeda are capable of causing a huge cost in human lives an material damage. In this case they used airplanes in civilian use. But in our worst case scenario, the *corpus delicti* would be an improvised device with HEU.[16] Luckily, the process of Uranium enrichment is a very complicated and expensive one which makes it very hard and almost impossible for non-state actors to engage in such a process.[17] In this way the aim

[11] *Id*, p. 75.

[12] Supra note 957, p. 18-19.

[13] International Convention for the Suppression of Acts of Nuclear Terrorism, 15 U.N.T.S. 2445, 13 April 2005, Art.i 2 para 1.

[14] For more on Al Qaeda see Kevin McGrath, *Conformting Al Qaeda: New Strategies to Combat Terrorism* (Naval Institute Press, Annapolis, 2011).

[15] For more see Stefan M. Aubrey, *The New Dimension of International Terrorism* (Strategie und Konfliktforshung, Zurich, 2004).

[16] Gaining a chain reaction and explosion in this case is much more feasible for an individual person than to to it with Plutonium, see supra note 950, pp. 725-726.

[17] Graham T. Allison, *Nuclear Terrorism: The Ultimate Preventable Catastrophe* (Time Books, New York, 2011), p. 10.

of international non-state organisations is to obtain one way or another, HEU from nuclear laboratories or stocks and use it to build an improvised nuclear weapon based on information which, today, may be easily accessed from the internet.[18] International organisations would not hesitate to put such material in their hands or even a nuclear warhead if possible but it seems that the overall security in such facilities is at a desirable level and the main attention is placed on facilities possessing nuclear material not in strict military use.[19]

In 1998, the Al Qaeda leader Osama Bin Laden declared that it is their "religious duty" to get hold of a nuclear weapon.[20] An Al Qaeda spokesperson, during a speech, argued that this organisation has the right to kill up to 4 million Americans as revenge against murders committed by Israel against Muslims.[21] During the shooting of Afghanistan scenes in Kabul the CNN network found evidence in the house of a high ranking Al Qaeda official Abu Khababa Al Masry, in the form of 25 pages with information on the types of nuclear weapons, physics and effects of nuclear explosions and features of nuclear material.[22] After experts had analysed these papers they concluded that the author may have had enough knowledge to realize a small nuclear explosion.[23]

The determination of such organisations to use any possible means to realize their aims is noticed also in the Tokyo attack of 20 March 1995 when a religious sect headed by Aum Shinrikyo attacked the metro system in the city with nerve gas. The Sarin gas used caused injury to around 5500 people.[24] After arrests and raids carried out at different facilities used by this sect, the police managed to unveil other activities related to this sect dealing with intensive programmes to develop nuclear, chemical and biological weapons.[25] Earlier, in 1993,

[18] John Foster, "Nuclear Weapons", *Encyclopedia Americana*, vol. 20 (Americana, New York, 1973), p. 520.

[19] Supra note 950, pp. 731-732.

[20] Christopher C. Joyner and Alexander Ian Parkhouse, "Nuclear Terrorism in a Globalizing World: Asses sing the Threat and the Emerging Management Regime", *Stanford Journal of International Law*, 45 Stan. J. Int'l L. 203 ver/ 2009, p. 212.

[21] See Suleiman Abu Gheith, "'Why We Fight America': Al Qa'ida Spokesman Explains September 11 and Declares Intentions to Kill 4 Million Americans with Weapons of Mass Destruction", *Middle East Media Res. Inst.* Special Dispatch No. 388, 12 July 2002.

[22] Supra note 966, p. 26.

[23] *Ibid.*

[24] John-Alex Romano, "Combating Terrorism and Weapons of Mass Destrucion: Reviving the Doctrine of a State Necessity", *Georgetown Law Journal*, 87 Geo. L. J. 1023, April 1999, p. 1024.

[25] *Ibid.* The leader of this sect predicted the end of the world in an imminent nuclear

terrorists failed to disperse the cyanide sodium gas when they placed a device at the World Trade Centre in the US. The initial explosion of the device destroyed the gas agents thus disabling its lethal effect.[26]

A potential risk from nuclear attack becomes real when we take into consideration that certain nuclear states may face difficulties in securing their nuclear stocks. The fact that an improvised nuclear device may be very easy to be realized is of high concern and it seems that there are such requirements in the market today.[27] The easiness of producing such a weapon was proved in 1977 by a Princeton University student named John Aristotle Phillips working on an individual project.[28] His methodology was very interesting, because he saw his endeavour from a terrorist's viewpoint of looking to build an inexpensive weapon and small enough to be able to transport it in a truck.[29] Phillips managed to get all the necessary technical information to build a nuclear bomb very easily. He managed to contact a company which were in a contract relationship with the American government to supply the latter with items for nuclear programmes.[30] Ultimately, Phillips successfully concluded his work entitled "*An Assessment of the Problems and Possibilities Confronting a Terrorist Group or Non-nuclear Nation Attempting to Design a Crude Pu239 Fission Bomb*". The cost of the whole project was $2,500.[31]

In 2003, research concluded that four out of ten Americans are concerned about the possibility of a terrorist nuclear attack.[32] Such scenarios are not out of the realms of reality taking into consideration that states

war between the US and Japan. According to him, the end of civilisation will start in 1996 and for this reason the only opportunity for survival wourld be to join his rituals and sect. In this way, he managed to gather many believers following him. For more see supra note 958, pp. 71-77.

[26] Supra note 973, p. 1024.

[27] Supra note 969, p. 209.

[28] Supra note 966, pp. 87-88, Phillips chosed this field of study to related to a research project he did during his studies.

[29] *Ibid.*

[30] Phillips bouthg copies of the Los Almos Primer "the First Lectures on How to Builed an Atomic Bobm" for 25 dollars, which at that time were declassified by the US Government, see supra note 966, pp. 88-89.

[31] The work wase evaluated with an excellent remark while the members of phicisc department at the University of Princeton who worked in the Manhattan Project believed that one such bomb as projected in Phillips thesis would work in reality. Concerned with this fact, the US Govenemnt calassified this work with "secret" label to keep it out of sight of individual who might missues it, see *Ibid.*

[32] *Id*, pp. 9-10.

which possess nuclear weapons and material may face different political and economic struggles making their stockpiles highly vulnerable. A report handed to President Bush in June of 2001, emphasised that a serious threat against the US nuclear security is the possibility that Russian nuclear material or arms may fall into the hands of international organisations.[33] After the 9/11 attack, the US commission which studied this attack recommended that the US should develop a general comprehensive programme for the prevention of terrorists obtaining weapons of mass destructions.[34]

In 2004, UN experts drafted a report focusing on high risks the world is facing today.[35] The GS Kofi Anan, in commenting on this report highlighted that *"nuclear terrorism is still often treated as science fiction- I wish it were. But unfortunately we live in a world of excess hazardous material and abundant technological know-how, in which some terrorists clearly state their intention to inflict catastrophic casualties."*[36] According to his report, if terrorists could manage to get 50 kg of HEU, they could improvise a device capable of destroying an average city. This amount of HEU may be easily carried in simple cardboard packages.[37]

According to the IAEA, nuclear terrorism may be manifested in four dimensions: 1) detonation of stolen or purchased nuclear weapons; 2) detonation of an improvised nuclear device processed from stolen or purchased nuclear material; 3) sabotage or attack against nuclear installations, locations or while transporting such material which may cause their dispersal into the environment; 4) detonation of a radiological dispersal device known as the dirty bomb.[38] As it may be seen from this report, terrorists would have somehow to acquire the nuclear material

---

[33] *Ibid.*

[34] Final Report of the National Commission on Terrorist Attacks Upon the United States, US National Commission on Terrorist Attacks Upon the U.S., the 9/11 Commission Report, (2004) p. 381.

[35] For more see Threats, Challenges and Changes, Report of High Level Panel on the UN, 2004.

[36] Supra note 969, p. 206.

[37] Supra note 984, p. 15 para 25.

[38] Nuclear and Radiological Security: Progress on Meassures to Protect Against Nuclear and Radiological Terroris", IAEA General Conference Resolution, IAEA Doc. GC(47)/Res/8, September 2003. The Dirty Bomb contains radioactive material which is not used for explosion. This bomb is a combination of conventional explosive devices containing radioactive material. The explosion of former disperses the latter thus causing environmental contamination effecting humans, see Inadequate Control of World's Radioactive Sources, IAEA Press Release 2002/09, 24 June 2009, visited on 13 August 2012, http://www.iaea.org/newscenter/pressreleases/2002/prn0209.shtml

using clandestine routes. This may be achieved in different ways and the source for such material would be states possessing such material and facing various political, economic and social problems affecting the proper functioning of the state. As the construction of a small capacity nuclear bomb requires a small quantity of HEU, it makes it very feasible for specific terrorists/criminal organisations to smuggle and transport that material, even by using postal services.[39] According to the chief executive of the CSX Lines, a company engaged in transporting goods by containers, if heroine may be smuggled by containers then the same can be said for nuclear bombs.[40]

Nuclear states possess weapons which are small in volume and weight, allowing for easy transportation. Tactical nuclear weapons which make up part of the American nuclear arsenal are designed to be carried by a single soldier in a bag weighting less than 30 kg.[41] Also, the same design is applied to nuclear warheads known as the Davy Crockett weighing only 25 kg with a destruction capacity of 0.25 kilotons, known as the babies of the US nuclear family.[42] The same may be said for Russia which possesses a similar nuclear arsenal.[43]

Another dangerous case would be the sabotage of nuclear systems used by states for military or peaceful purposes. This may be directed against nuclear plants for the production of electricity. If specific individuals are ready to steer an airplane to self-destruction then such individuals would find it much easier to hit a nuclear plant. The destruction of such plants could possibly cause a massive radioactive leak into environment. The cases of the two disasters in Chernobyl and Fukushima show what massive destruction may be caused by the uncontrolled destruction of a nuclear plant. Chechen rebels, headed by Dzhokar Dudayev, threatened to attack nuclear plants in Russia in 1992.[44]

[39] Supra note 966, p. 11.

[40] Could worse be Yet to Come, Special Report by the Economist, 01 November 2001. Accordign to statistics up to 11 Septebmer 2001 and which this percentage increase to 10%. This means that 90% of all container entering the US are submitted only to rutine controle which creates a huge space for smuggling of fission materials and explosives.

[41] Such weapons are used for destroying bridges, tunnels, commanding posts etc., see supra note 966, p. 48.

[42] *Ibid.*

[43] *Id*, p. 49.

[44] After establishing full control over Chechen territory, Russian authorities managed to discover personal archives of the Chechen rebel leader Dudayev revealing his plans he had in 1995 for two individual masked as Russian soldier entering Russian fleed and hijack one of

A third case would be the dropping of a so called dirty bomb with the purpose of dispersing radioactive material. Dispersing such material in the air may take human lives or inflict different diseases. Material such as caesium may cause damage to tissues and radiation intoxication of persons in the vicinity of the attack while to the persons at a greater distance away it may cause cancer due to gamma ray exposure.[45] Plutonium and other material which release Alfa particles may be dangerous only if they penetrate the body in which case they may cause certain cancers in certain organs or death from intoxication.[46] Clearing the contaminated area would take a long time and also financial support. For example, in the case of the anthrax letters addressed to senators Daschle and Patrick J. Leahy, the traces of anthrax were dispersed through the ventilation system throughout the building. In this case $20 million were needed and 3 months to clean the building from all traces. Furthermore, it took more than 2 years to re-open the postal office on Capitol Hill.[47]

In 1995, a group of Chechen rebels under the leadership of Shamil Basayev succeeded in placing a device in the Ismailovsky Park in Moscow.[48] After the opening of the device by competent authorities they determined that it contained radioactive material, a very small amount of cesium-137 but had it exploded it might have caused the immediate death of hundreds of people while thousands of other people may have become infected by cancerous diseases which could have been manifested years afterwards.[49]

Luckily, mankind has not yet experienced a nuclear terrorist attack but it seems that such an attack may be a possibility. This is so because there are states facing difficulties in protecting their nuclear material while on the other hand there is not the lack of will from different organisations to get hold of that material and to use it to achieve their ends. Fighting this feature is very complex taking into consideration the political issues revolving around such organisations. This may be seen in the struggle to design better international and national legislation to

---

its submarines carrying a nuclear warhead which would be used later to threaten Moscou and possibly force it to recognise the independence of Chechenya, see supra note 958, p. 78-79.

[45] Supra note 966, p. 57.

[46] *Ibid.*

[47] *Ibid.*

[48] Supra note 958, p. 79.

[49] *Ibid.*

fight terrorism and its feature which is necessarily reflected in terrorist activities involving nuclear material.

VII.2 THE PREVENTION AND FIGHT AGAINST NUCLEAR TERRORISM THROUGH INTERNAITONAL LAW

The prevention and fight against nuclear terrorism requires a multifaceted international cooperation in good faith. Terrorist groups, today, have spread their networks in different states and are supported by clandestine groups with international character which helps them to acquire the necessary means to achieve their ends. States have started with concrete cooperation in the prevention and fight against nuclear terrorism from the beginnings of the 1990s. The increasing mobility of people and goods facilitated by the latest technical and technological developments in the time of globalisation inherently includes the increased mobility of *"non-state actors, weapons of mass destruction and the increase of radical Islam of all forms"*.[50] The prevention and fight against such features is very difficult because such groups and organisations engaged in such activities are not based in a specific territory and do not often have one centralised commanding hierarchy.[51] These organisations sometimes look like a, hydra[52], a mythological animal with multiple heads the fight against which is very difficult.

Seeing the risk generated by the lack of security at nuclear facilities such as in the case of Russia during the 1990s, the GA established an *ad hoc*[53] committee with a mandate to prepare a text for the International Convention for the Suppression of Terrorist Bombings and the International Convention

[50] Antulio Joseph Echevarria, *Globalizaton and the Nature of War* (Strategic Studies Institute of the U.S. Army War College, Michigan, 2003), p. 3.

[51] David S. Jonas and Christopher Swift, "Reformulating the Nuclear Nonproliferation Regime: Al-Qaeda, Global Terrorism, and the Rouge State Paradigm", *University of California Journal of International Law and Foreign Affairs*, 13 UCLA J. Int'l L. & For. Aff. 337, Autumn, 2008, p. 340.

[52] In the Greek mythology, Hydra was a multi headed snake roaming around the swamps of Lerna and Argo. The number of heads varied depending on wirtings, for more see Encyclopedia www.encyclopedia.com.

[53] The Commity was established by the GA Resolution 201, UN. Doc. A/RES/51/201, 17 December 1996 under the moto of "Meassures to eliminate international terrorism".

for the Suppression of Acts of Nuclear Terrorism.[54] Up to the drafting of these conventions, the only international document dealing with this issue was the Convention on Physical Protection of Nuclear Material of 1980.[55]

The establishment of this committee with the aim of addressing international concerns over nuclear terrorism mirrored the belief that the expansion of UN activities and additional international cooperation is the best way of preventing, fighting and potentially eliminating terrorism in general.[56] The work of this committee was very effective which during its mandate managed to draft three conventions which were subsequently adopted by the GA. The three conventions which are now into force are: the International Convention on Suppression of Terrorist Bombings[57]; the International Convention for the Suppression of the Financing of Terrorists[58]; and the International Convention for the Suppression of Acts of Nuclear Terrorism.[59] This committee, also, drafted the text of the Comprehensive Convention on International Terrorism, which has not yet been adopted by the GA due to conceptual differences over the definition of Terrorism. The differences revolve around three main issues dealing with the: legal definition of terrorism; link between terrorism on one side and anticolonial and freedom movements on the other; and state and armed forces activities during armed conflicts in discharge of their official duties.[60]

The International Convention for the Suppression of Acts of Nuclear Terrorism (Convention on Nuclear Terrorism, CNT), emphasises the need for international cooperation and in particular the improvement of the rule of

[54] *Ibid.*

[55] Supra note 162.

[56] Paige Willan, "The Convention on the Suppression of Acts of Nuclear Terrorism: An old Solution to a New Problem", *Georgetown Journal of International Law*, 39 Geo. J. Int'l L. 527, Spring 2008, p. 530.

[57] International Convention on the Suppression of Terrorist Bombings, U.N. Doc. A/RES/52/164. 37 I.L.M. 249; 2149 U.N.T.S. 284, 15 December 1997.

[58] International Convention for the Suppression of the Financing Terrorism, U.N. Doc. A/RES/54/109, 09 December 1999.

[59] International Convention for the Suppression of Acts of Nuclear Terrorism, UN Doc. A/RES/59/290, 14 September 2005.

[60] According to draft conventions the terrorist is defined as *"a person's unlawfully and intentionally causing or threatening to cause violence by means of firearms, weapons, explosives, any lethal devices or dangerous substances, which results, or is likely to result, in death or serious bodily injury to a person, a group of persons or serious damage to property — whether for public use, a State or Government facility, a public transportation system or an infrastructure facility*". However even this definition is still being negotiated and might change in the future, see, "Draft Comprehensive Convention on International Terrorism", Center for Non-Proliferation Studies, visited on 7 March 2012, http://cns.miis.edu/inventory/pdfs/intlterr.pdf.

law and the role of each state in preventing nuclear terrorism. The text of the CNT was proposed by Russia which in its explaining letter to the proposal of this convention, emphasised that the Convention on the Physical Protection of Nuclear Material cannot help in itself in the fight against nuclear terrorism and the aim of this convention is to fight new and dangerous features of terrorism, in inciting states to adopt preventive measures in this field and the establishment of an international reliable mechanism for cooperation against nuclear terrorism at all phases.[61] This convention, in the first place, has a preventive character and focuses exclusively on individual acts and its scope of action is of nuclear non-proliferation or nuclear threats by states or intergovernmental organisations.[62] Due to contradictions among states, the states and armed forces acts were left outside the scope of this convention in order to achieve an international consensus for adoption of actual text.[63]

Article 2 para. 1 of the CNT determines actions which present a criminal act which includes every person who unlawfully and intentionally:

(a) Possesses radioactive material or makes or possesses a device:

(i) With the intent to cause death or serious bodily injury; or

(ii) With the intent to cause substantial damage to property or to the environment;

(b) Uses in any way radioactive material or a device, or uses or damages a nuclear facility in a manner which releases or risks the release of radioactive material:

(i) With the intent to cause death or serious bodily injury; or

(ii) With the intent to cause substantial damage to property or to the environment; or

(iii) With the intent to compel a natural or legal person, an international organisation or a State to do or refrain from doing an act.[64]

---

[61] Its is perhaps very symbolic that Russia proposed this convention which faced a lots of problems for securing its nuclear materials during, see, "Convention for Suppression of Acts of Nuclear Terrorism", Center for Non-Proliferation Studies, 7 March 2012.

[62] *Ibid.*

[63] David P. Fidler, "International Convention on Suppression of Acts of Nuclear Terrorism", *ASIL Insight*, vol. 11 issue 8, 5 July 2007.

[64] See supra note 1008, Art. 2 para. 1.

This convention incriminates the following acts: threat; illegal and intentional acquiring of radioactive material, device or facility; help in committing crimes determined in Article 2; and organisation or leading other persons to commit such a crime or in any other manner contributes to committing acts sanctioned in this convention.[65]According to the CNT, for an action to be qualified as a terrorist act it is required to establish cumulatively two essential elements that are the objective and subjective elements. The objective element deals with the manifestation of a concrete act determined by Article 2, while the subjective element has to do with the purpose of taking such an act. The purpose, as a subjective element is very hard to be demined and in many cases it becomes very controversial.[66]

The CNT is applicable only in peaceful times and not during armed conflicts. It also does not apply over the activities of armed forces which still remain subject to regulations by humanitarian law.[67] Article 4 contains compromising language between the nuclear and non-nuclear states. Nuclear states, in particular the non-aligned movement states, objected to the use of any word which might be understood as to legitimize the use of nuclear weapons by nuclear states.[68] This article on one side refrains from interfering thereupon the rights, obligations and responsibilities of states determined by the Charter and humanitarian law[69] while on the other side it excluded any sort of interpretation on the legality of threat or use of nuclear weapons.[70] Paragraph 4 of Article 4 was added after non-aligned states persisted during the drafting to include it.[71]

The CNT is applied strictly against actions with international character meaning that the person or the victim has a different citizenship from the person taking the action or in cases when the perpetrator resides in another state from the state where the action was carried out and no other state has jurisdiction over that act.[72] The convention

[65] See supra note 1007, Art. 2 para. 2,3,4.

[66] The Genocide Convention similar to the CNT foreseed for the fulfillement of two such elements: the according to Art. 2 and the purpose to commit genocide.

[67] Supra note 1008, Art. 4 para 2.

[68] "Inventory of International Nonproliferation Organizations and Regimes, International Convention for the Suppression of Acts of Nuclear Terrorism", Center for Nonproliferation Studies, visited on 5 December 2012, http://cns.miis.edu/inventory/pdfs/nucterr.pdf.

[69] Supra note 1008, Art. 4 para 1.

[70] *Id*, Art. 4 para 4.

[71] Supra note 1017.

[72] Supra note 1008, Art. 3. Art. 9 para 1 deals with the basis of jurisdiction according to which every state has jurisdiction to prosecute any offender if for an offense committed in

requires states to take necessary measures within their legal systems foreseeing adequate sanctions taking into consideration the nature and consequences of such acts.[73] In other words, it requires states to consider such acts with aggravated consideration and to foresee higher penalties as compared to similar acts which do not involve nuclear terrorism. Also, the state is obliged to take necessary measures including legislative ones, so that such acts are not covered by political, ideological, racial, ethnic, religious or similar blanket.[74]

Genuine international cooperation is very important in fighting such acts with transnational character to fulfil the objective and purpose of this convention. For this reason, the CNT requires states to take all measures to facilitate cooperation in preventing such acts.[75] States have sovereign authority over their territories making them responsible for taking action to prevent such activities within a state so that it prevents any person, group or organisation to use its territory to harm another state.[76] The circulation of information, confidentiality and cooperation during the investigation phase is of paramount importance.[77]

One of the most important issues in the fight against nuclear terrorism is the extradition of persons from one state to another. The CNT obliges all states to consider such acts as extraditable meaning that persons involved in such acts may be extradited even in cases when the states involved in the process do not have any extradition agreement.[78] The political purpose provision cannot cover these acts for the purpose

the territory of a sate; aircraft or ship carrying the flaf of that state or is registered in that state; the offense is commiteed by the person holding citizenship of that state. According to para. 2, the state may expand its jurisdiction even in cases when the victim is a citizen of that stae; the offense is committed against the governemt or state outside of its terrirotry such as embassy; the offense is committed by a stateless person with residence in that state; the offense is committed with a purpose of coercing that state for action or omission in a particular situation; the offense is committed in an aircraft or ship operated by that state. Jurisdiction according to para 2 is optional meaning that it is possible and concurrent because the offender migh be prosecuted by other states having jurisdiction under para 1 or 2 in case when it was faster in getting hold of the offender. The convention does not foresse any provision for disputed management in which case states would have to solve it using diplomatic means.

[73] Supra note 1008, Art. 5.

[74] *Id*, Art. 6.

[75] *Id*, Art. 7.

[76] *Id*, Art. 7 para 1.

[77] *Id*, Art. 7 para 2 point b dhe para. 3, 4 and also Art. 14.

[78] *Id*, Art. 13 para. 1-3.

of preventing extradition.[79] However, a state may refuse the request for extradition in cases when it possesses substantial grounds to believe that the extradition request is made when the purpose of prosecuting or convicting a person is based on the basis of race, religion, nationality, ethnicity or political opinion or in case when admitting to extradite may cause prejudices against that person for reasons mentioned above.[80]

The convention foresees specific instructions for states which confiscate radioactive material or other fission material in order to take all measures to avoid any further damage and to cooperate with the IAEA in managing such material.[81] The confiscated material should be sent back to the originating state.[82] The CNT does not foresee any sanction against an originating state where the material is stolen, but it may be understood that that state should take concrete measures to secure radioactive material in the future. The conventions contain a disposition which requires states to guarantee the rights of persons accused of committing acts determined by Article 2.[83] The accused persons should enjoy a free and fair trial including all the rights guaranteed by internal legislation or international human rights instruments.[84]

The CNT does not interfere with the rules of international law over the jurisdiction of states to investigate such actions perpetrated in vessels carrying the flag of a particular state. In these cases, the investigating state should cooperate with the state of the flag of which that vessel carries. The same rule applies in cases involving airplanes.[85]

The CNT is faced with different critics regarding particular provisions, language and measures proposed to prevent terrorism. It is a part of a broad corpus of international agreements aiming to fight this particular feature. Such agreements should contain specifications and standards in a more detailed way for physical protection of radioactive material and nuclear facilities from persons, groups or organisations or other provisions to improve a state's endeavours for physical protec-

[79] *Id,* Art. 15.

[80] *Id,* Art. 16.

[81] *Id,* Art. 18.

[82] *Id,* Art. 18 para. 2.

[83] *Id,* Art. 12.

[84] *Id,* Art. 12.

[85] "Convention for Suppression of Acts of Nuclear Terrorism", Center for Non-Proliferation Studies, visited on 12 December 2012, http://cns.miis.edu/inventory/pdfs/nucterr.pdf.

tion within its borders.[86] During the drafting process of the CNT, Larry D. Johnson, who was a legal advisor to the IAEA, proposed more effective preventive measures going beyond the mere incriminating and preventing of such terrorist acts. According to him, such conventions have only reactive effect.[87] The convention is more focused on using traditional means of law enforcement which in specific cases cannot yield their desired effect because in suicide cases for example, the perpetrator does not care at all about the consequences of his acts. In these cases, the concept of deterrence is incapable of producing any result.[88] States should focus more on forensic cooperation which would enable them to trace, in advance, nuclear crimes before they become reality.[89] Also, the CNT is criticized for not having foreseen any concrete measure for improving the protection of radioactive material or nuclear facilities but that it only requires states to take *"appropriate measures"* to secure such material.[90] Cooperation with the IAEA is encouraged only after states confiscate nuclear material from terrorist groups in which case it might be better if such disposition encourage cooperation before an eventual confiscation happened. In general, the CNT instead of focusing more on how to protect such nuclear material, it focuses more on incriminating and controlling illegal activities.[91]

The CNT seems to have a deficiency in Article 2 which determines the role of the nuclear facilities employees in nuclear terrorism. In order to incriminate such a person for nuclear terrorism that person should have had knowledge in advance of the purpose of the particular person or group to commit an act foreseen by the convention.[92] Here, we are dealing with the subjective element in which case the suspect may very easily defend himself by saying that he did not have any prior knowledge about the purpose of that particular person or group which would then be very hard to prove the opposite. The justification from the employee in this case would be that the fission or radioactive ma-

[86] David Fidler cituar n/ John F. Murphy, *The Evolving Dimensions of International Law: Hard Choices for the World Community* (Cambridge University Press, New York, 2010) pp. 188-189.

[87] *Ibid.*

[88] Supra note 1005, pp. 532-533.

[89] *Id*, p. 534.

[90] *Ibid.*

[91] *Id*, p. 535.

[92] *Id*, p. 537.

terial was required for scientific purposes by that particular person or group.[93] Another deficiency relates to the general lack of consensus regarding the definition of terrorism which seems to require more time to reach an international consensus.

For a more successful fight against nuclear terrorism, international instruments should foresee clear responsibility for persons and granting jurisdiction to prosecute such acts by an international body such as the International Criminal Court. This would give more insurance that persons involved in preparing, inciting, assisting or perpetrating such acts would be brought to justice. At the same time, giving the International Criminal Court the jurisdiction over nuclear terrorism might have a positive impact in lowering international contradictions taking into consideration international disputes over the definition of terrorism. Apart from this, genuine international cooperation in the field of intelligence would create a better security climate in preventing an eventual nuclear terrorist attack. Prevention is always a better remedy than healing, therefore states cooperation in forensics and intelligence gathering is crucial.

Other important international bodies such as the SC acting under Chapter VII of the Charter undertook concrete steps to address nuclear terrorism. This is very important because resolutions taken under this chapter are binding and should be respected by all states.

[93] *Id,* p. 538.

VII.3 PREVENTION AND FIGHTING NUCLEAR TERRORISM BY OTHER INTERNATIONAL ACTS

The International community has enacted other documents which play a significant role in the fight against nuclear terrorism. First and foremost is the Convention on Physical Protection of Nuclear Material (CPPNM) of 1980. This convention is the sole international binding agreement in the field of physical protection of nuclear material. The scope of this convention relates only to the protection of nuclear material during transportation. According to Article 2 of the convention it *"shall apply to nuclear material used for peaceful purposes while in international nuclear transport"*.[94] It requires states to carry such transactions only with states party to the agreement[95], and in exceptional circumstances with other states, which are capable of offering safeguards and security measures as recommended by the Convention.[96]

The CPPNM incriminates all acts which include *"the receipt, possession, use, transfer, alteration, disposal or dispersal of nuclear material and which causes or is likely to cause death or serious injury to any person or substantial damage to property"*.[97] All states are obliged to foresee these acts as such in their legislation with the purpose of taking effective measures in realization of the objective and purpose of this convention.[98] It expressly requires states to penalise, using internal legislation, all acts which are listed in the CPPNM.[99] The Convention gives jurisdiction to state parties in prosecuting such acts in cases when they are committed in the territory of a state party, vessel carrying flag of that state or airplane registered in that state or if the perpetrator

---

[94] Convention on the Physical Protection of Nuclear Material, 1456 UNTS 101, 03 March 1980, Art. 1.

[95] *Id*, Art. 4 para. 1 and 2.

[96] The level of physical protection related to the transportation of fission material is foressen in Annex I of the Convention while chategorising them is done according to Annex II which includes Plutonium, Uranium U-235, Uranium U-233 and other fuels (depleted or natural Uranium, Torium, low enriched fuel), see *Id*.

[97] *Id*, Art. 7 para 1.

[98] *Id*, Art. 3.

[99] *Id*, Art. 7.

has citizenship of that state.[100] This Convention is a basis for extradition of persons involved in such acts, because it requires states to consider them as extraditable even if states do not have any specific agreement for extradition stating that *"If a State Party which makes extradition conditional on the existence of a treaty receives a request for extradition from another State Party with which it has no extradition treaty, it may at its option consider this Convention as the legal basis for extradition in respect of those offences"*[101]

The CPPNM set a standard for the protection of nuclear material and penalise attempts to steal it. However, the Convention has a deficiency as it focuses only on the protection of nuclear material while during transportation and does not apply cases of nuclear material used for peaceful purposes during times when they remain deposited in a facility.[102] In 2005, the CPPNM was amended to include provisions related to the protection of deposited nuclear material but it has not yet entered into force, leaving it with this deficiency.[103] This amendment requires states to take concrete measures for the physical protection of deposited nuclear material used for peaceful purposes as well as nuclear material during transaction.[104] Even though this amendment is considered to be very important it seems that it will take some time for it to come into force and until then the CPPNM will stay limited in the realization of its objective and purpose.[105] Even with its limited scope, the CPPNM directly helps in the prevention of nuclear terrorism because taking necessary measures for the physical protection of nuclear material makes it harder for terrorists to get hold of it in the first place which is perhaps the best way to prevent nuclear terrorism. To achieve its efficacy it is still required that its amendment comes into force so it covers also nuclear deposition facilities.

Another important document is the Convention for Suppression of Financing of Terrorism (CSFT) which further strengthens the legal infrastructure in the fight against terrorism. According to this

[100] *Id,* Art. 8.

[101] *Id,* Art. 11 para 1 and 2.

[102] Supra note 969, p. 228.

[103] "Convention on the Physical Protection of Nuclear Material", IAEA, International Conventions and Agreements, visited on 10 March 2012, http://www.iaea.org/Publications/Documents/Conventions/cppnm.html.

[104] *Ibid.*

[105] Supra note 969, p. 228.

Convention, a person commits a crime if *"by any means, directly or indirectly, unlawfully and wilfully, provides or collects funds with the intention that they should be used or in the knowledge that they are to be used, in full or in part, in order to carry out"*.[106] For the purpose of this Convention, it is not important whether the fund in itself was established to help committing terrorist acts.[107] Such language used is important because it acts as a preventive measure in the fight against such activities from the phases when such acts are planned and organized. From the preventive point of view, the CSFT requires states to take measures to prohibit illegal activities of persons or organisations that knowingly encourage, instigate, organise or engage in committing such crimes.[108] The CSFT incriminates any activity with the purpose of causing death or serious bodily injury to a civilian or any other person not engaged actively in an armed conflict and when such an act is committed with the purpose of intimidating the population or to compel a government or an international organisation to do or abstain from doing any act.[109] This Convention does not apply in cases when the offence is committed within the borders of a single state by an offender with that nationality and is present in the territory of that state and no other states have jurisdiction to prosecute that crime determined by Article 7 of the Convention.[110]

The CSFT requires all Member States to adopt adequate legislative means to punish acts as determined by this Convention as criminal offenses by also foreseeing specific penal measures and allowing for extradition of persons involved in such acts.[111] Such acts are extraditable and this Convention is the basis for extradition in cases when there is a lack of specific extradition agreement[112] and no person may hide behind any political motivation to prevent extradition.[113] In the network of financial transaction a key role is played by financial institutions and their cooperation is very important in fighting acts foreseen by this Convention. The CSFT determines specific obligations for these institutions

[106] Supra note 1007, Art. 2.
[107] *Id,* Art. 2.
[108] *Id,* Art. 18.
[109] *Id,* Art. 2 para b.
[110] *Id,* Art. 3.
[111] *Id,* Art. 14.
[112] *Id,* Art. 12 para. 1 and 2.
[113] *Id,* Art. 12 para. 4.

which should take all necessary measures to cooperate with states and other institutions and to trace and report any existence of such funds.[114]

The CSFT plays a very important role in fighting terrorism because tracking down and freezing financial activities has a huge impact in obscuring activities of terrorist organisations. Organisations which deal with nuclear terrorism will need sufficient sums of money which is earned by different legal or semi-legal ways. This money may be used to purchase nuclear material and for corrupting different persons involved in the process such as employees at nuclear facilities or law enforcement officers.

Aside from these Conventions, an important role was played by the SC which in 2004 adopted Resolution 1540 which established more effective measures against the proliferation of weapons of mass destruction and their means for delivery.[115] The importance of this resolution lies in the fact that it is adopted under Chapter VII of the Charter[116] and is binding on all states. The resolution prohibits all states from "*providing any form of support to non-State actors that attempt to develop, acquire, manufacture, possess, transport, transfer or use nuclear, chemical or biological weapons and their means of delivery*".[117] It also calls upon all states to enact specific internal legislation[118], and to take all necessary measures for effective control of their territory[119] and fight such features. This resolution established a committee with a two year mandate which would report to this organ in the implementation of this resolution by states and states on the other hand are required to report on their measures to implement it within 6 months.[120] The mandate of this committee was extended by ten years in 2011.[121] The extension of its mandate by ten years is a sign that the fight against terrorism requires more time and using long-term activities to achieve concrete results.

[114] This includes reporting over extraordinary money transfer; ban on registering bank accounts for unidentified persons; detection of freeze of funds which are used for criminal purposes foreseen in this convention, see *Id*, Art. 18 para. 1 point b.

[115] Supra note 969, p. 232.

[116] See supra note 121.

[117] Security Council Resolution 1540, UN. Doc. S/RES/1540, 28 April 2004, Art. 1.

[118] *Id,* Art. 2.

[119] *Id,* Art. 3.

[120] *Id,* Art. 4.

[121] Earlier the mandate of the Committee was extended for two year to 2006 with Resolution 1673, see Security Council Resolution 1810, UN. Doc. S/RES/1810, 25 April 2008.

The main functions of this committee are to coordinate and facilitate technical assistance for the implementation of the resolution and makes specific recommendations drafted by experts of the field. The committee reports on a two year basis to the SC. [122]

In its report of 2011, the committee concluded that a marked success had been achieved from 2004 in the fight against nuclear terrorism but a lot of work still remains to be done as the *"the gravity of the threat remains considerable."*[123] According to this report, an increased number of states have adopted legislative measures as a response to the requirements of the resolution related to nuclear weapons and their means of delivery. Up to the drafting of this report, 115 states have national legal legislation in place prohibiting the manufacture/production of nuclear weapons by non-state agents.[124] At the same time, 92 states have enacted specific sanctioning measures to punish these acts.[125] With regards to delivery means, states have improved their legal infrastructure and according to the report 39 states have regulated production activities for delivery means of nuclear weapons.[126]

Resolution 1540 calls on taking measures for punishing any person engaged as an accomplice, assisting or financing activities foreseen in the resolution. The report considered that there is also progress in this aspect and 103 states have taken specific measures to prevent such activities.[127] An important factor is the taking of efficient measures for the physical protection and securing of nuclear material. In this aspect, the report draws attention to the fact that there was an overall improvement in the security of states. Presented below are some data regarding the accounting, securing and physical protection of nuclear material according to this committee.

---

[122] For more on the activities of this Committee see "The 1540 Committee", visited on 15 December 2012, http://www.un.org/sc/1540/index.shtml.

[123] Letter dated 12 September 2011 from the Chair of the Security Council Committee established pursuant to resolution 1540 (2004) addressed to the President of the Security Council submitting the report of the Committee on compliance with resolution 1540 (2004), p. 2, UN. Doc. S/2011/579, 14 September 2011.

[124] In 2008 the number of these states was 97. See *Id*, p. 10.

[125] In 2008 th enumber of these states was 76. See *Ibid.*

[126] In 2008 the number of these states was 0, See *Id*, pp. 11-12.

[127] In 2008 the number of these states was 99. See *Id*, p. 12.

Obligation	*Nuclear*
Accounting	
Production	164/73
Use	165/73
Storage	165/71
Transport	78/72
Securing	
Production	81/72
Use	90/81
Storage	89/80
Transport	101/100
Physical protection	
Protection	74/61.[128]

The report encourages states to take measures to improve border security, control of trade and international brokering in licensing and also the control of technology which may be used in the field of nuclear material and delivery systems.[129] At the end, the report concludes that there is a need for further measures to fully implement the requirements of the resolution and for the need of increased international cooperation including cooperation with the committee.[130] The resolution, despite the fact of it being adopted by the SC acting under Chapter VII, is criticized for a weak legal language using words like *"appropriate effective",* which leave a lot of room for different interpretations.[131] Furthermore, the committee does not have any executive competences against states which do not cooperate fully in the strict implementation of the resolution.[132]

The SC has approved other resolutions which help in the fight against international terrorism in general and which also include nu-

[128] The figures present the number of Member States with legal frameworks and adequate implementation measures according to the data approved by the Committee, see *Id*, p. 13.

[129] *Id*, pp. 15-18.

[130] *Id*, pp. 28-31.

[131] Supra note 969, p. 233.

[132] These two deficiencies are characteristics to other legal instruments designed to fight terrorism, *Id*, p. 233.

clear terrorism. With this aspect in mind the SC approved Resolution 1267 (1999) and 1373 (2001) acting under Chapter VII. These two resolutions establish their respective committees which monitor the implementation of their requirements. The 1540 Committee together with these two other committees are obliged to cooperate together in complying with the requirements of Resolution 1810 (2008) which extended the mandate of the 1540 Committee.[133]

Resolution 1267 deals directly with Al Qaeda and the Taleban in Afghanistan. It required the Taleban regime at that time to handover Osama Bin Laden[134] and enacted a sanction regime against that regime until the fulfilment of the requirement.[135] The committee established by this resolution monitors the implementation and drafts a list of persons and entities engaged in activities incriminated by the resolution.[136] The SC continued to adopt other resolutions referring to particular persons and entities connected to Al Qaeda. From Resolution 1267 the SC adopted 9 other resolutions related to this issue.[137] Sanction measures foreseen by the latest Resolution 1989 (2011) include: freezing of funds and other financial and economic assets of individuals, groups and entities connected to Al Qaeda; entry or transit prevention of those individuals and the prevention of sale, supply or direct or indirect transfer of those individuals, groups, undertakings or entities from its territory or by their nationals outside their territory or arms and related materiel of all types.[138]

---

[133] Supra note 1071, para. 12.

[134] Security Council Resolution, 1267, UN. Doc. S/RES/1267, 15 October 1999, paragrafi 2. Osama Bin Laden was localised and killed in the meantime on 2 May 2012, for more see Christine Fair, "The bin Laden aftermath : The U.S. shouldn't hold Pakistan's military against Pakistan's civilians", *Foreign Policy*, visited on 12 December 2012, http://afpak.foreignpolicy.com/posts/2011/05/04/the_bin_laden_aftermath_the_us_shouldnt_hold_pakistans_military_against_pakistans_c.

[135] *Id*, para. 3 and 4. Sanction measures include flight ban operated by the Taleban; fund freeze which are generated directly or indirectly by the Taleban.

[136] See "The List established and maintained by the Committee pursuant to resolutions 1267 (1999) and 1989 (2011) with respect to individuals, groups, undertakings and other entities associated with Al-Qaida", visited on 10 November 2012, http://www.un.org/sc/committees/1267/aq_sanctions_list.shtml.

[137] See "Security Council Committee Pursuant to Resolution 1267 (1999) and 1989 (2011) concerning Al-Qaida and associated Individuals and Entities", visited on 19 October 2012, http://www.un.org/sc/committees/1267/.

[138] Security Council Resolution 1989, UN. Doc. S/RES/1989 (2011), 17 July 2011.

The Resolution was adopted at a very sensitive time in international relations related to the 9/11 attacks.[139] It was adopted on 28 September 2001 and represented the first SC Resolution against international terrorism. This resolution calls on all states to implement a number of measures in order to improve the legal and institutional infrastructure to fight terrorist related activities. It considered terrorist acts as a threat to international peace and security. Specifically, the resolution requires states to incriminate the financing of terrorism; freezing of funds related to persons engaged in terrorist acts; prohibit all forms of financial aid for terrorist groups; abrogate provisions providing support or safe havens for terrorists; exchange of information between states regarding any group planning to commit terrorist acts; cooperate in investigating, detection, arrest, extradition and prosecution of persons involved in such acts; incriminate by national legislation active and passive assistance to terrorist activities and bringing to justice perpetrators of such acts.[140] It calls on all states to become, as soon as possible, parties to international treaty instruments against terrorism.[141]

The resolution establishes an Anti-Terrorist Committee with responsibility to monitor its implementation.[142] The work of this committee consists of: visits to all UN Member States; technical assistance; drafting of state reports; and application of good practices in fighting terrorism.[143] The committee can call for special meetings if necessary to address any particular issue.[144] Resolution 1373 failed to define acts which incite the commission of a terrorist act. To fill this gap, the SC adopted Resolution 1624 (2005) condemning the incitement to commit a terrorist act and calls on all states to prohibit such acts by national legislation and to take adequate measures to prohibit the safe haven against anybody *"with respect to whom there is credible and relevant information giving serious reasons for considering that they have been guilty of such conduct."*[145]

---

[139] Security Council Resolution, UN. Doc. S/RES/1373 (2001), 28 September 2001.

[140] *Id*, para. 1-3.

[141] *Id*, para 3 point d.

[142] *Id*, para. 6.

[143] See "Security Council Counter-Terrorism Committee", visited on19 October 2012, http://www.un.org/en/sc/ctc/.

[144] *Ibid.*

[145] Security Council Resolution 1624, UN. Doc. S/Res/1624, 14 September 2005, para. 1.

The fight against terrorism in general and nuclear terrorism in particular, was pushed ahead to a great extent after the 9/11 attack when the world realized the worst possible capabilities of terrorist organisations. The 9/11 attacks woke up international leaders to set aside, as much as possible, all political divergences to unite against such features as a real threat against mankind. For the implementation of international commitments taken by states genuine international cooperation is necessary and which seems to flounder in some aspects. The case of Osama Bin Laden tells the bitter truth that he was hiding in Pakistan while, at least officially, Pakistani authorities never admitted to have known that fact.[146] Other different international initiatives have been established on a bilateral and multilateral basis to help states which have shown willingness to cooperate and fight terrorist activities but have run into difficulties in yielding specific results.

VII.4 OTHER BILATERAL AND OTHER MULTILATERAL APPROACHES IN PREVENTION AND THE FIGHT AGAINST NUCLEAR TERRORISM

The potential risk from nuclear terrorism incited necessary cooperation between states at the bilateral and multilateral level independent of international forums. International cooperation may be difficult in particular fields. Successful cooperation requires the fulfilment of some criteria: common purpose; 2) cooperation will; 3) cooperation capacity; 4) definition of the issue involved and 5) determination of means to approach the issue.[147] Achieving a broad international consensus on these criteria, in particular in issues related to terrorism may become very controversial and here we could start with the definition. Today, even among close allies the definition of terrorism is different

[146] Christine Fair, "The bin Laden aftermath: The U.S. shouldn't hold Pakistan's military against Pakistan's civilians", *Foreign Policy*, visited on 12 December 2012, http://afpak.foreignpolicy.com/posts/2011/05/04/the_bin_laden_aftermath_the_us_shouldnt_hold_pakistans_military_against_pakistans_c

[147] Erica Chenoweth, "A Contested Threat: The Politics of Security Collaboration for Combating Terrorism" *n/ Handbook of Defence Politics: International and Comparative Perspectives: International and Comparative Perspectives* ed. *Isaia "Ike" Wilson III, James J. F. Forrest,* (Routledge, United Kingdom 2008), p. 66.

and details are what matters.[148] However in the struggle against nuclear terrorism and the seriousness of the situation, states have established different initiatives on an individual basis to help with these features and which are mostly supported by the US.

An increased level of bilateral and multilateral cooperation is facilitated today through the following initiative: the Nuclear Threat Reduction Initiative (NTI); the Global Nuclear Threat Reduction Initiative (GNTI); the Proliferation Security Initiative; (PSI) and the Global Initiative to Combat Nuclear Terrorism (Global Initiative). The NTI and GNTI are focused on strengthening the security capacities to secure nuclear infrastructure in states possessing nuclear material and providing assistance in the safe return of nuclear material in the US and Russia.[149] The Global Initiative focuses on the strengthening of partnership between states to combat nuclear terrorism in harmony with the principle determined by the Convention for Suppression of Acts of Nuclear Terrorism; the Convention on Physical Protection of Nuclear Material and its amendment; and the SC 1540 Resolution.[150]

Nuclear Threat Reduction Initiative (NTI)

The NTI is the first programme initiated by the US the purpose of which is to respond to the situation after the collapse of the former USSR which had a huge nuclear arsenal and nuclear material in its possession including the knowhow for Uranium enrichment and other processes in this field.[151] Senators Nunn and Lugar proposed a bill in 1991 which initially focuses on the strengthening of security systems and demolition of the nuclear arsenal in Russia and other states rising out of the collapse of the former USSR.[152] The US, through this initiative, provided financial support and technical expertise to secure the demolition

[148] For example the US has in its list of terrorist organizations the Hamas Movement which is not the case with the EU, *Ibid.*

[149] *Id,* p. 223.

[150] *Id,* pp. 223-224.

[151] Bonie Jenkis, "Adopting to the Times: The Evolution of U.S. Threat Reduction Programmess", Arms Control Association, January/February 2011, visited on 20 October 2012, http://www.armscontrol.org/act/2011_01-02/Jenkins.

[152] Supra note 969, p. 223.

of nuclear weapons, supporting infrastructure, additional material and delivery systems.[153]

After the 9/11 attacks, there was a need to redesign the role and function of this initiative to cover other states and non-state organisations. In this way, after the year 2001, the NTI expanded its focus onto the prevention of any state or non-state organisation, particularly terrorist ones, to put on hold any nuclear weapons or weapons of mass destruction in general.[154] To address new coming challenges the NTI is engaged in activities to include projects focused and related to the biological and chemical security such as: the prevention of reduction of contagious diseases and other biological threats; improvement of border security; strengthening of export controls; development of nuclear forensics; interception of illegal trafficking; and prevention of radiological terrorism.[155] The results of this initiative are important. According to the 2006 data, 106 kg of nuclear material was returned to Russia and 71 kg of the same units to the US as a result of this initiative.[156]

Today, the object and purpose of this initiative has changed from its initial phase and is considered as a part of American government programmes and initiatives to address complex challenges coming from WMD perceived as a threat to national security and global stability. Also, the name of the initiative has lately been changed and today it is known as the Global Security Engagement.[157]

---

[153] Chen Kane, "From Donor to Partner: The Evolution of U.S. Cooperative Threat Reduction into Global Security Engagement", Nuclear Threat Initiative, 12 May 2011, visited on 20 October 2012, http://www.nti.org/analysis/articles/donor-partner-evolution-us-cooperative-threat-reduction-global-security-engagement/.

[154] After 2001 the US, through this initiative, managed to cooperate in different project with Afghanista, Pakistan, Iraq, Lybia, Indonesia, Malaysia with attempts to get involved more with different states of Afrika, see *Ibid.*

[155] *Ibid.*

[156] Supra note 969, p. 223.

[157] Formaly, wtill this inititative is know as GNTI because changing its name would require another legislation to be passed by the Congress which complicates it, see supra note 1096.

Global Nuclear Threat Reduction Initiative (GNTI)

The GNTI was established by the American Department of Energy with the purpose of reduction and protection of vulnerable nuclear and radiological material locations and civilian facilities in the world.[158] This initiative attempts to prevent the nuclear and radiological material from falling in the hands of different groups for the production of WMD. The three main focuses of this initiative are: conversion; removal and protection of nuclear and radiological material.[159]

Through conversion, the initiative assists in the conversion of HEU at civil and scientific laboratories and also from the facilities for the production of LEU isotopes which is used only for peaceful purposes. It has helped to eliminate and reduce to a great extent the risk of misusing the HEU stored in such facilities and targets of particular terrorist groups.[160]

Through removal, the initiative attempts to remove or eliminate excessive nuclear and radiological material locations and civilian facilities in the world which could be used for the production of WMD. Its scope of action is mainly focused on the removal of nuclear material originating from the US and Russia but also of material with other origins. It also includes the removal or elimination of radiological material which could be used for the production of a "dirty bomb".[161] Through protection activities, it tries to support different states in the protection of nuclear and radiological material from theft and possible sabotage in the world until a final solution is found.[162]

In the year 2004, the US and Russia have together organised a conference in the framework of this initiative with more than 90 states participating and which committed $450 million for a 10 year period to be used in realizing its projects around the world.[163] According to

[158] For more see "Office of the Global Threat Reduction", visited on 6 September 2011, http://nnsa.energy.gov/aboutus/ourprogrammess/nonproliferation/programmesoffices/officeglobalthreatreduction

[159] *Ibid.*

[160] *Ibid.*

[161] *Ibid.*

[162] *Ibid.*

[163] Amy F. Woolf, Mary Beth Nikiting, Paul K. Kerr, Arms Control and Nonproliferation: A Catalog of Treaties and Agreements, Report for Congress, Congressional Research

the Energy Department, from May 2004 up to 2010, a large quantity of HEU was returned to the US and Russia capable of the production of 80 nuclear weapons and it also achieved raising the security level at more than 600 locations in the world. At the same time, 57 scientific nuclear reactors were converted from their use for the production of HEU into using them for the production of LEU while 7 such reactors were dismantled.[164]

Proliferation Security Initiative (PSI)

The PSI was established in the year 2003 under the leadership of President George Bush who in May 2003 publicly announced that the US would lead the new struggle to intercept the WMD deliveries and related materials to terrorist groups and states contribution in further proliferation.[165] Initially, the establishment of this initiative gathered 10 states but now it has more than 73 including Russia which contributes in the realisation of its objective and purpose.[166] Its strength comes from the fact that the stepping stone of its work and cooperation is the signing of bilateral agreements between states which allow them to conduct their activities beyond general rules of international law such as for example, it allows them to board a vessel, search, hold and confiscate cargo from any vessel suspected of trafficking nuclear material or weapons.[167] Besides this, such actions may be carried out against vessels of other states which are not party to such arrangements in cases when they are located in the territorial waters of participating states and are suspected of carrying nuclear material or weapons.[168] In other cases, such activities are carried out in compliance with the Sea Convention according to which states are not allowed to interfere with vessels located on the high seas and carry a flag of another state.[169] In these cases, a

Service, 2 February 2010, p. 34.

[164] *Ibid*, p. 34. See also supra note 950.

[165] Supra note 655.

[166] China still remains outside the frameworks of this initiative, see *Ibid.*

[167] Supra note 969, p. 223.

[168] *Ibid.*

[169] The United Nations Convention on the Law of Sea, 1833 U.N.T.S. 3, 10 December 1982 , Art. 10.

vessel carrying the flag of a non-participating state may not be stopped on the high seas even in cases when it is suspected of carrying nuclear material or weapons.[170]

Participating states, in September 2003, agreed to determine four basic principles to help realise its objective and purpose.[171] These principles are: 1) taking of effective individual and collective measures to intercept the transfer or transportation of WMD's, their delivery means and related material carried between states or non-state actors contributing in their proliferation; 2) adoption of adequate procedures for exchange of information related to proliferation, protection of classified material, dedication of enough means and sources to enable the interception of these transactions and maximising of international cooperation between states in this process; 3) review and work with national authorities to strengthen their capacities to fight these features and in strengthening of international legal framework; 4) taking of concrete action to assist struggles to intercept WMD's deliveries, their means of delivery or other related material.[172]

This initiative is an informal structure and does not empower states with additional competences in the fight against WMD's trafficking and related material. It has 15 key states and more than 70 other participating states.[173] In the year 2004, President Bush proposed expanding the competences of this initiative (to not address only the delivery and transfer activities) in order to suppress the activities of different facilities, confiscation of materials and freezing of assets related directly or indirectly with WMD's. However, up to now nothing has moved in this direction.[174] Interception of the vessel sailing from Indonesia towards Libya carrying centrifuges components for Uranium enrichment, according to American officials, was a success of international cooperation in this initiative.[175]

---

[170] Supra note 969, p. 223.

[171] The principles of this initiative can be found at the State Department official webpage, visited on 13 September 2011, http://www.state.gov/t/isn/c27726.htm

[172] *Ibid.*

[173] Supra note 1114, p. 35.

[174] *Ibid.*

[175] Supra note 655.

Global Initiative to Combat Nuclear Terrorism (Global Initiative)

The Global Initiative is the most concrete one designed to combat nuclear terrorism. This initiative was established under the leadership of the US President George Bush and the Russian President Vladimir Putin in 2006.[176] Its mission is to strengthen global capacity in prevention, detection and response against nuclear terrorism through international cooperation.[177] Today, this initiative has 82 state partners in the world.[178] Apart from Member States it has also four observers who play a very important role in fighting terrorism: the European Union, IAEA, INTERPO and the UN Drugs and Crime Office.[179] It plays a specific role in the implementation of the objective and purpose of the International Covenants for Suppression of Acts of Nuclear Terrorism; the Convention on Physical Protection of Nuclear Material and its Amendment of 2005 and that of the SC 1540 Resolution[180].

Partner countries in this initiative have determined eight principles for their work: 1) improvement of accounting, control and protection of nuclear and radiological material; 2) increase the security level at nuclear civilian facilities; 3) detection and prohibition of nuclear traffic with nuclear and radiological material; 4) capacity improvement to search, confiscate and establishment of secure controls of nuclear and radiological materials; 5) prohibition of safe havens and supply sources for terrorists seeking to obtain nuclear or radiological material; 6) securing necessary legal infrastructure to combat activities related to nuclear terrorism7) response against and mitigation of nuclear terrorism consequences; 8) share of information to prevent and response against acts of nuclear terrorism.[181]

Despite the good-will behind this initiative, it is faced with financial problems because it does not have any specific provisions about its funding. This may impact on exercising its function and in achieving

[176] For more see The Global Initiative to Combat Nuclear Terrorism, US State Department, visited on17 October 2011, http://www.state.gov/t/isn/c18406.htm.

[177] *Ibid.*

[178] *Ibid.*

[179] *Ibid.*

[180] Supra note 969, p. 224-225.

[181] Supra note 1119.

concrete results.[182] This initiative is expected to yield its results in the future. According to a State Department official, the purpose of this initiative is to create a *"steady and growing network"* of participants, because combating terrorism cannot be done by one state only.[183] The work of this initiative was pretty much focused on Africa because a number of countries from this continent do not perceive nuclear terrorism as a real threat and hesitate to join such international initiatives. To break this stance, the US, through this Global Initiative was engaged with different African countries to raise their awareness on the impact and the role of nuclear terrorism in the world.[184]

The Global G8 Partnership Against the Proliferation of Materials and Weapons of Mass Destruction

The Global G8 Partnership was established in the year 2002 at the summit of the 7 most industrialised nations plus Russia at the time.[185] By establishing this partnership states committed themselves to specific amounts of money to finance it, among which the US alone committed financial support of $10 billion to be disbursed over a 10 year period, with an objective to reach at least $20 billion for the same period for which other states committed to finance the remaining $10 billion.[186] During the May summit of 2011, the state leaders of the most industrialized countries committed to secure the same amount of money for the

[182] Supra note 1114, p. 36.

[183] Wade Boese, "Anti-Nuclear Terrorism Principles Issued", Arms Control Association, visited on 20 March 2012 http://www.armscontrol.org/act/2006_12/AntiNuclear.

[184] Up to now the following African states are part of this intitiative: Cape Verde, Côte d'Ivoire, Libya, Mauritius, Morocco, the Seychelles, and Zambia, see Bonnie Jenkins, "Adopting to the Times: The Evolution of U.S. Threat Reduction Programmess", Arms Control Association, January/February 2011, visited on 18 August 2011, http://www.armscontrol.org/act/2011_01-02/Jenkins.

[185] Seven most industrialise nations at that time were: The US, Great Britain, Germany, Italy, japan, France and Canada. Today, this partnership is supported by other states: Australia, Belgium, Check Republic, Denmark, Finland, Ireland, Holland, New Zealand, Norway, Ploand, South Korea and Switzerland, see "Global Partnership Against the Spread of Weapons and Materials of Mass Destrucition, programmes 10+10 over 10", Nuclear Threat Initiative, visited on 30 March 2012, http://www.nti.org/treaties-and-regimes/global-partnership-against-spread-/eapons-and-materials-mass-destruction-10-plus-10-over-10-programmes/.

[186] *Ibid.*

next decade.[187] Other financial sources are allowed to contribute to the functioning of this partnership.[188]

This partnership is based on a non-proliferation framework with four main objectives: destruction of chemical weapons; destruction of nuclear weapons; nuclear and radiological security; and peaceful employment of former scientists involved in the field of armament.[189] The main focus of its work was Russia in the first place but as time went by, the activities of this partnership have been expanded to other countries.[190]

In its summit of 2002, states agreed to design 6 principles as a basis for preventing terrorists or states providing safe havens to terrorists from obtaining material or weapons of mass destruction. These principles consist of 1) strengthening international treaties and instruments and other institutions to prevent proliferation; 2) improve accounting and securing of material and weapons during the phases of production, use, stocking or international and national transportation; 4) strengthening of border controls; 5) control of national and international transactions and deliveries; and 6) strengthening of efforts in managing and eradicating stockpiles of fission materials which are out of use for defence purposes.[191] This summit also approved specific guidelines for the functioning of this partnership.[192] According to the guidelines, states may enter into bilateral and multilateral agreements to achieve the objective and purpose of this partnership.[193] The mandate of this partnership expired in 2012, however it is expected to be extended taking into consideration results achieved and the readiness of states to continue with financial support for another decade. The annual summit of the G8 held in Canada in June of 2012 issued the Global Partnership Report emphasising the achieved progress in the elimination of chemi-

---

[187] *Ibid.*

[188] For the moment, this partnership has partner countries from Africa, Latin America and Middle East, see supra note 1126.

[189] Supra note 950, p. 748.

[190] Today, this partnership is doing some important work in Ukranie, see Amy F. Wolf, Nonprolfieration and Threat Reduction Assistance: U.S. Programmes in the Former Soviet Union, Congressional Research Services, Report for Congress, 04 February 2010, p. 55.

[191] The Global Partnership Against the Spread of Weapons and Materials of Mass Destruction, Statement by G8 Leaders, visited on 27 June 2002, http://www.g8.utoronto.ca/summit/2002kananaskis/arms.html.

[192] *Ibid.*

[193] Supra note 1126.

cal weapons stating that 45% of all existing chemical weapons had been destroyed at the global level as a result of this partnership.[194]

Different initiatives exist at the international level foreseeing objectives and purposes in fighting international terrorism and nuclear terrorism in particular. However, it seems that they are faced with different problems including financial ones but also the number of participating states which does not give them a universal character and thus not all states participate in their activities. On the other side the existence of several initiatives with similar objectives and purposes may impact the overlap of tasks and duties with direct effect in coordination activities. An adequate forum which would also centralise such efforts would come under the UN umbrella which on the other side is facing a lack of meaningful activities arising first and foremost from different political perspectives and viewpoints on specific issues coming from Member States with voting rights. After the 9/11 attacks, there have not been any terrorist attack of the same scale however no one can be sure that it will not happen again and which could involve nuclear weapons or other WMDs. The current situation at the international level seems to point to the fact that still, international cooperation and coordination to prevent terrorism in general will still need to be developed at different terrains through bilateral and multilateral cooperation. This, in the first place, impacts the overall coordination efforts and financial burden for which some countries cooperate only in selective initiatives or in the worst case to be reluctant to cooperate. Ultimately, without universal support and engagement, the objectives and purposes of these initiatives may be only good words on the paper without diminishing the results achieved so far.

[194] *Ibid.*

CHAPTER VIII

CONCLUSION

Nuclear material and energy will be part of our lives in one way or another for years to come and with this the concern related to the control of activities related to its production and use. Nuclear energy can play a crucial part in supporting the development of mankind by responding to the ever increasing need for energy but the same sources of energy may be misused by state and non-state actors in a way becoming a major threat to mankind. The US gave the green light in 2012 to continue construction of new nuclear reactors for the production of electricity.[1] Poland is reviewing its plans to construct nuclear reactors for the production of electricity which caused reactions from Germany which in turn has put in place an agenda for shutting down all its nuclear reactors by 2022.[2] More than 45 states all around the world have currently at least one nuclear reactor and are seriously considering continuing to construct new ones.[3] The trend of demand for nuclear energy supply is on the rise taking into consideration the trends of urban development in the developed and underdeveloped world. It seems that states under development will present the highest need for such energy which is understandable in order to support their expanding economies.[4]

Increasing demand for nuclear energy at the same time increases the possibility of misusing it by state and non-state actors which may easily have a great impact on international peace and security. There is a relatively good legal infrastructure to fight the misuse of nuclear energy but it still needs to be improved for the better management of different

[1] See "Nuclear Power in the USA", World Nuclear Association, visited on 2 May 2012, http://www.world-nuclear.org/info/inf41.html.

[2] See Aaron Wiener, "German Oppose New Plants Next Door", *SpiegelOnline International*, visited on 13 January 2012, http://www.spiegel.de/international/europe/0,1518,808794,00.html.

[3] Included here are states like Kosovo, Albania, Croatia, Serbia and other states in Europe, Asia, Africa and Latin America, see "Emerging Nuclear Energy Countries", World Nuclear Association, visited on02 April 2012, http://www.world-nuclear.org/info/inf102.html.

[4] *Ibid.*

situations. A very important agreement is the Comprehensive Test Ban Treaty and has not yet come into force. The management of this situation requires a more liberal approach by the international community but also by using technological development. From the technological aspect, it would be highly desirable if it became possible to develop such machinery which could be used only for Uranium enrichment at a lower scale for peaceful use and not military. This could possibly ease at a high level the international control of Uranium enrichment activities and in the removal of all dilemmas regarding nuclear programmes of different states. At the same time this would make it very easy for states wishing to acquire such technology for peaceful use and in harmony with their rights to produce such energy as stipulated in the NPT. However, even in these cases, states which are willing to do so may modify those devices and use them for military purposes. Today, most of the states in the world possess the scientific capacities who understand the process of Uranium enrichment which could be used to achieve particular interests of a state. States, while passing through difficulties, have managed to develop their military programmes, even through clandestine methods, which makes the hypothesis less reliable that the development of a separate technology for Uranium enrichment would make the world a safer place from its misuse.

The other approach in international cooperation would favour a more liberal approach in international relations which would entail a general transfer of competences in the realization of the NPT objective and purpose on international organisations in which case the IAEA would take the cornerstone position. This would necessarily require the establishment of an LEU reserve to supply states requiring it and managed by the IAEA. Such an authority was initiated by the IAEA Board of Governors resolution in November of 2009 which authorised the General Director to establish it.[5] In compliance with this an agreement was signed by Russia which agreed to take over the construction of a reserve facility and its maintenance with a capacity of 120 metric tons, free of charge.[6]

[5] Request by the Russian Federation regarding its Initiative to Establish as Reserve of Low Enriched Uranium (LEU) for the Supply of LEU to the IAEA for its Member States, Board of Governors Resolution, IAEA Gov/2009/81, 27 November 2009, para 2.

[6] In December of 2001, Russia completed construction of this facility, while the SPI commited financial support of 50 million dollars while the US committed 50 million, EU 32 million, UAE 10 million, Norway, 5 million and Kuwait 10 million, see "Russia Inaugurates World's First Low Enriched Uranium Reserve:, IAEA top Stories and Features, 17 decem-

Prima facie this initiative sounds very good, however there are obstacles because the role of this reserve is supposed to be in supporting states with LEU supply in cases of international market disturbances in nuclear material.[7] States would still reserve their unlimited right to acquire technology for the production of nuclear energy for peaceful use in compliance with Article VI of the NPT.[8] For the realization of the objective and purpose of the NPT it would be necessary to prohibit any state from producing nuclear energy on its own and on the other hand to give guarantees for the uninterrupted supply of nuclear energy for peaceful use at an affordable price which could revolve around the amount or expansion of the production of nuclear energy of that state. Of course, one has to pay attention to the resistance of many states in this direction taking into consideration that in the first place we deal here with the removal of control of a state from over their energetic sources and transfer it to an international authority. It has to do a lot with how much trust states show to developing such arrangements and whether they will be able to receive a constant supply of energy as they had determined the demand and uninterrupted. It also has to do with the prestige of a state which wants to show its technological development to the world. A lot of attention should be paid to internal factors, political and economic situation of a particular state which impacts the whole decision making process and thus determine the positioning of a state in international relations.

Securing a common international reserve to meet the needs of every state for nuclear energy for peaceful use under the IAEA management may impact world security in two aspects. On one side, it would have an impact on the prevention of proliferation of nuclear energy and technology for military use and on the other side it would increase the level of security at facilities storing nuclear material because these facilities would be built at a few locations and under IAEA supervision. A centralised management of nuclear energy would enable this material to be secured by specialised institutions and logically at a lower cost compared to what states pay for such services at the global level on an individual basis.

ber 2010, visited on 5 June 2011, http://www.iaea.org/newscenter/ne/s/2010/leureserve.html, also "IAEA approves global nuclear fuel bank", *World Nuclear News*, 06 December 2010, visited on 5 June 2011, http://www.world-nuclear-ne/s.org/ENF-IAEA_approves_global_nuclear_fuel_bank-0612105.html.

[7] Supra note 1150, para f of the preamble.

[8] *Id*, para. g of the preamble.

With regards to supply this reserve with nuclear material, it can be done by acknowledged nuclear states in which case the best ones would be the five ones recognized as such by the NPT. This could possibly avoid any controversies from states around the world. At the same time, this could directly impact on motivating states accelerating their disarmament efforts and possibly the elimination of all nuclear weapons, taking into consideration that the new security environment created could provide enough security to states that no state is hiding anything because none of them is allowed to produce nuclear energy at home. States supplying this reserve with necessary nuclear energy would sell it at a cost which would be enough to cover their expenses to produce it. The biggest beneficiary should be regarded to be the creation of a more secure environment and in the preservation of the international peace and security.

The five nuclear states could take the responsibility for constant supply with the necessary nuclear material while for accounting purposes it would require a professional group of persons with different backgrounds who could determine objectively the need of each state for nuclear energy in close cooperation with them. In such an arrangement, states would have taken on binding commitments in reporting their activities and clear balance between the amount of nuclear energy they acquire compared with the amount of electricity they produce. Full transparency and unlimited access at all times of the IAEA inspectors would be necessary for the process. To solve any potential disagreements a professional dispute settlement mechanism similar to what the WTO could be established the decision of which would be binding on all parties. The SC could play the key role in making sure of the implementation of the decisions of this mechanism because any disagreement of this nature may impact on international peace and security. In this case, it would require the amendment of international provisions and agreements discussed in this work. First and foremost it would require the amendment of the provision providing for the reserved rights of states to produce nuclear technology and energy for peaceful use.

If any, the role of the proposed IAEA reserve by its Board of Governors may play a crucial role towards the complete centralisation of nuclear reserves in this agency. For its success it would depend a lot on the stance of states vis-à-vis the centralisation of Uranium enrichment. The enriched Uranium in this reserve could be offered to states which have shown their willingness not to develop nuclear programmes at home and thus gradually increase the trust of other states to follow the same path and abandon their nuclear programmes willingly. In the meantime as the number of states entering this process accompanied with the established trust increases, they would be more ready to change the legal infrastructure which would place a general ban on all states to produce nuclear energy or technology at home.

The IAEA proposal may present only the first step but it will probably take many years to go further with more concrete steps. Until then, the NPT regime maybe should be reviewed in the realization of its objectives and purposes and above all, how all states could become party to the treaty, in particular states which possess nuclear capacity still remaining outside the regime. The NTP should stick with its policy of not allowing any new nuclear state aside from the five because it would go against the object and purpose of the treaty and also it would set a dangerous precedent to all states in and out of the regime. For the state outside the regime it would encourage them to stay in that position until they manage to develop nuclear energy and technology for military purposes and then apply to become party to the NPT but now as nuclear powers. For the states in the regime it could be understood that they could feel free to leave the regime if they wish to develop nuclear energy and technology for military use and return to the regime as nuclear powers. The case of North Korea, to which the SC made it clear that it would not be re-admitted into the regime as a nuclear state, is a good example of how the regime should continue to operate in this aspect. The prohibition of admitting new nuclear states has a direct impact on increasing the level of reliability of the regime towards all states.

Four states with military nuclear capabilities outside of the regime remain to be a great challenge to the international community in a struggle to allure them to become part of the NPT regime. In such a situation, perhaps the proposal of the former IAEA General Director ElBaradei for an international management of nuclear weapons would be the first step to deal with this situation. Nuclear weapons are closely linked with national interests of states as interpreted on their own criteria. States are rational actors and at a particular moment they can change their views on national security thus allowing them to possibly engage in international cooperation and collective control of national security. In this way, it would be possible for the creation of an international mini regime for the management of military nuclear capabilities of states which posess them which could open the way for them to become parties to the NPT in compliance with the requirements established by this regime. International management of their capabilities would allow them to be qualified conditionally as non-nuclear powers under international management because of their loss of direct control over their nuclear weapons. This may have a domino effect in inciting also the five nuclear states in the regime to follow the same suit toward full elimination of nuclear weapons.

The existence of huge amounts of nuclear weapons by nuclear states implies that they intend to use them at least in cases of self-defence as prescribed in their military doctrines and interpreted by them on any individual case while on the other hand there is no international provision expressly prohibiting the use or threat to use them in all situations. The ICJ confirmed this but it made a very general prohibition exclusion referring to the provision of humanitarian law. This stance was criticised even by the ICJ judges taking part in the voting in the advisory opinion regarding the use or threat to use nuclear weapons. This court at that time excluded the application of international legislation in the field of environment protection and their effect in the use of nuclear weapons. At that time legislation for the protection of the environment had not been developed as far as it is today and which is only based on some general principles and guidelines on how a man can move towards a sustainable development.

At the time of deciding on legal opinion only the UN Covenant Framework for Climate Change existed and which entered into force in 1994. But, after issuance of the advisory opinion on the legality of use or threat to use nuclear weapons important steps have been taken regarding the development of the legal infrastructure for the protection of the environment such as the entering into force of the Kyoto Protocol in 2005, the Copenhagen Accords in 2009 and also the Cancun Agreement in 2010 as the most important international acts in this field. Besides this, different studies were conducted and reports drafted on climate change in the protection of the environment and the effects of human activities on these changes.[9] Perhaps if the ICJ were to face the same question today vis-à-vis state obligations toward the environment, it could have reached another conclusion and maybe delegitimise the use of nuclear weapons because of their possible long-term effects on the environment. Anyhow, environmental law would still have to be developed further in order to give a strong argument against the use of nuclear weapons in all circumstances.

In the regional aspect, an important role is played by the nuclear free regimes which have now managed to create large territories free of nuclear weapons which put a ban on the production of nuclear technology or energy for peaceful use. These are very good examples which show that there is a possibility of increasing international trust and to achieve agreements to establish free nuclear zones in a region and the same could be achieved in other regions with additional commitments. These zones should be supported by the five nuclear states, especially the Central and South-East Asia zones where these nuclear states have not offered their necessary guarantees for the non-use of nuclear weapons against states of these zones. The five nuclear states can impact to strengthen further these zone and the release of pressure already in existence there.

In the struggle to fight non-state actors, the international community should do more in this endeavour such as in the case of the clandestine network of A.Q. Khan and other terrorist and criminal organisation with international character. This could be done by strengthening and improving international and national legal infrastructure. To fight clandestine networks such as that of A.Q. Khan it would be better if the international community could foresee specific international provision expressly dealing with non-state actors as organisations, groups or individuals with stricter and concrete measures to fight them and possibly empowered with jurisdiction of a respected international body to prosecute individuals engaged in such activities.[10] In this endeavour it would

[9] For more see official webpage of the United Nations Framwork Convention on Climate Change, visited on 4 May 2012, http://unfccc.int/2860.php.

[10] A.Q. Khan for his activities was sentenced to housarrest in 2009, which reprsents a modest sentence compared to the risk respresented by his activities towards international community, see Joby Warrick, "Nuclear Scientist A.Q. Khan is Freed From House Arrest", *Washington Post*, 7 February 2009, http://www.washingtonpost.com/wp-dyn/content/article/2009/02/06/AR2009020603730.html.

be very important that the Comprehensive Convention on International Terrorism would help a lot in the coordination of international activities to fight terrorism. The implementation of agreements in force and a closer cooperation between states, especially in the field of nuclear forensics could play a determining factor for a successful prevention of nuclear terrorism as the best way to suppress such activities.

LITERATURE

PRIMARY SOURCES

BOOKS

Adam Robert & Richard Guelff ed., *Documents on the Laws of War* (Oxford University Press, New York, 1989).

Alexei Arbatov, Vladimir Dvorkin, and Sergey Oznobishcheve, "*Contemporary Nuclear Doctrines,* (Institute of World Economy and International Relations and Russian Academy of Sciences, Nuclear Threat Initiative, MEMO RAN, Moscow, 2010).

Bowet D.W., *Self-Defence in International Law* (Praeger, Manchester, 1958).

Brian Michael Jenkins, *Will Terrorists Go Nuclear?* (Prometheus Books, New York, 2008).

David Halloway, *Entering the Nuclear Arms Race: The Soviet Decision to Build the Atomic Bomb 1939-1945* (Wilson Center, Washington, D.C, 1979).

Dietrich Schindler & Jiri Toman, *The Laws of Armed Conflicts* (BRILL, Leiden, 1988).

Frank Barnaby, *How Nuclear Weapons Spread: Nuclear Weapons Proliferation in the 1990s* (Routledge, New York, 2005).

Garry McCracken & Peter Stott, *Fusion: The Energy of Universe* (Elsevier Academic Press, Massachusetts, USA, 2005).

Graham Allison, *Nuclear Terrorism: The Ultimate Preventable Catastrophe* (Time Books, New York, 2011).

Graham T. Allison, Owen R. Cote, Jr., Richard A. Falkenrath, Steven E. Miller, *Avoiding Russian Anarchy: Containing the Threat of Russian Loose Nuclear Weapons and Fissile Material* (Centre for Science and International Affairs, Harvard, Massachusetts, 1999).

Henry D. Sokolski, *Getting Mad: Nuclear Mutual Assured Destruction, its Origins and Practice* (Strategic Studies Institute, 2004).

Hilaire McCoubrey & Nigel D. White, *International Law and Armed Conflicts* (Ashgate Publishing Group, Aldershot & London, 1992).

Ian Bellany, *Curbing the Spread of Nuclear Weapons* (Manchester University Press, Manchester 2005).

Ian Brownlie, *International Law and the Use of Force by States* (Clarendon Press, Oxford, 1963).

Ivan Sascha Sheehan, *When Terrorism and Counterterrorism Clash: The War on Terror and the Transformation of Terrorist Activity* (Cambria Press, New York, 2007).

Jack Carravelli, *Nuclear Insecurity: Understanding the Threat from Rouge Nations and Terrorists* (Praeger Security International, USA, 2008).

James E. Doyle, *Nuclear Safeguards, Security and Non-Proliferation* (Butteworth Heinemann, Massachusetts, USA, 2008).

John Burroughs, *The (Il)legality of Threat or Use of Nuclear Weapons: A Guide to the Historic Opinion of the International Court of Justice* (International Association of Lawyers Against Nuclear Weapons, Munster Lit Verlag, 1997).

John Tabak, *Nuclear Energy*, (Energy and the Environment, New York, 2009).

Joseph Cirincione, *Bomb Scare: The History and Future of Nuclear Weapons* (Columbia University Press, New York, 2007).

Keith A. Hansen, *The Comprehensive Nuclear Test Ban Treaty: An Insider's Perspective* (Stanford University Press, California, 2006).

Keith Mothersson, *From Hiroshima to the Hague: Guide to the World Court Project* (International Peace Bureau, Geneva, 1992).

Kevin McGrath, *Confronting Al Qaeda: New Strategies to Combat Terrorism* (Naval Institute Press, Annapolis, 2011).

Lori F. Damrosch & Ocsar Scheffer, *Law and Force in the New International Order,* (Westview Press, San Francisco, 1991).

Lori F. Damrosch, Louis Henkin, Richards Crawford Pugh, Oscar Schachter, Hans Smit, *International Law: Cases and Materials* (Fourth edition, West Group, St. Paul, 2001).

Mario Esteban Carranza, *South Asian Security and International Nuclear Order: Creating a Robust Indo-Pakistani Nuclear Arms Control Regime* (Ashgate, Burlington, 2009).

Mian, Zia, A. H. Nayyar, R. Rajaraman, and M. V. Ramana, *Fissile Materials in South Asia: The Implications of the U.S.-Indian Nuclear Deal*, (International Panel on Fissile Materials, September 2006).

Michael Krepon, Better Safe than Sorry: *The Ironies of Living with the Bomb* (Stanford Security Studies, Stanford University Press, California, 2009).

Michael Quinlan, *Thinking About Nuclear Weapons: Principles, Problems, Prospects* (Oxford University Press, Oxford, 2009).

O. Dahlman, S. Mykkeltveit, H. Haak, *Nuclear Test Ban: Converting Political Visions to Reality* (Springer, 2009).

Patrick M. Cronin, ed. *Double Trouble: Iran and North Korea as Challenges to International Security* (Praeger Security International, London, 2008).

Richard Rhodes, *Arsenals of Folly: The Making of the Nuclear Arms Race* (Knopf Doubleday Publishing Group, 2008, New York).

Robert Powell, *Nuclear Deterrence: Theory: The Search for Credibility* (Cambridge University Press, USA, 1990).

Robert W. Marrs, *Nuclear Terrorism: Rethinking the Unthinkable* (University Press of the Pacific, Hawaii, 2004).

Saira Khan, *Iran and Nuclear Weapons: Protracted Conflict and Proliferation* (Routledge, New York, 2010).

Sarah J. Diehl and James Clay Moltz, *History of Nuclear Weapons and Non-Proliferation: A Reference Handbook* (ABC Clio, California; Colorado; England 2002).

Scott D. Sagan, *The Limits of Safety: Organisations, Accidents, and Nuclear Weapons* (Princeton University Press, 1993).

Stanimir A. Alexandrov, *Self-Defence Against the use of Force in International Law* (Kluwer International, The Hague, 1996).

Stefan M. Aubrey, *The New Dimension of International Terrorism* (Strategie und Konfliktforshung, Zurich, 2004).

Weapons of Terror: Freeing the World of Nuclear, Biological and Chemical Arms, Weapons of Mass Destruction Commission (EO Grafiska, Stockholm, 2006)

Yoram Dinstein, *War, Aggression and Self-Defence*, (2nd ed. Cambridge University Press, Cambridge, 1994).

JOURNALS

"A. Q. Khan Nuclear Chronology", *Carnegie Endowment for International Peace*, Vol. VIII. No. 8, 07 September 2005.

"Nuclear Black Markets: Pakistan, A.Q. Khan and the rise of proliferation network: A Net Assessment", *The International Institute for Strategic Studies*, 2007.

"The Letters of Abdul Khan", *Bulletin of the Atomic Scientists*, Vol. 48. No. 6 July-August 1992.

"The NPT and Global Non-Proliferation Regime: A U.S. Policy Agenda", *Boston University International Law Journal*, 12 B.U. Int'l L.J. 407, autumn 1994.

Ali Ahmed, "Reviewing India's Nuclear Doctrine", *Institute for Defence Studies and Analyses*, 24 April 2009.

Antonio F. Perez, "Survival of Rights Under the Nuclear Non-Proliferation Treaty: Withdrawal and the Continuing Right of International Atomic Energy Agency Safeguards", *Virginia Journal of International Law*, 34 Va. J. Int'l L. 749, 1994.

Arsalan M. Suleman, "Bargaining in the Shadow of Violence: The NPT, IAEA, and Nuclear Non-Proliferation Negotiations", *Berkley Journal of International Law*, 25 Berkley J. Int'l L. 206, 2008.

Charles J. Moxcley, Jr. "The Sword in the Mirror: The Lawfulness of North Korea's use and Threat of Use of Nuclear Weapons Based on the United States Legitimization of Nuclear Weapons", *Fordham International Law Journal* , 27 Fordham Int'l L. J. 1379, April 2004

Christopher C. Joyner and Alexander Ian Parkhouse, "Nuclear Terrorism in a Globalizing World: Assessing the Threat and the Emerging Management Regime", *Stanford Journal of International Law*, 45 Stan. J. Int'l L. 203, summer 2009.

Christopher O. Clary, "The A.Q. Khan Network: Causes and Implications", (Master Thesis Naval Postgraduate School, California, December 2005).

Cody Coombs, "Blue Morning-Glories in the Sky: Correcting Sanctions to Enforce Nuclear Non-proliferation Iran", *Indiana International & Comparative Law Review*, 19 Ind. Int'l & Comp. L. Rev. 419, 2009.

David Albright & Mark Hibbs, "Pakistan's Bomb: Out of the Closet", *The Bulleting of the Atomic Scientists*, Vol. 48. No. 6 July-August 1992.

David P. Fidler, "International Convention on Suppression of Acts of Nuclear Terrorism", *ASIL Insight*, vol. 11 issue 8, 05 July 2007.

David S. Jonas and Christopher Swift, "Reformulating the Nuclear Nonproliferation Regime: Al-Qaeda, Global Terrorism, and the Rouge State Paradigm", *University of California Journal of International Law and Foreign Affairs*, 13 UCLA J. Int'l L. & For. Aff. 337, autumn, 2008.

David S. Yost, "France's New Nuclear Doctrine", *International Affairs,* Vol. 82, Issue 4, 2006.

Edda Kristjansdottir, "The Legality of the Threat or Use of Nuclear Weapons under Current International Law: The Arguments behind the World Court's Advisory Opinion", *New York University Journal of International Law and Politics*, 30 N.Y.U. J. Int'L. & Pol. 291, 1997-1998.

Edward Gunn, "The Moral Dilemma of Atomic Warfare", *Aegis, The Otterbein College Humanities Journal*, spring, 2006.

Eric Yong-Joong Lee, "The Six-Party Talks and the North Korean Nuclear Dispute Resolution Under the IAEA Safeguards Regime", *University of Hawaii Asian-pacific Law & Policy Journal*, 5 Asian-Pacific L. & Pol'y J. 101, 2004.

Geoffrey R. Watson, "ASIL Insight: The ICJ and the Lawfulness of the use of Nuclear Weapons", *ASIL Newsletter*, June 1995.

Geoffrey S. Carslo, "An offer They Can't Refuse? The Security Council Tells North Korea to Re-Sign the Nuclear Non-Proliferation Treaty", *Columbia Journal of Transnational Law*, 46 Colum. J. Transat'l L. 420, 2008.

Grant Guthrie, "Nuclear Testing Rocks the Sub-Continent: Can International Law Halt the Impending Nuclear Conflict Between India and Pakistan?", *Hasting International and Comparative Law Review*, 23 Hastings Int'l & Comp. L. Rev. 495, spring-summer 2000.

Gustavo R. Slauvienen, "Nuclear Non-proliferation and Unique Issues of Compliance", *ILSA Journal of International & Comparative Law*, 12 ILSA J Int'l & Comp L 593, 2005.

James C. Kraska, "Adverting Nuclear Terrorism: Building a Global Regime of Cooperative Threat Reduction", *American University International Law Review*, 20 Am. U. Int'l L. Rev. 703, 2005.

Jill M. Sheldon, "Nuclear Weapons and the Laws of War: Does Customary International Law Prohibit the Use of Nuclear Weapons in all Circumstance", *Fordham International Law Journal*, 20 Fordham Int'l L.J. 1891, 1996.

Kenneth Waltz, "The Spread of Nuclear Weapons: More May Be Better", *Adelphi Papers, International Institute of Strategic Studies*, No. 171, autumn 1981.

Mark E. Newcomb, "Non-Proliferation, Self-Defence, and the Korean Crisis", *Vanderbilt Journal of Transnational Law*, 27 Vand. J. Transat'l L. 603, October 1994.

Mathew Fuhrmann, "Spreading Temptation: Proliferation and Peaceful Nuclear Cooperation Agreements", *International Security* Vol. 34 no. 1, summer 2009.

Michael Spies, "Iran and the Limits of the Nuclear Non-Proliferation Regime, Symposium on the Nuclear Non-Proliferation Treaty: A Legal Framework in Crisis?", *American University of International Law Review*, 22 Am. U. Int'l L. Rev. 401, 2007.

Paige Willan, "The Convention on the Suppression of Acts of Nuclear Terrorism: An old Solution to a New Problem", *Georgetown Journal of International Law*, 39 Geo. J. Int'l L. 527, spring 2008.

Raven Winters, "Preventing Repeat Offenders: North Korea's Withdrawal and the Need for Revision to the Nuclear Non-Proliferation Treaty", *Vanderbilt Journal of Transnational Law*, 38 Vand. J. Transnat'l L. 1499, November 2005.

Roxana Vatanparast, "International Law Versus the Preemptive Use of Force: Racing to Confront the Spectre of a Nuclear Iran", *Hastings International and Comparative Law*, 31 Hastings Int'l & Comp. L. Rev. 783, summer 2008.

Steven E. Miller, "Proliferation gamesmanship: Iran and the Politics of Nuclear Confrontation", *Syracuse Law Review, 57 Syracuse L. Rev.* 551, summer 2008.

Suleiman Abu Gheith, "'Why We Fight America': Al Qaida Spokesman Explains September 11 and Declares Intentions to Kill 4 Million Americans with Weapons of Mass Destruction", *Middle East Media Res. Inst.* Special Dispatch No. 388, 12 July 2002.

Wendy L. Mirsky, "The Link Between Russian Organized Crime and Nuclear-Weapons Proliferation: Fighting Crime and Ensuring International Security", *University of Pennsylvania Journal of International Business Law*, 16. U. Pa. J. Int'l Bus. L. 749, 1995.

Winston P. Naga, "Nuclear Arsenals, International lawyers, and the Challenge of the Millennium", *The Yale Journal of International Law*, 24 Yale J. Int'l L. 485, summer 1999.

INTERNATIONLA AGREEMENTS AND RESOLUTIONS

International Agreements

African Nuclear Weapon-Free Zone Treaty, 35 I.L.M. 698.

Charter of the United Nations, 59 Stat. 1031, T.S. 993, 26 June 1945.

Convention on Prohibitions or Restrictions on the use of Certain Conventional Weapons Which May Deemed to be Excessively Injurious or to Have Indiscriminate Effects, UN Doc. A/Conf.95/15, Annex I (1980), 10 October1980.

Convention on the Physical Protection of Nuclear Material, T.I.A.S. 11080, 03 March 1980.

Additional Model Protocol, IAEA Doc. INFCIRC/540 (corrected).

International Convention for the Suppression of Acts of Nuclear Terrorism, 15 U.N.T.S. 2445, 13 April 2005.

International Convention for the Suppression of Acts of Nuclear Terrorism, UN Doc. A/Res/59/290, 14 September 2005.

International Convention for the Suppression of the Financing Terrorism, U.N. Doc. A/Res/54/109, 09 December 1999.

International Convention on the Suppression of Terrorist Bombings, U.N. Doc. A/Res/52/164, 2149 U.N.T.S. 284, 15 December 1997.

Protocol III of the South Pacific Nuclear Free Zone Treaty, 24 I.L.M. 1442, 06 August 1986.

Model Safeguards Agreement, IAEA Doc. INFCIRC/26, 30 March 1961.

Protocol I of the African Nuclear Weapon-Free Zone Treaty, 35 I.L.M. 698.

Protocol II of the African Nuclear Weapon-Free Zone Treaty, 35 I.L.M. 698.

CTBT Protocol on the International Monitoring System and International Data Centre Functions.

Protocol II of the South Pacific Nuclear Free Zone Treaty, 24 I.L.M. 1442, 06 August 1986.

Protocol II of the Treaty for the Prohibition of Nuclear Weapons in Latin America and the Caribbean, 634 U.N.T.S. 326, 22 April 1967.

The Statute of the International Court of Justice, 3 Bevans 1179, 26 June 1945.

The Text of the Agreement between Belgium, Denmark, the Federal Republic of Germany, Ireland, Italy, Luxembourg, the Netherlands, the European Atomic Energy Community and the Agency in Connection with the Treaty on the Non-Proliferation of Nuclear Weapons, IAEA Doc. INFCIRC/193, 14 September 1973.

The Treaty Banning Nuclear Weapons Tests in the Atmosphere, in Outer Space and Under Water, 480 U.N.T.S. 43, 05 August 1963.

Treaty Banning Nuclear Weapons Tests in the Atmosphere, in Outer Space and Under Water, 480 U.N.T.S. 43, 05 August 1963.

Treaty Between The United States of America and The Union of Soviet Socialist Republics on the Limitation of Underground Nuclear Weapon Tests, 13 I.L.M. 906, 3 July 1974.

Treaty Between the United States of America and the Union of Soviet Socialist Republics on Underground Nuclear Explosions for Peaceful Purposes, 15 I.L.M. 891, 28 May 1976.

Treaty for the Prohibition of Nuclear Weapons in Latin America and the Caribbean, 634 U.N.T.S. 326, 22 April 1967.

Treaty on the Non-Proliferation of Nuclear Weapons, 729 U.N.T.S. 161, 1968.

Treaty on the Prohibition of the Emplacement of Nuclear Weapons and other Weapons of Mass Destruction on the Sea-Bed and the Ocean Floor and in the Subsoil Thereof, 955 U.N.T.S. 115, 11 February 1971.

Treaty on the South East Asia Nuclear Weapon-Free Zone, 35 I.L.M. 635, 15 December 1995.

South Pacific Nuclear Free Zone Treaty, 24 I.L.M. 1442, 06 August 1986.

Treaty on a Nuclear-Weapon-Free Zone in Central Asia, UN/Res/51/45, 08 September 2006.

The Antarctic Treaty, 402 U.N.T.S. 71, 01 December 1959.

Agreement of 13 December 1991 between the Republic of Argentina, the Federative Republic of Brazil, the Brazilian-Argentine Agency for Accounting and Control of Nuclear Materials and the International Atomic Energy Agency for the Application of Safeguards, IAEA Doc. INFCIRC/435, March 1994.

Agreement of 30 January 1992 between the Governments of the Democratic People's Republic of Korea and the International Atomic Energy Agency for the Application of Safeguards in Connection with the Treaty on the Non-Proliferation of Nuclear Weapons, IAEA INFCIRC/403, May 1992.

Agreed Framework of 21 October 1994 between the United States of America and the Democratic People's Republic of Korea, IAEA INFCIRC/457, 02 November 1994.

The Statute of the IAEA, 276 U.N.T.S. 3, 26 October 1956.

Resolutions

Declaration on the Prohibition of the Use of Nuclear and Thermo-Nuclear Weapons, General Assembly Resolution 1653, UN. Doc. A/5100 (1961), 08 November 1961.

General Assembly Resolution "Measures to eliminate international terrorism", UN. Doc. A/Res/51/201, 17 December 1996.

General Assembly Resolution on Condemnation of Nuclear War, UN. Doc. A/Res/38/75, 15 December 1983.

General Assembly Resolution on General and Complete Disarmament: A Prohibition of the Dumping of Radioactive Waste, UN. Doc. A/Res/49/75 (1994).

Health and Environmental Effect of Nuclear Weapons, WHA RES. 46.40, U.N. WHO, Agenda Item 33, U.N. Doc. WHA 46.40 (1993).

Implementation of the NPT Safeguards Agreement between the Agency and the Democratic People's Republic of Korea, IAEA General Conference Resolution, IAEA Doc. GC(48)/RES/15, September 2004.

Implementation of the NPT Safeguards Agreement between the Agency and the Democratic People's Republic of Korea, IAEA General Conference Resolution ,IAEA Doc. GC(49)/Res/14, September 2005.

Implementation of the NPT safeguards agreement and relevant provisions of United Nations Security Council resolutions in the Islamic Republic of Iran, IAEA Board of Governors Resolution, IAEA Doc. GOV/2011/69, 18 November 2011.

Implementation of the NPT Safeguards Agreement in the Islamic Republic of Iran, IAEA Board of Governors Resolution, IAEA Doc. GOV/2006/27, 12 June 2006

Implementation of the NPT Safeguards Agreement in the Islamic Republic of Iran, IAEA Board of Governors Resolution, IAEA Doc. GOV/2006/38, 12 June 2006

Implementation of the NPT Safeguards Agreement in the Islamic Republic of Iran, IAEA Board of Governors Resolution, IAEA Doc. GOV/2006/53, 14 September 2006

Implementation of the NPT Safeguards Agreement in the Islamic Republic of Iran, IAEA Board of Governors Resolution, IAEA Doc. GOV/2006/64, 14 November 2006

Nuclear and Radiological Security: Progress on Measures to Protect Against Nuclear and Radiological Terrorism, IAEA General Conference Resolution, IAEA Doc. GC(47)/Res/8, September 2003.

Nuclear Security Report 2007: Measures to Protect Against Nuclear Terrorism, The IAEA Board of Governors General Conference, IAEA Doc. GOV/2007/43-GC (51)15, 15 August 2007.

Security Council Resolution 1441, UN. Doc. S/Res/1441 (2002), 08 November 2002.

Security Council Resolution 1540, UN. Doc. S/Res/1540, 28 April 2004.

Security Council Resolution 1624, UN. Doc. S/Res/1624, 14 September 2005.

Security Council Resolution 1695, UN. Doc. S/Res/1695 (2006), 15 July 2006.

Security Council Resolution 1718, UN. Doc. S/Res/1718 (2006), 14 October 2006.

Security Council Resolution 1737, UN. Doc. S/Res/1737/2006, 23 December 2006.

Security Council Resolution 1804, UN. Doc. S/Res/1804/2008, 03 March 2008.

Security Council Resolution 1804, UN. Doc. S/Res/1804/2008, 03 March 2008.

Security Council Resolution 1810, UN. Doc. S/Res/1810, 25 April 2008.

Security Council Resolution 1969, UN. Doc. S/Res/1969/2006, 31 July 2006.

Security Council Resolution 1989, UN. Doc. S/Res/1989 (2011), 17 July 2011.

Security Council Resolution 687, UN. Doc. S/Res/687 (1991), 08 April 1991.

Security Council Resolution 825, UN. Doc. S/Res/825, 11 May 1993.

Security Council Resolution 984,UN. Doc. S/Res/984/1995, 11 April 1995.

Security Council Resolution, 1267, UN. Doc. S/Res/1267, 15 October 1999.

Security Council Resolution, 1373, UN. Doc. S/Res/1373 (2001), 28 September 2001.

The implementation of IAEA safeguards in the Democratic People's Republic of Korea (DPRK), Resolution of the Board of Governors, IAEA GOV/2002/60, 29 November 2002.

OTHER LEGAL ACTS, DOCUMENTS AND SPEECHES

Other Legal Acts

Federal Constitutional Act concerning a Nuclear Free Austria, MGBL/OS/199990813/1/0149, 01 July 1999.

Law of Mongolia on its Nuclear-Weapon-Free Status, 03 February 2000.

Documents

The CTBT Annex on the List of Characteristic Parameters for the International Data Centre for Standard Event Screening.

Communication dated 20 June 1995 from the Embassy of Egypt together with the Written Statement of the Government of Egypt to the President of the ICJ.

Declaration of Judge Vereshchetin, Decl. Vereshchetin, Legality of the Threat or Use of Nuclear Weapons, Advisory opinions and orders", General List no. 95, pp. 279-181.

Declaration of President Bedjaoui, Decl. Bedjaoui, Legality of the Threat or Use of Nuclear Weapons, Advisory opinions and orders", General List no. 95, pp. 268-274.

Declaration on Atomic Bomb by President Truman, and Prime Ministers Atlee and King, 15 November 1946.

Dissenting Opinion of Vice President Schwebel, Diss. Op. Schwebel., Legality of the Threat or Use of Nuclear Weapons, Advisory opinions and orders", General List no. 95, pp. 311-329.

Dissenting Opinion of Judge Koroma, Diss. Op. Koroma, Legality of the Threat or Use of Nuclear Weapons, Advisory opinions and orders", General List no. 95., pp. 556-582.

Dissenting Opinion of Judge ODA, Diss. Op. Oda., Legality of the Threat or Use of Nuclear Weapons, Advisory opinions and orders", General List no. 95, pp. 330-374.

Dissenting Opinion of Judge Shahabuddeen, Diss. Op. Shahabuddeen, Legality of the Threat or Use of Nuclear Weapons, Advisory opinions and orders", General List no. 95, pp. 375-428.

Dissenting Opinion of Judge Weeramantry, Diss. Op. Weeramantry. Legality of the Threat or Use of Nuclear Weapons, Advisory opinions and orders", General List no. 95, pp. 556-582,

Einstein letter to President Roosevelt, 02 August 1939.

Final Declaration and the Measures to Promote the Entry into Force of the Comprehensive Nuclear-Test-Ban Treaty, New York, CTBTO, 23 September 2011.

IAEA Board of Governors Adopts Resolution on Safeguards in North Korea, IAEA Media Advisory, 2003/48,12 February 2003.

Inadequate Control of World's Radioactive Sources, IAEA Press Release 2002/09, 24 June 2009.

Adv. Op. Interpretation of the Agreement of 25 March 1951 between the WHO and Egypt, Advisory Opinion, I.C.J., Reports 1980.

Joint Declaration of South and North Korea on the Denuclearization of the Korean Peninsula, 19 February 1992.

Letter dated 12 September 2011 from the Chair of the Security Council Committee established pursuant to resolution 1540 (2004) addressed to the President of the Security Council submitting the report of the Committee on compliance with resolution 1540 (2004) , UN SC S/2011/579, 14 September 2011.

Letter Dated 13 June 1995 from the Ambassador of Finland, together with the written statement of the Government of Finland to the President of the ICJ, Embassy of Finland in the Hague, No. 1185, ICJ, Advisory Proceedings, Legality of the Threat or Use of Nuclear Weapons, Written Statements, 3.

Letter dated 14 June 1995 from the Minister at the Embassy of Japan, together with written statement of the Government of Japan to the Registers Office of the ICJ, Embassy of Japan, the Netherlands, ICJ, Advisory Proceedings, Legality of the Threat or Use of Nuclear Weapons, Written Statements, 2.

Letter dated 16 June 1995 from the Legal Adviser to the Foreign and Commonwealth Office of the United Kingdom of Great Britain and Northern Ireland, together with the written comments of the United Kingdom to the Registers Office of the ICJ, Foreign & Commonwealth Office, London SW1A 2AH, ICJ, Advisory Proceedings, Legality of the Threat or Use of Nuclear Weapons, Written Statements, 5.

Letter dated 19 June 1995 from the Ambassador of the Russian Federation together with written statement of the Government of the Russian Federation to the Registars Office of the ICJ, Russian Federation Embassy, the Hague.

Letter Dated 20 June 1995 from the Acting Legal Adviser to the Department of State, together with written statement of the Government of the United States of America to the Registers Office of the ICJ, US Department of State, Washington D.C. 20520, ICJ, Advisory Proceedings, Legality of the Threat or Use of Nuclear Weapons, Written Statements, 18.

Letter dated 20 June1995 from the Ambassador of the Federal Republic of Germany, together with written statement of the Government of the Federal Republic of Germany to the Registars Office of the ICJ, Der Botschafter Der Bundesrepublic Deutschland, the Hague, ICJ, Advisory Proceedings, Legality of the Threat or Use of Nuclear Weapons, Written Statements, 20.

Note Verbale dated 19 June 1995 from the Embassy of Mexico, together with written statement of the Government of Mexico to the President of the ICJ, Embassy of Mexico, the Hague, ICJ, Advisory Proceedings, Legality of the Threat or Use of Nuclear Weapons, Written Statements, 15.

Records of the Chief of Engineers, Manhattan Engineer District, Harrison-Bundy File, US National archive, Record Group 77, folder #76, published on Nuclear Files, visited on 08 September 2012, www.nuclearfiles.org.

Request by the Russian Federation regarding its Initiative to Establish a Reserve of Low Enriched Uranium (LEU) for the Supply of LEU to the IAEA for its Member States, Board of Governors Resolution, IAEA Doc. Gov/2009/81, 27 November 2009.

Separate Opinion of Judge Fleichhauer, Sep. Op. Fleichhauer, Legality of the Threat or Use of Nuclear Weapons, Advisory opinions and orders", ICJ General List no. 95, pp. 305-310.

The Atomic Energy Act of 1946, 42 U.S.C. 2011-2396 (1988 & Supp. 1992).

The Structure and Content of Agreements between the agency and States Required in Connection with the Treaty on the non-Proliferation of Nuclear weapons, IAEA Doc. INFCIRC/153 June 1972.

Speeches

Ambassador Javad Zarif speech at The Liechtenstein Colloquium on European and International Affairs me titull "Iran's Security Challenges and the Region", Lichtenstein Colloquium Report Vol 1, Princeton, August 2005.

President Harry S. Truman Message to Congress on the Atomic Bomb, Washington DC, 03 October 1945, Harry S. Truman Library and Museum, Public Papers of the Presidents: Harry Truman 1945-1953.

Remarks at the Review Conference of the Nuclear Non Proliferation Treaty by Hillary Rodham Clinton, The US State Department, 03 May 2010.

Statement by the Iranian Government and Visiting EU Foreign Ministers, 21 October 2003, IAEA, visituar on 20 June 2012.

Statement by the President of the Security Council, UN. Doc. S/ PRST/2006/15, 29 March 2006.

The Global Partnership Against the Spread of Weapons and Materials of Mass Destruction, Statement by G8 Leaders.

REPORTS, CASES AND INTERVIEWS

Reports

Global Fissile Material Report 2011, (International Panel on Fission Material, September 2011.

IAEA Annual Report, IAEA Doc. GC (48)/3 (2004).

IAEA Mission Report of the Great East Japan Earthquake Expert Mission", IAEA International Fact Finding Expert Mission of the Fukushima Dai-Ichi NPP Accident Following the Great East Japan Earthquake and Tsunami, 24 May-02 June 2011, 16 June 2011.

Implementation of NPT Safeguards Agreement in the Islamic Republic of Iran, Report of the Board of Governors, IAEA Doc. GOV/2005/67, 24 September 2005.

Implementation of NPT Safeguards Agreement in the Islamic Republic of Iran, Report of the Board of Governors, IAEA Doc. GOV/2006/14, 04 February 2006.

Implementation of the NPT Safeguards Agreement and relevant Provisions of Security Council Resolutions in the Islamic Republic of Iran, Report of the Director General, IAEA Doc. GOV/2011/65, 08 November 2011.

Implementation of the NPT Safeguards Agreement in the Islamic Republic of Iran, Report by the Board of Governors, IAEA Doc. GOV/2004/34, 01 June 2004.

Implementation of the NPT Safeguards Agreement in the Islamic Republic of Iran", Report of the Board of Governors, IAEA Doc. GOV/2006/27, 12 June 2006.

Innovation in Nuclear Technology, NEA/OECD (OECD, Paris, 2007).

Jonathan Medalia, Comprehensive Nuclear Test-Ban Treaty: Background and Current Developments (Congressional Research Service, Report for Congress, 28 January 2009).

Joop Boer, Henk van der Keur, Karel Koster and Frank Slijper, A.Q. Khan, Urenco and the Proliferation of Nuclear Weapons technology: The Symbiotic relation between nuclear energy and nuclear weapons, Report Commissioned by Greenpeace International, May 2004.

Nuclear Safety Review of the Year 2012, IAEA Doc GC (56)/INF/2.

Nuclear Weapons Testing, WHO Report, WHO/69-12, September 1995.

Pakistan's Nuclear Weapons Arsenal Safety Endangered, Report by Dr. Subhash Kapila for South Asia Analysis Group, 25 May 2011.

Report of the Canberra Commission on the Elimination of Nuclear Weapons, Australian Government, Department of Foreign Affairs and Trade, August 1996.

Report of the U.N. First Committee U.N. Doc. A/49/PV/90 (1994).

Report of the U.N. First Committee U.N. Doc. A/C.1/48/SR. 3 (1993).

Report of the U.N. First Committee U.N. Doc. A/C.1/49/L.36 (1994).

Report of the U.N. First Committee, U.N. Doc A/49/699 (1994).

Risks and Benefits of Nuclear Energy, OECD NEA Report, 2007.

The Agency's inability to verify the Non-Diversion of Material Required to be Safeguarded, Report by the Director General of the IAEA on Behalf of the Board of Governors to all Members of the Agency, IAEA Doc. INFCIRC/419, 08 April 1993

The Non-Compliance of the Democratic People's Republic of Korea with the Agreement Between the IAEA and the Democratic People's Republic of Korea for the Application of Safeguards in Connection with the Treaty on the Non-Proliferation of Nuclear Weapons, Report by the Director General of the IAEA on Behalf of the Board of Governors to all Members of the Agency, IAEA Doc. INFCIRC/419, 08 April 1993.

The US-Russia Joint Threat Assessment of Nuclear Terrorism, Report by Belfer Center for Science and International Affairs, Harvard Kennedy School and Institute for US and Canadian Studies, May 2011.

Threats, Challenges and Changes, Report of High Level Panel on the UN (2004).

Uranium 2009: Resources, Production and Demand, (OECD NEA & IAEA, 2010).

Cases and interviews

Adv. Op. Legality of the Threat or Use of Nuclear Weapons, Advisory opinions and orders, General List no. 95, 08 July 1996.

Interview with Petter Stania, Director of the Vienna Peace Institute on the role of nuclear energy on international security.

INTERNET SOURCES AND OFFICIAL WEBSITES

"About Safeguards, What do we do", IAEA, visited on 24 January 2012, http://www.iaea.org/OurWork/SV/Safeguards/what.html.

"Arms Control and Proliferation: China", Arms Control Association, visited on 09 June 2011, http://www.armscontrol.org/factsheets/chinaprofile

"Arms Control and Proliferation: France", Arms Control Association, visited on 10 June 2011, http://www.armscontrol.org/factsheets/franceprofile.

"Arms Control and Proliferation: India", Arms Control Association, visited on 10 June 2011, http://www.armscontrol.org/factsheets/indiaprofile.

"Arms Control and Proliferation: Iran", Arms Control Association, visited on 10 June 2011, http://www.armscontrol.org/factsheets/iranprofile.

"Arms Control and Proliferation: Israel", Arms Control Association, visited on 10 June 2011, http://www.armscontrol.org/factsheets/israelprofile.

"Arms Control and Proliferation: North Korea: Arms Control association, visited on 10 June 2011, http://www.armscontrol.org/factsheets/northkoreaprofile.

"Arms Control and Proliferation: Pakistan", Arms Control Association, visited on 10 June 2011, http://www.armscontrol.org/factsheets/pakistanprofile.

"Arms Control and Proliferation: Russia", Arms Control Association, visited on 09 June 2011, http://www.armscontrol.org/factsheets/russiaprofile.

"Arms Control and Proliferation: The United States", Arms Control Association, visited on 08 June 2011, http://www.armscontrol.org/factsheets/unitedstatesprofile.

"Arms Control and Proliferation: The United States", Arms Control Association, visited on 08 June 2011, http://www.armscontrol.org/factsheets/unitedstatesprofile.

"Arms Control and Proliferation: United Kingdom", Arms Control Association, visited on 10 June 2011, http://www.armscontrol.org/factsheets/ukprofile.

"Chronology of Libya's Disarmament and Relations with the United States", Arms Control Association, visited on 11 February 2012, http://www.armscontrol.org/factsheets/LibyaChronology.

"Convention for Suppression of Acts of Nuclear Terrorism", Centre for Non-Proliferation Studies, 07 March 2012, visited on 29 November 2012, http://www.miis.edu/academics/researchcenters/nonproliferation.

"Convention on the Physical Protection of Nuclear Material", IAEA, International Conventions and Agreements, visited on 10 March 2012, http://www.iaea.org/Publications/Documents/Conventions/cppnm.html.

"Country Profile: North Korea", Nuclear Threat Initiative, visited on 10 June 2011, http://www.nti.org/e_research/profiles/NK/Nuclear/chronology.html.

"Draft Comprehensive Convention on International Terrorism", Centre for Non-Proliferation Studies, visited on 07 March 2012, http://www.miis.edu/academics/researchcenters/nonproliferation .

"France "would use nuclear arms", *BBC*, 19 January 2006, visited on 20 September 2012, http://news.bbc.co.uk/2/hi/europe/4627862.stm.

"France on edge after accident at nuclear site", *The Independent*, 13 February 2011, visited on 20 September 2012, http://www.independent.co.uk/news/world/europe/france-on-edge-after-accident-at-nuclear-site-2353692.html.

"Fukushima Accident 2011", World Nuclear Association, November 2012, visited on 25 June 2012, http://www.world-nuclear.org/info/fukushima_accident_inf129.html.

"Global Partnership Against the Spread of Weapons and Materials of Mass Destruction, programmes 10+10 over 10", Nuclear Threat Initiative, visited on 30 March 2012, http://www.nti.org/treaties-and-regimes/global-partnership-against-spread-/eapons-and-materials-mass-destruction-10-plus-10-over-10-programmes/.

"Hydroaccoustic Monitoring", CTBTO, 06 February 2012, visited on 15 December 2012, http://www.ctbto.org/verification-regime/monitoring-technologies-how-they-work/hydroacoustic-monitoring/page-2/.

"IAEA Chief Calls for International Nuclear Fuel Bank", *Voice of America*, 07 November 2005, visited on 15 December 2012, http://www.voanews.com/english/news/a-13-2005-11-07-voa46-66368037.html?moddate=2005-11-07.

"Illicit Trafficking Database", IAEA visited on 15 December 2012, http://www-ns.iaea.org/security/itdb.asp.

"Increasing Transparency in the U.S. Nuclear Stockpile", US Departmet of Defence Fact Sheet, 03 May 2011, visited on 15 January 2012, http://www.defence.gov/npr/docs/10-05-03_Fact_Sheet_US_Nuclear_Transparency__FINAL_w_Date.pdf.

"Infrasound Monitoring", CTBTO, 06 February 2012, visited on 15 December 2012, http://www.ctbto.org/verification-regime/monitoring-technologies-how-they-work/infrasound-monitoring/page-2/.

"Inventory of International Nonproliferation Organisations and Regimes, International Convention for the Suppression of Acts of Nuclear Terrorism", Centre for Nonproliferation Studies, 05 December 2012, visited on 10 November 2012, http://cns.miis.edu/inventory/pdfs/nucterr.pdf.

"It was Others Who Failed", Interview of Mohamed Elbaradei, *Spiegel,* 18 May 2009, visited on 15 January 2012, http://www.spiegel.de/international/world/0,1518,625600,00.html.

"Khan Research Laboratories", Global Security, 09 February 2012, visited on 10 June 2012, http://www.globalsecurity.org/wmd/world/pakistan/kahuta.htm.

"North Korea Agrees to Freeze Nuclear Work: US to Give Aid", *The New York Times*, 29 February 2012, visited on 30 March 2012, http://www.nytimes.com/2012/03/01/world/asia/us-says-north-korea-agrees-to-curb-nuclear-work.html?_r=1&hp=&pagewanted=print.

"North Korean Leader Kim Jong Il Dead, state TV report", *CNN*, 18 December 2011, visited on 20 February 2012, http://articles.cnn.com/2011-12-18/asia/world_asia_north-korea-leader-dead_1_state-tv-reports-north-korean-leader-kim-jong?_s=PM:ASIA.

"North Korean Rocket Fails Moment after Liftoff", *The New York Times*, 12 April 2012, visited on 11 June 2012, http://www.nytimes.com/2012/04/13/world/asia/north-korea-launches-rocket-defying-world-warnings.html?_r=1&hp.

"Nuclear Phaseout is an historic Moment", *International Spiegel Online*, 30 May 2011, visited on 11 March 2012, http://www.spiegel.de/international/germany/0,1518,765681,00.html.

"Nuclear Testing Tall", Arms Control Association, 02 February 2012, visited on 10 June 2012, http://www.armscontrol.org/factsheets/nucleartesttally.

"Nuclear Testing", CTBTO, 1949-2009, visited on 15 September 2012, http://www.ctbto.org/nuclear-testing/history-of-nuclear-testing/nuclear-testing-1945-2009/page-7-nuclear-testing-1945-2009/.

"Nuclear Weapons: Who Has What at a Glance", Arms Control Association, 08 June 2011, visited on 15 January 2012, http://www.armscontrol.org/factsheets/Nuclearweaponswhohaswhat.

"Radionuclide Monitoring", CTBTO, 06 February 2012, visited on 10 June 2012, http://www.ctbto.org/verification-regime/monitoring-technologies-how-they-work/radionuclide-monitoring/page-3/.

"Security Council Committee Pursuant to Resolution 1267 (1999) and 1989 (2011) concerning Al-Qaida and associated Individuals and Entities", UN, visited on 19 October 2012, http://www.un.org/sc/committees/1267/.

"Seismic Monitoring", CTBTO, 06 February 2012, visited on 19 October 2012, http://www.ctbto.org/verification-regime/monitoring-technologies-how-they-work/seismic-monitoring/page-2/.

"The Manhattan Project", Nuclear Files, visited on 09 September 2012, http://www.nuclearfiles.org/menu/key-issues/nuclear-weapons/history/pre-cold-war/manhattan-project/index.htm.

"Weapons of Mass Destruction: AQ Khan Network", Global Security, 11 February 2012, visited on 10 June 2012, http://www.globalsecurity.org//md//orld/dprk/khan-dprk.htm.

"Weapons of Mass Destruction", US Arms Control and Disarmament Agency Fact Sheet, visited on 02 November 2011, http://dosfan.lib.uic.edu/acda/factsht.htm.

Alicia Godsberg, "CTBT Ratification and fact-twisting argument", Federation of American Scientists, visited on 07 February 2012, visited on 10 June 2012, http://www.fas.org/blog/ssp/2010/03/ctbt-ratification-and-fact-twisting-arguments.php.

Bonie Jenkis, "Adopting to the Times: The Evolution of U.S. Threat Reduction Programmess", Arms Control Association, January/February 2011, visited on 20 October 2012, http://www.armscontrol.org/act/2011_01-02/Jenkins.

Chen Kane, "From Donor to Partner: The Evolution of U.S. Cooperative Threat Reduction into Global Security Engagement", Nuclear Threat Initiative, 12 May 2011, visited on 20 October 2012, http://www.nti.org/analysis/articles/donor-partner-evolution-us-cooperative-threat-reduction-global-security-engagement/.

Christine Fair, "The Bin Laden aftermath: The U.S. shouldn't hold Pakistan's military against Pakistan's civilians", *Foreign Policy*, visited on 12 December 2012, http://afpak.foreignpolicy.com/posts/2011/05/04/the_Bin_laden_aftermath_the_us_shouldnt_hold_pakistans_military_against_pakistans_c.

Comprehensive Test Ban Treaty Organisation (CTBTO), visited on 06 February 2012, http://www.ctbto.org/the-treaty/.

Convention for Suppression of Acts of Nuclear Terrorism", Center for Non-Prolifearton Studies, 12 December 2012, visited on 20 December 2012, http://cns.miis.edu/inventory/pdfs/nucterr.pdf.

Daniel A. Pinkston, "North Korea's Nuclear Weapons Programmes and the Sixth-Party Talks", Nuclear Threat Initiative, 01 April 2006, visited on 20 November 2012, http://www.nti.org/analysis/articles/north-koreas-nuclear-weapons/.

Daryl G. Kimball, "Why We Don't Need to Resume Nuclear Testing", Arms Control Association, Arms Control Today, November 2009, visited on 15 September 2012, http://www.armscontrol.org/act/2009_11/focus.

David E. Sanger, "Pakistan Leader Confirms Nuclear Exports", *New York Times*, 13 September 2005, visited on 20 November 2012, http://www.nytimes.com/2005/09/13/international/asia/13musharraf.html.

Federation of American Scientists, visited on 09 September 2012, visited on 20 November 2012, http://www.fas.org/sgp/othergov/doe/lanl/docs1/00349710.pdf.

IAEA approves global nuclear fuel bank", *World Nuclear News*, 06 December 2010, visited on 05 June 2011, http://www.world-nuclear-ne/s.org/ENF-IAEA_approves_global_nuclear_fuel_bank-0612105.html.

International Atomic Energy Agency, visited on 15 October 2012, www.iaea.com.

Kamrahn Khan, "Pakistanis Exploited Nuclear Network", *The Washington Post*, 28 January 2004, visited on 10 November 2012, http://www.washingtonpost.com/wp-dyn/articles/A54334-2004Jan27.html.

Legality of the Threat or Use of Nuclear Weapons, ICJ, visited on 10 February 2012, http://www.icj-cij.org/docket/index.php?p1=3&p2=4&k=e1&p3=4&-case=95.

North Korea agrees to nuclear moratorium, *BBC*, 11 March 2012, visited on 10 October 2012, http://www.bbc.co.uk/news/world-asia-pacific-17208755.

Nuclear Chain Reactions", Atomic Archive, visited on 20 March 2012, www.atomicarchive.com/Fission/Fission2.shtml.

Nuclear Weapons Free Zones", Arms Control Association, visited on 01 February 2012, http://www.armscontrol.org/factsheets/nwfz.

Nuclear Weapons Free Zones", Project of the Nuclear Peace Foundation, visited on 31 January 2012, http://www.nuclearfiles.org/menu/library/treaties/nuclear-free-zones/trty_nuclear-free-zone-index.htm.

Office of the Global Threat Reduction", visited on 06 September 2011, http://nnsa.energy.gov/aboutus/ourprogrammess/nonproliferation/programmesoffices/officeglobalthreatreduction.

Pakistan Profile", Nuclear Threat Initiative, visited on 10 June 2011, http://www.nti.org/e_research/profiles/Pakistan/Nuclear/index.html.

Peter Crail and Dariyl G. Kimbal, "Nuclear Weapons Free-Zones at a Glance", Arms Control Association, visited on 30 January 2012, http://www.armscontrol.org/factsheets/nwfz.

Peter Lavoy, "Pakistan's Nuclear Posture: Security and Survivability," Nonproliferation Policy Education Center, January 2007, visited on 10 February 2012, http://www.npolicy.org/article_file/Pakistans_Nuclear_Posture-Security_and_Survivability.pdf.

Safeguards Overview" IAEA, Publications, Factsheet, visited on 25 January 2012, visited on 10 June 2012 http://www.iaea.org/Publications/Factsheets/English/sg_overview.html.

Security Council Counter-Terrorism Committee", visited on 19 October 2012, http://www.un.org/en/sc/ctc/.

The Acheson-Lilienthal & Baruch Plans, 1946", US Department of State, Office of the Historian, visited on 15 January 2012, http://history.state.gov/milestones/1945-1952/BaruchPlans.

The Frisch-Peierls Memorandum, March 1940", Atomic Archive, visited on 08 September 2012, http://www.atomicarchive.com/Docs/Begin/FrischPeierls.shtml.

The UN First Committee, visited on 10 October 2011, http://www.un.org/ga/60/first/.

United Nations Office for Disarmament Affairs, visited on 15 November 2012, http://www.un.org/disarmament/WMD/Nuclear/NPT.shtml.

US State Department, The Global Initiative to Combat Nuclear Terrorism, visited on 17 October 2011, http://www.state.gov/t/isn/c18406.htm.

Wade Boese, "Anti-Nuclear Terrorism Principles Issued", Arms Control Association, visited on 20 March 2012, http://www.armscontrol.org/act/2006_12/AntiNuclear.

World Court Project/International Law, The Lawyers Committee on Nuclear Policy, visited on 30 April 2012, http://lcnp.org/wcourt/.

SECONDARY SOURCES

BOOKS

A.S. Muller, D. Raic & J.M. Thuranszky, *The International Court of Justice: Its Future Role after Fifty Years*, (Martinus Njihoff Publishers, The Hague-Boston-London, 1997).

Angus Martyn, *The Right of Self-Defence under International Law: The Response to the Terrorist Attacks of 11 September* (Department of the Parliamentary Library, Canberra, 2001).

Antulio Joseph Echevarria, *Globalizaton and the Nature of War* (Strategic Studies Institute of the U.S. Army War College, Michigan, 2003).

Bert Chapman, *Military Doctrine: A Reference Handbook* (ABC-CLIO, California 2009).

David Armstrong, Lorna Lloyd & John Redmond, *International Organisations in World Politics* (third edition, Palgrave Macmillan, New York, 2004).

David Edwin Mathews, *The Division of Korea: How it Came to Be and the Possibility of Unificatio*n (University of Adelaide, Department of Politics, Australia, 1998).

David Held & Anthony McGrew, *David Goldblatt & Jonathan Perraton, Global Transformations: Politics, Economics and Culture* (Stanford University Press, California, 1999).

David R. Snock *Religious Perspectives on War: Christian, Muslim and Jewish Attitudes Toward Force* (Revised Edition, US Institute of Peace, Washington, 2002).

Geoffrey Best, *War and Law Since 1945* (Clarendon Press, Oxford, 1994).

Geoffrey Parker ed., *The Cambridge History of Warfare* (Cambridge University Press, New York, 2005).

Hangs Morgenthau, *Politics Among Nations* (Knopf, New York, 1948).

Helmut Philip Aust, *Complicity and the Law of State Responsibility* (Cambridge University Press, New York, 2011).

Hugo Grotius, *De Jure Belli Ac Pacis Libri Tres*, ed. Francis W. Kesley ed. & James B. Scott trans., *The Classics of International Law* (1964).

Imanuel Kant, *Perpetual Peace: A Philosophical Essay* (1795).

Isaia "Ike" Wilson III, James J. F. Forrest, *Handbook of Defence Politics: International and Comparative Perspectives: International and Comparative Perspectives* (Routledge, United Kingdom 2008).

Jean Jacques Rousseau, *Social Contract* (1972), Donald A. Cress ed. & trans, *Basic Political Writings,* (Hacket Publishing, Indianapolis/Cambridge, 1987).

John F. Murphy, *The Evolving Dimensions of International Law: Hard Choices for the World Community* (Cambridge University Press, New York, 2010).

John Foster, *"Nuclear Weapons," Encyclopedia Americana*, vol. 20 (Americana, New York, 1973).

John Keegan, *The Second World War*, (Random House, New York, 2011).

Jutta Brunnee and Stephen J. Toope, *Legitimacy and Legality in International Law: An International Account* (Cambridge Studies in International and Comparative Law, Cambridge University Press, Cambridge, 2010).

L. F. L. Oppenheim, *International Law: A Treatise* (Vol. 2, 7th edition, London, 1952).

Louis Henkin, *How Nations Behave: Law and Foreign Policy*, (2nd edition, Columbia University Press, New York, 1979).

Lt. Col. Charles W. Durr Jr. *United States Army, Nuclear Deterrence in the third Millennium* (USAWC Strategy Research Project, US Army War College Carlisle Barracks, Pennsylvania, 2002).

Martin Gilbert, *The Second World War: A Complete History* (Henry Holt and Company, New York, 2004).

Michael Graham Fry, Eric Goldstein, Richard Langhorne, *Guide to International Relations and Diplomacy* (Continuum, New York, 2002).

Nigel D. White, *Democracy Goes to War: British Military Deployments under International Law* (Oxford Univeristy Press, 2009).

Oscar Schachter, *International Law in Theory and Practice* (Martinus Njihoff Publishers, Leiden, 1991).

Paul R. Viotti, Mark V. Kauppi, *International Relations Theory*, (Pearson, 2010, New York).

Philip C. Jessup, *A Modern Law of Nations: An Introduction* (Mac Millan, New York, 1948).

Robin Herman, *Fusion: The Search for Endless Energy* (Cambridge University Press, US, 1990 Reprinted 1991).

William R. Slomanson, *Fundamental Principles of International Law* (Fourth edition, Clark Baxter, California 2003).

JOURNALS

Albright, David, "Global Stocks of Nuclear Explosive Materials", *Institute for Science and International Security,* 30 June 2005.

Anthony Clark Arend, "International Law and the Preemptive Use of Military Force", *The Washington Quarterly*, 26(2) The Wash. Quarterly 89, 91 (2003).

Anthony Fainbert, "Osirak and International Security", *The Bulletin of Atomic Scientists* (Educational Foundation for Nuclear Science Inc., 1981).

Barry Kellman & David S. Gualtieri, "Barricading the Nuclear Window: A legal Regime to Curtail Nuclear Smuggling", *The University of Illinois Law Reviews*, 1996 U. Ill. L. Rev. 667, 1996.

Christopher Greenwood, "International Law and the Pre-emptive Use of Force: Afghanistan, Al-Qaida, and Iraq", *San Diego International Law Journal*, 4 San Diego Int'l L.J. 7, 2003.

D'Amato, "Israel's Air Strike Upon the Iraqi Nuclear Reactor", *American Journal of International Law*, 77 A.J.I.L 584, 1983.

David Albright, and Susan Basu, "Neither a Determined Proliferator Nor a Responsible Nuclear State: India's Record Needs Scrutiny", *Institute for Science and International Security*, 05 April 2006.

David Eshel, "Izraeli's Nuclear Deterrence Faces First Scrutiny", *Jane's Intelligence Review*, Vol. 12, No. 7, July 2000.

Franck, "Who Killed Article 2(4)? Or Changing Norms Governing the Use of Article 2(4)", *American Journal of International Law"*, 64 A.J.I.L. 809, 1970.

Hans M. Kristensen and Robert S. Norris, *"Russian Nuclear Forces 2011", Bulletin of the Atomic Scientist*, 67(3), (SAGE, 2011).

James D. Fry, "Arbitrating Arms Control Disputes", *Stanford Journal of International Law*, 44 Stan. J. Int'l L. 359, summer 2008.

John A. Stoop and James P. Kahan, "Flying is the Safest Way to Travel: How Aviation was a Pioneer in Independent Accident Investigation", *European Journal of Transport and Infrastructure Research*, EJTIR, Vol. 5, no. 2, 2005.

John-Alex Romano, "Combating Terrorism and Weapons of Mass Destruction: Reviving the Doctrine of a State Necessity", *Georgetown Law Journal*, 87 Geo. L. J. 1023, April 1999.

Kate Dawes and Commander Robert Green RN, "The World Court Project: How a Citizen Network Can Influence the United Nations", *Pacifica Review, La Trobe University, Melbourne, Vol 7 No 2, October/November 1995.*

Kristen E. Eichensehr, "Targeting Teheran: Assessing the Lawfulness of Preemptive Strikes Against Nuclear Facilities", *University of California Los Angeles Journal of International Law*, 11 UCLA J. Int'l L. & For. Aff. 59, 2008.

Louis Henkin, "The Reports of the Death of Article 2(4) Are Greatly Exaggerated", *American Journal of International Law*, 65 A.J.I.L. 544 (1971).

Louis Henkin, "The UN and Its Supporters", *Political Science Quarterly*, 78 Pol. Sci. Q. 504, 1963.

Maac Chesney, "Some Comments on the "Quarantine" of Cuba", *American Journal of International Law*, 57 A.J.I.L. 592 (1963).

Marjoie Whiteman, "Threat or Use of Limited Force: The Cuban Missile Crisis, 1962", *Digest of International Law*, Vol 4, 1965.

Matthew Allen Fitzgerald, "Seizing Weapons of Mass Destruction from Foreign-Flagged Ships on the High Seas Under Article 51 of the UN Charter", *Vancouver Journal of International Law*, 49 Va. J. Int'l L. 473, 2008.

Miriam Sapiro, "Preempting Prevention: Lessons Learned", *New York University Journal of International Law*, 37 N.Y.U. J. Int'l L. & Pol. 357, 2005.

Oscar Schaster, "The Right of States to Use Armed Force", *Michigan Law Review*, 82 Mich. L. Rev. 1620, 1984.

R. Y. Jennings, "The Caroline and McLeado Cases", *American Journal of International Law*, 32 Am. J. Int. L 82, 1938.

Uri Shoham, "The Israeli Aerial Raid Upon the Iraqi Nuclear Reactor and the Right of Self-Defence", *Military Law Review*, 109 Mil. L. Rev. 191, 1985.

INTERNATIONAL AGREEMENTS, RESOLUTIONS, DOCUMENTS AND SPEECHES

International Agreements

Agreement Between the Government of the United States of America and the Government of the Russian Federation Concerning the Management and Disposition of Plutonium Designated as no Longer Required for Defence Purposes and Related Cooperation, 01 September 2000.

Convention on the Prevention and Punishment of the Crime of Genocide, 78 U.N.T.S. 277, 09 December 1948.

Convention on the Privileges and Immunities of the United Nations, 1 U.N.T.S. 15, 13 February 1946.

Convention on the Prohibition of Military or Any Other Hostile Use of Environmental Modification Techniques, 1108 U.N.T.S. 151, 10 December 1976.

Convention Respecting the Laws and Customs of War in Land, Hague 1899, U.S.T.S. 539, 2 A.J.I.L. Supp. 90.

Hague Convention (V) Respecting the Rights and Duties of Neutral Powers and Persons in Case of War on Land, U.S.T.S. 540, 2 A.J.I.L. Supp. 117, 18 October 1907.

Hague Convention (XIII) Respecting the Rights and Duties of Neutral Powers in Naval War, U.S.T.S. 545, 2 A.J.I.L. Supp.247, 18 October 1907.

International Covenant on Civil and Political Rights, 999 U.N.T.S. 171.

Kellogg-Briand Pact 1928, 93 L.N.T.S. 343.

Protocol for the Prohibition of the Use of Asphyxiating, Poisonous or Other *Gases*, and of Bacteriological Methods of Warfare, 94 L.N.T.S. 65, 17 June 1925.

The 1925 Geneva Protocol.

The League of Nations Covenant, 13 AJIL Supp. 128 (1919).

The United Nations Convention on the Law of Sea, 1833 U.N.T.S. 3, 21 I.L.M. 1261, 10 December 1982.

The Vienna Convention on the Law of Treaties, 1155 U.N.T.S. 331, 22 May 1969.

Treaty on Principles Governing the Activities of States in the Exploration and Use of Outer Space, including the Moon and other Celestial Bodies, 610 U.N.T.S. 205, 19 December 1966.

Resolutions

Declaration on Principles of International Law concerning Friendly Relations and Co-operation Among States in accordance with the Charter of the United Nations, 24 October 1970, UN.Doc. A/Res/25/2625.

Declaration on the Enhancement of the Effectiveness of the Principle of Refraining from the Threat or Use of Force in International Relations, 18 November 1987, UN.Doc. A/Res/42/22.

Protection of the Environment in Times of Armed Conflict, General Assembly Resolution, UN.Doc. A/Res/47/37, 25 November 1992.

Question of General and Complete Disarmament, General Assembly Resolution 1884, UN.Doc. A/5515 (1963), 17 October 1963.

Documents and Speeches

Final Act of the International Peace Conference Hague 1899.

Final Act of the Second Peace Conference Hague 1907.

General Dwight Eisenhower, US Responses to Dropping the Bomb, 1945.

Letter of American Secretary of State Daniel Webster addressed to the Lord Ashburton, dated 27 July 1842.

Rio Declaration on Environment and Development 1992.

Special Briefing on the Nuclear Posture Review, U.S. Department of Defence, News Transcript, 09 January 2002.

The Hague Declaration 1899.

The List established and maintained by the Committee pursuant to resolutions 1267 (1999) and 1989 (2011) with respect to individuals, groups, undertakings and other entities associated with Al-Qaida.

The President's State of the Union Address, 29 January 2002, The White House.

The Secretary-General Address to the General Assembly, New York, Sept. 23, 2003.

UN Secretary-General on the Question of Defining Aggression, UN. Doc. A/2211, 03 October 1952.

REPORTS, CASES AND INTERVIEWS

Reports

Amy F. Wolf, Nonproliferation and Threat Reduction Assistance: U.S. Programmes in the Former Soviet Union, Congressional Research Services, Report for Congress, 04 February 2010.

Amy F. Woolf, Mary Beth Nikiting, Paul K. Kerr, Arms Control and Nonproliferation: A Catalogue of Treaties and Agreements Report for Congress, Congressional Research Service, 02 February 2010.

Comprehensive Report of the Special Advisor to the Director of Central Intelligence on Iraq's Weapons of Mass Destructions, 30 September 2004.

Could worse be Yet to Come, Special Report by the Economist, 01 November 2001.

Final Report of the National Commission on Terrorist Attacks Upon the United States", US National Commission on Terrorist Attacks Upon the U.S., the 9/11 Commission Report, (2004).

ICJ Yearbook, I.C.J. Yb. 1996-1997.

Multilateral Approaches to the Nuclear Fuel Cycle, The report of the Independent Expert Group on Multilateral Approaches to the Nuclear Fuel Cycle, commissioned by the Director General, IAEA Doc. INFCIRC/640, 22 February 2005.

Nuclear Nonproliferation: Comprehensive U.S. Planning and Better Foreign Cooperation Needed to Secure Vulnerable Nuclear Materials Worldwide, US Governmental Accountability Office, Report to the Chairmen and Ranking Member, Subcommittee on Energy and Water Development, Committee on Appropriations, House of Representatives, December 2010.

Nuclear Non-Proliferation: Security of Russia's Nuclear Material Improving; Further Enhancements Needed, United States General Accounting Office, Report to Congressional Requester, February 2011.

Report Forms and Explanations for their Use, IAEA, Department of Safeguard, Agency No. SG-FM-1171, version date 02-11-2011.

The Chernobyl Accident, United Nations Scientific Committee on the Effect of Atomic Radiation, 30 May 2011.

World Energy Outlook: 2009, OECD/IEA (OECD, Paris, 2009).

Cases and Interviews

Adv. Op. Accordance with International Law of the Unilateral Declaration of Independence in Respect of Kosovo", ICJ General List No. 141, 22 July 2010.

Interview with Kreshnik Gashi, Head of the Kosovo Commission for Investigation of Aeronautical Accidents and Incidents, Prishtina, 15 July 2012.

Military and Paramilitary Activities in and Against Nicaragua (Nicaragua v. United States), Jurisdiction and Admissibility, ICJ REP, 392., 27 June 1986.

The Case of the S.S. "Lotus", PCIJ Series A.-No. 10, 7 September 1927.

INTERNET SOURCES AND OFFICIAL WEBSITES

"2011 Key World Energy Statistics", International Energy Agency, visited on 20 September 2012, http://www.iea.org/textbase/nppdf/free/2011/key_world_energy_stats.pdf.

"Albert Einstein Site Online", visited on 30 December 2012, http://www.alberteinsteinsite.com/quotes/einsteinquotes.html.

"Atoms for Peace" President Eisenhower's Speech at UN GA, 8 December 1953, Atomic Archive, Historical Documents, Arms Control, Deterrence and Nuclear Non-Proliferation, visited on 20 January 2012, http:/www.atomicarchive.com/Docs/Deterrence/Atomsforpeace.shtml.

"Chernobyl Accident, 1986",World Nuclear Association, December 2012, visited on 20 September 2012, http://www.world-nuclear.org/info/chernobyl/inf07.html.

"Chinas' National Statement on Security Assurances", Nuclear Threat Initiative, 05 April 1995, visited on 15 December 2012, http://www.nti.org/db/china/engdocs/npt0495a.htm.

"Cold War: A Brief History" Atom Archive, pp. 28, visited on 20 September 2012, http://www.atomicarchive.com/History/coldwar/page19.shtml.

"CTBT ratification and fact-twisting arguments", Federation of American Scientists, 07 February 2012, visited on 20 April 2012, http://www.fas.org/blog/ssp/2010/03/ctbt-ratification-and-fact-twisting-arguments.php.

"Deterrence", Project of the Nuclear Age Peace Foundation, Nuclear Files, visited on 20 April 2012, http://www.nuclearfiles.org/.

"DPRK Factsheet", IAEA, visited on 30 February 2012, http://www.iaea.org/newscenter/focus/iaeadprk/fact_sheet_may2003.shtml.

"Emerging Nuclear Energy Countries", World Nuclear Association, visited on 02 April 2012, http://www.world-nuclear.org/info/inf102.html.

"Establishment of Preparation Commission", CTBTO, 06 February 2012, visited on 02 April 2012, http://www.ctbto.org/the-treaty/developments-after-1996/1996-97creating-actbto-preparatory-commission/page-1-1996-97-creating-the-ctbto/.

"Excerpts from Obama Interview for New York Times", *New York Times*, visited on 09 November 2011, http://www.nytimes.com/2010/04/06//orld/06armstext.html?pagewanted=2&sq=obama%20interview&st=cse&scp=1.

"Fact Sheet: Climate change science-the status of climate change today", UN Framework Convention on Climate Change, visited on 26 March 2012, http://unfccc.int/press/fact_sheets/items/4987.php.

"History of the ICJ Court", ICJ, visited on 28 December 2011, http://www.icj-cij.org/court/index.php?p1=1&p2=1#International.

"International Court of Justice, Permanent Court of International Justice", visited on 03 November 2011, http://www.icj-cij.org/pcij/index.php?p1=9.

"International Court of Justice", visited on 03 November 2011, http://www.icj-cij.org/homepage/index.php.

"International Humanitarian Law and Related Legal Regimes", International Committee of Red Cross, visited on 26 October 2011, www.icrc.org.

"International Panel on Climate Change", visited on 13 October 2012, http://www.ipcc.ch/.

"Iranian Leader: Wipe out Israel", *CNN,* visited on 27 October 2005, http://articles.cnn.com/2005-10-26/world/ahmadinejad_1_israel-jerusalem-day-islamic-world?_s=PM:WORLD.

"Israel's Airstrike on Syria's Nuclear Reactor: Preventive War and the Nonproliferation Regime", Arms Control Association, visited on 09 November 2011, http://www.armscontrol.org/node/3404.

"Izraeli PM warns about danger of nuclear Iran", *CBS News*, visited on 31 October 2011, http://www.cbsnews.com/8301-501713_162-20127919/israeli-pm-warns-about-danger-of-nuclear-iran/.

"Merkel's Government Extends Nuclear Plants Lifespan" *International Spiegel Online*, 30 May 2011, visited on 11 March 2012, http://www.spiegel.de/international/germany/0,1518,715833,00.html.

"Nuclear Power in France" World Nuclear Association, April 2011, visited on 20 September 2012, http://www.world-nuclear.org/info/inf40.html.

"Nuclear Power in the USA", World Nuclear Association, visited on 02 May 2012, http://www.world-nuclear.org/info/inf41.html.

"Pervez Muhsaraf on Pakistan Nuclear Weapons" interview with, Fareed Zakaria, *CNN GPS*, 04 November 2011, visited on 10 June 2012, http://globalpublicsquare.blogs.cnn.com/2011/11/05/this-week-on-gps-pervez-musharraf-on-pakistani-nuclear-weapons-plus-bill-gates-and-arne-duncan-on-education/.

"Revolutionary railroad: Atomic train being developed in Russia", *RT*, 20 February 2011, visited on 15 June 2012, http://rt.com/news/sci-tech/revolutionary-locomotive-russia-atomic/.

"Russia Inaugurates World's First Low Enriched Uranium Reserve:, IAEA top Stories and Features, 17 December 2010, visited on 05 June 2011, http://www.iaea.org/newscenter/ne/s/2010/leureserve.html.

"Signatories and Parties to the Treaty on the Non-Proliferation of Nuclear Weapons", Federation of Nuclear Scientists, visited on 23 January 2012, http://www.fas.org/nuke/control/npt/text/npt3.htm .

"Status of Signature and Ratification", CTBTO, 06 February 2012, visited on 12 April 2012 http://www.ctbto.org/the-treaty/status-of-signature-and-ratification/.

"Switzerland Decides on Nuclear Phase-out", *The New York Times*, visited on 25 May 2011, http://www.nytimes.com/2011/05/26/business/global/26nuclear.html.

"Ten Fact About Nuclear Weapons", Nuclear Age Peace Foundation, visited on 10 January 2012, http://www.wagingpeace.org/articles/2009/09/facts_myths.pdf.

"The 1540 Committee", UN, visited on 15 December 2012, http://www.un.org/sc/1540/index.shtml.

"The Caroline", Max Planck Encyclopaedia of Public International Law, visited on 13 April 2012, http://www.mpepil.com/sample_article?id=/epil/entries/la/-9780199231690-e261&recno=12&.

"The President's State of the Union Address", 29 January 2002, The White House, visited on 28 June 2012, http://georgewbush-whitehouse.archives.gov/news/releases/2002/01/20020129-11.html.

"Three Mile Island Accident", World Nuclear Association, 30 May 2011, visited on 20 September 2012, http://www.world-nuclear.org/info/default.aspx?id=500&terms=three%20miles%20island.

"Timeline of Nuclear Age", Atomic Archive, visited on 09 September 2012, http://www.atomicarchive.com/Timeline/Time1940.shtml.

"Timeline of the Nuclear Age", Nuclear Files, visited on 08 September 2012, http://www.nuclearfiles.org/menu/timeline/timeline_page.php?year=1943.

"US to resume building nuclear plants", *New Scientists,* visited on 14 February 2012, http://www.newscientist.com/article/dn21476-us-to-resume-building-nuclear-plants.html.

"What is nuclear fission", Nuclear Files, visited on 10 March 2012, http://www.nuclearfiles.org/menu/key-issues/nuclear-weapons/basics/what-is-fission.htm.

Aaron Wiener, "German Oppose New Plants Next Door", *Spiegel Online International*, visited on 13 January 2012, http://www.spiegel.de/international/europe/0,1518,808794,00.html.

Country Profiles, Argentina and Brazil", Global Security Initiative, Disarmament and Peace Education, visited on 13 January 2012, http://www.gsinstitute.org/dpe/countries/argentina_brazil.html.

Encyclopaedia, visited on 18 March 2012, www.encyclopedia.com.

Greg Myre, "Olmert Inadvertently acknowledges Israel has the bomb", World Security Network, 13 December 2006, visited on 15 January 2012, http://www.globalsecuritynews.com/showArticle3.cfm?article_id=13787.

ICRC, International Humanitarian Law: Treaties and Documents, visited on 16 January 2012, http://www.icrc.org/ihl.

Jane Perlez, "Continuing Buildup, China Boosts Military Spending More Than 11 Percent", *The New York Times*, 04 March 2012, http://www.

nytimes.com/2012/03/05/world/asia/china-boosts-military-spending-more-than-11-percent.html?_r=0.

Jefferson Lab Glossary", visited on 18 March 2012, http://education.jlab.org/glossary/index.html.

Jeffrey Goldberg & Marc Ambinder, "The Ally from Hell", *The Atlantic Magazine*, December 2011, visited on 19 March 2012, http://www.theatlantic.com/magazine/archive/2011/12/the-ally-from-hell/308730/.

Joby Warrick, "Nuclear Scientist A.Q. Khan is Freed From House Arrest", *Washington Post*, 07 February 2009, visited on 19 March 2012, http://www.washingtonpost.com/wp-dyn/content/article/2009/02/06/AR2009020603730.html.

Martin Lamonica, "How nuke power bested solar in latest March mission", *CBS News*, 22 November 2011, visited on 22 April 2012 http://www.cbsnews.com/8301-205_162-57329453/how-nuke-power-bested-solar-in-latest-March-mission/.

Micah Zenko, "Controlling Tactical Nuclear Weapons", International Relations and Security Network 11 November 2010, visited on 16 September 2011, http://www.isn.ethz.ch/isn/Current-Affairs/ISN-Insights/Detail?lng=en&ots627=fce62fe0-528d-4884-9cdf-283c282cf0b2&id=123743&contextid734=123743&contextid735=123741&tabid=123741.

Miles A. Pomber "Editor's Note", Arms Control Association, visited onon 16 September 2011 http://www.armscontrol.org/act/2008_04/EditorsNote.

Kosovo Ministry of Foreign Affairs, www.mfa-ks.net.

Nazila Fathi, "Wipe Isreal 'off the map' Iranian says", *The New York Times*, 27 October 2005, visited on 18 April 2012 http://www.nytimes.com/2005/10/26/world/africa/26iht-iran.html.

Paul Watson and Mubashir Zaidi, "Death of N. Korean Woman Offers Clues to Pakistani Nuclear Deals", *Los Angeles Times*, 01 March 2004, visited on 14 April 2014 http://articles.latimes.com/2004/mar/01/world/fg-murder1.

Permanent Court of Arbitration, visited on 17 September 2012 www.pca-cpa.org.

The US State Department, visited on 11 November 2012 http://www.state.gov/t/isn/c27726.htm .

UN Oil for Food Programmes", visited on 11 November 2012 http://www.un.org/depts/oip/.

United Nations Framework Convention on Climate Change, visited on 15 September 2012 http:www.unfccc.int/2860.php.

United Nations Office for Outer Space Affairs, visited on 3 October 2012 http://www.oosa.unvienna.org/oosawSpaceLaw/outerspt.html.

Urenco, visited on 3 October 2012 http://www.urenco.com/custom/1/homepage/default.aspx.

INDEX

Symbols

11 September 19, 208, 275
1540 Committee 227, 229

A

Abandon 194, 195, 245
Abu Khababa Al Masry 210
Accident 39, 40, 41
Accountability 203
Acheson-Lilienthal Report 50
Acquisition 156
Additional Protocol 118, 148
Advisory opinion 15, 17, 93, 96, 101, 102, 103, 105, 106, 107, 108, 109, 110, 111, 112, 113, 116, 124, 125, 246
Africa 34, 37, 46, 52, 59, 151, 152, 155, 156, 157, 158, 159, 177, 182, 238, 239, 241
African Nuclear Weapon Free Zone Treaty 155
Aggressor 66
Agriculture 31
Albert Einstein 11, 12, 21, 24
Algeria 34, 155, 161
Amendment 224, 232, 244
American Department of Defence 83
American Intelligent Service 192
Anarchic system 62
Ancient Greece 61
Antarctic Treaty 135, 159
Anthrax 208, 214
Anticipatory self-defence 78, 85
Applied sciences 31
A.Q. Khan 13, 18, 57, 59, 171, 172, 173, 174, 175, 176, 177, 178, 183, 192, 197, 203, 247
Arak 59, 180
Arbitrator 149
Arms race 49, 50, 52, 87, 104, 138, 170, 174, 189, 199
Arsenal 204
Asia 16, 46, 56, 151, 155, 156, 157, 158, 160, 174, 204, 241, 247
Asphyxiating gases 65
Associations against Nuclear Weapons 107
Atlee 50, 51, 261
Atmosphere 135, 162
Atomic bomb 24, 26, 27, 28, 29, 178
Atomic nuclei 14, 22, 24, 35
Atoms for Peace 134, 135, 181, 284
Attack 25, 26, 49, 63, 66, 72, 74, 76, 77, 78, 79, 80, 81, 82, 83, 84, 85, 86, 88, 90, 91, 92, 93, 96, 104, 129, 151, 153, 161, 162, 195, 196, 201, 204, 208, 209, 210, 211, 212, 213, 214, 222, 231, 240
Australia 34, 45, 83, 107, 111, 155, 159, 189, 238
Austria 46, 111, 150, 156
Authority for Atomic Development 51
Axis of evil 180, 192

B

Babylonia 61
Balance of power 51, 87, 88
Ballistic missiles 53, 56, 85, 92, 146, 176, 178, 194, 195
Bangkok Treaty 155, 157
Baruch Plan 51, 134
Battlefield 68
Belgium 37, 53, 150, 159, 172, 238
Belligerent 66
Belorussia 40
Berlin Tegel Airport 200
Bernard Baruch 51
Bhopal 171
Bilateral cooperation 50
Bill Clinton 164
Black market 200
Board of Governors 145, 147, 149, 184, 185, 186, 187, 190, 191, 192, 193, 198, 242, 244
Bona fide 138
Brain 31, 42
Brazil 34, 37, 45, 150, 152, 157

Breach 72, 108, 139, 184
British Prime Minister 26
Bushehr 182

C

Caesium-137 31
Calder Hall 36
Canberra 107, 154, 155, 208, 266, 275
Canberra Commission 154, 155
Cancer 31, 41, 214
Capability 25, 59, 74, 168, 180
Capitol Hill 214
Carbon 43, 44, 47
Caroline case 77, 79, 80, 81
Catholic University of Leuven 172
Central and South-East Asia 247
Centralise 19, 240
Centrifuge designs 176
Chagos archipelago 157
Chain reaction 23
Chapultepec Treaty 77
Charter 17, 49, 50, 69, 70, 71, 72, 75, 76, 77, 78, 81, 98, 101, 104, 105, 108, 109, 111, 113, 115, 119, 124, 125, 128, 131, 135, 168, 195, 218, 222, 226
Chechen rebels 209, 213, 214
Chechnya 209
Chelyabinsk 201
Chernobyl 38, 40, 41, 42, 213
Chicago 26, 28
China 34, 36, 37, 38, 46, 52, 55, 61, 80, 90, 91, 97, 105, 111, 161, 165, 169, 173, 175, 177, 183, 187, 188, 193, 235
Christopher Greenwood 81, 84
Civil engineering 31
Civilian 21, 22, 61, 62, 82, 123, 127, 200, 209, 225, 234, 237
Clandestine network 18, 174, 247
Clean energy 42
Coal 43, 44
Coalition of the Willing 83
Cobalt-60 31
Coercion 71
Cold War 17, 40, 49, 70, 88, 134, 160, 164, 199
Collapse 197, 199, 232
Columbia 23, 70, 190, 208
Combatant 62
Commitment 93, 143, 144, 145, 146, 151, 187, 196, 197, 233, 246, 249
Communist 49
Comprehensive Test Ban Treaty 165, 169, 242, 272
Condemning 191, 230
Conduct of war 62
Confiscated 198, 201, 220
Congress 29, 107, 134, 164, 165, 180, 192, 233, 234, 239
Consensus 18, 19, 64, 86, 208, 217, 222, 231
Constraints. *See* Constraint
Contentious matters 101
Convention for the Amelioration of the Condition of the Wounded and Sick in Armed Forces in the Field 68
Convention for the Prevention and Punishment of the Crime of Genocide 118
Convention for the Suppression of Acts of Nuclear Terrorism 198, 209, 215, 216, 218, 256, 269
Convention for the Suppression of the Financing of Terrorists 216
Convention on the Civil and Political Rights 117
Convention on the Physical Protection of Nuclear Material 217, 223, 224
Convention on the Prevention of Development, Production and Stockpiling of Chemical Weapons and their Destruction 120
Convention on the Prohibition of the Development, Production and Stockpiling of Bacteriological and Toxin Weapons 120
Convention on the Territorial Sea and Contiguous Zone 160
Conversion 234
Corpus delicti 209
Corpus legis 116

Court of International Arbitration 96
Criminal Court 179, 222
Criminal organisations 198, 200, 208, 213
CTBT 165, 166, 167, 168, 169, 256, 261, 271, 284
CTBT Conference 167
Cuba 74, 155
Cuban Crisis 74, 86, 162
Cure 31
Customary law 66, 68, 77, 97, 101, 121, 122, 128, 129, 130, 131, 136, 156
Cyanide sodium 211
Cyclotron 22
Czech 25, 34, 37, 201

D

Dai-Ichi 39
Daniel Webster 79
Dante Alighieri 95
Data base for illegal trafficking and other unauthorized activities related to fission materials 198
David Lilienthal 50
Dean Acheson 50
Declaration for the Prevention of the Use of Nuclear and Thermonuclear Weapons 117
Declaration on Friendly Relations 71
Declaration on the Effectiveness of the Principle of Refraining from Threat or Use of Force in International Relations 71
De Jure Belli Ac Pacis 62, 63, 276
Delegitimize 15, 67, 68, 111, 130, 131, 136
Delft 171
Demand 34
De Monarchia 95
Department of Defence 83, 164, 202
Department of Energy 202, 234
Depleted Uranium 47, 193
Destroy 32, 56, 60, 63, 82, 126
Destruction 29, 66, 78, 120, 159, 176, 202, 208, 210, 238, 239
Destruction capacity 11, 25, 146, 161, 213
Detection 26, 151, 154, 167, 226, 230, 237
Deterrence 49, 58, 88, 135, 199
Deterrent 30, 49
Detonation 146, 212
Deuterium 24
Device 22, 24, 143, 146, 207, 209, 211, 212, 214, 217, 218
Director General 35, 141, 150, 185, 190, 196
Disarmament 66, 67, 105, 111, 135, 157, 162, 177
Discretion 101, 102
Discrimination 117, 137, 153
Diseases 31, 41, 214, 233
Dismantling 47, 54, 74
Disputes 65, 71, 75, 85, 86, 95, 96, 97, 99, 149, 150, 170, 222
Diversion 190
Double standards 15, 17
Dum-dum bullets 65
Dwight Eisenhower 29
Dzhokar Dudayev 213

E

East Asia 16, 46, 155, 174, 247
Eastern Karelia 110
Ehud Olmert 58
Electricity 11, 12, 21, 22, 30, 31, 32, 35, 36, 38, 39, 41, 42, 43, 44, 45, 46, 47, 48, 57, 136, 181, 213, 241, 244
Elihu Root 96
Emilio Segre 24
Energy convertor 35
England 21, 36, 61, 66
Environment 35, 43, 118
Environmental catastrophe 118
Erga omnes 70, 80, 178
Ernest Lawrence 21
Ernest Rutherford 21
European Space Agency 32
European Union 237
Eventual attack 76, 77, 78, 81, 84, 88, 161
Executive Council 166, 167, 168
Exploitation 33
Explosives 65, 213, 216
Expressis verbis 130
Extract 33, 44, 48
Extradite 220

F

Factories 56, 144, 177
Fait accompli 142
Fat Man 28
Finland 34, 37, 112, 113, 150, 238
First Committee 110, 111, 266, 273
First World War 61
Fission 23, 54, 211
Florence 95
Fossil fuel 43
Framework agreement 191, 192, 193
France 34, 35, 37, 44, 52, 56, 58, 61, 64, 89, 91, 92, 105, 106, 107, 111, 112, 134, 159, 161, 164, 182, 183, 238
Franklin Roosevelt 25
Frits Veerman 172, 173
Fuel 35, 135
Fukushima 38, 39, 41, 42, 46, 213
Fusion 24

G

G8 46, 238, 239
Gaddafi 177
Gas 23, 35, 40, 41, 43, 59, 167, 177, 181, 192, 210, 211
Gas centrifuges 23, 59, 192
Gaseous diffusion 23
General Assembly (GA) 50
General Secretary 77
General Treaty for the Renunciation of War 61
General Treaty on Renunciation of War as an Instrument of National Policy 67
Geneva Conference 67
Geneva Eighteen Member Commission on Disarmament 162
Geneva Law 122
George Bush 84, 180, 192, 235, 237
Germany 11, 25, 26, 27, 28, 34, 37, 38, 46, 53, 66, 96, 111, 112, 114, 122, 150, 177, 182, 183, 238, 241
Glen Seaborg 24
Global electricity 43
Global Initiative to Combat Nuclear Terrorism 232, 237
Global jihad 203
Global level 15, 153, 161, 240, 243
Global Nuclear Threat Reduction Initiative 232, 234
Global reserve 19
Global warming 43
Good faith 63, 124, 138, 215
Graphite 35
Great Britain 25, 26, 52, 53, 64, 77, 78, 82, 112, 113, 141, 238
Greenhouse 41
Grotius 62, 63, 83
Ground zero 169
Guarantees 198
Gun boat diplomacy 73
Gun-type 27

H

Hague Conference 64, 66, 96, 120
Hague Law 122
Handfor 26
Hannes Alven 31
Harold Evans 107
Harry Truman 27, 28, 30
Hatfield-Exon-Mitchel 164
Heart 31
Heat capacity 43, 44
Helium 14
Henri Dunant 68
Henry Kissinger 174
Hezbollah 86
Highly Enriched Uranium 13, 47
Hiroshima 11, 27, 28, 29, 30, 49, 104, 106, 128, 133, 250
Holland 53, 65, 171, 172, 238
Hugo de Groot 62
Human condition 126
Human error 40
Humanitarian law 17, 18, 63, 65, 116, 118, 122, 123, 124, 126, 127, 128, 131, 179, 218, 246
Human suffering 11
Hundred Years War 61
Hungarian 20, 111
Hydro acoustic 166
Hydrogen bomb 24

I

Igor Kurchatov 52
Imminent attack 79
Implement 147
Implosion-type 27
Improvised nuclear device 211, 212
Incident 41
Incriminate 221, 230
India 18, 34, 36, 37, 38, 52, 56, 92, 105, 112, 140, 150, 152, 158, 161, 163, 165, 169, 170, 171, 174, 182, 204, 252, 254, 267, 278
Industrial development 21
Infrasound 166, 167, 269
Infringing 15, 48, 135
Inspection 190, 193
Instant attack 79
Intercept 77, 235, 236
International 9, 10, 12, 13, 14, 15, 16, 17, 18, 19, 20, 29, 32, 38, 42, 48, 49, 50, 51, 52, 57, 58, 59, 62, 63, 64, 65, 66, 67, 68, 69, 70, 71, 72, 73, 74, 75, 76, 77, 79, 80, 81, 82, 83, 85, 86, 87, 88, 93, 95, 96, 97, 98, 99, 101, 103, 104, 105, 107, 108, 110, 111, 114, 115, 116, 118, 119, 120, 121, 123, 124, 125, 126, 127, 128, 129, 130, 131, 134, 135, 137, 138, 139, 144, 148, 152, 153, 154, 155, 156, 159, 168, 169, 170, 171, 177, 178, 179, 180, 181, 187, 188, 193, 195, 196, 197, 198, 199, 204, 208, 210, 212, 214, 215, 216, 217, 218, 219, 220, 222, 223, 225, 228, 230, 231, 235, 236, 237, 238, 239, 240, 241, 242, 243, 244, 245, 246, 247, 248, 258, 267, 270, 272, 285, 287
International Atomic Energy Agency 16, 19, 20, 134, 137, 139, 146, 150, 189, 253, 258, 272
International Court of Justice 15, 17, 18, 66, 97, 98, 108, 110, 111, 250, 257, 275, 285
International Criminal Court 179, 222
International governance 98
International initiative 15
International Lawyers 107
International markct 42, 243
International Peace Bureau 106, 108, 250
International Physicists for the Prevention of Nuclear War 108
Invention 11, 22, 25, 31, 49, 122, 126
Investigate 59, 83, 220
Iodine 31
Iranian Atomic Energy 181
Iranian programme 59
Iraq 52, 56, 81, 82, 83, 84, 85, 171, 177, 178, 180, 181, 182, 233, 277, 282
Iraqi Observation Group 83
Islamic revolution 181, 182, 183
Ismailovsky Park 214
Isotopes 22, 23, 31, 32, 35, 36, 167, 234
Israel 18, 52, 56, 58, 59, 73, 74, 81, 85, 93, 105, 129, 140, 153, 165, 180, 183, 210, 267, 278, 285, 287
Italy 34, 53, 112, 150, 208, 238, 257

J

Japan 11, 26, 28, 29, 30, 34, 37, 38, 39, 42, 50, 80, 97, 111, 112, 116, 159, 193, 211, 262, 265
Javad Zarif 181, 264
Jean Jacques Rousseau 63, 276
John Aristotle Phillips 211
Joint Declaration of South and North Korea on the Denuclearization of the Korean Peninsula 189, 262
J. Robert Oppenheimer 26
Judge 125, 126, 127, 128, 130, 131, 261, 262, 263
Judge Koroma 131, 261
Judge Oda 131, 261
Judge Vereshchetin 131, 261
Judicial regimes 131, 261
Jurisdiction 70, 97, 99, 100, 101, 102, 103, 106, 146, 163, 165, 179, 218, 219, 220, 222, 223, 225, 247
Jus ad bellum 5, 61
Jus cogens 70
Jus in bella 5, 61
Just and unjust wars 67

K

Kashmir 92
Kazakhstan 34, 45, 52, 161, 199, 202
Kim Jong Il 196
King 50, 51, 261
Knowhow 12, 13, 17, 57, 104, 105, 178, 205, 232
Kofi Annan 82
Korean peninsula 58, 189, 190, 193, 194
Kosovo 41, 101, 151, 152, 241
Kurdish 82

L

Laboratory 28, 172
Latin America 120, 121, 151, 155, 157, 239, 241
Laws and customs of war on land 65
Lawyers Committee on Nuclear Energy 107
League Council 96
League of Nations 68, 96
Leak 38, 39, 40, 44, 151, 162, 163, 197, 213
Legal infrastructure 15, 224, 227, 237, 241, 245, 246, 247
Legitimate targets 63
Leo Szilard 22, 25, 28
Leslie Groves 26
Lethal effect 211
Liberal 49, 242
Libya 52, 55, 57, 86, 152, 177, 181, 236, 238
Light elements 24
Limited Test Ban Treaty 162
Little Boy 28
London Tribunal for Nuclear Warfare 106
Los Almos 26, 211
Los Almos Primer 211
Louis Henkin 69, 70, 74, 80
Low Enriched Uranium 242, 263, 286

M

Mahmoud Ahmedinejad 74
Malaysia 34, 112, 155, 177, 233
Manhattan Engineering District 26
Manhattan Project 12, 26, 27, 28, 211
Mankind 11, 15, 21, 24, 25, 30, 41, 42, 43, 47, 60, 61, 126, 160, 214, 231, 241
Maritime warfare 65
Mars 32
Martens clause 17, 108, 122
Material breach 139
Material damage 11, 61, 198, 209
Means of delivery 226, 227, 236
Means of warfare 17, 114
Medicine 11, 31, 32
Memorandum 25
Metallurgical Laboratory 28
Middle East 46, 58, 73, 93, 174, 180, 210, 239, 255
Milisieverts 40
military activities within and against Nicaragua 70
Military confrontation 191
Military doctrines 17, 79, 84, 86, 88, 89, 104, 129, 246
Military purposes 9, 11, 13, 21, 28, 36, 48, 56, 57, 105, 133, 138, 140, 141, 143, 150, 152, 153, 154, 160, 174, 179, 182, 185, 187, 189, 200, 242, 245
Military Tribunal of Nuremberg 79
Military use 12, 14, 15, 17, 22, 27, 32, 35, 48, 53, 54, 55, 56, 57, 59, 152, 171, 180, 188, 210, 243, 245
Moderator 35
Mohajerani 183
Mohamed El Baradei 16
Mongolia 34, 156, 200, 261
Moral 62, 254
Moratorium 58, 164, 165, 169, 195, 272
Morocco 111, 238
Motive 84, 116, 208
Multilateral cooperation 19, 232, 240
Multiple 32, 35, 215
Multiple use 32
Murmansk 201
Mutually Assured Destruction 208

N

Nagasaki 11, 27, 28, 29, 30, 104, 128, 133
Namibia 34, 45

NASA 32
Natanz 59, 180, 184
National Nuclear Safety 202
National security 12, 14, 73, 74, 87, 88, 104, 133, 139, 142, 172, 233, 246
Natural disaster 12, 14, 73, 74, 87, 88, 104, 133, 139, 142, 172, 233, 246
Natural resources 42, 181
Nature 10, 22, 23, 24, 32, 35, 42, 119, 154, 169, 198, 219, 244
Nauru 112, 155
Navy facility 201
Navy Island 78
Near East 140
Necessary 10, 14, 17, 29, 30, 72, 76, 77, 78, 83, 103, 104, 118, 119, 122, 129, 141, 143, 144, 148, 175, 176, 180, 181, 182, 186, 192, 211, 215, 219, 224, 226, 230, 231, 237, 243, 244, 247
Necessity 22, 210, 278
Nerve gas 210
Neutron 22, 23, 24, 36
New Mexico 26, 27
New world order 69
New York 11, 22, 23, 35, 38, 61, 62, 67, 68, 70, 73, 77, 78, 80, 81, 84, 97, 104, 106, 107, 154, 162, 165, 177, 180, 181, 196, 208, 209, 210, 221, 249, 250, 251, 252, 254, 262, 270, 272, 275, 276, 277, 279, 282, 285, 286, 287, 288
New Zealand 106, 107, 112, 155, 238
Niagara River 78
Nicaragua case 80
Nightmare 14, 48, 197
Nobel Prize 11
Non-aligned movement 107, 111, 218
Non-Compliance 190, 266
Non-deployed 53, 89
Non liqet 128, 130
Non-nuclear states 89, 105, 133, 136, 143, 153, 218
Non-state actor 136
North America 46
North Korea 9, 18, 52, 55, 57, 58, 86, 105, 129, 139, 140, 148, 152, 153, 165, 169, 170, 171, 175, 176, 177, 178, 180, 188, 189, 190, 191, 192, 193, 194, 195, 196, 201, 202, 205, 245, 251, 253, 254, 255, 262, 268, 270, 272
NPT 6, 9, 14, 15, 18, 19, 48, 55, 58, 59, 85, 89, 91, 105, 106, 120, 129, 130, 133, 136, 137, 138, 139, 140, 141, 142, 143, 144, 145, 146, 148, 149, 150, 151, 152, 153, 158, 164, 179, 181, 182, 183, 184, 185, 187, 188, 189, 190, 191, 192, 193, 194, 195, 242, 243, 244, 245, 246, 252, 253, 259, 265, 274
Nuclear energy 9, 10, 12, 13, 14, 15, 16, 17, 19, 20, 21, 22, 24, 25, 27, 32, 36, 38, 41, 42, 44, 46, 47, 48, 49, 50, 51, 57, 59, 73, 86, 105, 120, 131, 133, 134, 135, 136, 137, 138, 139, 140, 142, 143, 144, 146, 147, 148, 153, 156, 171, 172, 179, 181, 182, 189, 197, 241, 243, 244, 245, 266, 267
Nuclear energy bank 135
Nuclear free zones 135, 151, 152, 154, 155, 157, 158, 159, 160
Nuclear missiles 74
Nuclear Non-Proliferation Treaty 14, 139, 143, 189, 190, 253, 254, 255
Nuclear Terrorism 198, 207, 208, 209, 210, 216, 217, 218, 220, 232, 237, 238, 249, 251, 253, 254, 255, 256, 259, 266, 268, 269, 272, 274
Nuclear Test 161, 162, 164, 250, 251, 265
Nuclear Test Ban 161, 162, 250, 251
Nuclear Testing Threshold 164
Nuclear Threat Reduction Initiative 232, 234
Nuclear weapon 11, 16, 17, 19, 30, 50, 51, 52, 88, 109, 122, 129, 133, 134, 136, 153, 154, 156, 161, 162, 163, 165, 174, 180, 183, 186, 194, 199, 203, 204, 210
Nuclear weapon free zones 17

O

Oak Ridge 26, 27
OECD 33, 34, 36, 37, 44, 47, 265, 266, 267, 283
Offence 225
Oil 43, 82, 177, 181
Oil for Peace 82
Opinion juris 70, 129
Ordinary centrifuges 23
Organization 43, 191
Osiraq 56, 85
Otto Frisch 25
Oxidized 33

P

P1 175
P2 176
Pacific Ocean 38, 39, 157
Pacific settlement of international disputes 65
Pakistan 18, 37, 52, 55, 57, 92, 105, 140, 153, 158, 161, 163, 165, 169, 170, 171, 172, 173, 174, 175, 176, 177, 178, 197, 199, 203, 204, 229, 231, 233
Pakistani Commission for Atomic Energy 173
Pakistani Engineering Research Laboratory 172
Paris Agreement 184
Paris Pact 67
Paul Henri Spaak 98
Peaceful purposes 11, 15, 21, 32, 48, 50, 51, 54, 85, 134, 135, 136, 137, 141, 142, 150, 152, 157, 159, 169, 182, 189, 213, 223, 224, 234
Peaceful use 11, 12, 14, 19, 21, 24, 32, 41, 59, 86, 133, 135, 143, 156, 159, 179, 181, 188, 191, 209, 242, 243, 244, 247
Pearl Harbour 26
Pelindaba Treaty 155, 157, 158
Pennsylvania 39, 49, 255, 276
Permanent Court of International Justice 66, 96
Permanent Member 51
Pervez Musharraf 175, 203
Phosphates 33
Physics laboratory in Moscow 201
Plasma energy 24
Plutonium 24, 26, 27, 28, 32, 35, 36, 53, 54, 55, 56, 57, 58, 59, 143, 182, 190, 198, 199, 200, 201, 202, 209, 214, 223
Podolsk 201
Political elite 21, 195, 196
Political struggle 197
Political turmoil 175
Possession 12, 14, 189
Potsdam Conference 27
Power 44, 241
Prague 201
President Bedjaoui 124, 126
Preventive force 15
Prima facie 243
Princeton University 154, 211
Procurement 173, 175
Programme 43
Prohibit 62
Prohibition 67, 111, 117, 120, 121, 135, 155, 159
Projectiles 63
Proliferation 14, 21, 22, 53, 54, 55, 56, 57, 58, 59, 80, 89, 105, 133, 134, 135, 139, 143, 147, 150, 151, 172, 174, 180, 181, 189, 190, 195, 199, 216, 217, 220, 232, 235, 238
Proliferation Security Initiative 232, 235
Proportionality 78, 85, 86, 93, 118, 119
Protection 118, 198, 216, 217, 223, 224, 228, 232, 237
Protection of Environment in Times of Armed Conflict 118
Protocol for the Prohibition of the Use in War of Asphyxiating, Poisonous or other Gases, and of Bacteriological Methods of Warfare 67
Pu239 211

Q

Qom 59
Quartz 33
Queen of Holland 65
Quorum 100, 125

R

Radioactive 31, 32, 40, 111, 198, 212
Radioisotope 31
Radionuclide 167
Railway tracks 31
Raison d'etre 130
Rarotonga Treaty 155, 156, 157
Reactive self-defence 76
Reactor 73, 79, 81
Realism 62, 154
Realpolitik 87
Rebus sic standibus 139, 140
Red Cross Movement 68
Regime 73, 134, 143, 174, 192, 200, 207, 210, 215
Regulation 179
Release of energy 11, 23
Religion 61, 181, 220
Religious duty 210
Removal 156, 196, 234, 242, 243
Reprocessing 35, 47, 173, 184, 186, 188, 190, 195
Resolution 82, 83, 111, 117, 118, 121, 129, 135, 186, 187, 191, 192, 193, 194, 195, 198, 212, 215, 226, 227, 229, 230, 232, 237, 242
Resolution 47/37 118
Resolution 49/75 K 111
Resolution 948 121
Resolution 1267 229, 271
Resolution 1373 230
Resolution 1540 198, 227, 262
Resolution 1624 230, 259, 302
Resolution 1653 121, 129, 135, 258
Resolution 1673 226
Resolution 1695 194, 260
Resolution 1718 195, 260
Resolution 1810 226, 229, 260
Richard Falk 107
Rio Declaration 118
Robert Serber 27
Robots 32
Roman Empire 61
Rudolf Peierls 25
Ruhollah Mostafavi Musavi Khomeini 180
Russia 29, 32, 36, 37, 40, 45, 52, 53, 54, 58, 63, 64, 90, 105, 141, 161, 169, 175, 183, 187, 193, 197, 199, 200, 201, 202, 203, 207, 209, 213, 215, 217, 232, 233, 234, 235, 238, 239, 242
Russian Czar 65
Russian Foreign Intelligence Service 201, 202
Russian Kingdom 64

S

Sabotage 212, 213, 234
Saddam Hussein 82, 83, 178
Safeguard agreement 137, 144, 145, 146, 147, 149, 150, 151, 152, 179, 182, 185, 189, 190, 193
Sanctions 187
Sand stones 33
San Francisco 77, 80, 97
Sapphire 202
Sarin gas 210
Scientist 54, 247
Sean MacBride 107
Second Declaration of The Hague 120
Second Declaration of The Hague Conference 120
Secretary of State 67, 79
Security Council (SC) 49
Seismic 166
Self-defence 76
Sellafield 36
Semi-Palatinsk-21 52
Shah Mohammad Reza Pahlavi 181
Shamil Basayev 214
Shia 82, 181
Siamese Twins 31
Six party talks 193, 194, 195
Social disturbances 199
Solferino 68
South Africa 34, 37, 52, 59, 152, 155, 156, 159, 177, 182

South America 46
South-East Asia 46, 247
South Pacific 106, 120, 121, 151, 155, 158, 161
South Pacific Nuclear Free Zone Treaty 120, 121, 155
Sovereignty 9, 13, 62, 69, 80, 119, 139, 188
Soviet Lawyers Association 107
Splitting atoms 11
Stalin 51
State Department 90, 203, 236, 237, 238
Statute 63, 96, 98, 101, 102, 105, 108, 109, 112, 113, 125, 137, 144, 145, 146, 190
Steel 31
Stephen Rademaker 168
Stockholm 29, 107
St. Petersburg 63, 64, 117
St. Petersburg Declaration 63, 64, 117
Strategic 29, 173, 208, 215
Strategic Bombardment 29
Structure of the atom 22
Suez Canal 81, 176
Super-state 95
Surrender 11, 22, 28, 29
Suspend 149, 167, 184, 186, 192, 195
Switzerland 37, 38, 68, 238
Syria 54, 73, 177, 178

T

Tactical 128, 213
Taleban 229
Technetium-99 31
Technical provisions 15
Technical University in West Berlin 171
Technology 47, 169
Teheran Centre for Nuclear Research 182
Territorial integrity 9, 13, 69, 71, 79, 80, 119, 188
Terrorism 198, 207, 208, 209, 210, 215, 216, 217, 218, 220, 224, 230, 231, 232, 237, 238, 248
Terrorist networks 19
Terrorist organizations 232
Test 161, 162, 164, 165, 169, 242
The Code of Conduct on the Safety and Security of Radioactive Sources and Supplementary Guidance on the Import and Export of Radioactive Sources 198
Third World War 12
Thirty Years War 61, 62
Threat to use force 71, 72, 73, 75, 119
Three Mile Island 38, 39, 40, 287
Tlatelolco Treaty 120, 155, 156, 157, 158
TNT 25, 27
Tokyo 210
Total war 62
Toxic gases 67
Treaty 14, 15, 18, 61, 67, 77, 89, 105, 120, 121, 133, 134, 135, 136, 137, 138, 139, 143, 146, 150, 153, 155, 156, 157, 158, 159, 160, 162, 163, 164, 165, 167, 169, 189, 190, 195, 242
Treaty Banning Nuclear Weapons Tests in the Atmosphere, in Outer Space and Under Water 135, 162, 257
Treaty for the Prohibition of Nuclear Weapons in Latin America 120, 121, 155
Treaty on a Nuclear Weapon Free Zone in Central Asia 155
Treaty on Principles Governing the Activities of States in the Exploration and Use of Outer Space, including the Moon and other Celestial Bodies 135, 159, 160, 281
Treaty on Scientific Nuclear Explosions 164
Treaty on the Prohibition of the Emplacement of Nuclear Weapons and other Weapons of Mass Destruction on the Sea-Bed and the Ocean Floor and in the Subsoil Thereof 159, 257
Treaty on the South East Asia Nuclear Weapon-Free Zone 155, 257
Treaty regime 170
Trinity Alamogordo 27
Tritium 24
Truman 27, 28, 29, 30, 48, 50, 51
Tumour 31
Turbines 35
Turkey 34, 53, 177

U

U-235 22, 23, 26, 27, 35, 201, 223
U-238 23, 24, 35, 36
U-239 36
Ukraine 34, 37, 38, 40, 111, 199, 201
Ultra-Centrifuges Holland 172
UN Commission for Atomic Energy 51
UN Commission on Disarmament 162
Undeclared 148, 151, 157, 190
United Kingdom 35, 52, 55, 83, 91, 96, 97, 98, 105, 108, 112, 113, 114, 122, 123, 159, 161, 162, 231
United Nations 40, 49, 50, 51, 67, 69, 70, 71, 72, 76, 97, 98, 101, 105, 106, 113, 135, 155, 159, 163, 187, 235, 247, 256, 259, 274, 278, 280, 281, 283, 289
United Nations Declaration 97
United States 34, 37, 49, 53, 70, 112, 113, 114, 164, 177, 191, 193, 199, 212, 253, 257, 258, 263, 268, 276, 280, 282, 283
Universal membership 14, 138
University of California-Berkley 22, 24, 26
UN Special Commission for Iraq 178
Uranium 12, 13, 14, 16, 19, 21, 22, 23, 24, 25, 26, 27, 28, 31, 32, 33, 34, 35, 36, 37, 40, 42, 43, 44, 45, 46, 47, 48, 58, 59, 141, 143, 172, 173, 174, 176, 178, 180, 182, 183, 184, 185, 188, 190, 192, 193, 199, 201, 209, 223, 232, 236, 242, 245
Uranium deposits 32
Uranium metallic hemispheres 185
Uranium mine 188
Uranium ore 44, 45, 182, 188
Uranium resources 16, 47
Uranium waste 173
Urenco 172, 173
Use of force 14, 17, 63, 64, 65, 69, 70, 71, 72, 75, 76, 78, 79, 84, 104, 116, 117, 119, 128, 130, 168
US National Defence Research Committee 26
US President 28, 65, 237
USSR 49, 50, 51, 54, 97, 107, 110, 134, 156, 159, 161, 162, 164, 188, 189, 197, 199, 200, 201, 202, 232

V

Vannevar Bush 26
Verification 137, 144, 146, 147, 148, 154, 162, 166, 167, 169, 186, 193, 195, 196, 269, 270, 271
Vicious cycle 14, 49
Victims 29, 41, 117, 208
Vienna Convention on the Law of Treaties 139, 140
Vietnam War 181
Violation 71, 72, 75, 81, 152, 184, 185, 186, 192, 193
Vladimir Putin 237
Voting 100, 103, 111, 121, 124, 125, 126, 129, 240, 246
Vulnerability 198, 200, 202, 204

W

Warfare 61, 62, 67, 106, 117, 118
Warhead 210, 214
Weak states 197, 198, 204
Weapon 155, 156, 164
Weapons of Mass Destruction 29, 66, 78, 159, 176, 210, 238, 252, 255, 257, 271, 278, 279
Wellington 107
Werner Heisenberg 26
Western block 48
WHO Assembly 108, 109
Winston Churchill 26
Withdraw 14, 15, 47, 107, 139, 140, 191, 192, 209
World Congress 107
World Court 15, 98, 101, 106, 250, 254, 274, 278
World Court Project 15, 101, 106
World Health Organisation 101, 108
World order 69, 98
World Trade Centre 211
World War II 11

Y

Yellow Cake 33
Yongbyon 57, 188, 195

Z

Völkerrecht und internationale Beziehungen

Nora Matthiesen
Wiedergutmachung für Opfer internationaler bewaffneter Konflikte
Die Rechtsposition des Individuums bei Verletzungen des humanitären Völkerrechts

Kriege töten Menschen, verletzen sie, berauben sie ihrer Lebensgrundlage. Häufig missachten Konfliktparteien die Regeln des humanitären Völkerrechts, die Individuen gerade hiervor schützen sollen. Es stellt sich dann die Frage, ob die Opfer einen eigenen Wiedergutmachungsanspruch haben, den sie selbst prozessual durchsetzen können. Die Autorin gibt unter Einbeziehung der zunehmenden Individualisierung des Völkerrechts Antworten. Zur Überwindung eines Durchsetzungsdefizits im Völkerrecht schlägt sie die Errichtung eines internationalen Gerichtshofs für Menschenrechte und humanitäre Rechte vor.

Bd. 5, 2012, 568 S., 55,90 €, br., ISBN 978-3-643-11506-5

Jacqueline Neumann
Die Förderung der Rule of Law in der Entwicklungszusammenarbeit
Ein Beitrag zur Herausbildung einer völkerrechtlichen Verfassungsnorm

Das Buch analysiert erstmals die Bedeutung der Rechtsstaatsförderung durch die Entwicklungszusammenarbeit für den Prozess der Konstitutionalisierung des Völkerrechts. Hierzu untersucht der klar strukturierte Beitrag die entwicklungspolitischen Konzepte in der Mehrebenenordnung von Weltbank, EU und Deutschland, und sichert die theoretischen Ergebnisse mit einer Fallstudie zu Kenia ab. Auf der Grundlage der zwischen Gebern und Partnern übereinstimmend anerkannten Inhalte der *Rule of Law* werden Anforderungen für die Planung, Durchführung und Kontrolle der Kooperation herausgearbeitet. Die Autorin schließt mit dem Hinweis, dass die drei untersuchten Geber in diesem Bereich Defizite aufweisen, und macht Reformvorschläge.

Bd. 6, 2013, 904 S., 74,90 €, gb., ISBN 978-3-643-12323-7

LIT Verlag Berlin – Münster – Wien – Zürich – London

Auslieferung Deutschland / Österreich / Schweiz: siehe Impressumsseite